D1285135

Reviews for *"The Way of Psychosynthesis"*

"The science of psychology was born and developed ___ ___ ___ ___, course of the past century. In that same fertile period Roberto Assagioli created Psychosynthesis. In this book Petra Guggisberg Nocelli outlines with depth and clarity its history to this day, its main ideas, techniques, aspects and applications. An essential work for those who want to understand this adventure of the spirit."

> Piero Ferrucci, Philosopher, Training Psychotherapist, Clinical Supervisor and Author, SIPT

"'The Way of Psychosynthesis' is the first comprehensive view of how Psychosynthesis fits into the entire field of psychology, noting how it helped to define the 4th force, transpersonal psychology, and via 'psychoenergetics' how it leads the future of the field. A work of great love and deep scholarship, it is an amazingly thorough book and one we need. Dr. Nocelli has taken on a challenge in Psychosynthesis literature which has not yet been engaged in. I am so very happy to have it in the world."

> Dorothy Firman, Professor, Author, Trainer and Director of The Synthesis Center

"Each chapter of 'The Way of Psychosynthesis', while having autonomy in a monographic sense, is an organic whole and offers a real path of research and development of psychosynthetic theory and practice. You have the impression of being in front of a harmonious and richly colored mandala, which allows us to look through Psychosynthesis in the multidimensionality of space and of time."

> Gianni Yoav Dattilo, Psychologist, Training Psychotherapist and Clinical Supervisor, SIPT

"Welcome to this 'guide' to the 'Way of Psychosynthesis'. The young author, of the latest generation of psychosynthesists, creates a truly large framework that tends toward an essential completeness. This volume deserves to occupy a significant place in the recent development of psychosynthetic literature. It is recommended to anyone interested in understanding Psychosynthesis, not in a superficially informative way but essentially and with a broad breadth."

> Massimo Rosselli, Psychiatrist, Training Psychotherapist and Clinical Supervisor, SIPT, and Past President, EFPP

"A great achievement: well written, informative, interesting and engaging. Every training organization should have it on their essential reading list and I will certainly be recommending it to my students."

> Will Parfitt, Psychotherapist, Psychosynthesis Trainer, Director of PS Avalon and Author

JOIN AND SUPPORT THE PROJECT "THE TREE ON THE MOUNTAIN"!

This book is the realization of the first part of a larger project titled "The Tree on the Mountain" to which I have dedicated myself for many years with a spirit of Service, love and will. This project also includes the translation and publication in English of my second work: "Know, Master, Transform Yourself-A collection of practical tools for inner harmony, development of potential, and personal and transpersonal psychosynthesis" (Xenia, 2016).

"Know, Master, Transform Yourself" is a wonderful manual that collects and organizes more than 280 exercises and techniques of Psychosynthesis, including explanations of its theoretical aspect. A very useful tool for anyone working in the fields of psychotherapy, counseling, coaching, interpersonal relationships and education.

As Piero Ferrucci commented: "*Here one understands that Psychosynthesis is not the idea of a single individual, but the result of a collaboration between thousands of people all over the world - a real movement.*"

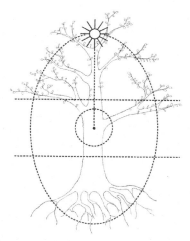

The intent of "The Tree on the Mountain" is the contextualization, organization, synthesis, and complete updating of the various aspects of Psychosynthesis: historical and cultural, theoretical and conceptual, methodological, pragmatic, and technical.

If you want to know more about the second part of the project and how to participate and support it, please write to:
p.g.nocelli@hotmail.com.

Thank you so much for your kind attention!

Petra Guggisberg Nocelli

Petra Guggisberg Nocelli

THE WAY OF
PSYCHOSYNTHESIS

A complete guide to
origins, concepts, and the fundamental experiences

with a biography of Roberto Assagioli

Lugano 2017

© Petra Guggisberg Nocelli

English edition: December, 2017

ISBN 979-12-200-3333-6

Synthesis Insights
Easton, Maryland 21601
USA

Editor: William Burr

Translated by: Edward Seagraves

Layout & Cover Graphics: Synthesis Insights.

Cover Illustration: The Cosmic Egg (Hildegard von Bingen)

Author's website: www.psicosintesi.ch

Email: p.g.nocelli@hotmail.com

CreateSpace Self-Publishing (www.createspace.com)

To Luca, Viola, and Emiliano
with love and gratitude;

to all those who follow the Way,
especially those who fear they may have strayed from it;

to Life: singular, precious, unrepeatable,
and to its each and every moment;

...and to Massimo Rosselli
with deep affection and gratitude.

DEVELOPMENT- JIAN
"The tree on the mountain is visible from afar, and its development influences the landscape of the entire region. It does not shoot up like a swamp plant; its growth proceeds gradually. Thus also the work of influencing people can be only gradual. No sudden influence or awakening is of lasting effect."
I CHING

"But by my love and hope I beseech thee:
cast not away the hero in thy soul!
Keep sacred thy highest hope!"
Friedrich Nietzsche- *"Thus spoke Zarathustra"*

ACKNOWLEDGMENTS

To create the English edition of this first book, which I consider to be a very useful tool for dissemination and in-depth study of Psychosynthesis, I knocked on the door of almost everyone I imagined might want to support the project. I am really grateful to those who responded to my appeal by participating with a donation. The gesture of each one of you was so precious to me! Your generosity enabled me to collect about 60% of the total amount needed. I financed the remainder by investing the royalties I have gained so far from the sale of my books in Italian and the income I received in 2017 from being invited here and there to hold courses and seminars.

Three special thanks go to Fernando Maggini (Switzerland), Michael Wolde (Sweden), and Aurora and Adalberto Guggisberg (Switzerland), whose contribution was incredibly generous and decisive.

Thank you very much also to Nadine Aernouts (Spain), Erika Agresti (Italy), Paolo Assandri (United Kingdom), Robert Bakker (Netherlands), Rebeca Bandeira (Portugal), Sheila Bartlett (United Kingdom), Lucia Bassignana Ceccarelli (Italy), Andrea Bonacchi (Italy), Maria Gabriella Cavallari (Italy), Gianni Yoav Dattilo (Italy), Alessandro Di Giovanni (Italy), Samuel Djian-Gutenberg (France), Fez film (Italy), Manuel Guggisberg (Canada), Keith Hakwood (United Kingdom), Alan Haras (USA), Colette Hartgill (United Kingdom), Leehee Holley (Israel), Julia Jameson (United Kingdom), Adrienne Jeffries (Australia), Diane Keel (United Kingdom), Angelique Kruip (Netherlands), Isabelle Clotilde Küng (Switzerland), Ann Marie Lamb (Sweden), Pablo Lentini Riva (France), Alessandra Giuliana Marson (Italy), Marianne Marthinussen (Norway), Audrey McMorrow (USA), Veronica Mecchia (France), Rita Montisci (Italy), David Nelson (USA), Monica Nocelli (Australia), Ursula Noll (Germany), Will Parfitt (United Kingdom), Gloria Paz (Ecuador), Cristina Pelizzatti (Italy), Stefano Pelli (Italy), Stephen Rekab (Ireland), Irene Rizzo (Italy), Renzo Rossin (Italy), Sue Salmela (USA), Andrée Samuel (Bresil), Franco Salvini (France), Elena Savino (Italy), Maria Bernadette Schenker (Italy), Linda Simmons (United Kingdom), Kenneth Sørensen (Denmark), Ivan Strigin (Russia), Kay Taylor (USA), The Synthesis Center (USA), Giuseppe Vercelli (Italy), Anne Yeomans (USA).

I'd like also to thank Cristina Pelizzatti for listening to me when, almost by chance, I told her of my intention to translate my texts into English. Shortly thereafter, Cristina enthusiastically offered me concrete possibilities, resources and contacts. I would like to thank William Burr, to whom I entrusted the management of the project, Edward Seagraves, who did the primary translation of the text, and the proofreading team: Patricia A. Elkins, Dorothy Firman, Amy Spalding-Fletcher, Marjorie Hope-Gross, Becky Jones, Jane Katz, and Barbara Veale Smith. Without your many skills, and knowing little and poor English, it would not have been possible to accomplish all this.

I also thank those who took the time to respond in detail to my emails and phone calls by giving me useful information, sharing their experiences and making their knowledge available in a variety of ways: Andreas Barella, Marina Bernardi, Piero Ferrucci, Dorothy Firman, Isabelle Clotilde Küng, Jan Kuniholm, Mariella Lancia, Catherine Ann Lombard, Mike Malagreca, Fernando Maraghini, Will Parfitt, Massimo Rosselli, Kenneth Sørensen, Mauro Ventola and Vittorio Viglienghi.

Finally, there were really many people and institutions who sent me encouraging words and helped me in the spreading of information about this project. It would be impossible to nominate everyone! I will just mention those who allowed me to share crowdfunding information in a variety of ways: The Psychosynthesis Institute founded by Roberto Assagioli, The Istituto Internazionale di Psicosintesi Educativa (IIPE), The Gruppo alle Fonti, the European Federation for Psychosynthesis Psychotherapy (EFPP) and the Psychosynthesis London Trust. I hope I have not forgotten anyone, and thank you all.

PRESENTATION

It is with joy and heartfelt appreciation that I welcome the English edition of this excellent guide to the path of Psychosynthesis.

As a matter of fact Roberto Assagioli, the Italian psychiatrist, decided to publish his major books first in English, and paradoxically never saw the Italian translation of his masterpiece, The Act of Will, which appeared after his death.

The founder of Psychosynthesis was clearly aware of the importance of the English language in the international scientific community; and Psychosynthesis is in its essence international, going far beyond all cultural boundaries and barriers of any kind, in an overall spirit of synthesis and integration.

Petra Guggisberg Nocelli's lovely book was created in a period of fresh blossoming of works on Psychosynthesis, each having its own special physiognomy, a sign of creative evolution of our concept. Each chapter of this work, although having its thematic independence, is an organic whole and offers a real path in the research and development of psychosynthetic theory and practice. It gives the impression of viewing a harmonic Mandala, rich in colors, allowing us to look through psychosynthesis into the multidimensionality of space and time.

The Way of Psychosynthesis opens with a detailed personal and cultural biography of Roberto Assagioli, which makes it possible for a deeper understanding not only of the person, but also of the very genesis of his new concept of the psyche.

The second part examines the environment in which psychosynthesis is born and develops. Our orientation is re-examined and compared to the panorama of contemporary psychology: behaviorism, psychoanalysis, analytical psychology, the humanistic-existential trend, transpersonal psychology and the new frontiers of psychoenergetics.

The third part allows one to fully enter the psychosynthetic experience by exhaustively expanding the times and the ways of the path, the concepts and the fundamental diagrams, while taking into account the proposals for change and development. All this is essential if you hold to the idea of psychosynthesis as a dynamic process in continuous evolution in the various areas of application, rather than a static and definitive theory.

In the fourth part, among other things what is striking is that the fundamental ideas of our model, "the seven fundamental experiences of psychosynthesis" as the author calls it, are made accessible to the inexperienced public, while at the same time also very useful for the expert reader, offering new and original ideas of thought and experimentation. For example, issues such as disidentification and self-identification, will, the subpersonalities, 'I' and Self, the Superconscious, the principle of Synthesis—none of which are simple from a conceptual point of view—are dealt with clarity and depth.

Psychosynthesis does not come from nowhere and in a vacuum; it has complex roots, still not yet sufficiently discovered and explored. The pragmatic spirit of our research has often favored the empirical and applicative aspects, but here we are faced with a true, complete guide to the visceral experience of psychosynthesis, where clear theories and practical ideas find a wonderful balance. The various themes are studied in light of the sources, thus favoring the possibility of new investigations, without weighty text and always bearing in mind that Psychosynthesis is basically a psychological practice to be experienced.

It is not often that a work is both a clear and complete introduction to a theme and also an in-depth study with spurts of originality.

Petra Guggisberg Nocelli was a brilliant pupil of the psychotherapy school of SIPT, and it is my great pleasure to welcome her contribution, written with a genuine psychosynthetic spirit which enriches our bibliography. This book will surely contribute to the dissemination of Psychosynthesis worldwide and I deeply trust it will be an invaluable general introduction for beginners and a precious tool for the seasoned practitioner as well.

Dr. Gianni Yoav Dattilo

Psychologist, Training Psychotherapist and Clinical Supervisor, SIPT (*Italian Society for Psychosynthesis Psychotherapy*), member, APA

PREFACE TO THE ITALIAN EDITION

39 - OBSTRUCTION, JIAN
There is water on the mountain:
the image of obstacles.

53 - DEVELOPMENT, JIAN
There is a tree on the mountain:
the image of development.

I CHING

This book is born out of an attempt to answer a question often put to me by friends, patients, scholars and therapists of other orientations: "What is Psychosynthesis?" This question, despite years of practice and study, fortunately succeeds yet again and always to get me into trouble.

In trying to outline an inevitably compound and multifaceted response, I have been guided by the general purpose of providing the reader with a comprehensive and ample view of the evolution of psychosynthetic teaching, starting with the first writings from Roberto Assagioli at the beginning of the 1900s, up to the invaluable contributions of his own students and other contemporary psychosynthesists.

It was a difficult a decision to finalize the writing of this text as Psychosynthesis is wonderfully vast, inclusive and fruitful, and I dare say "infinite": an adequate mirror for the spirit of the human being. Therefore, many of the topics discussed would require further insights, for which I suggest with pleasure a reading of the volumes published by the various authors widely cited in the course of this work.

The Way of Psychosynthesis springs from the complete rewriting of my degree thesis that I presented in July 2000 at the Università Statale di Milano. At the time, I had devoted much effort, energy and passion to that work. And so, after 10 years, driven by an inner desire that is bringing me back to reconnect the threads of the present with those of the past, I decided to resume what I had developed and update it entirely.

Writing this book really meant a lot to me, and marks the symbolic fulfillment of a long, difficult, and troubled period. I consider this text as the tangible fruit of a surprising process that involved me on multiple levels, reconciling myself with parts of myself and my past, relieving me and liberating an unexpected amount of will, joy, pleasure and satisfaction. The hope is that some of this energy can filter through the pages to reach those who read it.

I would like to conclude with a practical recommendation. This text lends itself to be read in an orderly and progressive manner, but can also be readily consulted as a manual, in its individual parts, chapters or paragraphs, according to the needs and interests of the moment: discover the biography of Roberto Assagioli, get an idea of the relationship between Psychosynthesis and Psychoanalysis, or between Psychosynthesis and Transpersonal Psychology, study the evolution of thought regarding the image of the individual illustrated in the Egg Diagram, learn about the techniques of the psychosynthesis process, analyze specific topics such as subpersonalities, superconscious, Ideal Model, and so on. I refer the reader to the Contents for a total overview.

Petra Guggisberg Nocelli

Miglieglia, Switzerland, March 13, 2011

PREFACE

Taormina 02 June 2016

"COURAGE - The will to risk. The acceptance of insecurity.
A wise will must at times and places know how to dare,
assuming responsibility and risk. You must have the courage to err, to give the right
part of life to the 'divine unforeseen'."

R. Assagioli, handwritten notes

I'd like to tell you a story that accompanied the birth and development of this book and which, in a certain way, is also the partial history of a broader task which I either chose or was assigned (who knows?) for this stage of my life.

We're in 1999. I'm twenty-five years old and I'm descending, full of emotion, the steps of a steep garden leading to a house on the shores of Lago Maggiore. The light is unmistakable, marvelous, and is reflected in the dark blue waters along with the green of the August trees. I feel very excited because I'm returning to find an elderly and very mysterious gentleman who has conceded me the honor of teaching me to consult the I CHING[1].

A little in awe, I knock on the door. A man opens, whom I remember tall, with white hair cascading on his shoulders. It is Rudolf Ritsema, for many years director of the Eranos Foundation[2] in Ascona, Switzerland.

I had met Mr. Ritsema a few months earlier. I had contacted him in the search for any traces left by the passage of Roberto Assagioli to Monte Verità, and because I wanted to view the mandalas painted by Olga Fröbe Kapteyn, a friend of the father of Psychosynthesis who had kindly hosted him in the '30s, along with other illustrious guests, precisely in that ancient farmhouse now the seat of the prestigious Foundation.

On that occasion I had discovered that Ritsema had translated the I CHING directly from the original Chinese according to completely new criteria and using

---

[1] The I CHING, or "Book of Changes" is considered the first of the Chinese classical texts. Considered a book of wisdom by Confucius, it has been used for over 4,500 years by scholars to explore questions of mathematics, philosophy, and physics, and, more in general, to obtain indications and responses relative to important questions in the lives of those who consult it.

[2] The "Eranos Sessions" were begun in 1933 by Olga Fröbe-Kapteyn (1881-1962) with the intention to gather, in a sort of "school of spiritual research" the pre-eminent researchers and scholars of Eastern and Western religion and spirituality of the time. In addition to Roberto Assagioli, Eranos was frequented by names of the caliber of Carl Gustav Jung, Mircea Eliade, Károly Kerényi, James Hillman, Martin Buber, Erich Neumann, Adolf Portmann, Paul Tillich, Marie-Louise von Franz- to name only a few.

a revolutionary method favoring access to that archetypal dimension of the unconscious which manifests itself usually in dreams. He said to consult it in that way was a bit like dreaming: dreaming around a specific question. The question that brought me there that day was "what situation accompanies my decision to become a psychotherapist?"

Ritsema has me sit at a table in a fairly dark room, furnished with a lot of wood and with a beautiful window overlooking the light of the lake. He takes the yarrow sticks, explains briefly the procedure used to consult the oracle, and we begin. At the end of the third passage—every divination foresees six in total, one for every line which will make up the final hexagram- he pauses, rubs his forehead and looks me straight in the eye, asking if I'm truly certain I want to continue. I can assure you that his look and the question took my breath away for a few interminable seconds, and then, naturally, I decided that I preferred to know. Ignorance would have surely been worse than whatever response.

The reply of the oracle consists of two hexagrams, 39 and 53. The first says: "*The mountain above possesses the current. Limping Jian*". The second: "*The mountain above possesses the tree. Infiltrating Jian*". Ritsema asks me if I plan to attend the Jung Institute in Zürich. I tell him no, that my intention is to go to Florence, where SIPT, the Società Italiana di Psicosintesi Terapeutica (Italian Society for Psychosynthesis Psychotherapy) is situated. He tells me with satisfaction that the oracle approves because for me it is propitious to head South, whereas it is not to go North. He also tells me that I have to confront a dangerous abyss, but to not fear because the outcome of that situation will be positive: a tree on the mountain.

I take my leave of the courteous Mr. Ritsema. Shortly after I begin writing my graduate thesis that will become this book, and I start to "limp", blatantly. In truth, even today my progress through life is sometimes difficult, but this is another story. I graduated on the 4th of July, 2000, I delivered my dissertation to a few psychosynthesis educators and trainers, and forgot for a long time that morning spent at Eranos.

Ten years later, walking in a wood alongside a pretty waterfall in the company of my daughter born a few months earlier, a sudden thought passed through my mind: "why don't you publish your thesis?". I sent some abstracts to Dr. Gianni Yoav Dattilo, at that time President of SIPT. Gianni was enthusiastic and passed them on to Dr. Alberto Alberti, a direct pupil of Roberto Assagioli and editor, who welcomed my request. Work on the text then began, lasting about a year and a half with the objective of completely updating it.

In April, 2011 it is all ready for delivery. The last thing I have to do is a graphic[3] for insertion in the book that illustrates symbolically how the Egg Diagram developed by Assagioli succeeds in embodying the profound dynamism which

---

3   See Part 3, Chap. IV, Para. 6.

characterizes the bio-psychic-transpersonal constitution of the human being. I print a sheet on which the famous tripartite design is reproduced and begin to move the pencil, trying to superimpose the image of a tree: the roots which dig into the depths of the earth, the horizontal extension of the trunk and lower branches, the crown projected toward the sky and the light of the sun. I think I haven't tried to draw something since middle school. All the same the lines flow, possessing a certain elegance and harmony.

At a certain point, everything stops. I hold my breath, suspended. Something is about to flower with force in my consciousness.
It emerges! After 12 years I return suddenly in that room overlooking Lago Maggiore. I return to the eyes of Rudolf Ritsema that tell me, reassuringly: "There will be a good outcome, there will be a tree on the mountain. This is a very good thing!". I look at the drawing that I've almost completed, the tree inserted in the ovoid. I'm living that which we define in psychosynthesis as a "transpersonal experience", a revelation. The pieces of the mosaic come together: my entire journey of 12 years reveals its significance, or I succeed finally in seeing it. It's an intense emotion, a moment of profound comprehension. It's wonder and amazement, which move me to tears.

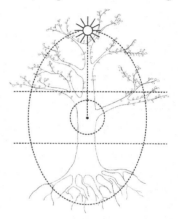

In reality the synchronicities with the image of hexagram 53 don't finish here and are truly incredible, but maybe I'll have the occasion to tell you about them another time. However I would like to tell you how I arrived at the decision to throw myself into the mad enterprise of translating this text into English, even though being capable neither of speaking it nor of writing it sufficiently well.

I had recently published my second book and was unable to choose, between two new themes that I liked a lot, which to develop first. One day I received a call from a colleague who invited me to participate in an innovative training program on Psychosynthesis Life Coaching in the Italian language, originally conceived and developed in the USA. At the end of our conversation, with a certain amazement, I heard myself say; "I've been thinking of translating my books into English for a while now. Do you know if there are any possibilities?" And here we are!

That evening of 2011, while I drew the image of the tree in the ovoid, I was referring only to that first publication in Italian. Now instead, after several years, "the tree on the mountain" gives title to a much wider and organic project which includes, in addition to *"La Via della Psicosintesi"* / *"The Way of Psychosynthesis"*, the over 500 pages which make up my second book *"Conosci, possiedi, trasforma te stesso - Una raccolta di strumenti pratici per l'armonia interiore, lo sviluppo del potenziale e la psicosintesi personale e transpersonale"* (*"Know, Master, Transform Yourself - a collection of practical tools for inner harmony, the development of potential and personal and transpersonal psychosynthesis"*). The purpose of this project is not so much the expression of my personal vision of Psychosynthesis, as it is the contextualisation, organization, synthesis and complete re-actualization of its various aspects: historical and cultural, theoretical and conceptual, methodological, pragmatic, and technical. The two books have been added to the bibliographies of the leading Italian institutes for psychosynthesis training, including SIPT and the IIPE. Completion of the entire project foresees that these are translated into English, rendering them available to that greater part of students, educators, and enthusiasts who don't read Italian.

As Shanteena Sabbadini wrote—who, with others of the caliber of James Hillman was one of the researchers who greatly helped Ritsema in his work of translating the I CHING—"maybe it is only an illusion that the images of the oracle speak to us, that they precisely respond to our questions. Maybe 'synchronicity' is only a name for purely casual coincidences. Yet…"

20 September is arriving, the date chosen for "World Psychosynthesis Day". It is a propitious time to give voice to the hope which accompanies this project. I hope from my heart that it can sustain the enthusiasm of all those who feel a resonance with the message of Psychosynthesis, permitting each to recognize—independently from group or institutional affiliation, and beyond the numerous and inevitable differences which are to be respected and supported—that which unites us, that which moves us, at times on different paths, in the direction of the same common destination. This challenge has never been more urgent or vital. Succeeding in meeting it means to develop and improve the extraordinary potential of the monumental vision that has been given to us. Roberto Assagioli's legacy gives us all the tools to realize this, as well as the methods for activating our Good Will.

> *The tree on the mountain is seen from afar, and its development influences the landscape of the entire region. It doesn't grow in the blink of an eye like the denizens of the swamp, but its growth proceeds gradually. An action on humankind can also only be gradual. No sudden influx or awakening can be permanent. Slowly, slowly, must progress be made.*
>
> *I CHING*

> *"But by my love and hope, I beseech thee: cast not away the hero in thy soul! Keep sacred thy highest hope!"*
>
> **Friedrich Nietzsche-** *"Thus spoke Zarathustra"*

Petra Guggisberg Nocelli

Miglieglia, Switzerland, September 18, 2017

CONTENTS

PART ONE

THE FOUNDER
OF PSYCHOSYNTHESIS

A biography of Roberto Assagioli

The first part of this book introduces Psychosynthesis through the biography of its founder in an attempt to outline a relationship between his formative experiences, his personality traits and the development of his thought.

I believe that this preliminary biographical text is useful since, as the psychologist and psychoanalyst Sebastiano Tilli[1] writes, "Today the prevailing idea is that the salient points of a psychological theory lead back to certain fundamental and unconscious elements of the personality of the creator of that theory." However, is important to remember that a work tends to go beyond its author, changing form according to the need that those who relate to it have to reflect on themselves and the world.

Retracing the life of the father of Psychosynthesis was not easy. Unlike other founders, for example Sigmund Freud and Carl Gustav Jung, he was always very reserved and did not write any memoirs. This is quite unusual and certainly significant: one has the impression that Assagioli wanted to keep his life intentionally hidden, an impression confirmed by the fact that he asked a certain discretion of his students. He said: "The need is to advance Psychosynthesis, not my name."

The only autobiographical testimony that comes to us refers to an experience he considered highly formative and which he detailed only because "a living example has more influence than many other forms of teaching and reaches a wider audience than purely scientific essays"[2]. The reference is to stories related to his imprisonment during the Fascist era.

Add to this the destruction of materials that would surely have been very interesting. The father of Psychosynthesis was Jewish and during the period of anti-Semitic persecution, two fires, one in his home in Rome and the other in his summer residence in Tuscany, destroyed a large part of his archives. Thus many years of his biography remain practically unknown.

Fortunately, the valuable testimonies collected by writer and journalist Paola Giovetti in her essential book entitled *Roberto Assagioli*[3], the interviews he gave shortly before dying to American philosopher Sam Keen[4] and other journalists, as well as several letters, allowed me to reliably outline his human aspect. In addition, the correspondence with Prezzolini, Papini and Vailati, the writings, early articles and accounts of his participation in numerous scientific and cultural initiatives, give reliable testimony to the evolution of his thought.

---

1   S. Tilli, *Spunti per una lettura prospettica della "psicologia" di Roberto Assagioli,* in *I nuovi paradigmi della psicologia,* (edited by) M. Rosselli, Cittadella ed., 1992.

2   R. Assagioli, cit. in P. Giovetti, *Roberto Assagioli,* Ed. Mediterranee, 1995.

3   Paola Giovetti, op. cit.

4   S. Keen, *La proporzione aurea di Roberto Assagioli,* Psychology Today, 1974.

In the *first chapter*, I considered the years of training, of which we know a considerable amount thanks to the good work of Dr. Alessandro Berti[5] and Dr. Di Sazio[6], as well as the contributions of Giorgio Luti[7], who was Professor Emeritus of Italian Literature at the Faculty of Letters of the University of Florence, and also Carlo Tonini[8], archivist at the Archivio Contemporaneo Gabinetto G. P. Vieusseux. This period is very important because Assagioli outlined the essential points of his thinking that never changed significantly. In fact, he said he had received the framework of Psychosynthesis at the age of eleven, while admiring a Venetian sunset: "then for the rest of my life I put my flesh on that skeleton".[9]

In the *second chapter* I attempted to retrace the life of Assagioli and his family during the years between the start of the First World War and the end of the Second. In the search for the implications that these experiences had in formulating his ideas, it was inevitable to emphasize the period of his imprisonment and persecution by the Nazis, also because, paradoxically, these events seemed to have marked the culminating moment of his inner fulfillment.

In the *third chapter*, however, I retraced the expansion of Psychosynthesis on an international level through the participation of its founder in countless cultural and scientific events, through the publication of the first books entirely devoted to the subject, and also through the intense training activity of his students. I concluded this first part with a human portrait of Roberto Assagioli as described by about fifteen friends and acquaintances in a series of interviews.[10]

---

5   A. Berti, *Roberto Assagioli: profilo biografico degli anni di formazione*, Ed. Istituto di Psicosintesi, 1987.

6   C. Di Sazio, *Roberto Assagioli: un contributo storico al padre della psicosintesi,* graduate thesis, Università degli Studi di Roma, academic year 1986- 87.

7   G. Luti, *Roberto Assagioli e l'avanguardia fiorentina nel primo novecento*, in *I nuovi paradigmi della psicologia*, op. cit.

8   C. Tonini, *Il carteggio Assagioli-Prezzolini*, in *I nuovi paradigmi della psicologia,* op. cit.

9   R. Assagioli, cit. in P. Giovetti, op. cit.

10   Ibid.

CHAPTER I

THE FORMATIVE YEARS

1. Childhood and early youth

Roberto Marco Greco was born to Jewish parents on February 27, 1888 in Venice. His mother, a Venitian native named Elena Kaula, was born in Alessandria, Egypt, while his father, Leone, was an engineer from Verona who died suddenly when Roberto was just two years old. Shortly thereafter, young Roberto became ill and was hospitalized where he was lovingly cared for by Dr. Emanuele Todesco Assagioli. A year after, Elena and Emanuele were married.

The family situation in which Assagioli grew up was very stimulating and the considerable financial status of his adoptive father allowed him to travel frequently and enjoy various environments, providing him also with the opportunity to learn a multitude of languages. He himself writes in the essay *Come si imparano le lingue con l'inconscio (How To Learn Languages With The Unconscious)*[11] how he learned Italian, French and English almost at the same time. He will later add a bit of Russian, German—which he knew so well that, at still a very young age, he was able to do difficult translations which Freud himself defined "impeccable"[12] —and the study of Sanskrit.

We know very little of his infancy, but psychologist and anthropologist Peter Roche De Coppens, a student of Assagioli, repeats in an interview a story that the maestro told him just before passing away. At the age of just eleven, looking at the sunset, he had an intuition into the structure of the psyche and the mystery of the Self. He said:

"That day I received the skeleton of Psychosynthesis, and I spent the rest of my life putting meat on those bones."[13]

Young Roberto graduated at the age of sixteen from the Liceo Foscarini upper school. His studies centered on the humanities and sciences which honed in him a keen interest for both medicine and philosophy.[14]

At the age of fifteen, he started to write and publish. In 1903 two of his articles appeared in the "Giornale di Venezia" (The Venice Journal). The first was titled *Lavoro cosciente e pretese incoscienti* (Conscious Work and Unconscious Presumptions)

---

11   R. Assagioli, *Come si imparano le lingua con l'inconscio,* Ed. Istituto di psicosintesi.

12   *Lettere tra Freud e Jung,* edited by W. McGuire, translation, Torino, 1974.

13   P. Roche De Coppens, cit. in P. Giovetti, op. cit.

14   A. Berti, *Roberto Assagioli - profilo biografico degli anni di formazione,* Edizioni Istituto di Psicosintesi, 1987.

and was about a student protest against the Public Education Ministry; the second, *La crisi del libro in Francia* (*The Book Crisis in France*), denounces the lack of professionalism in the publishing sector and its inability to stimulate readers with appropriate publications.

2. The move to Florence: the literary *avant-garde* and the years at university

In 1904 the Assagioli family moved to Florence, residing in Via degli Alfani 46. It was time for Roberto to register at the university. He chose Medicine and Surgery, but soon directed his attention to psychiatry, the only discipline that connected the physical and behavioral sciences. In those times, psychology was not recognized as an individual science: it was considered to be part of the literary faculty, particularly in philosophy, or in the faculty of medicine, linked to psychiatry and neurology. The so-called insane asylum was the only environment in which therapeutic techniques could be explored. Assagioli's psychiatry professor was Eugenio Tanzi who combined an interest in mental alienation, paranoia, and hypnosis with that of a fascination for the spirit medium.

The first years of the century saw the most fruitful period of psychological activity in Italy, and in 1905, Rome was chosen to host the 5th International Convention of Psychology organized by psychiatrist Sante De Sanctis (1862-1935). The convention, while on the one hand proclaiming the personal success of American psychologist and philosopher William James (1842-1910), on the other unfortunately marked the highest point in the arc of Italian psychology in the international arena.

The message of James was acknowledged by the pragmatist group of the "Leonardo" journal, which inserted themselves in the vein of the great crisis at the close of the century, pointing out the failure of natural sciences in their goal to present themselves as a guide toward the advancement of humankind. In fact, one of the key points in the journal's study was the controversy involving positivism, which opposed individualism and glorious action, opening the door to intuitionism, the philosophy of action, and from this, through James, to magical idealism.[15]

The future father of Psychosynthesis approached Florence's *avant-garde* group just as his studies on pragmatism intensified. Assagioli was intensely involved in the activities of the Leonardians but was never completely one of them. He felt close to the interpretation that young Giovanni Papini (1881-1956) gave to pragmatism, in which the concept of a will which finds itself between the human self and material things assumes fundamental importance, a kind of magical power capable of commanding and changing those same material things, but he would never share the tendency toward the philosophy of the "superman".

---

15   Ibid.

2.1. Friendship with Giovanni Papini

There are references to the relationship between Roberto Assagioli and Giovanni Papini going back to 1904, when the future father of Psychosynthesis was just sixteen. But the first official evidence of his being introduced to the *avant-garde* environment is a letter written in April of 1905.

In that period, Assagioli, wanting to make contact with the cultural circles suggested to him by Papini and Prezzolini, began a long series of trips through Switzerland, Germany, England and Russia that saw him assume the role of foreign representative of the group. It's quite probable that the good level of distribution obtained by the "Leonardo" publication in that period was due to his notable practical skills.[16]

Letters from that year indicate Assagioli's uncertainties and need for security in a relationship that was not felt to be on an equal level, but in a short time there seems to be a consensus between the two, not only regarding their common interests, but regarding a true ideological-spiritual complicity. In fact, our young student wrote to Papini from Berlin, in response to a letter in which he was reprimanded for the scarcity of his correspondence, claiming that the silence between them is attributable to the "(...) vivid displeasure of us both having had to break the dear communion of our souls and not knowing how to maintain it over a distance"[17].

In 1906 Assagioli travels continuously and the friendship with the head of the *avant-garde* seems increasingly tight and intimate. Letters and postcards full of affectionate messages are many. During his numerous journeys, he also visits Geneva, where he meets psychologists Edouard Claparède (1873-1940) and Theodore Flournoy (1854-1920), with whom he will stay in touch for a long time. They invite him to introduce the Florentine experience to the Geneva circles. He wrote to Papini: "(...) I have been commissioned to write a long article on the 'movement' for their Archives"[18].

On returning to Florence, a group is formed which includes Giovanni Papini, Giovanni Vailati (1863-1909), Arturo Reghini (1878-1946) and Assagioli himself, the objective being a meeting with the famous Neapolitan medium Eusapia Paladino.

The association between Papini and Assagioli flattened in the early months of 1907. The latter acquired a degree of independence and well-defined personal interests. Though correspondence had become more rare, the letters that arouse most interest are those of this period.

Papini, perhaps to reaffirm that he is still the only one able to decide, suspends the publications of "Leonardo" definitively without asking anyone's opinion, not

---

16   G. Luti, *Roberto Assagioli e l'avanguardia fiorentina nel primo novecento,* in *I nuovi paradigmi della psicologia,* op. cit.

17   R. Assagioli, cit. in A. Berti, op. cit.

18   Ibid.

even that of Assagioli who was the journal's administrator, one of its financiers and the chief editor. A letter from the end of August shows that the immediate reaction of our young student was to stay out. He wrote: "... indeed, I'm glad I have no official bond with you now so I can take my position clearly and freely"[19]. And he again writes to Papini, commenting on his article in the final issue of "Leonardo", appropriately titled "The End": "(...) it was done very well and very skillfully; your position seems to me too 'ideal'-logical-coherent and therefore gives the impression that it was found ingeniously, rather than actually something experienced."[20].

But we cannot yet speak of a definitive breaking of relationships. The end of the journal resulted in a year of silence between them. Then in 1909, with the founding of "La Voce" (The Voice), contact was resumed albeit with a more formal tone. The two exchange letters of an informative character, news of activities, encounters and literary interests. Assagioli claims to have chosen to dedicate his time to scientific, medical and above all psychological studies: "... they seem to me the most suitable to satisfy my preeminent need to know the mysteries of the human soul and to use that knowledge for the liberation of souls." He also tells his friend, probably in response to some veiled accusation, of not having chosen to devote himself to psychology "for reasons of opportunity"; on the contrary, such studies "bring me difficulties and struggles in the field of science"[21].

The last saved letters are from 1911, however, after the closing of "Leonardo" and in the early days of "La Voce", their paths take very different directions. We will find the name of Assagioli again in Papini's diary many years later, in 1948. He tells of an interesting episode that took place at the end of a lecture in Ricasoli's home by Clement Rebora on writer George Bernard Shaw: "...a short, bald man with a half-white, half-black beard is coming toward me and beginning to speak as if he knew me. I respond but without realizing who he is. They told me afterward that it was Dr. Roberto Assagioli, who came to see me, no less, in 1904. I hadn't seen him for nearly forty years. He presented a thesis on Freud (the first in Italy) and now he was trying to found Psychosynthesis."[22]

This memory lapse sounds a little strange considering it was Papini himself who introduced Assagioli to the *avant-garde* environment, establishing with him friendships that, according to the letters and the importance of the role played by the young Roberto in the Florence journal, we can judge to be anything but episodic and superficial. Papini's attempt to suppress that memory was certainly influenced by his religious conversion and having supported a regime that, with its racial laws, persecuted the Jewish Assagioli.

---

19   Ibid.

20   Ibid.

21   Ibid.

22   G. Papini, *Diario*, Florence 1962, dated 12 January 1948, cit. in M. David, *La psicoanalisi e la cultura italiana*, Boringhieri, 1966.

2.2. Relationships with Prezzolini

From the documents we have available, it is certain that writer Giuseppe Prezzolini (1882-1982) also closely followed Roberto Assagioli. We know of diverse personal and literary assignments entrusted by Prezzolini to his young friend while he was in various European cities. Testimony to their friendly and playful relationship is found in a letter that Prezzolini sent to Papini in 1905, saying: "How I miss Assagioli! A gentle man who speaks of friendship, what a brilliant substitute and confessional dodger! How can I talk about myself, or about you, now that I don't have an Assagioli? Where can I find an Assagioli?"[23]

The first contact between Assagioli and Prezzolini dates back to the first months of 1905 when the latter urged him to compose a work to be put into a collection of mystic writings.[24] The project came to fruition in 1908 with the publication of the difficult translation of *Sibyllinische Blätter Des Magus In Norden* by Prussian philosopher Johann Georg Hamann (1730-1788), supported by the pleasing approvals of Benedict Croce who considered Hamann one of the darkest writers that ever existed. The work is preceded by a rich introduction, also written by Assagioli, in which he defines Hamann as "an insanely inquisitive soul, a passionate scholar of philosophical and religious subjects (...) the typical example of the infinite complexity of human nature."[25]

Assagioli, just twenty years old, had another opportunity to discuss the topics of his work at the *International Congress of Philosophy* in Heidelberg, held in early September 1908. The subject of his communication was to compare Hamann's philosophy to that of Ralph Waldo Emerson (1803-1882). His aim was to demonstrate the grossness of the error committed by those who "seek the genesis of the highest conceptions of the philosophers in their personal characteristics and the influences exerted upon them by the environment and the times"[26]. Indeed, in his report, Assagioli pointed out that although the two scholars had taken different paths, and despite the significant diversity of their psychological, human, and religious characteristics, they came to very similar results: both affirmed the existence of an intuitive knowledge to which logical activity must be subordinated; they considered the visible world as a product and at the same time symbol of an inner, spiritual world, the only true and real one; and they denied the dualism between spirit and matter to support the intimate unity of everything.

After the experience with "Leonardo" and the publication of Hamann's essay,

---

23   C. Tonini, *Il carteggio Assagioli-Prezzolini dell'archivio contemporaneo del gabinetto Vieusseux di Firenze*, in *I nuovi paradigmi della psicologia*, op. cit.

24   A. Berti, op. cit.

25   R. Assagioli, cit. in A. Berti, op. cit.

26   R. Assagioli, *Johann Georg Hamman e Ralph Waldo Emerson- Alcune curiose coincidenze fra le loro idee*, in *Verhandlungen des III Internationalen Kongresses Für Philosophie Heidelberg*, 1908.

contact between Assagioli and Prezzolini resumed at the time of the founding of "La Voce". Assagioli responded to Prezzolini's call by promising financial support and, in return, asked for the position of editorial secretary. From the correspondence of that period, the concern that Prezzolini felt about being economically dependent on Assagioli was apparent. But the real obstacle to the financial participation of our author was due to the diversity of ideas and interests, as made clear in a letter dated September 9, 1908. In it, Prezzolini writes: "It seemed to me to be an obstacle in relation to theological and worldly environments." In fact, "La Voce" was intended to counteract these environments and to entrust important assignments to someone that adhered to them would appear at a minimum to be inconsistent. Assagioli replied, showing a freedom of spirit that would characterize him until the end of his days, explaining that he wanted to enter, for educational purposes, different environments and adds that he was "absolutely unattached to any group, society or church, and I am ready to declare it publicly."

The future father of Psychosynthesis was a gifted young man with intense personal interests and, most likely, Prezzolini feared that his proposal concealed the desire to give the nascent journal a personal imprint, as had been the case for the last issues of "Leonardo". Having Assagioli as secretary could mean the possibility of having to follow his plans. However, Prezzolini points out that this is not a rejection of other forms of collaboration and his intention to involve him in the project is real. In fact, Assagioli will publish four articles for "La Voce", the last of which, the one on Freud, anticipates the topics discussed at the *Conference on the Sexual Question* organized by the journal itself.

It was this conference that would be the cause of reciprocal tension between the two friends. David[27] writes that Prezzolini, a bit annoyed by the applause given to Assagioli at the end of his presentation, wrote in "La Voce" of November 17, 1910: "These theories are nothing but masked and complicated positivism. The last part (on sublimation) trades punches with the first one. (...)". Assagioli protested vigorously against this undeserved accusation. On the other hand, Prezzolini would always look with suspicion on psychoanalysis, also because of "a bit of distrust due to Freud's Semitic origins"[28].

After the events of the Conference, the two will grow more and more distant, especially because of the diversity of their interests. In the following years, there would be sporadic missives. The war will then mark the halt of all the activities of the Florence group, although in 1919 Assagioli still wrote to his old companion from Palmanova's field hospital, where he served as a doctor with the rank of lieutenant.

More than half a century later, it would be Prezzolini seeking out Assagioli in order to obtain permission to publish his article on Freud in the anthology collection of "La Voce". The father of Psychosynthesis, near death, declared that

---

27   M. David, *La psicoanalisi nella cultura italiana,* Boringieri, 1966.

28   Ibid.

he did not exactly remember the contents of the writing, but would gladly allow the publication because "as far as I know, it was the first to come out in a literary journal, a 'historical fact' according to the correct use of the term", adding "in the name of our old friendship even if our paths diverged."[29]

3. Philosophical and spiritual interests: the love of the Orient

For our young author, 1906 was a particularly important year because it marks the beginning of a series of parallel experiences, all fundamentally on the formative level. In the "Journal of Applied Psychology" directed by psychiatrist Giulio Cesare Ferrari (1867-1932), he published the first article in which he showed that he is already aware of Freud; his friendship with the "Leonardo" group and with Papini was consolidated; he devoted himself intensely to the study and reading of various scientific, literary and mystical-philosophical subjects. 1906 was also the year of frequent travels abroad and, as I have already pointed out, this period marks his first contacts with Claparède.

In addition to the new friendships, the subject that interested him most was theosophy, pushing him to broaden his preparation on Eastern thought. For this purpose he gathered his friends in order to study Sanskrit and he avidly read the Bhagavad-Gita, which, as he wrote, showed him:

> "how much the introspective psychology of the Indians, especially with regard to higher states of consciousness, had come to such a point of complexity and depth as to by far surpass contemporary psychology"[30].

In that same year, he went to Rome where he would have the opportunity to meet David Santillana (1855-1931), one of the most expert students of Muslim religious law with a profound knowledge of oriental philosophies, particularly Islamic mysticism, i.e. Sufism. Santillana will introduce him to Indian spirituality, the thinking of Swami Vivekananda, and Ramacharaka's yoga. He will also become a friend of physiologist Luigi Luciani (1840-1919) who will motivate him to become interested in mediumship.

Assagioli would, however, distance himself on several occasions from the interest in spiritualism he had as a youth, considering it responsible for a passive attitude that may hold the risk of "remaining too entangled in the chameleontic sphere of phenomenal psychism"[31].

His encounters with the mystical and oriental traditions resulted in an interior transformation in which Arturo Reghini's influence would be of decisive

---

29   R. Assagioli, cit in A. Berti, op. cit.

30   R. Assagioli, cit. in P. Giovetti, op. cit.

31   R. Assagioli, notes, cit. in A. Berti, op. cit.

importance. It is no accident, therefore, that the latter and Assagioli focused on this in the third and last series of the "Leonardo" journal.[32]

It is important to emphasize how spirituality freed from any dogmatism advocated by theosophy, which acknowledged that all religions share a common basis of truth, met naturally with the modernist aspirations of the Florentine philosophical environment which demanded religious freedom of conscience and considered all individual religions fundamentally authentic. This natural opening toward syncretism then provided the necessary support for the spread of Eastern philosophies and theosophy which, by virtue of its opposition to materialism and positivism, represented a very important spiritual revival movement throughout Europe.

3.1. The *Philosophic Library*: a complete concept of the individual

Arturo Reghini was a mathematician and philosopher from Florence linked to Freemasonry, who founded the Italian headquarters of the Theosophical Society in Rome in 1898. In 1903 he became president of the *Philosophical Library*, commissioned with giving it a new, more serious image.

Augusto Hermet[33] writes that Reghini started "kicking the various spiritic and theosophic crowds out from the salons" using "witty and intelligent quips against the naivety and tricks of more or less exotic occultists". The new president organized a program of conferences, which, after a moment of initial distrust, the Leonardians joined, resulting in very interesting collaborations. He himself published some articles in the *avant-garde* journal.

The Library and the group of young intellectuals were allied by the common desire to revive the reaction to positivism and to promote a spiritual rebirth toward a more complete concept of the individual, seen not only as rationality, but also as feeling, intuition and spirit. The purpose of the Library was to educate: as the minutes of the meetings emerged, the project consisted in transforming it into a "sort of free university for philosophical and religious studies".

Roberto Assagioli was one of its most frequent visitors. At the end of 1907 he held a lecture entitled *Umanismo Ariano (Aryan Humanism)* and in January 1908 he proposed a series of philosophical poetry readings introduced by his essay *Poesia e Filosofia (Poetry and Philosophy)*, followed by contributions from Papini on the poems of Thomas Campanella, from Guido Ferrando on Coleridge, and from Pierce Ronzy on Guyon.

The Philosophy Circle

The formation of the *Philosophy Circle*, as conceived by Papini, is considered to be "the first act of the change in orientation, tending to overcome the uncertain

---

32   A. Berti, op. cit.

33   A. Hermet, *La ventura delle riviste,* cit. in A. Berti, op. cit.

occultist and theosophical past"[34]. Assagioli regularly attended the meetings and, as a testament of the important position he occupied, the members nominated him their representative at the International Convention of Psychology in Geneva.

In 1909 the Philosophy Circle decided to join with the Italian Philosophical Society, but in that year, when Italian journalist and politician Giovanni Amendola (1882-1926) was elected secretary in place of Ferrando, the membership of the Circle at the Philosophical Library ceased due to contrasting directions. Assagioli and some others dissociated themselves from the decision of their comrades by reaffirming their memberships individually.

4. Early writings and ideas

The different character of the journals with which young Roberto collaborated makes us think he was already free of the conformist-anticonformist dichotomies. As we have seen, his very first writings appeared in two very different publications: the serious and traditional "Journal of Psychology" directed by Ferrari and the anti-academic and controversial "Leonardo" of Papini and Prezzolini which proposed a radical vision of positivism through pragmatism. [35]

4.1. The articles between pragmatism and spirituality in "Leonardo": the revelation of his own existential project

"Leonardo" was published from 1903 to 1907, and the issues are traditionally divided into three periods: the first "cultural-political-demagogical", the second "cultural-philosophical-divulgative" and the third "cultural-mystical-metaphysical". During the second period, Assagioli published an article titled *L'arte della creazione* (*The Art of Creation*) on English philosopher and poet Edward Carpenter (1844-1929) in which one can perceive the echo of his embracing magical pragmatism. The other text was on Austrian writer Peter Altenberg (1859-1929) of which he was quite critical. However, most of his writings come out of the third period.[36]

The first of these is called *Fantasia in Re interiore* (*Fantasy in the Inner King*) and came out in February 1907. The story tells of a time long ago, yet inwardly recent, and a city at the foot of a high mountain always hidden by clouds. The ascent of the mountain was apparently impossible. The elders remembered a strange, ancient legend about an invisible castle on the summit, in which a king, imprisoned by a spell, waited for his release. One day an old wise man came to

---

34   Ibid.

35   C. Di Sazio, *Roberto Assagioli: un contributo storico al padre della psicosintesi,* graduate thesis, Facoltà di Magistero di Roma, academic year 1986-87.

36   Ibid.

the town who, after gathering the inhabitants, told them a fantastic story. He said he had lived in a similar city, also lying at the foot of a mountain, and saw several men climb up and perish because they were unprepared. Afterward, many of his fellow citizens cursed the castle and some considered it merely an illusion, denying its existence, until one day a pure-hearted young man of undeniable will discovered a secret passage inside the mountain. He reached the summit but never returned. The wise man could not continue his story because the authorities arrested him and sentenced him to death. But as soon as the sentence was executed, the clouds opened, revealing to everyone the luminous castle sitting on the top of the mountain.

Sebastiano Tilli[37] offers a double interpretation of the fable. From an allegorical point of view, it may be a theosophical or spiritual interpretation. Let's not forget that this writing came at a very precise period in Assagioli's development, that of the birth of his interest in Oriental thought and philosophy, and his friendship with Arturo Reghini. From another point of view, however, the story appears to symbolically precede those which would be the fundamental concepts of Psychosynthesis, such as the subdivision of the psyche into different levels, the principle of elevation and evolution, the need to find an inward path to accomplish such a climb, the importance of intuition and purity of motives in this process, the difference that exists between voluntarism and will, the archetype of the old wise man (who is killed to symbolize the reaction of the conventional to what is new but also the overcoming of any identification with an external master to instead become the masters of ourselves) and the theme of the struggles and obstacles that are met on the path of integration.

But this is not the only intepretation. The fable also becomes a possibility of alluding to the unspeakable, bringing the Self of the person who narrates closer by understanding the inner evolution of that irreducible subjectivity. The story provides a unique and invaluable testimony of an existential path. Indeed, in this short fairy tale one can see the foreshadow of the existential project and the attitude that Assagioli will always retain: as a pure-hearted young man, oblivious to the skepticism and disillusionment that often surrounded him, following his intuition for the rest of his life, seeking an inner way that leads to the soul, to the Self of the individual. As the old man condemned to death indicates, he has and will maintain a deep and unshakable confidence in the fundamental goodness of the human being, the lofty goals, the great potential of the human soul, sacrificing, in the name of higher values, fame and personal recognition, serenely accepting the scientific isolation and the ironic smiles of colleagues.

The second article published is titled *Per Un Nuovo Umanesimo Ariano (For A New Aryan Humanism)* and is complementary to *Fantasy*. With this essay Assagioli aims to bridge some gaps in Eastern studies, attempting to repropose the original

---

37   S. Tilli, *Concetti della psicologia umanistica di Roberto Assagioli,* Ed. Istituto di Psicosintesi, 1980.

teachings of that ancient culture. According to our author, after the failure of the mechanistic explanation of the individual and the universe, the need for a radically new approach to the great problem of life appeared to be urgent. For Assagioli, humankind's task consists in the "unification of our individuality," understood as the different selves that inhabit the bio-psycho-spiritual world of the human being. However, it is not about negating parts of us, but rather harmonizing the various internal trends in a new synthesis.

He was inspired by the classical tradition of the Orphic and Eleusinian Mysteries, by the Christian tradition of the great mystics, and by the Indian culture that can be of help to modern humankind precisely because it lacks the disagreement, characteristic of the West, between feeling and thought, faith and reason. Even back then, the father of Psychosynthesis formulated the prophecy that the advancement of psychology in Europe would require the heritage of Eastern thought.[38]

By quoting Alessandro Berti, we can claim that "if *Fantasy in the Inner King* represents the moment of illumination and ascent, and *For a New Aryan Humanity* represents the guide in this ascent, Assagioli's third essay represents the practical moment to travel the inner path"[39].

In this third article, titled *Il Nuovo Pensiero Americano* (*The New American Thought*), Assagioli proposes the will as a suitable instrument to aid the inner ascent, recognizing it as having a fundamental role in the transformation of oneself. It is intended not as a voluntaristic dream of personal power, but as an inner conquest towards higher tasks, an inner force that works through images and mental depictions. Assagioli says that our psychic life is not something unmovable, but rather "an impetuous mental current of images" on which it is difficult to concentrate; for this reason, they rarely turn into external or internal acts capable of producing change. The article goes on to say that if we could "concentrate our will for a long time on the same image or purpose, it would acquire an incredible, terrible power, capable of leading our consciousness to completely different states, vastly superior to the ordinary."

What differentiates the mysticism that Assagioli borrows from 'the new American thought' from that of east and west is that in these higher states of consciousness, one does not lose the sense of one's own identity. Our author seems to want to clear the field of the "misunderstanding of annihilation", to abandon dualism, abandon the struggle between spirit and matter, to exalt the redemption of the body, which is not considered an impediment to the development of consciousness, but a necessary instrument for doing the work. The young Assagioli has identified hindrances to the attainment of a spiritual consciousness in erroneous psychological attitudes and not in physicality.

---

38   A. Berti, op. cit.

39   Ibid.

In conclusion, the essays in "Leonardo" can be traced back on one hand to a pragmatic and formative psychology. In this regard we can see how the future father of Psychosynthesis was struck by the *Varieties of Religious Experiences* of William James whose psychological implications foreshadow Abraham Maslow's existential-humanistic psychology in many respects. On the other hand, the Leonardo essays can be traced to an imposition of spiritualistic thinking the adherence to which is not attributable to a fashion, but to a deep and personal search in line with that of other great scholars such as, for example, Swiss psychiatrist Carl Gustav Jung (1875-1961).[40]

4.2. The incompleteness of the human soul and modern psychagogy

Starting in 1909, Assagioli contributed to the publication of the journal "La Voce", writing four articles, the last of which, the one on Freud, was to be part of the so-called "historical issue" of February 1910, anticipating the themes dealt with at the *Convegno sulla Questione Sessuale* (*Conference on the Sexual Issue*) organized by the journal itself in November of that year. But of Assagioli's position on psychoanalysis and sexual matters, I will deal more thoroughly later on.

Instead, of fundamental importance were the three articles of 1909 titled *Per una moderna psicagogia, L'educazione morale degli studenti universitari* (*For a Modern Psychagogy, The Moral Education of University Students*), both published in "La Voce", and *La psicologia delle idee forze e la psicagogia* (*The Psychology of the Ideas of Force and Psychagogy*) which appeared in "The Journal of Applied Psychology".

Assagioli is just 21 years old, but in his mind he already has a clear idea of what he considers "true education". In the above-mentioned articles he attacks the old educational system, denouncing the harmfulness of the methods used; the uselessness of exasperated superficial factual knowledge forced on students without taking into account their interests and their attitudes; the absence of courageous sexual education; the social consequences of an education that he calls "shamefully low". He also calls out for a full preparation for life, not just for a profession. For our young college student, it is time to act radically, replacing old and obsolete pedagogy with a new applied science that he intends as "a set of practical methods, rules for action, and not a theoretical science or part of philosophy".

He named this new science *Psychagogy* (a term used by Plato in *Encomium of Elena*), meaning an education of the psyche, a learning process that does not stop at childhood but lasts for a lifetime and embraces the whole of the person. However, it is right to specify, so as not to confuse the terms, that psychagogy is not an eclectic mix of pedagogy and psychology. It could be defined first and foremost as an attitude that implies the ability to extract the most fertile and useful assumptions from different spheres in order to grasp the essential points

---

40   Ibid.

of humankind's development. Assagioli wanted to make psychagogy something more than a method: it would be an "art of education" which, since its elements already exist, doesn't create something from nothing. The work consisted in knowing how to draw those elements from the various disciplines, then to coordinate and harmonize them. The largest reservoir from which to draw these elements was psychology: not the experimental kind, nor, as we have seen, the theoretical kind, but the kind derived from "observing life, works of art, and the practice of pedagogy"[41].

Psychagogy is therefore not a theory, nor a technique, nor a mere fusion of psychological theories with the pedagogical. The Greek term implies an active and dynamic conception of education. In fact, it gives the sense of guiding, of developing what is already potentially present. It is not about forming mental patterns, but about cultivating the spontaneous development of what is implicit in human nature.[42]

Psychagogy differs from psychology above all because it looks not only at the ill part of the human being but also at the healthy part, and secondly because it is not a theoretical science. Then, it differs from pedagogy because it is not limited to the education of the child. The new discipline is directed to the adult, indeed, to the human being throughout his/her existence because "man is never something definitive, static, fulfilled ... he is continually developing"[43].

And so Assagioli proposes a global study of the human mind in terms of an active, practical and operational application in which whatever is within the child or the adult can emerge and strengthen with the participation and help of the guide-therapist. Psychagogy is concerned with the development and organization of the internal energies that are waiting to be used correctly, and concerns the Self of an individual.[44]

The sources of inspiration were Western mystics, Christian religious psychologists, the "true geniuses of introspection and inner action" of the orient, both Hindu and Buddhist, and the Anglo-American *new thinkers*, who "even with exaggeration and naiveté are carriers of ingenious psychological intuitions and offer very practical and effective methods".

4.3. Assagioli and psychoanalysis: a courageous and misunderstood pioneer

It is now unanimously acknowledged that Assagioli, at the age of only sixteen, was the first in Italy to deal with psychoanalysis and to have translated Freud, recognizing the revolutionary extension of his discoveries.[45] This was no small

41   R. Assagioli, cit. in A. Berti, op. cit.

42   S. Tilli, op. cit.

43   R. Assagioli, *Psicosintesi - Armonia della vita*, op. cit.

44   S. Tilli, op. cit.

45   S. Maharaba, *Lineamenti della psicologia italiana: 1870-1945*, Giunti-Barbera, 1981 and

achievement if we think about how psychoanalysis was initially ostracized in Italy. Professor and psychoanalyst Emilio Servadio (1904-1995) recalls in a personal interview with Paola Giovetti[46]:

> "Psychiatrists back then didn't understand or accept psychoanalysis. Also holding it hostage was the idealist philosophy of Croce and Gentile, the leftists, fascism and the Catholic Church (…)."

Humorism and smiling wisdom

The first article in which Assagioli proves to already have an initial knowledge of the Freudian writings was published in 1906 in the *"Rivista di psicologia applicata alla Pedagogia e alla Psicopatologia"* (*"Journal of Psychology Applied to Pedagogy and Psychopathology"*), founded in 1905 to investigate the possibilities of adopting principles of pure science into people's lives, to offer young people the opportunity to express their hypotheses and to hear the ideas of others on the topics they themselves cultivated.[47] The director was Giulio Cesare Ferrari, professor of psychology in Bologna, a strict experimentalist and disseminator of William James in Italy.

The article's title is *Gli effetti del riso e le loro applicazioni pedagogiche* (*The Effects Of Laughter And Their Pedagogical Applications*). In it our young passionate psychologist argues that laughter can have an exciting effect on intelligence, developing critical sense and capacity of observation, and that it can have a relaxing and regenerating effect, re-establishing inner equilibrium. Laughing at something, he writes, is basically recognizing our moral independence from it. Assagioli refers to the book *Jokes and Their Relation to the Unconscious* by Freud, whom he calls "one of the most educated and ingenious modern scientists" although he does not further examine Freudian concepts in this article, holding to the purpose of showing the possible pedagogical applications of laughter and good humor.

The article is worthy of attention because it marks the beginning of his interest in psychoanalysis and also because it foretells of a trait that will remain a steady part of Assagioli's personality, that is, considering optimism, sense of humor and joy as inspirational principles of his philosophy of life.

Freud, Jung, Bleuler, Kraepelin and Jones

Towards the end of 1907, probably through Claparède, whom he met the year before, Assagioli was introduced to the Burghölzli psychiatric hospital. Attending this famous University of Zurich clinic for two years, which also hosted Carl Gustav Jung, then considered Freud's heir apparent, the future father of Psychosynthesis decided to prepare his thesis on psychoanalysis.

M. David, op. cit.

46   P. Giovetti, op. cit.

47   S. Marhaba, op. cit.

In 1908, to complete his studies, he went to the Nervenklinik sanitorium in Munich and attended the courses of German psychiatrist Emil Kraepelin (1856-1926), an anti-Freudian known for his studies on early dementia. Here he had the opportunity to meet and associate with British neurologist and psychoanalyst Ernest Jones (1879-1958), a follower and future biographer of Freud. Jones himself, recalling this episode of his life, claimed that Assagioli was "introduced to psychoanalysis by me during the time we spent together at Kraepelin's clinic(...)"[48]. In truth, we know that it would be rather more precise to talk about a more profound study of Freudian theories that Assagioli had already approached in Geneva with Claparède and in Zurich with Bleuler and Jung.

Still in 1908, when he finished his time in Munich, Assagioli participated in two conferences held respectively in Oxford and London, the first on the history of religions, the second on moral and scholastic education. He reviewed them in French for the "Scientia" journal which Michel David[49] defined as "a beautiful instrument of high-level scientific dissemination and true cultural Europeanization, open to all disciplines and professions." Our author later reviewed the writings of Freud, Stekel and Ellis.

Participation in these conferences by the future father of Psychosynthesis was of particular importance as it provides us with a testimony of his early interest in pedagogical issues that as we have seen above, will find its best expression in the articles on psychology in the following year.

In July 1908 Assagioli returned to the Burghölzli clinic, where Jung, writing to Freud reserved for him some quite friendly words:

"Among these (migratory birds) there is a very kind and perhaps astute acquaintance, a certain Dr. Roberto Assagioli of Florence, of that city's psychiatric clinic. Professor Tanzi had him write his degree thesis in psychoanalytic theory. He is a very receptive young man who seems to have vast medical knowledge and is also an enthusiastic follower, who ventures into new territory with the impetus that is needed. He wants to come and see you next spring"[50].

The Geneva Congress on Psychology and founding of the Italian Psychological Society

The period spent at the Burghölzli psychiatric hospital was interrupted by his participation in the *Convention of Psychology* in Geneva held from August 2nd to August 7th, 1909. Assagioli was particularly interested in the work dealing with the psychology of religious expression. In his review of the convention for the "Coenobium" journal, he highlights a substantial difference between the speakers who did not have a real experience of what they were talking about, such as the Danish philosopher Harald Hoffding (1843-1931) and American psychologist

---

48   Jones, cit. in A. Berti, op. cit.

49   M. David, op. cit.

50   Letters between Freud and Jung, cit. in A. Berti, op. cit.

James H. Lueba (1867-1946) whom he defined as "intellectual, abstract and too metaphysical," compared to those who have "passionately explored the inner worlds rising to the peaks of spiritual consciousness"[51], like Polish philosopher Wincenty Lutoslawski (1863-1954) who immediately became a good friend. Assagioli polemically says that those who talk about such subjects without having gone through them personally are to be considered incompetent.

The Geneva Congress was important for another fact: noting the disproportion between the value and the number of Italian participants and the beneficial effect of their participation, the idea arose of establishing an association uniting those involved in research and psychological studies in order to coordinate the efforts of the various researchers. Assagioli was among the first to associate himself with the Psychological Society whose first meeting, held right in Florence at the Philosophical Library, registered fifty-three participants.

Association with the Psychoanalysis Society and the first thesis on psychoanalysis in Italy

Assagioli dedicated the last period of 1909 to writing his graduate thesis and in September of the same year he returned to the Burghölzli clinic. His interest in psychoanalytic theories allowed him, though not yet a graduate, to be admitted to the Freudian Society of Zurich and, as a member, to write in the yearbook of the Society, the "Jahrbuch". At the same time, he began corresponding with Freud who then writes to Jung: "Yesterday I had a nice letter from Assagioli from Florence, written, by the way, in an impeccable manner." Freud expected the young Italian student to work to spread the psychoanalytic movement. The opportunity to do so would be offered, as we shall see, by the "La Voce" journal that in February 1910 devoted an entire issue to the topic of sexuality.

In March 1910, a convention was held in Nuremberg, attended by all major proponents of the movement: Jung, Adler, Abraham, Stegmann and of course Freud, whose presentation titled *The Future Possibilities of Psychotherapy* was the first and the most fascinating for Assagioli. He followed with fervid interest all the reports and debates, then reviewed them for the "*Rivista di Psicologia Applicata*" ("*Journal of Applied Psychology*")[52]. From the words of the article he seems to have remained favorably affected by the climate created by the participants, so much so that he wrote: "Freudians are distinguished by vivacity and 'wit', they make ingenious comparisons, and generally show an extraordinary understanding of lower psychic life."

The Convention marked a major step forward towards the recognition of psychoanalysis together with the foundation of the International Psychoanalytical

---

51   R. Assagioli, *La psicologia della religione al Congresso di Ginevra,* Coenobium, 1909, n. 4.

52   R. Assagioli, *Seconda riunione psicoanalitica,* Rivista di Psicologia Applicata, a. VI, n. 3, 1910.

Association. Assagioli, the only Italian, became a member and began to participate intensively in the activities by making contact himself with the first French member, Dr. Pierre Morichau-Beauchant and writing in the "Jahrbuch" an article titled *Freudian Teachings in Italy*[53]. Assagioli argues that "surprisingly, Freudian doctrines have not aroused great interest in Italy" and finds the cause in the methods of psychiatric research where Italian researchers are looking for either "a clinical direction", aimed at the study of symptoms and the classification of psychoses or "anatomical direction", pointed at histological and biochemical issues. Then he followed with a quick review of the first Italian writings on Freud.

On July 1, 1910, Assagioli presented his thesis on psychoanalysis, the first in Italy, with Prof. Eugenio Tanzi scoring 105 points out of 110. After finishing his studies he was finally free to follow his vocation. The interest with which he heard Freud's report on psychotherapy in Nuremberg was an indication of the direction his research would take. After graduating, in the autumn of the same year he embarked on a study trip with the aim of deepening his knowledge of psycho-therapeutic techniques. The first stage was once again the Burghölzli clinic. He would tell himself: "I went to Zurich to study with Eugenio Bleuler, the discoverer of schizophrenia, and when I returned, I practiced psychoanalysis, but I soon discovered its limitations."[54]

The Sex Question: "The Ideas of Sigmund Freud on Sexuality" and the Convention on the sex issue

Entering the lively debate that was developing on the sexual question in the puritan environment of Umbertine society, in February 1910 the editors of "La Voce" published an issue entirely dedicated to the subject. With his contribution, the article titled *Le idee di Sigmund Freud sulla sessualità* (*Sigmund Freud's Ideas On Sexuality*), Assagioli aimed to briefly illustrate the new discoveries of the Viennese neurologist by adopting the advice of the latter to overcome "that mixture of lubricity and *prudery* with which this topic is usually treated".

Our author wrote that "the profound and unbiased study of the sexuality question will highlight many animalistic and perverse parts of human nature", and went on to say that only by recognizing "all the blind instinctive forces that dwell in man we can validly fight and dominate them". With great clarity, and without the inaccuracies that are easily found in other articles on Freud in that period, Assagioli penned the *Tre saggi sulla teoria della sessualità* (*Three Essays On The Theory Of Sexuality*) and completely expounded on the theory of libido without skirting any topic, certainly salacious for the time, such as that of childhood sexuality.

---

53   R. Assagioli, *Die Freudschen Lehren in Italien*, "Jahrbuch der Psychoanalytische und Psychopatologische Forschungen", a. 1910.

54   S. Keen, *The Golden Mean of Roberto Assagioli*, interview, Centro Studi di Psicosintesi "R. Assagioli", 1987.

His objective expounding of Freudian ideas was followed by critical remarks. First of all, he distinguished the scientific content of psychoanalysis, defined as "of extraordinary practical importance" from the particular characteristics that were determined by the Middle-European environment and culture of the time. He then pointed to Freud's "tendency to attach extraordinary importance to the inferior and instinctive sides of sexuality, and above all to its aberrations", believing that this was due to the fact that Freud worked predominantly with people afflicted with pathologies, and that this led to undue and premature generalizations and neglecting other important aspects of the psyche, such as the higher manifestations of love.

However, the strongest criticism of Freud concerned the concept of will, a decisive element of Assagioli's thinking that gradually led him away from psychoanalysis. He rebuked the Viennese master for not having made a clear distinction between the mechanism of repression and the conscious and harmonious domination of instincts, and consequently had not given the necessary importance to the study of sublimation. Assagioli supported the possibility of conscious transformation of the instincts precisely thanks to the process of sublimation, and concluded the article by affirming the importance of sexual education which must be imparted from early childhood. In this context, he said:

> "Only those who know and understand how to fearlessly face and tame the obscure monsters that crawl in the lower realms of their being can, aware of their pitfalls, explore the brightest peaks of their soul and study the highest mysteries of human life."

And so the newest science of psychoanalysis came forth to bring reassertions and contributions to ancient wisdom that viewed knowledge of oneself as the beginning and end of all human knowledge.[55]

After devoting an entire issue to the subject of sexuality, "La Voce" organized a conference on the same subject, held in Florence in November 1910. The idea of the conference was developed by Prezzolini and the various presentations were then published in the next issue of the journal.

Assagioli presented an account on the transformation and sublimation of sexual energies, a natural development of the article on Freud, but the prestigious journal never published it. During the conference, a controversy arose between Prezzolini and the future father of Psychosynthesis (see Chapter I, Para. 2.2) who was accused of supporting a veiled positivist position. David wrote: "The affluence of young people validated Prezzolini's idea of organizing the Convention on Sexual Issues, ... but the applause received by Assagioli and the idea formed of psychoanalysis after listening to his presentation made Prezzolini immediately distrustful. We will see that this distrust never diminished. In any case, it may not

---

55   A. Gasparini Riondino, *Scritti giovanili di Roberto Assagioli,* typescript.

be impossible to find the echo of Assagioli's words in some Florentine intellectual's diaries from that time. For now, I'm just hoping for it."[56]

The Assagioli presentation was published the following year in the *Rivista di Psicologia Applicata* (*Journal of Applied Psychology*). The article shows an increase in his appreciation for Freud, probably due to the reading of the Viennese psychologist's *Five Lessons On Psychoanalysis* that led him to improve his knowledge of Freudian thought. But Assagioli did not hold back criticism of those who, dealing with sublimation, believed that they could explain it completely by reducing this "higher manifestation" to a "product of the transformation of a phenomenon of a lower order". He believed that connecting the higher manifestations of human nature with those inferior is methodically incorrect and reductive.

The last part of the article is an *exposé*, which he described as "summary and incomplete", of some fundamental requirements valid for any sublimation process: a mental inclination toward sincerity and courage with regard to sexuality; a consideration of the instinct as a biological function and not according to morality; the development of the will to actuate such sublimation; engaging in creative activities. For Assagioli the demonstration of the infinite capacity of humankind to sublimate is found in the autobiographies and biographies of great artists.

5. The friendship with Carl Gustav Jung

As I have said, after graduating, Assagioli spent a period at the Zurich clinic to study with Bleuler. But Zurich held more interest than just the activities that took place at Burghölzli. Indeed a favorite destination in the city was a cottage on Lake Zurich, the residence of psychiatrist and psychoanalyst Carl Gustav Jung. Assagioli recalled his meetings with the great Swiss psychiatrist:

> "Jung graciously welcomed visitors who came from everywhere, and I treasure a living memory of the animated conversations with him in his big study, its walls all carpeted with books and full of curious exotic objects." [57]

One can suppose that there was a friendship between them, defined by our author as "more than cordial", due not just to the common interest in research and psychoanalytic practice. Both, in fact, shared a passion for oriental cultures, paranormal and occult phenomena, divination, alchemy and astrology.

Their relationship lasted for a long time and through the few communications in our possession (only Jung conserved Assagioli's letters) we can see how they greeted each other as "brother", which could suggest that their bond originated from a shared ideal of brotherhood for humanitarian purposes. This hypothesis seems to find confirmation in the "collective letter to friends" written by Assagioli at the end of the Second World War, in which he told of his intention to "reconnect

---

56   M. David, op. cit.

57   R. Assagioli, *Carl Jung e la psicosintesi*, typescript, 1966.

as much as possible the good threads that connected us in the past"[58]. I will return to this letter, a precious account of the period when Assagioli was persecuted by the Nazis, in the next chapter, transcribing it in its entirety.

On the occasion of the death of his friend and colleague, Assagioli held a series of lessons at the Institute of Psychosynthesis entitled *Jung e la Psicosintesi* (*Jung and Psychosynthesis*) in which he commemorated Jung in words that indicate how much esteem he held for him:

> "... he was an ingenious investigator and therapist of the human soul, one who bravely worked with a mind free of prejudices and academic constraints. (...) His qualities were great and diverse: he had a profound human sense, an intense thirst for knowledge, an admirable rectitude and intellectual modesty, a sincere awareness of his own shortcomings and of those of others. (...) He never claimed that he created a complete and definitive system; he always stated that psychology is a new science (...) he's been a brave pioneer who has opened new paths and dimensions to the human soul." [59]

Assagioli considered the contributions of Jung precious, even genial. He recognized the fact that Jung expanded the field of psychology by freeing it from the strict limitations of purely descriptive objectivism, demonstrating the existence and value of higher psychic functions and spiritual needs, and to have always kept in mind the relativity of any knowledge and the inevitable presence of the subjective dimension in every researcher. Our author could not help describing him as "... among all the psychotherapists, the one closest to the positions and the practice of Psychosynthesis."[60]

But it was not only from a human point of view that the two masters shared the same determination to carry out personal research outside formal schemes and acknowledgments, even at the cost of enormous sacrifices. The qualities Assagioli attributes to Jung we can likewise attribute to Assagioli himself. In fact, like Jung, he appreciated the limits of psychoanalysis, and even before his colleague, detached himself from them to independently formulate his own psychological conception.

6. The "Psiche" Journal

The years 1910 and 1911 saw the greatest commitment to psychoanalysis, but already in 1912 Assagioli moved away from the orthodox Freudian teachings to develop his theories and founded the journal "Psiche" with the collaboration of professors Guido Villa, Sante De Sanctis (1862-1935) and Enrico Morselli (1852-1929). The publication pursued a precise purpose of dissemination and

---

58   R. Assagioli, cit. in A. Berti, op. cit.

59   R. Assagioli, op. cit.

60   Ibid.

education, as is apparent from the programmatic words written by Assagioli on the title page of the first issue of January 1912:

> "We decided to give it a try: to bring together a group of psychologists who are convinced that a more lively and flexible psychology needs to be developed; a psychology that, albeit not alienated from analysis, focuses mostly on synthesis, as in our conscious and subconscious activity, a psychology whose results are not a cold theoretical notion, but lend themselves to important and fruitful applications in everyday life and contribute to the moral uplifting of men." [61]

The journal came out in Florence every two months, from January 1912 until 1915, and had as its master of ceremonies Roberto Assagioli himself. The program was interesting and ambitious, but from the first issue, our author had to point out the difficulty of adhering to it due to the lack of preparedness and the lack of coordination amongst Italian scientists.

The controversial target of the journal is organicism, positivistic materialism and the strict experimentalism of the Wundtian tradition, which Assagioli contrasts with a "total human psychology" open to all fields of knowledge: 1) Psychology and Philosophy 2) Physiological and Experimental Psychology 3) Comparative Psychology and Psychobiology 4) Pathological Psychology 5) Child and Pedagogical Psychology 6) Psychology of the Personality (Ethology) and Psychagogy 7) Collective and Social Psychology 8) Ethnic Psychology 9) Supernormal Psychology 10) Psychoanalysis and the Study of the Subconscious 11) Psychology of Religion 12) Aesthetic Psychology 13) Sexual Psychology 14) Judicial Psychology 15) Study of Autobiographies and Contributions to Psychology found in Poetical and Literary Works 16) History of Western Psychology 17) Oriental Psychology.

Another great merit of "Psiche" was that it published the translation of many pages from Freud and Adler and the essential contributions of the philosopher Francesco De Sarlo (1864-1937) and his group. At the journal Assagioli contributed both with his work as chief editor and also with numerous interesting articles, amongst which I cite: *La psicologia del subconscio - La psicoanalisi, Il metodo psicoanalitico, Psicologia e psicoterapia, Gli errori degli scienziati, I cavalli pensanti e i loro critici, Psicologia individuale e comparata* and *Le dottrine di Alfred Adler.* (*The Psychology of the Subconscious - Psychoanalysis, The Psychoanalytic Method, Psychology and Psychotherapy, The Errors of Scientists, Thinking Horses and Their Critics, Individual and Comparative Psychology,* and *The Doctrines of Alfred Adler.*)

The publications were brutally interrupted by the outbreak of the First World War. Along with the "Psiche" journal, the first phase of the biographical trail of Roberto Assagioli also closes. This experience will mark the completion of his detachment from Freud, although he continued to have great respect for him and to consider psychoanalysis as an indispensable technique for the exploration of the unconscious: the transition from psychoanalysis to Psychosynthesis.

---

61   R. Assagioli, cit. in S. Maharaba, op. cit.

CHAPTER II

CONSOLIDATION

If up to 1914 Assagioli wrote many articles, we can still follow the evolution of his reflections quite well between 1915 and 1926, although his production became less copious and relevant. Yet, precisely in these years, his thought came to almost definitive maturity with very few subsequent revisions. His friendship with Carl Gustav Jung and the clinical experience accumulated during the war period was certainly decisive in this regard.[62]

The mature Assagioli personified the natural evolution of the young psychiatrist, founder and contributor of "Psiche".

1. The years around the First World War

1.1. A soap pistol

As I have already pointed out, the outbreak of the First World War interrupted Assagioli's activities; he was called to arms to serve as a lieutenant in the medical corps. Little is known about this period. He neither talked nor left written notes about it. He only said that he not only never fired a shot, but that he never carried a real pistol. To give the impression of being armed, he made a gun out of soap and painted it black.

The tremendous spectacle of war does not seem to have affected his innate optimism, nor did it significantly influence his thinking, except to convince him even further of wanting to dedicate his life to the cure and liberation of humankind's existence. The ultimate aim of his commitment and his work was to transform the individual, indeed to help the individual transform himself, and, through the individual to create a society characterized by upright human relationships in which people are aware and responsible, capable of exercising their own will to express themselves creatively and to be fully realized in the world.

1.2. Marriage and moving to Rome

After the war, Assagioli resumed his activities and began to study and work as a psychotherapist. We know he had a first, short and childless marriage, ending in divorce: an unusual thing for the time. Shortly thereafter, in 1922, Roberto

---

62   C. Di Sazio, op. cit.

married Nella Ciapetti, a woman of a solid and sure temperament. In 1923, Ilario, their only son, was born, and in 1926 the entire family moved to Rome for reasons that are unknown, although we can assume that Rome, being less provincial, was more open and stimulating than Florence, offering Assagioli an interesting environment and space suitable for carrying out his studies and his work.

2. From Psychagogy to Psychosynthesis

2.1. The Institute of Culture and Psychic Therapy

The years between the two world wars were those in which our author's thought deepened and consolidated.

1926 is definitely an important date because in that year Assagioli founded the *Istituto di Cultura e Terapia Psichica* (*Institute of Culture and Psychic Therapy*) in Rome and began to use the word "psychosynthesis" publicly. However, it would be necessary to wait until 1933 for the Institute to be named the *Istituto di Psicosintesi* (*Institute of Psychosynthesis*). On May 4, during the inaugural session, Assagioli held a lecture titled *Come si educa la volontà* (*How To Educate the Will*), a topic that would always be one of the cornerstones of his thinking.

The purpose of the Institute was to contribute to the renewal of the individual and society by "promoting a better and more effective expression of inner energies and carrying out a work of psychic prevention and treatment"[63] through the teaching of psychological training techniques and integral development of the psyche. The program revived the ideas that, from a very young age the father of Psychosynthesis had matured and expressed in articles written for "Leonardo", and even more so in those on psychagogy published in "La Voce".

At the Institute, Assagioli held conferences, gave lectures and received individual patients, but he mostly worked with small groups of people: in this he was also a forerunner. In a commemorative article published in *"La Nazione"* (*"The Nation"*) ten years after Assagioli's death, Alfredo Scanzani wrote that the Institute could rightly be regarded as a progenitor "of those growth centers that became fashionable in the 1970s in America and subsequently in Europe"[64].

Also in 1926, our author published the booklet *Psychosynthesis: A New Method of Healing* in English, translated into Italian the following year with the title *Un nuovo metodo di cura: la psicosintesi*. It explains how, after using various psychotherapeutic methods, including suggestion, persuasion, psychoanalysis and other active techniques, he developed a new approach aimed at reconstructing the patient's entire personality. He stressed the importance of body-psyche interaction, outlining the principles that underpin psychosomatic medicine today, but added

---

63   Art. 2 of the Statutes, *Istituto di Psicosintesi*.

64   A. Scanzani, article in "La Nazione", 24 Dec. 1983.

that Psychosynthesis finds its application not only in the treatment of psycho-physical disorders: it is also a method for education of children as well as adults, in self-training and for the harmonization of interpersonal and social relationships, as it represents, "not just an ideal of health and harmony, but also of development and growth."

And so, Psychagogy gave birth to Psychosynthesis, in which Assagioli summed up all his pioneering insights, demonstrating his great openness to every branch of science, especially human sciences, and to spiritual disciplines. His intent was to educate the individual in self-transformation, to make him or her co-author of their own destiny.

2.2. "Nemo propheta in patria"

The founder of Psychosynthesis was an isolated character on the Italian cultural landscape. As I have already mentioned in the premise, he was always more interested in meeting with the individual or working with small groups rather than accepting personal awards and prestige. He did not want to belong to static institutions and he liked to repeat, quoting philosopher and dear friend Hermann Keyserling: "Whoever deals with the future, cannot pay heed to the squabbles of the present"[65] but with a touch of bitterness sometimes lamented: "Nemo propheta in patria"- "no one is a prophet in his own land".

The years between 1926 and immediately before the war were full of activity of a psychiatric and psychological nature, as well as spiritual. Assagioli traveled extensively in Europe as well as to America in order to meet scholars and make Psychosynthesis known abroad. He was in correspondence and personal contact with some of the most important scientists and scholars of his time. Of Freud and Jung I have already spoken. In addition, among others, he became acquainted with the prophet of progressive Judaism Martin Buber (1878-1965), German thinker Hermann Keyserling (1880-1946), the genius of the century Albert Einstein (1879-1955), writer James Joyce (1882-1941), Zen master Daisetz Teitaro Suzuki (1870-1966), poet Rabindranath Tagore (1861-1941), for whom he also acted as a translator and with whom he passionately studied pedagogical ideas, anthropologist Alexandra David-Neel (1868-1969), Lama Anagarika Govinda (1898-1985) as well as many of the major exponents of contemporary psychology.

And it was from abroad that the first important awards came. I have already mentioned the booklet of 1926, *Psychosynthesis: A New Method of Healing* written in English. But a major contribution in making Assagioli's work known outside Italy was the publication of two articles written at the beginning of the 30's in the prestigious English *Hibbert Journal*. In Italy, we had to wait until 1973 to read them![66]

---

65   P. Giovetti, op. cit.

66   R. Assagioli, *Principi e metodi della psicosintesi terapeutica,* Ed. Astrolabio, 1973.

2.3. The human drama and a "pluridimensional" concept of the personality

The first of these two articles, titled *Psicologia dinamica e psicosintesi* (*Dynamic Psychology and Psychosynthesis*), traces a brief history of the psychology of the unconscious, starting from Janet and Breuer and passing through Freud, subsequently addressing the developments and modifications that, at the conception of the latter, were advanced by some of his students and followers such as Abraham, Ferenczi, Adler, Jung, Rank, Steckel, Melanie Klein and Binswanger. Assagioli subsequently took into consideration the innovative movements which, in his view, contributed to a more complete knowledge of human nature: the nascent field of psychosomatic medicine, the psychology of religion, anthropological and social studies, research on the superconscious and its manifestations, research on parapsychological phenomena, oriental psychology, holistic psychology, and existential psychology.

Assagioli aimed to coordinate all this material in a synthesis to reach a "'pluri-dimensional' conception of human personality, which is certainly not perfect and definitive, but wider and more responsive to the multiform reality than what has been formulated so far"[67], a conception that allows for "a wider knowledge of human drama, travails and problems that weigh on each of us, and show us the path leading to inner freedom" [68]. For our author, this drama could be synthetically defined as that of the man who "by obscurely intuiting to be 'one' and then finding himself manifold, does not understand himself, and not understanding, does not therefore possess himself"[69]. He then finds in the ancient Delphic imperative "Know yourself" the first step towards freedom, the second step in the domain of known elements possible thanks to the process of disidentification, the third in the gradual transformation of these elements from their own existential plan. Thus, depending on the case, or at different stages of the process, psychosynthesis can become a method for curing neuro-psychic and psychosomatic disorders, a means of self-training, or a psycho-spiritual development method.

The second article, *Realizzazione di sé e disturbi psichici (Realization of Self and Psychological Disorders)*, introduced an absolutely fundamental theme in psychosynthesis. Assagioli opened this paper criticizing the pathological direction of psychoanalysis and ascribing to it, as he had done twenty years ago, "an exaggerated accentuation of morbid manifestations and inferior aspects of human nature"[70], an attitude that led to "undue generalization of the many discoveries from psychopathology to psychology of normal men." Assagioli, however, saw the beginning of a healthy reaction to this obscure and pessimistic vision, although he admitted that he did not fall victim to the opposite extreme, which is to look at a conception of the individual "as a unified personality, which unfortunately is

---

67   Ibid.

68   Ibid.

69   Ibid.

70   Ibid.

quite far from being true." In the psychosynthetic vision, organic unity is a goal that can be visualized, gradually approached and, to a certain extent, achieved, rather than an already existing reality.

Further on in the paper he exposed the various stages of self-realization, stating that it "can be reached at different levels and does not necessarily include what can be defined as the transpersonal or spiritual level." After having thus distinguished a personal realization of self (personal psychosynthesis) from a spiritual achievement (transpersonal psychosynthesis), he continued by emphasizing the importance of making a clear distinction between "common" pathological disorders and disorders arising from inner awakening characterized by a process that can be divided into five different phases:

- crises that precede spiritual awakening
- crises generated by the awakening
- reactions to awakening
- phases of the transmutation process
- the dark night of the soul

I will go back to the details of the particular phases in the fourth part of the book (see Part 4, Chapter VII, Par. 4.2). For now, I'll just emphasize the importance of a review of diagnostic criteria for therapeutic purposes. In fact, our author found that the same disorder may, while presenting the same symptomatology, have a regressive or progressive character depending on whether it is related to ordinary patients or people who are going through a period of spiritual awakening. The two cases call for very different interventions.

The '30s marked an increase in Assagioli's activity. In addition to the aforementioned articles and the activities and writings of which I will speak shortly, he again looked toward Freud and gave several lessons on various subjects such as: *L'animo molteplice (The Multiple Mind)*, *Le energie latenti in noi e il loro uso nell'educazione e nella medicina (The Dormant Energies In Us and Their Use In Education and Medicine)*, *La struttura dell'inconscio e i suoi rapporti con la coscienza (The Structure of the Unconscious and Its Relations With the Conscience)*, *Il subcosciente e la suggestione (The Subconscious and Suggestion)*, *La natura e le leggi della suggestione (Nature and Laws of Suggestion)* and *La pratica della suggestione (The Practice of Suggestion)*.[71]

2.4 Writings on the Transpersonal

We know of articles on the transpersonal subject going back to 1921. The first, titled *Il risveglio dell'anima (The Awakening of the Soul)*[72], brings many accounts "from every era and every part of the world" by the "souls who have received the

---

71   R. Assagioli, *Corsi di lezioni sulla psicosintesi*, Istituto di Psicosintesi.

72   Published in "Ultra", XV, 1-2, 1921.

light"[73]. Assagioli, examining the documentation of such "strange inner states", wondered what their significance was: whether they were purely morbid facts, fatigue or imbalances of the mind or body, or if they were rather the accounts of "a new and wonderful event". He noted that although the various writings presented a number of differences at a first reading, in fact these differences were only formal, linked to the different religious beliefs or the temperamental characteristics of the awakened. He also emphasized that all those who have tried to talk about their transpersonal experiences have emphasized the inadequacy of human language and of every description.

The article goes on to consider the accounts left by two famous contemporary authors; the first from Russian writer Leo Tolstoy (1828-1910), who in his *Confessions* gives a detailed account of the existential crisis he experienced at the height of his maturity and reputation; the second, that of the Indian poet Rabindranath Tagore, who recalls in *My Reminiscences* many of the spiritual experiences he had since early childhood.

It is interesting to mention the article also because it reveals a fundamental method used in Psychosynthesis to study human nature. It always starts from the subjective experience of an individual, or better yet from the individual's account of the experience, and so the privileged sources from which the information is drawn, rather than accurate scientific studies, are autobiographies, biographies, letters and diaries, or even firsthand declarations.

From 1923 we have the article titled *Marta e Maria (Marta and Maria)*[74], in which our author describes the characteristics of active and contemplative life, and supports the need for proper integration or synthesis between the two; while from 1925 we have *Mistica e medicina (Mysticism and Medicine)*[75] in which, following the article written in 1921, he criticizes the reductive and pathological vision with which medicine considers mystic phenomena.

Starting in 1930, remembering that Assagioli moved to Rome in '26, writings became more abundant. Even before that date, he wrote *Stadi e crisi dello sviluppo spirituale (Stages and Crises of Spiritual Development)*. In 1932, in *La purificazione dell'anima (The Purification of the Soul)*[76], he faced the problem of morality, sustaining that "any immorality, amoralism or supermorality ... renders us the more enslaved the more we are deluded and unaware of our chains." Still in '32 he held a series of lessons on transpersonal elements in the personality titled *Psicologia individuale e sviluppo spirituale (Individual Psychology and Spiritual Development)*. Here he deals with qualities that can connect the personal self to higher dimensions of conscience and explains that these higher dimensions may vary according to

---

73   Ibid.

74   Published in "Delta", year 1, n. 9-10-11, 1923.

75   Published in "Ultra", XIX, n. 1, 1925.

76   Published in "Alba spirituale", n. 5, 1959.

personal typology: for some, the driving element is beauty, for others, love, and for yet others, joy, or will.

From 1935 there is an essay on *Spiritualità del '900 (Spirituality of the 1900s)*[77]. Assagioli opened the article by noting the clearly materialistic features of the period, denouncing intellectualism—dressed as transcendence—as one of the worst obstacles to genuine spirituality and the misunderstandings and confusion to which the term "spirit" lends itself. After having postulated that the spirit cannot be accepted intellectually since it transcends the human mind, he specifies what can be considered its manifestation in man, that is, "all that causes him to transcend his self-centered exclusiveness, his fears, his inertia, his hedonism; all that leads him to discipline, to dominate, to direct the disorderly, instinctive and emotional forces that stir within him, all that induces him to recognize a reality that is wider, superior, social or ideal, and to enter into it by overcoming the limitations of one's own personality."

He continued, stating that, despite the impressive technological developments and general standardization, a great change was under way. He saw the signs in the new discoveries of physics, in the revolt against positivism seen in the field of philosophy, in the flourishing of psychology which was increasingly open to input from other branches. Above all, he noted the growing interest in the spiritual dimensions of existence that was leading more and more people to recognize the relativity of every doctrinal formulation and every formal arrangement, to learn about methods of discipline and internal conquest that can favor a direct and personal experience of truth, attempting to bring spirituality into daily life.

In particular Assagioli indicated two fundamental aspects of the new era: the emergence of "an integral spirituality, which includes the whole of man, without stagnant compartments, without opposition between mind and heart, between soul and body, between inner life and practical life which extends to social life ..." and the "rapid extension of the struggle, research and awakening to an increasing number of human beings." To support all this he cites Jung, who in his book *Modern Man In Search of a Soul* makes the following statement:

> "Over the last 30 years, people from every corner of the Earth have come to consult me. I have cared for many hundreds of the sick ... Of all those who were in the second half of life, that is, those over 35, there was not even one whose problem wasn't, in the end, to find a religious vision of life."

The meaning every individual attributes to their own existence is the great theme that fascinated Assagioli, a theme that will be resumed more than twenty years later by American humanistic psychologists.

In 1938 Assagioli held another series of lectures on transpersonal psychosynthesis, in which he dealt with the subject of obstacles to spiritual development. He identified three main categories: mental, emotional and voluntary. His focus

---

[77] Published in "La cultura del mondo", Bologna, anno XVIII, n. 6, 1962.

was above all the emotional as he felt that skepticism and doubt about the dimensions of meaning, the sacred and the mysterious in reality hide an infinite variety of fears: the fear of death, solitude, weakness, the unknown, mystery, and above all the fear of suffering. Another hindrance is the tendency toward attachment, not only active toward things and people, but also passive, such as inertia or wallowing in the past. Finally, he took into consideration aggressiveness in its various manifestations of anger, resentment, condemnation, blame, and especially criticism.

The last article we have news of prior to the outbreak of war was titled *Trasmutazione e sublimazione delle energie affettive e sessuali (Transmutation and Sublimation of Emotional and Sexual Energies)*[78]. This writing provides us with an important demonstration of the interest and importance that Assagioli constantly attributes to the issues raised by psychoanalysis. I think it is important to emphasize this point so as not to clumsily misunderstand Psychosynthesis. Assagioli always considered a good personal psychosynthesis to be fundamental and indispensable, in which the integration of sexual and aggressive energies has a primary role. For him it was very important to build on solid foundations, firmly anchored to *bios* before going into the territories of transpersonal development.

3. The Second World War

3.1 Freedom in jail and realization of the Self[79]

Starting in 1936, work became ever more difficult for Assagioli due to increasing anti-Semitism and the hostility that his humanitarian activities aroused in the Fascist government.[80] In 1938 the Institute was closed and Roberto retired with his family to the countryside. In 1940, when he returned from a study conference in England, he was arrested in his home in Chianti on charges of being a pacifist and internationalist. In Rome's Regina Coeli prison, he was kept in isolation for the whole of August. He never knew exactly who his accusers were.

During his stay in prison, Assagioli took quite a few notes which he entitled *Libertà in prigione (Freedom in Jail)*. But he was very reluctant to make them public because he considered his difficulties insignificant compared to the tragic experiences lived through by the many victims of the conflict. He wrote in the preface of the text:

---

78   Published in "Il Loto", Giuntina typography, anno IX, n. 3, 1938.

79   In 2016 The Istituto di Psicosintesi published *Freedom in Jail* (ed. Catherine Ann Lombard) for the new series *Quaderni dell'Archivio Assagioli*. This autobiographical work covers the time spent by Assagioli in the Regina Coeli prison in 1940 under the fascist regime.

80   R. and B. Schaub, *Freedom in Jail: Assagioli's notes*, in "Rivista dell'Istituto di Psicosintesi", anno XIII N. 1, April 1996.

"I hesitated a lot before deciding whether or not to write this 'prison diary'. First of all, my little adventure was not heroic or dramatic in any way. A month of imprisonment without physical hardship and suffering is a banal incident compared to certain heroic deaths, or compared to the terrible suffering of innumerable protagonists of the World War. I also feel a strong reluctance to attract public attention to myself. On the other hand:

1. I felt the strong and spontaneous need to write my experience when I was still in prison.

2. Biographies and autobiographies have a high educational value and I remember how much help and inspiration I have received from many of these. A living example exerts more influence than many other forms of teaching. It reaches a wider readership than purely scientific essays.

3. One of the purposes and uses is to show (and implicitly teach) how to rise continuously from personal situations, events, incidents and experiences toward general problems, principles and laws of impersonal nature; how to use every circumstance for constructive purposes, to exercise and evolve some part of one's very being; how to keep one's serenity and to obtain interest and joy from everything."[81]

Regarding how Assagioli passed his time in jail, it is worth focusing on this briefly as the experience reveals many interesting details of this personality.

The autobiographical text continues with some brief comments on the interrogation that was conducted just after the arrest. Judging by his description, it seems he was in quite a good mood, even though it was out of place: "Taken into custody by the police ... listening to the quick reading of the charges ... I responded and acted like a buffoon."[82] When he was asked to describe his work, he seems to have spoken for a long time. He says that the interrogators listened very carefully and that in the end told him that they found his ideas "interesting". Roberto was happily amused as it was the first official acknowledgment that Psychosynthesis achieved in Italy. But at that point the official, trying to find a way to accuse him of a precise crime, shouted at him that he was a pacifist. Assagioli replied by explaining what pacifism was for him:

"Everyone has an ideal of peace. No one wants war in and of itself, but, in my capacity as a psychiatrist, I do not think peace can be achieved by political and lawful means ... and even less by means of a systematic and violent opposition to the war, waging a war on war. As a result I am not a pacifist in the usual sense of the word; I am deeply convinced that peace is a psychological problem (...) I believe that only by educating (...) everyone to resolve the problem inside ourselves (...) and in the surrounding environment, becoming living examples of peace found in ourselves, in our families, in our work, demonstrating the possibility of fair and harmonious relationships (...) It is a slow process, but in my opinion, the only sure one (...)"

---

81   R. Assagioli, *Libertà in prigione*, unedited manuscript.

82   Ibid.

In this essay, some of the basic ideas conceived by the father of Psychosynthesis come back: to transform society, one has to focus on individual growth, promoting the need for inner growth and developing a culture of lifelong education.

At that point the official asked him how he educated his disciples and who were his main followers. Assagioli, in order not to incriminate anyone, said he was very tired and did not remember. He recalled, "I was determined not to talk, no matter what kind of pressure they could put on me, and he (the official) probably sensed it." He was then brought to an adjacent room and handcuffed, and then put in a cell. He wrote that the handcuffs canceled any doubts about his destiny and that he felt a tightening of the solar plexus: "but it was an instinctive reaction, mainly due to the surprise and the novelty, a feeling that lasted only a few moments. I 'awakened' immediately; a sense of inner dignity, calm but strong, developed and pervaded my consciousness."

Assagioli was put in isolation: his notes tell us very little about the prison itself and instead examine the psychological and transpersonal experiences he had in which he recognized a "sense of boundlessness, an absence of separation from all that exists, a union of the Self with everything ... a push towards the outside, a pouring out and expanding in all directions like a sphere in perpetual expansion. A sense of universal love ... A wonderful union, without any separation; only different aspects of a single wonder."

After the passage quoted, the notes tell of an inarticulate phase described by many mystics:

> "Essential Reality is so far above any mental concept. It is inexpressible. It must be lived (...) The joy inherent in life itself (...) The realization of one's own Self, which is based on oneSelf and resides in oneSelf (...) The 'I' without 'I' (...) The three aspects of the supreme paradox: absence of the 'I' (Buddhist aspect), United with God (mystic aspect), Realization of the True Self (Vedic aspect)."

The notes assume a professional and clinical tone, and our author describes the techniques of meditation he employed during isolation, concluding the writing with the fundamental intuition to which he devoted his whole life:

> "I realized that I was free to choose between two different attitudes towards my situation: giving it a certain meaning, or alternatively, using it in one way or another. I could rebel or submit passively, vegetating, or I could indulge in the unhealthy pleasure of self-pity, assuming the role of a martyr. Or I could even see the situation with humor by considering it as a new and interesting experience. I could turn it into a period of rest, or a period of intense thinking on personal matters, reflecting on my past life, or on scientific and philosophical problems; or I could take advantage of the situation to place myself under training of the psychological faculties and conduct well-defined psychological experiments on myself. Or, in conclusion, I could turn it into a spiritual retreat: far from the world at last. I had no doubt: it was up to me."

In jail Assagioli experienced the illusion of our usual perceptions, understanding that real prisons are those we build ourselves, using sclerotic ways of thinking and reacting instinctively to situations. He realized that he was free to choose what attitude to take in the circumstances and clearly predicted what precise effects this choice would have had. In his mind there was no doubt about this essential freedom, about the privileges it offered to him, and his responsibility towards himself, his friends, and his life. Not a sad and helpless resignation, but a serene, positive and virile acceptance, an active search for the best use of the opportunities and gifts offered by the new situation.

His detention enabled him to achieve independence in relation to the circumstances, to gain inner freedom "without which all others are inadequate". In prison he now understood without a shadow of a doubt that the task of his life was to "help men and women to free themselves from their inner prisons".

3.2 Nazi persecution and the letter "to Friends"

Assagioli was released thanks to the intervention of some influential friends, but was kept under close surveillance. In 1943 he was denounced as a Jew to the Nazis and was actively pursued by these until the end of the war. The father of Psychosynthesis was not a simple Jew, but a "differentiated Jew": his wife and son were, in fact, baptized. He was forced to hide in remote mountain villages and was barely saved on two occasions. His family's homes were destroyed with dynamite and burned.

Of the actual period of the war we do not know much. As I have already mentioned, Roberto, with his wife and son Ilario, left Rome and moved to the countryside, first in Chianti then in Capolona, in the area surrounding Arezzo. It is known that he and Ilario spent various periods hiding in shepherd's cottages.

With the war still not over, Assagioli began to think about reviving cultural activities and wrote a letter to his friends (including Carl Gustav Jung), in which he talked about the years of forced hiding, the difficulties experienced, those not yet finished, and of his great desire to be together in peace, harmony and goodwill. The letter was written in September 1944 in Capolona and is kept at the ETH-Bibliothek Wissenschaftshistorische Sammlungen in Zurich (ETH Library Science and History Collection). I transcribe the text translated from the original German[83]:

"Dear friends,

Eager to re-establish as much as possible the good ties that connected us in the past, I thought to begin by sending you this first collective letter, given the practical limitations of the moment. I am glad to be able to tell you that my loved ones

---

83   R. Assagioli, cit. in A. Berti, op. cit.

and I are alive and free. The Germans and the fascists have given me the honor (if not the pleasure) of personally searching for me; so I have had to play hide-and-seek with them for several months in the area of the Alpe di Catenaia (in the province of Arezzo) and in the upper Val Tiberina. With the help of God and many good people (local friends, farmers, a paratrooper and various British people whose fate I shared in part), the searchers have always arrived too late. Regarding living conditions, I preferred to keep things humorous in footnote 1. Our house at Nussa, Capolona, was looted and then destroyed with dynamite. In the basement, I found piles of notes and papers which represented my work of more than 35 years spread all over the floor. I began to clean them up and put them in order. We are currently staying in the part of the farm less affected by the grenades. Of Villa Serena we still have no news. I'm ready for the worst because even there, I had ... a bad political reputation. As many of you know, I was arrested in 1940 under the charge of elevating and spreading prayers for peace and other international crimes. For the near future I'm not yet able to make precise plans. When I can, I will make a trip to Rome, and one to Florence. In the first few, relatively quiet months of my 'secret life' (autumn 1943 - winter 1944) I worked at reviewing my writings in Italian, so that I could then put them together in two or three volumes, and also the editing of a book in English on psychosynthesis. I also wrote an essay: Politica e Psicologia (Le vie della ricostruzione) (Politics and Psychology- The way of Reconstruction). Now I have various and not simple problems of practical life to deal with, but I have also resumed my spiritual and cultural activities and I mean to intensify them and extend them as much as I will have the opportunity. I feel the inner command, and I join you with all of myself, to play my small part in the great and joyful work toward individual, national and world renewal. There are wonderful possibilities that will be implemented if each and everyone of us want and know how to do our part in harmonious cooperation with all men and groups of good will.

1. 'Grand Hôtel des Ètables', a first class... ruin. Running water in all rooms ... when it rains. Archaic graffiti on the walls. Authentic antique feed troughs. All the hay you can eat at no extra cost. Waking up to strong percussion ... English and German drums. Security locks (do not even open with the key). Rich assortment of local insects having exceptional liveliness and resourcefulness. From August 1st (arrival of Anglo-Americans): every afternoon intercontinental meeting with competition in language acrobatics. Great 'unscheduled surprise events' (without notice): accurate imitation of volcanic earthquake with rain of flaming splinters. 'Branch office: Châlet des Mansardes in Castagneto' (Upper Val Tiberina). Selected public and high culture Library (Nouvelle Revue Française, etc.). Great ricotta cheese. Adjacent corn fields, the ideal hideout recommended by Italian and English experts.

2. Unfortunately, I have been an able prophet! Villa Serena has also been looted and targeted by cannon fire."

This letter is a wonderful testimony to the personality of the father of Psychosynthesis. He shows truly surprising serenity and humor, a sign of a real inner liberation he attained. Although the strains of war irredeemably undermine the already precarious health of his only son Ilario, stricken with tuberculosis, friends said that they never heard him rebuke anyone or make a single negative comment in the darkest period of his life.

4. Spiritual Vision

Roberto Assagioli always strove greatly to keep his psychological and scientific interests separate from the spiritual, although it is undeniable that Psychosynthesis includes aspects derived from oriental philosophies and esoteric disciplines. However, he was particularly interested in the applicative aspect of such knowledge, their curative and transformative potential, and he reworked these elements in psychological terms that were accessible to the modern Western mentality. He was attracted to the fact that they "worked". In this regard, he liked to mention Goethe's motto *"Wirklichkeit ist was wirkt"*: "Reality is what works".

Assagioli was convinced of the phenomenological reality of transpersonal experiences and the realization of the Self. He declared that he was dealing with "facts and with spiritual conscience" but was not interested in the discussion "of what the 'Spirit' in its essence may be", in that "Psychosynthesis can be considered neutral toward these last issues ... and in the face of philosophy and religion"[84]. He thus clearly distinguished the spiritual, existential experience from the theological or metaphysical formulations of such experiences and from the institutions which, during various historical periods and within the various cultures, were founded to communicate the fruits of those experiences to others. He wrote:

> "Psychosynthesis decisively affirms the reality of spiritual experience, the existence of higher values, the 'noetic' or 'noological' dimension as Frankl calls it, but is neutral with regard to... formulations and institutions. Its purpose is to help achieve the experience."[85]

Consistent with this approach, Assagioli studied the religious and esoteric traditions of many cultures, and became interested in theosophy, but it cannot be said that he had ever subscribed exclusively to any one of them. He was born Jewish and went a long way to further the Jewish cause, even though he always said he did not believe in any particular religion. He dealt with esotericism, but more than indiscriminately accepting esoteric theories, he maintained an open, possibilistic attitude; he was interested and understanding in the widest sense of the term. He considered that

> "psychologists should not be tied to any one system (…) they must make contact with the vital reality of psychic life with its immediate dynamism and draw from it the theoretical and practical consequences."[86]

---

84   R. Assagioli, *Principi e metodi della psicosintesi terapeutica*, op. cit.

85   Ibid.

86   R. Assagioli, *Psicosintesi - Armonia della vita*, op. cit.

4.1. Roberto Assagioli and the Jewish tradition

Formally, Assagioli belonged to the Jewish faith for which he had maximum respect, and there was no doubt that being Jewish had a certain influence, both in his life and in his thinking. In this regard, psychotherapist and psychosynthesist Giovanni Dattilo[87], in a recent article, identifies some essential core principles of Psychosynthesis that can be better understood in the light of Jewish tradition. In particular: the idea of multiplicity in us, the concept of polarity and synthesis, and that of the will.

In the *Zohar*, the most important book of the kabbalistic tradition, the distinctive task assigned to the individual in creation is to "reduce and bring unity to multiplicity", both in the multiplicity that distinguishes the microcosm, meaning the individual himself, and in the multiplicity of the macrocosm. For his part, Assagioli defined Psychosynthesis as "a dynamic and, one could say, dramatic conception of psychic life, a struggle between a multiplicity of rebellious and conflicting forces, and a unifying center that tends to dominate them, to bring them into harmony, using them in the most productive and creative ways."[88]

As for the subject of polarity and synthesis, we can find deep analogies between the concept that the father of Psychosynthesis had of psychic dynamics and the vision borrowed from the Sephirotic tree of the kabbalists. The latter, also called the Tree of Life, consists of a diagram that is articulated along three parallel vertical pillars in which the creative polarities are represented in their manifestation in the world. These three pillars correspond to the three existential paths that every human being can take, but only the middle way, also called the "royal pathway", has the ability to unite opposites. The pillars on the right and left also represent the two basic polarities of the whole reality: the male and female, from which all the other opposing pairs in the creation emerge. The main teaching contained in the kabbalistic doctrine of the Tree of Life is therefore the integration of male and female components, to be carried out both within the individual and also in the relationship between the couple. How can we not accept the obvious similarities with the Egg Diagram, with the Assagiolian vision of the concept of synthesis and with the importance attributed to sexuality and therefore a total vision of the individual?

Finally we look at the concept of will. I defer to the words with which Dattilo[89] concluded his captivating essay:

"A Jewish saying recites that 'there is nothing that can oppose the will', a phrase common to almost all traditions. And perhaps man, with his will, performs his most specific human function in that Heaven and Earth within himself, the Self and the

---

87   Giovanni Yoav Dattilo, *Roberto Assagioli: psicosintesi e tradizione ebraica*, in "Rivista di Psicosintesi Terapeutica", Anno X - Nuova serie, N. 19, March 2009.

88   R. Assagioli, *Principi e metodi della psicosintesi terapeutica*, op. cit., p. 36.

89   Giovanni Yoav Dattilo, op. cit., p. 26.

personality, join in a passionate kiss. Perhaps this is the *mysterium coniunctionis*, the core of Psychosynthesis."

Friendship with Martin Buber and progressive Judaism

Additionally, Assagioli had a cordial friendship with Martin Buber, the German-Jewish philosopher, humanist and anthropologist, who dealt with adult education in the years when Nazism had excluded Jews from schools. There are two central motives of Buber's thinking to which the father of Psychosynthesis should have felt very close: Hassidism and the dialogic principle. The first—whose fundamental characteristics are a widely popular mysticism, thus accessible to ordinary men and women; opposition to asceticism and escape from the world, the abolition of many penitential practices, and the insistence on the joy of the heart and on righteous intention—was conceived as a dialogue between Heaven and Earth, as sanctification of daily life, as an expression of a faith not practiced intellectually. Instead, the dialogic concept claimed that only in a relationship can an individual really become a person. The dialogic principle is the manifestation of the ability to be in a total relationship with nature, with other men and with spiritual entities, by placing yourself in an I-Thou relationship. In this, Buber traced the fundamental meaning of human existence.[90]

As a testament to how much he felt involved in the Jewish cause—more precisely in the cause of progressive Judaism, open and supportive of peace amongst peoples and interreligious dialogue—in the early 1950s the father of Psychosynthesis founded the Unione italiana per l'ebraismo progressivo (Italian Union for Progressive Judaism), which advocated these principles. In the article *L'ebraismo progressivo e la psicologia (Progressive Judaism and Psychology)*[91], Assagioli clearly outlined the nature of his relationship with Jewish tradition and the contribution this had given to the birth of Psychosynthesis:

> "In the development of the theory and practice of psychosynthesis, I draw inspiration from the Jewish tradition.. Looking toward the future, progressive Judaism may and should, in my opinion, assume the task of taking from the long and rich Jewish tradition together with the life experiences of its mystics and 'zaddikim', the many and precious psychological data found therein, using it in combination with the best that modern psychology has to offer. In this way, progressive Judaism would help this new science to overcome materialistic tendencies and academic apprehensions that limit its development and prevent the recognition of the superconscious sphere of human nature and the appreciation of its spiritual sphere.

---

90   *Le garzantine: Filosofia*, Ed. Garzanti, 1993.

91   R. Assagioli, *L'ebraismo progressivo e la psicologia*, in "La Voce dell'Unione Italiana", 3 March 1955.

In this way, psychology will really become what it can and should be according to its own name: the 'science of the spirit', and would help man to develop and utilize all the latent abilities of his 'real being' for the good of everyone."

In another article titled *Scialom* (*Shalom*), he explained the authentic meaning of the word:

The original meaning of 'shalom' is 'health' or 'wholeness', and therefore means wellness of the individual and the community, both physically and spiritually. To achieve 'shalom' in this deeper and wider sense, the first step is, of course, a reciprocal tolerance that excludes any fanaticism, imposition or aggression. But this is only a first step that by itself is inadequate. It must be followed by the recognition, indeed the positive appreciation, of the necessity and usefulness of differences. Unity does not require uniformity; it consists in the organic union of different parts. It is therefore a question of accepting and maintaining the diversities, while at the same time recognizing that they are relative and not absolute." [92]

For Assagioli, the fields in which *shalom* was to be implemented were the same as those in which the psychosynthetic work takes place: first and foremost in ourselves, among the various conscious or unconscious elements of our complex and multiform essence; then among individuals, starting with the family and then extending to the multiple social relationships; among peoples, when they recognize themselves as parts of a single planetary organism; in the field of religion, within each religion and between different religions "which are historical manifestations of the same universal truth (...)". In this declaration, the echo of theosophical teachings is heard.

4.2 Theosophical studies and the Arcane school

His belonging to Judaism and the great respect that Assagioli nourished for Christianity did not diminish his interest in Oriental spirituality and philosophy[93]. This, and the fact that both his mother and wife were students of theosophy, naturally brought his interest to such subjects.

The term theosophy, in its traditional meaning, means "intellectual knowledge of the divine". In modern times, it was reborn as an opposition to the rational dogmatism of scholastic philosophy in German Protestant mysticism by theologian Jakob Böhme (1575-1624) and later in the doctrine advocated by the Theosophical Society, founded in 1875 in New York by Helena Petrovna Blavatsky (1831-1891), a Russian noblewoman who at the age of sixteen began a long series of trips to Egypt, the Middle East, India, Ceylon and Tibet.[94] Theosophy was

---

92   R. Assagioli, cit. in P. Giovetti, op. cit.

93   P. Giovetti, op. cit.

94   S. Cranston, *Helena Blavatsky*, Armenia, 1994.

born in a time of fermentation, claiming to bring the modern individual to the sources of ancient wisdom, especially oriental.

At that moment in history, one of the recurring motives in French, English and Russian philosophical thought was the denunciation regarding the impossibility of science to grasp the deep roots of existence. The crisis of scientific reason involved the glorification of the cognitive possibilities of many different faculties of the spirit. Art and symbolism became privileged languages, the only ones able to penetrate the mystery.[95] In fact the theosophical movement influenced and inspired some great artists, among others, writers William Butler Yeats, George W. Russell, James Joyce, Jack London, D.H. Lawrence, T.S. Eliot and Thornton Wilder, painters Wassily Kandinsky, Piet Mondrian, Paul Klee and Paul Gauguin, and musicians Gustav Mahler, Jean Sibelius and Alexander Skryabin.[96]

The Theosophical Society had no dogma and did not ask anyone to forgo their own religion, but instead asked for the same respect for the religion of others as for their own. Its goals were, and still are, to spread the idea of a Universal Brotherhood of Humanity, without distinction of race, belief, sex, caste or color, to encourage the comparative study of religions, philosophies and sciences, and to investigate the unexplored laws of nature and the latent powers of the individual. Its only motto: "There is no higher religion than the truth."

All of these concepts were very close to Roberto Assagioli's thinking[97]: he was particularly concerned about the destiny of humanity and the growth of the individual, and the teachings of Blavatsky gave him inspiration for thoughts that he considered worthy of the utmost attention.

As we have seen, Assagioli had been interested in theosophy since the time of "Leonardo". During the 1920s he spent time with the theosophical group in Florence, and when he moved to Rome, his home was the meeting point of the theosophists in the capital city. He also wrote numerous articles for the group's journal. When in 1939 the Italian Theosophical Society was disbanded by the Fascist government for its opposition to racial policies, Assagioli resigned to avoid creating problems by writing: "I resign because I am a Jew." The Society was disbanded in any case, and several members had problems with the political police. During the war, Assagioli also experienced many difficulties, but once the conflict ended, he resumed the cultivation of his interest in theosophy and dedication to spiritual activities.

The father of Psychosynthesis was also in close contact with Alice Ann Bailey (1880-1949), the founder of the Arcane School, created in 1923 in order to prepare men for a new conscience through the teaching of meditation, considered the fundamental instrument for liberating the deeper resources of the human soul. Alice, an aristocratic English lady, said that, at the age of 39, she had come

---

95   G. Salvetti, *La nascita del Novecento*, E. D. T., 1977.

96   S. Cranston, op. cit.

97   P. Giovetti, op. cit.

into telepathic contact with a Master called "the Tibetan"[98]. He asked her to collaborate in writing some books. Initially, Bailey refused, fearing to be the victim of hallucinations and risking madness, but after several reassurances, she accepted, and in a period of about thirty years wrote about twenty volumes dealing with the principles of "Eternal Wisdom", meditation and service to humanity.

We know that Assagioli worked with Alice Bailey and was her representative in Italy for a long time. In the 1930s, the two met personally in Ascona, Switzerland, both guests of Olga Fröbe-Kapteyn in her villa on the shores of Lake Maggiore. A few years later, that villa would become the headquarters of the Eranos group, which was promoted by another brother-in-arms of Assagioli, Carl Gustav Jung, whom Fröbe-Kapteyn had met during a conference organized in Darmstadt by Hermann Keyserling's Schule der Weischeit (School of Wisdom). Jung himself believed that "the Tibetan" was the superior Self of Alice Bailey personified.

And it is Bailey, in her publication *The Unfinished Autobiography*, who provides us with a lovely description of Assagioli's charisma and personality in that period:

> "He's a man with a character of rare beauty. When he entered a room, his spiritual qualities signaled his presence. Frank D. Vanderlip calls him the modern Saint Francis of Assisi and says that the morning he spent with him marked the highest moment of his European trip. His talks were the highlight of the Ascona conferences. He spoke French, Italian and English, and the spiritual power that he emanated stimulated many to renew the consecration of life."[99]

4.3 Parapsychology

Assagioli was also interested in parapsychology, but his attention was mainly focused on "supernormal" faculties. He considered that the existence of these phenomena had been scientifically proven through observations and rigorous experiments conducted by scholars such as Eugene Osty, William Mackenzie, Emilio Servadio and Joseph Banks Rhine. In particular, Rhine had conducted research on so-called extrasensory perception (ESP) that, according to the name he assigned it, refers to the perception of an object, state or event without the use of the five ordinary senses. ESP includes clairvoyance, retrocognition, precognition and telepathy. According to Umberto Galimberti[100], although the explanations so far provided do not yet have a clear scientific expression, the results obtained by Rhine through extremely disciplined research are enough to justify the interest of science in the phenomenon.

Assagioli himself conducted experiments using the Rhine documentation, finding telepathic abilities in several subjects. He attributed an importance above all scientific, philosophical and even practical (for care and diagnosis) to studies

---

98   A. A. Bailey, *The Unfinished Autobiography*, Lucis Publishing, 1951.

99   Ibid.

100   U. Galimberti, *Psicologia*, Garzanti, 1999.

on parapsychological phenomena, but stressed the importance of underlining the dangers that could arise from an incorrect confrontation with these, such as credulity, fanaticism, exploitation and charlatanry. Our author invited researchers to investigate such manifestations with a scientific, serene, impartial, calm, prudent, but open attitude. He felt that these phenomena should not be ignored or, even worse, fought against by science because they correspond to an inexpressible tendency of the human spirit that, as Assagioli wrote in a note kept in his archive, "unless satisfied by science, is explained in a roundabout way, without control" with all the dangers that this may entail.

5. Resumption and consolidation of work

After the war, for the resumption of his work, Assagioli chose Florence where he had lived at the time of his university studies. He bought a small villa in the S. Domenico neighborhood (still home to the Institute of Psychosynthesis) on the road that leads from Florence to Fiesole. There he resumed his activities and studies, began to practice the professions of psychiatrist and psychotherapist, and held classes on psychosynthesis.

The Institute seemed to be very busy. Lessons were not reserved only to specialists, but open to anyone interested. As I have already pointed out, Assagioli greatly wanted to be understood by everyone and to involve people from every social class. Psychiatrist and psychologist Massimo Rosselli, a direct student, recalls that the father of Psychosynthesis was highly esteemed in Florence and that all of the city's cultural personalities went to the Institute at least once to hear him:

> "analysts, psychiatrists, psychologists, they all came. He was admired even if he was considered a bit special, not easily labeled. In those times, his inclusivity, his tying together of East and West was little understood...Assagioli was a pioneer and paid a price for it..." [101]

Assagioli followed not just seriously ill, psychotic patients, but also people who went to him for personal growth. Perhaps this was the aspect that most interested him, because Psychosynthesis is essentially a psychology for the healthy individual, or rather, is the art of educating oneself.

In addition to psychosynthesis courses, lessons, individual and group therapies, there were the trips: despite his precarious health, Assagioli always traveled a lot. He resumed this habit immediately after the war, and he frequently traveled to meet scholars, hold conferences and attend conventions. Every year, almost until the end of his long life, he went to England where he had meditation groups, and to Paris, where an important Psychosynthesis center existed and still exists. He also visited the United States, where his ideas had aroused a great deal of interest.

---

101   M. Rosselli in P. Giovetti, op. cit.

1957 marked an important date for dissemination of his ideas; with the help of a group of American friends and collaborators, the Psychosynthesis Research Foundation was established in New York. During the same period Assagioli was very active in conventions and international meetings, which laid the foundations for the subsequent establishment of centers and institutes in various parts of the world.[102]

Assagioli also received many visits from scholars, poets, writers and artists from all over the world and had regular guests who spent time with him working on their personal psychosynthesis. The great intellectual and human curiosity that enlivened him never diminished. His interests embraced all that could be humanly known and created; his attitude of openness and availability to others did the rest.

The father of Psychosynthesis was in the habit of spending the summer holidays with the family at Capolona where, starting in 1956, he began to organize a series of conferences on the topics that were closest to his heart: psychology, art, religion and culture. These conferences were attended by scholars of many different nationalities.

6. Nella and Ilario

In Assagioli's family, love reigned supreme. His wife Nella was considered a difficult and obstinate woman, but her goodness was out of the question. His niece, Donatella Ciapetti, who lived for several years with her aunt and uncle, said that theirs was a great marriage: "They were elderly and I heard them in their room playing like children, laughing and joking. They were very united and they both had the great willingness to let the other do what they wanted."[103]

Even Luisa Lunelli, a close family friend, writes in her own book[104] that their conjugal love had preserved juvenile nuances. When they went out to a show or reception, after Nella put on an elegant gown, Roberto would enter the room, select the jewelry that best suited his wife's attire and then admire her beauty with a satisfied look.

Roberto and Nella became parents with the birth of Francesco Ilario in 1923. Ilario was baptized because Assagioli's wife was Catholic and he believed that it was a mother's prerogative to give the child his first religious education. The boy was very intelligent, precocious, and endowed with great intellectual curiosity and an innate spirituality. During adolescence, at the age of fifteen, he became ill with tuberculosis. Nella and Roberto's suffering for the child's illness was enormous.

---

102   S. Tilli, *Concetti della psicologia umanistica di R. Assagioli,* op. cit.

103   D. Ciapetti, cit. in P. Giovetti, op. cit.

104   L. Lunelli, *Roberto Nella e Luisa,* Centro Studi di Psicosintesi "R. Assagioli", Firenze, 1991.

During the years of illness, Ilario read the works of great philosophers, writers and poets, gathering them in a collection of maxims that were published privately with the title *Dal dolore alla pace* (*From Pain To Peace*). In the preface he himself explained in what conditions and with what purpose he had performed that precious work:

> "When, during long years of illness, I would find in my many readings some maxim, aphorism or thought and I would transcribe them to form a collection, I did not think the time would come when it would be published. It was my own desire to make them known, because I knew from experience how much something like that can help to give joy, optimism and hope in the dark moments of life. The human value of this volume is given, apart from its content, from the fact that it is the harvest of real suffering, and that the first to have gained something from its pages is the compiler himself (...)"[105]

6.1. Ilario's death

In the years immediately preceding the war, and during the conflict, Ilario's health had high and low points, causing his parents to both hope and despair. After the end of the war, probably due to the struggles faced during the period of persecution when he had to hide in the mountains with his father, Ilario's condition worsened. From this time we have a beautiful and moving letter written by Assagioli to Jung asking help for himself and his stricken son:

> "My dear and esteemed colleague,
>
> grateful for your courteous welcome when, in 1939, I passed through Zurich on my way from England to return (imprudently!) to Italy, I write to give you news and to ask for a small favor.
>
> My family and I came out alive from the turbine of the war, but we suffered persecution and dangers, as I mentioned in the "Letter to Friends" that I attach. But, I did not mention a grave difficulty and complication we had during the war years: my son's serious illness, pulmonary tuberculosis. However, he has been surprisingly resistant to the hardships and since 1944 he has greatly improved.
>
> Now there is a very favorable opportunity to hasten his healing: "The Fédération Européenne de Secours aux Étudants" (European Federation of Student Aid) will almost certainly include him in the group of twenty Italian students who will be offered hospitality and care for six months in the university sanatorium at Leysin. He would very much like me to accompany him there and I, too, would like to go and talk with the colleagues in the clinic regarding his care. It seemed difficult for me to get permission from the Swiss authorities to enter the country, but the "Fédération" board hopes to get it by appointing me, as a physician, to accompany the entire group of students. But maybe the federal authorities will ask for information and references on me from some well-known Swiss citizen.

---

105   I. Assagioli, cit. in P. Giovetti, op. cit.

Therefore I have taken the liberty of giving them your name and if you are asked anything about me, I hope you will say I'm not an "unwanted" guest for a short stay in Switzerland.

Aside from that—as you know, I have always followed with vivid appreciation and admiration your pioneering work in psychology—I would like to know what your activities have focused on during these years and if you have published any new writings so that I can get them on my trip to Switzerland.

Please pardon me for the disturbance and accept my very best wishes and cordial regards.

Yours devotedly,

Roberto Assagioli"[106]

But despite the loving care of his parents and the arrival of penicillin, Ilario passed away: his weakened body could not tolerate the medication. It seemed that he had accepted not only the suffering, but also death. In fact, a few months prior to his demise in 1951, he wrote:

"Dying

is like leaving

home

at dawn"

said

the elderly Chung-Tzé.

"It is like quenching your thirst

with the fresh dew

of the radiant

prairies of Heaven,

to feel

light and free

in the blue

infinity

beyond all shadows

beyond any illusion.

Dying

is leaving time behind

entering reality.

---

106   Cit. in *Roberto Assagioli, 1888 - 1988*, edited by A. Berti, edited by Centro Studi "R. Assagioli", 1988.

Why are you crying, brother?
Why are you trembling?
We leave
the ephemeral
to gain
eternity.

Lift your eyes
and contemplate
the starry sky:
they are milestones
along the roads of the cosmos,
the supreme destination
of the human soul:
a return to the sublime
Divine Mansion."[107]

Death gathered Ilario serenely at dawn on November 6, 1951. Nella was devastated by her son's death: she suffered greatly and no longer wanted to see anyone. She only wished to be alone. Friends of the family recall that Roberto remained patiently and lovingly at her side for a long time until her wounded heart's bleeding subdued and she was able to gather herself to once more become the energetic woman she had always been.

Ilario's passing took a little of life's breath from the father of Psychosynthesis even if, thinking of his departed son, he would calmly say: "Now his eyes see a different sun!"[108]

---

107   Ibid.
108   P. Giovetti, op. cit.

CHAPTER III

THE FERTILITY OF THE FINAL YEARS

1. The '60s: an important period for the Psychosynthesis movement

1.1. 1961

With age, Assagioli's health declined, yet his work only became more demanding. We can say that he was never so active as in his later years, when he was already over 70.

1961 was a symbolic date for the beginning of a new season, both for Psychosynthesis and the countless activities of its founder. In June, the *Istituto di Psicosintesi (Institute of Psychosynthesis)* was established in Florence, with the aim of disseminating, transmitting and deepening its principles. In the same year Assagioli took part in the *5th International Psychotherapy Convention* and presented a report titled *Psicosintesi e psicoterapia esistenziale (Psychosynthesis and Existential Psychotherapy)*. On that occasion, he also presided over a symposium in which he presented his ideas, generating the lively interest of scholars who had come from various parts of the world, especially from the United States. In that same year he led the *Second International Week of Psychosynthesis*[109] in Vienna and the *Third International Week of Psychosynthesis* in Villeneuve, Switzerland. These were followed in 1964 by the *International Meeting* held in Capolona. In 1965, *International Psychosynthesis Week* was held again in Villeneuve, in 1966 in London, in 1967 in Rome, and in 1968 in Tunbridge Wells, England.

1.2. The 5th International Psychotherapy Convention: *Psychosynthesis and Existential Psychotherapy*

As I have mentioned, the *5th International Psychotherapy Convention* was held in Vienna, and Roberto Assagioli, in his presentation *Psicosintesi e psicoterapia esistenziale* (*Psychosynthesis and Existential Psychotherapy*) discussed the similarities and differences existing between his approach and other therapeutic methods that relate to the existential. He illustrated the tasks and aims of Psychosynthesis and proposed a complete cure that combined the use of active techniques with the existential approach.

Our author opened his presentation by clarifying what he meant by the term "existential": "This is used by different scholars in very different and sometimes

---

109   S. Tilli, *Concetti della psicologia umanistica di Roberto Assagioli,* op. cit.

even opposing ways." The erroneous tendency to consider the existential approach a unitary doctrine, said Assagioli, leads to confused and inaccurate ideas on philosophical existentialism. He went on to clarify that his objective, however, was not to start a theoretical discussion on "existentialisms"[110]. Indeed, when talking about "existential situations", Psychosynthesis does not refer to theories and philosophies, but to "real, experienced situations" such as birth, death, existential anguish, attitude toward evil, suffering, illnesses, the wide range of interpersonal relationships, the problem of isolation and communication, and finally the attitude towards nature, the world and the universe. For our author, the inevitable confrontation of the individual with these issues "demands 'the taking of positions' and therefore decisions": for Psychosynthesis, decision is considered one of the fundamental stages of the act of will.

He then traced the fundamental similarity between Psychosynthesis and the existential approach to psychotherapy in the common methodological attitudes starting with the "presence" of the individual, seen to be in constant development and containing latent potential. Psychosynthesis and existentialism also share the importance attributed to sense, to values, to choices and, consequently, to suffering and anxiety caused by lack of meaning, as well as the importance given to responsibility and motivation, emphasis on the future and recognition of the uniqueness of each individual that leads to a "new method for each patient".

Assagioli continued his presentation by pointing out the differences between the two approaches that were, however, considered relative. As the main point, he identified the emphasis that the psychosynthetic concept puts on the will as a specific function of the self. A second point of difference between the existential and the psychosynthetic approaches concerns the nature of the Transpersonal Self, considered by Psychosynthesis as pure self-awareness, a true phenomenal experience independent of any content of the field of consciousness. In addition, Psychosynthesis, unlike existential psychotherapy, recognizes positive, joyful and creative experiences along with those painful and tragic, and tries to promote and enhance them through the use of appropriate techniques and methods. In the end, for the psychosynthetic approach, the experience of solitude is not considered definitive but rather a temporary subjective condition that can alternate with a genuine experience of interpersonal communication. Above all, Psychosynthesis proposes, through the use of active techniques, the conscious and planned re-creation of personality through the transformation of sexual and aggressive energies, the reinforcement and maturation of under-developed psychological functions and the activation of latent potential.

Assagioli concluded his speech with "a friendly appeal to all psychotherapists to accentuate more the similarities rather than the differences, both in their concepts and in their methods, and to address not only the synthesis of therapies

---

110   R. Assagioli, *La psicologia e l'esistenza umana*, in *Situazioni esistenziali e loro soluzioni psicosintetiche*, Lessons, 1971.

but also a wider synthesis of science, philosophy, art and religion, towards an integrated knowledge of the 'phenomenon of man' and the achievement of his maximum realization"[111].

1.3. *Journées de Psychosynthèse (Days of Psychosynthesis)* in Paris and interindividual psychosynthesis

The following year, our author held a series of conferences in London and later attended the *Journées de Psychosynthèse* at Viry Châtillon in the outskirts of Paris, during which he spoke about the principles and methods of interindividual psychosynthesis.

Assagioli began his presentation by asserting how it is necessary to be more precise with the overly generic term of social psychology[112] and proposed to distinguish interindividual psychology, which deals mainly with interpersonal relationships, from group psychology (which is generally called social psychology) that instead deals with the relationships between individuals within a specific group, and between the individual and the group as a whole, as well as the relationships between different groups.

Our author continued by discussing the various theories and positions in social psychology (behavioral theory, psychoanalytic interpretation, cognitivist or personalistic and Gestalt conception, sociological conception). He then went on to consider the tasks of Psychosynthesis in the psycho-social field and clarified that in the psychosynthetic vision, synthesis always includes the following aspects: unity in diversity, diversity in unity, coordination and harmony, equilibrium of opposites, common direction towards a goal, a value or a unanimously chosen ideal. These fundamental principles apply to both personal and interindividual work.

Finally, Assagioli identified the methods that can be used in interindividual and group psychosynthesis. A first series, which he described as introductory, consists of techniques aimed at eliminating the main obstacles to good psychosynthesis, such as the natural self-centeredness of individuals, primary self-assertion (within certain necessary limits) and secondary (which is generally shown to be an overcompensation for a deficiency), hostility, or combativeness, and prejudices. A second series, on the other hand, consists of active techniques aimed at developing and promoting understanding, cooperation, the ability to empathize with others, generosity and goodwill, considered the expression of the highest and most effective method for implementing every form of interpersonal and interindividual psychosynthesis: *agape*.

---

111   R. Assagioli, *Principi e Metodi della psicosintesi terapeutica,* op. cit.

112   R. Assagioli, *Tecniche della psicosintesi interindividuale,* in *Corso di lezioni sulla psicosintesi,* 1965.

Our author concluded his presentation referring to the pioneering studies of Abraham Maslow and sociologist Pitirim Sorokin (1889-1968), proposing a scientific study on the higher sentiments since they "are real facts that determine human behavior".

1.4. The *Convention on Gifted Children*

In 1963, during the summer conventions that he regularly organized at Capolona, Assagioli presided over the *Convegno sui Superdotati* (*Convention on Gifted Children*) with the participation of about fifty people of different nationalities. As I have already pointed out, education in general, and especially the education of children with skills superior to the standard, was a topic that was very close to his heart: first of all because such children, according to Assagioli, incarnate the higher potentialities of human nature; secondly, because gifted individuals, if they are hindered or prevented from demonstrating their talents, can quite often easily become asocial or even antisocial. The father of Psychosynthesis denounced the fact that "in those places that are sadly and ironically called 'correctional facilities' there is a significant percentage of gifted persons"[113] and called on educators and parents to assume the task of "encouraging the training of such a group of pioneers, of renovators(...)"[114].

Our author also categorized children who are particularly gifted into two groups: the first is made up of those who can be called multi-gifted, meaning that they have excellent talents in all or in many fields; the second category includes those who, besides some brilliant ability, also have serious shortcomings in other facets of their personality. According to Assagioli, this second group presents difficult and delicate problems as far as education is concerned. Often, these children are physically weak, awkward, distracted, with an exuberant imagination and sensitivity, and are generally misunderstood by their family, teachers, and peers. If their talents are discovered, the mistake can be made of cultivating them too intensively, trying to create prodigies. In this regard, Assagioli denounced the exploitation of these children, both by families and by society, especially in America, and the excessive specialization that is usually given to their education.

For these youngsters, the father of Psychosynthesis called for integral education whose goal is the balanced and harmonious development of all aspects of the human being (physical, emotional, imaginative, mental, intuitive, volitional. spiritual) and their inclusion in organic synthesis. According to Assagioli, this education can be implemented with the combined and appropriately coordinated use of the following means:

---

113   R. Assagioli, *Lo sviluppo transpersonale*, Casa Editrice Astrolabio, 1988.

114   R. Assagioli, *L'educazione dei giovani particolarmente dotati*, Istituto di Psicosintesi, 1969.

- *active methods and "expressive techniques"* (active participation of the student in the educational process, "learning by doing"; movement, rhythm, dance, acting, modelling, drawing and painting, writing, performing and composing music...)

- *differential education* (adapted to the particular needs of each student)

- *physical education* (contact with nature: gardening, horticulture, caring for small animals, walking, hiking, gymnastics, sports...)

- *intellectual education* (not based on memorization but on the active development of all mental faculties and above all the capability to consult and use books intelligently by oneself)

- *education of the imagination and sentiments* (visualization exercises, imaginative creation, development of superior feelings by avoiding any repression and encouraging the constructive transformation of exuberant emotions)

- *education of the will* (the most neglected function both in family education and in school education; Assagioli believed that oppressive and authoritarian methods obtain the opposite result; effective methods are plentiful, and what can be especially useful is training children on the phases, quality and aspects of the act of will)

- *spiritual education* (in response to the needs of children, not as an imposition; all the natural spiritual manifestations: intuitions, aspirations, ethical, aesthetic, artistic inspiration are to be encouraged)

- *education on upright human relationships* (actually an integral part of spiritual education, in that spirituality is not meant as transcending the small self in a vertical sense, but also in a horizontal sense by widening the communion with others in concentric circles first to the family, to peers, to social relationships, and finally to the collective).

Assagioli concluded his presentation by emphasizing the importance of the environment and educators. An environment conducive to growth and learning must be imbued with harmony and beauty, be immersed in nature and include the use of art, especially music. Every educator should take responsibility for developing the most appreciated qualities of students: a cooperative and democratic attitude, benevolence toward and consideration of the individual, patience, wide-ranging interests, pleasant appearance and manners, fairness and impartiality, sense of humor, coherence, interest in student problems, adaptability, use of appreciation and praise, and particular competence in teaching a given subject.

1.5. The *6th International Conference on Psychotherapy: Synthesis In Psychotherapy*

In 1964 Assagioli participated again at the *International Conference on Psychotherapy* held in London with a paper on synthesis in psychotherapy. The paper is of great importance because it was decades ahead of its time, discussing a trend that is now gaining more and more acceptance in the frameworks of different psychotherapies. Assagioli proposed an integrative, synthetic and systemic orientation, capable of leading the various schools toward comparison and dialogue. He stated:

> "... the first thing that psychotherapists should do is to establish harmonious and cooperative relationships. This means, first of all, admitting that every point of view or partial system is correct in that it offers something positive, and is incorrect in that it excludes or negates. We must admit that every school, movement, point of view or technique has its merits and its limitations; therefore it is necessary to know, appreciate and use as many of them as possible."[115]

Our author, starting from the acknowledgment of the existence of many different methods in psychotherapy, proposed a general division into two groups. The first of these is composed of existential psychotherapies, based on depth psychology, which attach great importance to the human relationship and aim at eliminating the causes of discomfort; the second includes countless special techniques including suggestion, hypnosis and autogenic training aimed at eliminating the symptoms and disorders that the patient suffers.

Assagioli criticized the existential orientation in psychotherapy because it often does not help the patient "to use the new vision acquired of life and to modify their existence and, as a result, their relationships with others"[116]. He was also critical of the approach of specific techniques because it does not go into depth, and therefore does not eliminate the true cause or origin of the symptoms.

He proposed a combination of the two methods in an integral and differential psychotherapy, to be applied in a different way for each situation. According to the father of Psychosynthesis, some cases may be termed "Freudian" while others may be better understood in the light of the interpretations given by Adler, Jung, Horney, Franckl, et al. Of course, the distinctions proposed by Assagioli were not clear-cut because, very often, various pathogenic causes are present in different proportions.

As a consequence, the general scheme of a complete psychotherapy should include:

A. *analytical phase* (a wide-ranging examination of the patient's personality, in both its conscious and unconscious aspects, together with an investigation into existential issues)

B. *active phase* (the search for the most appropriate solutions and their actuation)

---

115   R. Assagioli, *Sintesi nella psicoterapia,* Lecture at the *VI International Congress of Psychotherapy*, London, 1964.

116   Ibid.

divided as follows:

- *elimination of obstacles*, dissolution of complexes, removal of repressions (psychoanalytical and cathartic phases)
- *regulation* of over-developed impulses, evolution of under-developed functions, activation and utilization of latent potential and energies
- *coordination in a harmonic synthesis*

Obviously the various tasks do not have to be kept separate or applied according to a strict chronological order, but rather coordinated in such a way as to converge toward the psychosynthesis of the individual.

At the Conference, Assagioli also chaired a *Symposium on Psychosynthesis* at the St. Ermin's Hotel, attended by physicians and psychologists of various nationalities. Interest in the educational and therapeutic conception proposed by Assagioli therefore grew rapidly and found, especially abroad, numerous supporters who requested personal and didactic training in this field.[117]

In 1966 another *Symposium on Psychosynthesis* was held once more in London at the Basil Street Hotel.

2. Bio-psychosynthesis and the psychosomatic conception

I would like to recall briefly that since 1909 Assagioli supported a psychological conception that foresaw mind-body interaction in his articles on psychagogy. Several times he came back to this topic, which he considered fundamental to the point of underlining that the term "psychosynthesis" was in reality nothing but an abbreviation of the more complete term "biopsychosynthesis". According to Assagioli, in order to heal, it is essential to use the psyche's influence on the body and that of the body on the psyche as a means of curing and strengthening.

In 1964's *Corso di lezioni sulla psicosintesi*[118] (*Course of Lessons on Psychosynthesis*), he worked on this theme, beginning with the analysis of the reasons why recognition of mind-body interaction meets with opposition and hostility. He identified the first and most important of these causes in the materialistic orientation of medicine, which deals with curing the body while neglecting the human being in his/her totality.

Combining to aggravate this negative attitude is the growing trend toward specialization that causes many doctors to not even deal with the body as a whole, but only with single organs. In addition the poor organization of social medicine forces the physician to perform his work hurriedly and superficially, making it impossible to have a human relationship with the patient, something that is considered essential in Psychosynthesis.

---

117 S. Tilli, op. cit.

118 R. Assagioli, *La medicina psicosomatica*, in *Corso di lezioni sulla psicosintesi*, manuscript, 1964.

To this state of affairs is added the orientation of psychiatry that not only does not recognize the psychogenesis of many physical disorders, but not even that of so many mental disorders. Assagioli decried the fact that doctors are taught neither normal nor pathological psychology, nor psychotherapy. He identified the causes of what he found to be an inexplicable shortcoming in meeting the difficulties, often of a personal nature, in the study of such a complex and difficult science. He wrote: "Many retreat, therefore, from the awareness of oneself ... so as not to face themselves."[119]

However, according to our author, this resistance to admit that some disorders may have psychic causes is not just from the medical profession. Even the same sufferers are afraid to face this hypothesis since psychic causes are sometimes considered to be a symptom of mental illness, madness, or that the disturbances are imaginary, not real.

Assagioli however warned that we should not be too strict. If, in fact, the administration of medicine can sometimes be even more damaging, preventing the patient from realizing the real origin of his disorders and thus deviating him from the most appropriate cure, there is often a real pairing of psychic and physical causes on which it is necessary to act wherever possible to relieve suffering. Our author also pointed out the suggestive action of drugs that can provoke an unconscious persistence within the patient of a magical mentality which is sensitive to ritual.

There is, finally, another reason that creates resistance in accepting psychosomatic influences that consists in the difficulty of understanding how psychic influences can produce material alterations. Faithful to his differential concept, Assagioli warned that "it is necessary to study the specific dynamics of actions and psychosomatic reactions, which can be very different from case to case"[120]. Disturbances may start from a physical cause, or a psychic cause, but there is always a mixing of both because "the very fact of getting sick causes a greater or lesser psychic trauma."

Assagioli explained that dealing with these issues would increase public pressure so that psychology and psychotherapy are finally given their important place in the teaching of medicine, thus raising awareness not only of our physical but also psychic health so that everyone can become "his or her own physician".

2.1. *The First International Psychosomatic Week*

In her book, Paola Giovetti[121] has collected an interesting account of the pioneering work performed in Italy by Roberto Assagioli to promote the dissemination and recognition of psychosomatic medicine. Some interesting

---

119   Ibid.

120   Ibid.

121   P. Giovetti, op. cit.

information emerges from her interview with Ferruccio Antonelli (1927-2000), a professor of psychiatry at the University of Rome and president of the Italian Society of Psychosomatic Medicine.

In 1967, the world's first psychosomatic convention was held in Rome; it was to be the 'presentation at the Temple', the temple of contemporary culture, of the Italian psychosomatic movement supported by incredible international sponsorship. [122] Assagioli gave his main lecture in the general session together with Hungarian psychoanalyst Michael Balint (1896-1970), inventor of "Balint training groups", Carlo L. Cazzullo (1915-2010), the first psychiatrist of the Palazzo Italia to be "open" to psychosomatics, French psychiatrist and psychoanalyst Leon Chertok (1911-1991), the pioneer of obstetric psychoprophylaxis, physician and founder of German psychosomatics Arthur Jores (1901-1982), Denis Leigh, of the European Group of Psychosomatic Research, and Juan R. Carballo, the supreme authority on psychiatry and psychosomatics in Spain. With these magnificent seven, the session was the highest moment of the week and Assagioli's masterful reading on *Medicina psicosomatica e Biopsicosintesi* (*Psychosomatic Medicine and Biopsychosynthesis*) was especially appreciated.

Finally, sixty years after his first articles, the father of Psychosynthesis was able to compare his beliefs with serious scholars and experts in the field. His presentation focused on the contributions that biopsychosynthesis can offer to psychosomatic medicine. At the beginning of the manuscript we obtained, our author defined Psychosynthesis as a development of psychoanalysis that proposes to eliminate the conflicts and obstacles that prevent the natural, complete and harmonious evolution of the human personality. He went on to say that: "... in the practice of psychosynthesis, it soon became necessary to include the body, that is, the recognition and utilization of close relationships, actions and reciprocal reactions between body and psyche"[123].

Among the many specific contributions to Psychosynthesis, Assagioli considered among the most important the recognition of the superior functions of the psyche and the demonstration of their importance in the pathogenesis of many nervous and psychosomatic disorders. He continued by illustrating the psychosynthetic conception of the individual's psycho-physical structure and explained how Psychosynthesis looks not only at the ways to cure and prevent diseases, but also at those applicable to promoting and achieving full humanity.

In this regard, a relevant place is assigned to the will, whose recognition and use is considered fundamental, especially as it concerns the "will to heal", without which any therapy is ineffective. The doctor's task would then be to solicit and strengthen this will of healing along with the recognition of the existential reality of the patient and his conception of life.

---

122   F. Antonelli, in P. Giovetti, op. cit.

123   R. Assagioli, *Medicina psicosomatica e biopsicosintesi*, Acta Medica Psychosomatica, 1967.

At this point, Assagioli asserted that philosophical conceptions can even produce psychosomatic disorders. He claimed that: "... every human being, even the simplest and most uncultured, necessarily has a conception of life, albeit rudimentary, even without being aware of it... On the other hand this philosophy, this conception of the world, is often not only rudimentary but contradictory, given the psychic multiplicity that exists in each of us"[124]. Therefore, the physician, in his interaction with the patient, must take into account this factor, since those who believe that life has meaning, and therefore value, are in a very different and more favorable mental condition than those who doubt it or deny it. He wrote:

> "The psychosomatic effects of the conception of the world and of life or, in other words, of the existential position or attitude of life can easily be explained. This attitude is not a mere mental conviction, but evokes emotions and feelings such as despair which are often intense and even violent; and these, like feelings and emotions of any other origin, produce physical reactions, that is, they are the cause of psychosomatic disorders."[125]

Our author further stated that Psychosynthesis, while dealing with existential problems, does not take any specific position, either metaphysical or religious, towards them, and that "it reaches the threshold of the mystery and stops there, so everybody can subscribe to it and use it, whatever their beliefs or metapsychological positions are."[126]

He then went on to explain what unhealthy attitudes can exist toward the body: on the one hand, one can fully identify with it, becoming slave to it and not recognizing any influence of the psychic faculties; on the other hand, one can live in a world of emotions and imaginations, or in the world of intellect, completely alienated from corporeality. These extreme attitudes can and should be changed through the use of various psycho-physical techniques.

The last point dealt with by Assagioli concerns the doctor-patient relationship. He attaches crucial importance to the influence of the doctor's personality on his client and makes it clear that Psychosynthesis distinguishes four main types of relationships, and each one is used, directed and deliberately set up for the purpose of therapy. First, there is *transfer* and the *countertransfer*, secondly the *relationship created by the therapeutic situation*, then the *human relationship* and finally the *resolution of the relationship*. He closed his report by highlighting the importance of the therapeutic group and group therapy.

---

124   Ibid.

125   Ibid.

126   Ibid.

3. The blossoming of the final years

3.1. Dissemination of Psychosynthesis in Italy and abroad

In 1965, the *Istituto di Psicosintesi* (*Institute of Psychosynthesis*) was elevated to the status of Ente Morale (Decree of the President of the Republic 1721, 1.8.1965), in recognition of the particular educational efforts of the Institute on cultural and social levels. This was an important acknowledgment of Assagioli's work.

Two years later, in 1967, the first *Centro italiano di Psicosintesi* (*Italian Center for Psychosynthesis*) was officially established in Rome as an offshoot of the Institute. The following year the center in Bologna was opened and in 1970 that of Perugia. The development of Psychosynthesis Centers began in this way and today they number 18 spread throughout Italy.

In the meantime, the blossoming of Psychosynthesis centers abroad continues: in India, the *Indian Psychosynthesis Research Institute* imparts the knowledge of Psychosynthesis in both English and Hindi; Greece hosts a Psychosynthesis Center in Athens; 1969 saw the opening of a Psychosynthesis Center in California; again in America we have the San Francisco institute with a university-style facility (*Synthesis Graduate School*); in 1972 the *Canadian Institute of Psychosynthesis* was officially established in Montreal; in the spring of 1974, the London Center was inaugurated. Other centers were established in New York, Los Angeles, Buenos Aires, Paris, Switzerland, Germany, Holland, Spain and Mexico.

3.2. Publications

The writings of Roberto Assagioli, dating back to 1906, are not yet organized in a well-defined and definitive system; there are more than three hundred pieces dealing with the most varied themes. Our author composed lessons and pamphlets, most of which have not yet been published. There is also an extraordinary number of handwritten notes, in many languages, that have been organized by some of his students including Dr. Massimo Rosselli and Dr. Piero Ferrucci: a goldmine still waiting to be discovered.[127] Some of the brochures and essays written by Assagioli have been published in nine languages (Italian, French, English, German, Spanish, Dutch, Russian, Polish and Japanese). With the exception of *The Act of Will*, his books were in fact created with collections of lessons and articles.

The first important publication is from 1965 with the release in the United States of *Psychosynthesis - A Manual of Principles and Techniques*[128], later translated

---

127 Thanks to the work of the *Gruppo alle Fonti*, many of these writings are now available online at www.archivioassagioli.com

128 R. Assagioli, *Psychosynthesis - A Manual of Principles and Techniques*, The Viking Press, New York, 1965.

into Italian and published in 1973 by Astrolabio[129]. The text is divided into three parts: the first, dedicated to the principles of Psychosynthesis, collects articles published in the thirties in the "Hibbert Journal"; the second relates to the explanation of the techniques used in Psychosynthesis and gathers the material accumulated by Assagioli during many years of therapeutic practice; finally, the third part deals with special applications of Psychosynthesis, such as the use of music, images, colors, symbols, and meditation as treatment methods.

The second text, published this time directly in Italian, dates back to 1966 and is called *Psicosintesi - Armonia della vita* (*Psychosynthesis - Harmony of Life*)[130]. The book is not of a technical nature and is not intended to deal with all the vast fields of Psychosynthesis. It contains the reprocessing of twenty lessons, held in Rome at the initiative of the Institute of Psychosynthesis, addressed to those who were interested in psychological and educational issues in the humanistic sense. The main vital or existential problems of the human being are discussed: what or who is the individual, the conscience and the unconscious, female psychology, sexuality and love, psychic conflicts, aggressiveness, latent potentialities in the human soul and their activation.

In 1973, we have the publication, again first in English, of *The Act of Will*[131]. This book has a singular story and is, as I have previously mentioned, the only one conceived and written as a book. At 77, Assagioli had to undergo a delicate operation. It seems that while in a semi-conscious state, he protested vigorously against something or someone and then consented, saying, "Okay, I'll do it!"[132]. He later told some of his closest associates that he thought about leaving, because for him death would only be a birth into more joyous levels, but he said, "They kicked me out." It seems that, in that semi-conscious state, he had seen a Master who had proposed a "postponement" if he would write some books. In fact, when he recuperated, he wrote *The Act Of Will*, after which he immediately started a new book, *La psicologia dell'alto e il Sé* (*Psychology of the High and the Self*). Piero Ferrucci claims that after Assagioli's operation there was actually a new flourishing:

> It was then that Assagioli laid the foundation for future work on psychosynthesis: new students, important acknowledgments, the book on will. If he had passed away at that moment, psychosynthesis may have died with its creator."[133]

Our author wrote *The Act Of Will* as an introduction, guide and tool for studying, developing and using it from the point of view of the latest developments in psychology, such as existential, humanistic and transpersonal psychology. In this book, he examined how the will works, and also how it works best, describing the qualities, various aspects, phases and objectives. Assagioli declared that this

---

129   R. Assagioli, *Principi e metodi della psicosintesi terapeutica*, Casa Ed. Astrolabio, 1973.

130   R. Assagioli, *Psicosintesi - Armonia della vita*, Ed. Mediterranee, 1966.

131   R. Assagioli, *The Act of Will*, The Viking Press, New York, 1973.

132   P. Giovetti, op. cit.

133   P. Ferrucci, in P. Giovetti, op. cit.

is a largely phenomenological study, based on statements, reports and his own experiences from many years of work, from his patients, students and colleagues. He wrote in the introduction:

"A historical overview of the problems related to the will shows that trying to solve this problem at the intellectual level not only does not lead to the solution, but results in contradictions, confusion and loss. And so I believe that the right procedure is to put off all the theories and intellectual discussions on the subject, and begin by discovering the reality and the nature of the will through direct existential experience."[134]

It is known that in the last days of his life, Assagioli was working on another book devoted to the theme he was most interested in and that he was going to call *La psicologia dell'alto e il Sé* (*Psychology of the High and the Self*). In this work he intended to bring together in a systematic and organic way all that he had learned, experienced and gathered on this subject during his long life. Unfortunately, the work was not completed, but Assagioli's desire was respected: on the occasion of the 100th anniversary of his birth (1988), the Astrolabio publishing firm released *Lo sviluppo transpersonale* (*Transpersonal Development*) in collaboration with Maria Luisa Girelli Macchia who organized his notes and added some other studies and essays.

The title is certainly suited to psychosynthetic orientation for which inner research and the realization of the Self represent a real and true practice that activates a dormant dimension in every human being: transpersonality. The first part of the book has a descriptive tone and introduces the concept of the superconscious. It is clear that Assagioli's intention was to liberate the spiritual content from the traditional framework in which it was relegated: religions, philosophies, and various occult ideologies. The second part is devoted to the problems and difficulties that can arise in the course of transpersonal development and looks at the approach best suited to addressing and overcoming such problems. The third part focuses on the transposition of spiritual research into everyday life by addressing practical issues such as the relationship with money, the transmutation and sublimation of sexual and aggressive energies, the synthesis of active and contemplative life, and the manifestation of transpersonal qualities in personality.

These were the actual books and publications. Among the many other writings, I have preferred to list a few of those in Italian published as works or pamphlets:

Le Religioni, i nuovi tempi e i giovani (in ALI, Rivista di Problemi Femminili, n. 11-12, 1948) [*Religions, Modern Times and Youth* (published in issue n° 11-12-48 of ALI, a women's journal]

La psicoterapia (in Medicina Psicosomatica, Vol. 2, n.1, 1957) [*Psychotherapy* (in Psychosomatic Medicine, Vol. 2, n° 1, 1957)]

---

134   R. Assagioli, *L'atto di volontà*, Casa Editrice Astrolabio, 1977.

La psicologia della donna e la sua psicosintesi [The Psychology of Woman and its Psychosynthesis]

Trasmutazione e sublimazione delle energie sessuali [Transmutation and Sublimation of Sexual Energies]

La purificazione dell'anima nel simbolismo del poema dantesco [Purification of the Spirit in the Symbolism of Dante's Epic Poetry]

La psicologia e l'Arte di Vivere [Psychology and the Art of Living]

Medicina psicosomatica e biopsicosintesi [Psychosomatic Medicine and Biosynthesis]

Saggezza sorridente [Smiling Wisdom]

I simboli del supernormale [Symbols of the Supernormal]

Come si imparano le lingue con l'inconscio [How to Learn Languages Using the Unconscious]

Equilibramento e sintesi degli opposti [Balancing and Synthesis of Opposites]

Modi e ritmi della formazione psicologica [Ways and Rhythms of Psychological Training]

Psicologia dinamica e piscosintesi [Dynamic Psychology and Psychosynthesis]

Note sull'educazione [Notes on Education]

La Psicologia nell'Avvenire [Psychology in the Future]

Educazione dei giovani particolarmente dotati [The Education of Exceptionally Gifted Children]

La psicologia e la Scienza della Sessualità [Psychology and the Science of Sexuality]

Spiritualità del Novecento [Spirituality in the 1900s]

Per vivere meglio [To Live Better]

Parole stimolo [Evocative Words]

I tipi umani [Human Types]

(all published in collaboration with the *Institute of Psychosynthesis*, Florence)

3.3. The language of Roberto Assagioli

Those who personally knew him assert that Assagioli had the ability to express great and profound ideas with "small" words, in a way that was simple and accessible to all.[135] He considered the truth something simple, a direct existential experience, not a mental complication or a conceptual definition. In turn, the language he used in his writings was clear and instructive, exempt from any intellectual presumption. According to his pupil, psychotherapist and psychosynthe-

---

135   A. Alberti, *Roberto Assagioli: Note e Ricordi, in Psicosintesi*, "Rivista dell'Istituto di Psicosintesi", anno XVI, n. 2, 1999.

sist Sergio Bartoli[136], the clarity, fluency, coherence, continuous exemplification of concepts, absence of any "hermetism", and the absolute respect of semantic values, made Assagioli a distinctive writer, constantly dedicated to clarifying his thoughts. As Assagioli himself wrote in the preface of *The Act of Will*, he addresses the subject in the simplest style possible with deliberate repetitions aimed at drawing the reader's attention several times to the same fundamental point.

It is therefore very probable that Assagioli considered writing as an additional opportunity to demonstrate how the spirit of synthesis could work in a scientific context. The simplicity and form of the contents cannot be reduced to a simplistic vision of the human being and his/her intrinsic complexity, but rather to the consciously pursued intent of favoring an integrative and inclusive vision while avoiding academicism for the sake of academicism, sterile criticism and meticulous, intellectualist analysis of the topics. More than anything else, his aim was to be understood by all; although he was an educator by trade, he was more a traveling companion than a professor.

4. The end and a new beginning

The last years of Roberto Assagioli's life were intense, prolific and rich with satisfaction. Psychosynthesis was being disseminated worldwide and he followed the progression of his creation. Up to the very last years before his death, he continued to travel tirelessly to participate in conventions in Austria, France, Switzerland and England.

Even during this time, his life was very full: in addition to traveling abroad, there were Psychosynthesis courses in Florence, counseling, organization of material for students and collaborators and meetings with people from all over the world. These were the years when Assagioli found those who would carry the torch of Psychosynthesis. In addition to this, he also worked as a member of the editorial board of the *Journal of Humanistic Psychology* and the *Journal of Transpersonal Psychology*, publications of the two respective psychological branches whose birth he had contributed to greatly. This level of activity would have tired a young and healthy man, and he was no longer either one or the other.[137]

4.1. Nella's illness and death

Then came the difficult times of Nella's illness, a degenerative disease that created many problems regarding assistance; she suffered anxiety, a desire to not leave the home, gradual loss of memory, and growing inability to recognize people. Assagioli never entertained the option of consigning his wife to a nursing home and cared for her with tender love until the end. In 1972, although Nella

---

136   S. Bartoli, in *Lo Sviluppo transpersonale,* op. cit.

137   P. Giovetti, op. cit.

was very ill, the couple celebrated their golden anniversary. A cake was prepared and Roberto recited a poem by Trilussa to his wife that spoke of being together in joy and sorrow. Then, in 1973, he was alone.

We know that in the last period, he had lost his hearing, but he did not complain about it; on the contrary, he joked and said that he could now hear only what he wanted to hear. He was serene and active until the end.

How Assagioli was just prior to his death was revealed in an extraordinary interview given by American philosopher and journalist Sam Keen.[138] Keen had gone to Florence in the spring of 1974 just to meet the founder of Psychosynthesis and provided an invaluable account of Assagioli's life and work environment:

> "Assagioli's office is a small room in his apartment, which is above the headquarters of the Institute. Books line two of the walls: Ralph Waldo Emerson, Herman Keyserling, Abraham Maslow and Carl Gustav Jung seem to be favorites. On the next to the bottom shelf *Jonathan Livingston Seagull* is perched between Rollo May and Erik Erikson. The desk is antique and covered with objects and papers (talismans of the shaman), fresh cut flowers (like tiger lilies I knew in Tennessee); a barometer; a clock; a kitchen timer; scales; a flag of the United Nations; a star globe; two word-cards: ENERGY and GOOD-WILL. The walls, once white, have now yellowed like old bones. A stuffed Victorian love seat squats in one corner of the room.
>
> Assagioli rises to greet me. He is old, fine-boned and frail, but the liveliness and delight in his face make his presence vigorous. His pointed goatee and salmon-colored-velvet smoking jacket lend an air of old-world authority. (…)."

4.2. The passing of Roberto Assagioli

From Sam Keen's long interview, it's worth mentioning Assagioli's last answer. Keen asked him how he faces the idea of death and his answer contained the convictions of a lifetime. His answer shines light on the serenity, balance and faith that always were part of his personality. Here's what he said:[139]

> "Death looks to me primarily like a vacation There are many hypotheses about death and the idea of reincarnation seems the most sensible to me. I have no direct knowledge about reincarnation but my belief puts me in good company with hundreds of millions of Eastern people, with the Buddha and many others in the West. Death is a normal part of a biological cycle. It is my body that dies and not all of me. So I don't care much. I may die this evening but I would willingly accept a few more years in order to do the work I am interested in, which I think may be useful to others. I am, as the French say, *disponible* (available). Also humor helps, and a sense of proportion. I am one individual on a small planet in a little solar system in one of the galaxies."

---

138 S. Keen, *La proporzione aurea di Roberto Assagioli*, Centro Studi di Psicosintesi "R. Assagioli", 1987.

139 P. Giovetti, op. cit.

Commenting on these words, Keen wrote: "… in speaking about death there was no change in the tone or intensity of Assagioli's voice and the light still played in his dark eyes, and his mouth was never very far from a smile."

Assagioli died several months later, on August 23, 1974, in the peace of Villa Ilario in the Capolona countryside. He had just turned 86 a few months prior. Ida Palombi, his faithful secretary, says that the last word he uttered before slipping into unconsciousness was "Ilario", his son's name. He passed away rather quickly, without prolonged suffering. It was a moment for which Assagioli had prepared himself for quite some time. Another account on the master's death comes from his student, psychiatrist Alberto Alberti, in a touching commemorative article:

> "An important event I was witness to was his death in Capolona. That night, some other students and I watched over him, and there was an 'air of sanctity'. Assagioli left us in that moment which he had consciously taught us about, but we would have to wait many years for the seeds he planted in our unconscious to sprout.
>
> Despite the sadness of the moment, I felt that something profound had occurred, that each of us students carried within us that potential, each in his/her own way, a 'promise of continuity' of the project, that 'blossoming' that Assagioli himself experienced, and showed us, the 'gardener and his plot'. Today maybe the time is beginning to be ripe."[140]

Assagioli's remains were cremated in a wood pyre in Arezzo on August 30th. As we have seen, he was inclined to believe in reincarnation, and based on that doctrine, cremation is performed so that the surviving spiritual essence can more easily leave the physical world. And so the earthly parabola of the father of Psychosynthesis came to an end. The advancement of his creation is still in the trusted hands of the students that Assagioli trained, and who continue to "water the good plant."[141]

5. Assagioli: the portrait of a new humanity

In her book, Paola Giovetti quotes the accounts given regarding the human figure that was Roberto Assagioli, interviewing about fifteen of the people closest to him: relatives, friends, neighbors and students. Among these are Ms. Luisa Lunelli, his niece Donatella Ciapetti Assagioli, Prof. Sergio Bernardi, Dr. Sergio Bartoli, Prof. Ferruccio Antonelli, Ms. Teresa D'Amico, Dr. Piero Ferrucci, Prof. Bruno Caldironi, Dr. Massimo Rosselli, Dr. Andrea Bocconi, Dr. Matilde Santandrea, Vittorio Arzilla, secretary of the Institute of Psychosynthesis in Florence from 1968 to 1982, Ms. Ada Cini, Sousanne Nouvion, founder of the French Institute of Psychosynthesis, and Prof. Peter De Coppens. By reading all of these accounts,

---

140   A. Alberti, op. cit.

141   P. Giovetti, op. cit.

a concise and accurate picture of the personality of the father of Psychosynthesis emerges, and I will now try to render it as complete as possible.

Everyone interviewed describes Assagioli as a simple and serene man who managed to maintain these qualities even in the most difficult and painful moments of his life, for example when they arrested and imprisoned him, or when he lost his son and then his wife. But his serenity had nothing to do with fatalism or resignation; it was rather, according to testimony, the ability to take the best from any situation, even if negative. His simplicity was thought to be the fruit of a long passage of maturity that brought him from complexity, perceivable in his first articles, to clarity, the effect of synthesis seen in the last writings. It was the simplicity of one who reached the wisdom and breadth of extraordinary vision; the simplicity of one who had made synthesis the guiding star of his whole life.

Everyone agrees in saying that the quality that Assagioli expressed most, along with will, was joy. Humor and playfulness were strong in him, and he emanated an enormous quantity of joy and had a sense of wonder like that of children. His eyes were always smiling, infinite, warm, radiant, and he loved to repeat that they are not only the mirror, but also the "transmitters" of the soul. His knowing, radiant gaze had the power to dissolve any rigidity, infusing deep confidence, peace, tranquility, and total acceptance.

None of his neighbors remembers ever hearing a hostile phrase, a negative judgment, or seeing even the slightest animosity. He was contrary to controversy. He obviously had his views, but he did not judge, and always invited those around him to cultivate tolerance towards humanity. He was able to see in every person the healthy aspects projected toward the future. He trained his students to be receptive and open to every therapeutic method, teaching them not to rely solely on pathology, but also to see the other side, namely the healthy part of the individual.

Assagioli did not subscribe to direct teaching: he was the living testimony of his psychosynthesis. According to those who met him, he totally embodied his message, synthesizing in his persona the most beautiful aspects of all religions and philosophies. He transformed by example, with just his presence, wordlessly and, above all, without imposing his ideas. In fact, he respected the freedom of others and taught people not to base their lives on external reference points, but on what each person discovers in himself/herself. He did not want to create groups or suggest belonging to this or that church, but rather stimulated the higher and wiser side of those who met him by rendering them independent.

He could touch the soul of people. Being in contact with him transformed one, psychologically and spiritually. This, according to the interviewees, together with joy and sense of humor, were his main traits. They said that after getting to know him, they were no longer the same, not so much by what he was saying. but how he was. He created a special atmosphere all around himself, he knew how to make a deep impression, and stimulated the archetypes.

Whatever question he was asked, he always answered after a moment of silence, but the things he said had shocking effects because they were so wide-ranging that one could not grasp them immediately. His students say he had the ability to interpret events and situations with a vast vision and conscience. He gave short but deep answers, understandable according to the maturity of the person. In Assagioli everyone found different points of reference according to their degree of development. When he spoke, he transmitted confidence and good faith. He had the incredible gift to convey to those who listened to him a feeling of profound righteousness and truth in what he said and, with his affirmations, to shake the confidence of those who listened to him.

Everyone agrees on another point: Assagioli was a profoundly humble person. This humility made him respectful of others and always open to advice which he appreciated and accepted with pleasure. He was free to talk about every topic and kept informed on everything, but those close to him took years to realize the vastness of his literary, historical, scientific and musical culture, of the number of foreign languages he spoke and wrote, in addition to the ancient ones he read.

Assagioli did not have the appearance of a dean or professor. He never took advantage of or let his collaborators profit from Psychosynthesis, which he always considered to be a service to humanity. Assagioli knowingly dedicated his entire life to helping humankind.

People who knew or met him say they were initially struck by his physical fragility, yet all say that hidden beneath that fragility was an incredible, unexpected energy that he never flaunted: it seemed he could gain anything without the least effort.

Certainly one cannot define Assagioli an ordinary man. Those interviewed describe him as very fascinating, well-mannered and kind, infinitely patient, wise, thoroughly good-hearted with an extraordinary capacity to love which people could feel. He was generous and never asked anything for himself. He never became attached, and if one of his collaborators decided to take another path, he did not take it badly. He was an idealist, totally convinced of humankind's goodness.

A relationship with him was extremely fascinating. He was likened to a wise man, a master, an ancient spirit returned to teach, an enlightened one, a prophet. He definitely had the bearing of a holy man, an inspired man. He seemed to be in constant communication with the spirit. His dominant characteristic was a different state of consciousness. He was defined as a superior person who really sought to help others and who knew how to get others to make an effort; a very evolved person in contact with levels of consciousness unachievable for most. However, the interviewees explain that he did not want to be considered a guru, that he only wanted to be an educator, a psychologist. Yet, he was considered by everyone a Maestro "with a capital M".

Assagioli was totally and deeply authentic; everybody was aware of that and considered him a guiding light. He also gave the impression of being deeply complete and in continual meditation. He was a man who left his mark.

Assagioli was a good father, too. Those interviewed said their relationship with him was a very affectionate one, very fatherly. They fondly remember how nice he was with the youngsters, encouraging and stimulating them. They could ask him anything. He made them feel happy, stimulated their creativity and had a lot of faith in them. For many people, meeting him was an extraordinary experience, one of the loveliest of their lives, for many reasons: Assagioli was a catalyst in their development, capable of giving a jump-start to potential they didn't even know they had. He had the power to enliven people, to show people parts of themselves that may have been hidden, to help them make more of themselves. His students remember seeing very depressed, desperate people enter his studio and then come out completely transformed. Assagioli taught people how to walk through life, and saw life as a voyage. His student Dr. Andrea Bocconi recalls:

> "There's something special I'll always remember. On his desk he had a little boat, and when the cleaning service dusted there, he'd often find the boat out of place. He would always put it back where he wanted it, facing the window. Once, with the curiosity of a twenty-year-old, I asked him why he did that.
>
> 'Because, for me, it represents adventure', he told me. 'I can go off on a voyage at any time, change, put everything back into discussion.' "[142]

Getting on in years, he would repeat that he had not yet learned how to live, that one never stops learning how to live.

---

142   A. Bocconi, in P. Giovetti, op. cit.

PART TWO

THE BACKGROUND
OF PSYCHOSYNTHESIS

The Five Forces of Psychology

In this second part I propose to put Psychosynthesis into context compared to the major "forces" of psychology, illustrating what important contributions Roberto Assagioli has provided for their creation and development, not only in Italy but also abroad.

I'll begin by mentioning what Professor Luigi Peresson[1], a student of Assagioli, has written regarding this:

"I'd like to tell the reader about something that happened to me personally: back then, about 20 years ago, I was lucky enough to be given some training by Assagioli himself. In addition to reading his many publications, I marveled in listening to the lively voice of the master speaking of concepts that in more recent books were often lauded as new 'discoveries' of psychological science. I was so convinced that many of the things I was learning, (...) had already been clearly said and illustrated by Assagioli, perhaps without the pomposity (as was his style!)."

Obviously this is not meant to say that others "copied" Assagioli, but rather to emphasize that he was certainly a forerunner of ideas and guidelines that later scholars then perfected in their theoretical structure and in their applications.

These "forces" of psychology are usually identified as follows: *behaviorism* (first force), *psychoanalysis* (second force), *existential-humanistic psychology* (third force), and *transpersonal psychology* (fourth force). In his writings Assagioli added a fifth force called "*psychoenergetics*", an expression in psychology regarding the paradigm shift that was taking place in the scientific field following the revolutionary scope of the new discoveries of quantum physics. The father of Psychosynthesis felt that these discoveries would open the way to a new vision of the world and of human-kind, in which the great truths—acclaimed by all the sacred traditions over the millennia—would ultimately be considered without prejudice and recognized as storehouses of precious insights and indications for the future development of humanity.

Obviously, the goal of this part is not to write the exhaustive history of the aforementioned movements. After briefly reconstructing their origin and evolution, I will show how Psychosynthesis is positioned in relation to them. I will especially focus on the third and fourth "forces" since it was here that Assagioli's work made a major contribution to their origin and development.

---

1   L. Peresson, *La psicosintesi nel progresso delle scienze psicologiche*, in *I nuovi paradigmi della psicologia*, Cittadella editrice, Assisi, 1992, p. 25.

CHAPTER I

THE FIRST FORCE: BEHAVIORISM

For more than two thousand years, the object of the investigation of psychology has been been the soul. In fact, "psyche" (ψυχή) in Greek means "soul, mind, or spirit". With the birth of scientific psychology, the object remained the same even if it was no longer characterized as a substance, that is, the soul, but as a phenomenon, consciousness.

Within this tradition, behaviorism is considered a radical overturn as it rejects that psychology should have to deal with conscience, suggesting the study of psychological contents through their observable manifestation: behavior.[2]

In consideration of mind-body dualism, behaviorists opted for the behavioral body for both methodological reasons (behavior appeared more scientifically observable than the psyche) and for philosophical motives (behavior seemed a more important variable on which to draw for a real knowledge of the psychological person).[3]

Initially, behaviorism was a typically North American movement, interpreting the characteristic values of the *American way of life*, and only in the '50s did it begin to be known outside the United States. Though it was considered a compact school of thought, it was actually divided into various theoretical orientations. There was also an evolution in the internal approach to the models proposed by individual scholars.[4] However, to facilitate the discussion of the matter, I will take into consideration above all the thinking of its founder, psychologist John Watson (1878-1958).

1. The predecessors of behaviorism

In America in the early 1900s, two important schools dominated the psychological research field prior to behaviorism: structuralism and functionalism.

Structural psychology or "introspectionism", the leading exponent of which was Edward Titchener (1867-1927), one of the students of German psychologist Wilhelm Wundt (1832-1920), proposed to study the human mind through the breakdown of its elements (sensations, images and feelings) and the description

---

2   *Storia della psicologia*, edited by P. Legrenzi, il Mulino, 1980, pp. 141-142.

3   Ibid, p. 165.

4   L. Mecacci, *Storia della psicologia del Novecento*, Editori Laterza, 1992, pp. 211-212.

of the laws governing their combination. The preferred method of investigation was the introspective, consisting in the analysis of the psychic structure through rigorous self-observation of its own internal processes by specially trained researchers following specific procedures.

Functionalism, on the other hand, explicitly referring to Darwinian concepts, considered the research of mental activities related to the acquiring, storing, organizing and evaluating of experiences and their subsequent use in behavioral guidance. Attention was focused on learning processes, motivation, individual differences, evolutionary psychology and its educational applications, and on animal psychology. It had its main point of reference in William James's *Principles of Psychology* (1842-1910).

Behaviorism, advocated by John Watson, is traditionally considered the antithesis of Titchener's subjectivism, but it is equally true that it inherits diverse components. Among these: aversion to the metaphysical, the associational criterion, descriptive elementism, and a profound intolerance for the interpretations of so-called "common sense", considered the greatest enemy of scientific psychology.[5]

Therefore, with regard to functionalism, if on one side behaviorists decisively seized on the most original issues investigated by that school—the evolutionary idea that the individual is considered to be an animal that responds to the environment and the study of learning—on the other they denounced the many philosophical or prescientific components.[6]

2. Fundamental principles

Behaviorism was officially codified in 1913 when Watson published an article titled *Psychology as the Behaviorist Views It*. The entire behaviorist program is summed up in the first lines of the publication[7]:

> "Psychology as the behaviorist views it is a purely objective experimental branch of natural science. Its theoretical goal is the prediction and control of behavior. Introspection forms no essential part of its methods, nor is the scientific value of its data dependent upon the readiness with which they lend themselves to interpretation in terms of consciousness. The behaviorist, in his efforts to get a unitary scheme of animal response, recognizes no dividing line between man and brute."

The rejection of the conscience was certainly the central point in the manifesto of 1913. Of course, the target against which Watson directed his attacks was the introspective method, considered unscientific since the observer identified

---

5   P. Legrenzi, op. cit., p. 89.

6   Ibid, p. 90.

7   J. Watson, cit. in L. Mecacci, op. cit., pag. 200.

himself with the observed, and because it approached things that others could not see directly. The study of behavior would have made it possible to overcome these drawbacks.

Especially important afterward was the reference to the ability to control and/or manipulate behavior. This will be of crucial importance for its implications regarding education and the development of behavioral therapy.

Finally, the possibility of connecting animal and human behaviors led to animals being considered ideal laboratory test subjects for studying human psychology and that the results obtained on mice, monkeys and dogs were mechanically applied to human beings. This, however, prevented the particularities and complexities of various psychological conditions being taken into account.

In the years that followed, the problem of the analytical unit of psychology as a behavioral science was addressed, identified in the conditioned reflex and conditioning in general. There is no doubt that the Russian school, and especially physiologists Ivan Pavlov (1849-1936) and Vladimir Bechterev (1857-1927), had a great impact on Watson and his theoretical formulas.

Pavlov conducted experiments using dogs to show how animal and human organisms learn to associate one stimulus with another (conditional reflex principle). Ringing a bell while giving a steak to a dog conditioned the animal's brain, forming an association between the sound of the bell and the idea of something to eat. After a while, it was enough to ring the bell (stimulus) for the dog to begin salivating (response) while waiting for the food. Pavlov deduced that salivation was induced in the dog by an artificially induced conditioned reflex.

Starting with those findings, Watson hypothesized that complex behavior of humans was the result of long-term conditioning. For this reason all behaviorists attached special importance to the study of learning processes.

3. The image of the individual and behavioral therapy

According to the behaviorist view, a baby is born without instinct, intelligence or other innate characteristics, and only experience will shape him/her psychologically. The human being is therefore considered the totality of their experience.

Watson tried to apply these ideas in the psychopathological field. Through classical conditioning techniques he was able to induce a phobic neurosis in a child, the famous "Little Albert". In this way, he believed that the neuroses were not innate, but could be defined in the terms of learned emotional responses. It thus opened the way for behavioral therapies that would have a huge success in the United States after World War II.

The main proponents of behavioral therapy were American psychologists Joseph Wolpe (1915-1997), Burrhus Skinner (1904-1990), and German-born

English psychologist Hans Eysenck (1916-1997) who summarized the central idea[8]:

> "The behaviorial model of abnormal behavior simply states that every behavior is learned, and that 'abnormal' behavior is learned according to the same laws of 'normal' behavior. (...) The symptoms displayed by the patient are therefore merely the behaviors that he has learned; there is no cause or underlying 'complex' that produces and feeds the symptoms and makes them reappear after they have been eliminated by a purely 'symptomatic' cure. Based on this way of considering the problem, it also follows that behaviors, once learned, may be unlearned (...)"

By treating symptoms rather than identifying deep-seated dynamics, behavioral therapy has been proposed as a clearly defined alternative to interpretive psychotherapies such as psychoanalysis. The position of some well-known psychologists in the behavioral area of psychoanalysis has often been radical, even complete refusal. They considered the body to be like a *black box* into which the psychologist cannot enter unless he starts applying metaphysics. So psychoanalysis, and more generally depth psychology, could only be rejected as a set of concepts and practices that cannot be verified according to the criteria of modern science.

4. Psychosynthesis and "surface" psychology

Certainly Psychosynthesis could not join with either the behavioral doctrine or its therapeutic and educational ideal. Assagioli's position with regard to the scientific method diverged radically from that used by scientific psychology.

4.1. The psychosynthetic vision of the scientific method

According to Psychosynthesis, psychology, being a science of humankind, should provide the means to understand and deal with the totality of the human being. Assagioli held that the scientific method was erroneously identified with the experimental and quantitative technical specifications used in natural sciences. In this way:

> "when psychology freed itself from the bonds to philosophy, (...) its practitioners believed it was possible, indeed necessary, to use the same techniques—and only those—that were used in natural sciences, excluding from its field of investigations everything that is qualitative and subjective (...). But in doing so, they eliminated what is specifically human, which is the real object of psychology."[9]

---

8   Hans Eysenck, cit. in L. Mecacci, op. cit., p.234.

9   R. Assagioli, *Le nuove dimensioni della psicologia*, Corso di lezioni sulla psicosintesi, 1973, p. 4.

According to Assagioli this exclusion is in no way justifiable. First of all, because physical science itself had to recognize the presence of a subjective factor in all observations. Secondly, because, with Psychosynthesis, everything that is capable of modifying all that exists has its own reality. Feelings, ideas, images, goals, and values are therefore considered as facts, since they have a powerful effect on the individual and his/her behavior and therefore, as facts, can be scientifically studied.

For Assagioli, the true scientific mind is one that functions correctly, avoids quibbling, rationalizing, errors in judgment and, above all, errors in language. Indeed, the true scientific mind is able to avoid all the "idols" mentioned by the English philosopher Francis Bacon (1561-1626):

- *idola tribus*: illusions due to the very constitution of the human psyche and common to all men;
- *idola specus*: deriving from the individual temperament, the education, the various dispositions and moods of each individual;
- *idola fori*: dependent on the transmission through language (in this regard it is worth pointing out that Assagioli considered modern semantics a huge step forward in this regard);
- *idola theatri*: the erroneous notions due to the academic and systemic spirit, accepted without discrimination and based on the authority of others;
- *idola scholae*: consists of having blind faith in rules at the expense of personal judgment.

According to our author, only a psychology free of these prejudices can truly call itself a science and, at the same time, study the human being as a whole.

> "There is nothing that limits vision as much as a system; it excludes all those facts of reality that do not fall into the enchanted castle of that intellectual structure. Now, psychologists—more than any other scholar—should be free from any system. They have to come into contact with the living reality of psychic life, with its evident dynamism, and from this draw theoretical and practical consequences; not start from a preconceived idea of what psychic life should be."[10]

Psychosynthesis therefore distinguishes the scientific method from the many research techniques available, and considers the former single and the latter multiple. This absolutely does not want to deny the importance of using quantitative techniques: quite the contrary. In Psychosynthesis the quantitative/objective and the qualitative/subjective approaches are not in contrast with each other but complementary. In this regard, I recall that Assagioli asked for this reassessment of research methods long before the subject began to be discussed, albeit timidly, in Italy's academic environment.

---

10   R. Assagioli, *Psicosintesi - Armonia della vita*, Edizioni Mediterranee, Roma, 1971, p. 24.

4.2. Dialogue with behaviorism

Although Psychosynthesis does not share the scientific and theoretical orientation of behaviorism, considering its view of the human being unilateral, it does not oppose it with an attitude of complete rejection. In his writings, Assagioli has repeatedly stated that behaviorism must be recognized as having provided a good deal of useful data for various psychological applications. Certainly the representatives of the mechanistic conception "did not take into account—or have done so in a very partial and totally inadequate fashion—that in the psyche there is a fundamental tendency: that of union, synthesis, which is something deeper and more vital than the simple mechanical association of sensations and ideas."[11] Nevertheless, Assagioli credits them with investigating the aspects of human behavior that are more similar to that of the animal, thus providing, though not intentionally, the basic knowledge necessary to adequately manage these inclinations.

In addition, Psychosynthesis uses some processes that are very close to behavioral therapy: suggestion and autosuggestion, progressive muscle relaxation, autogenic training, bio-feedback, and so forth. Indeed, we can say that Assagioli, proposing techniques such as imaginative evocation, Ideal Model, and guided vision, was actually many years ahead of some of the methods widely used by behaviorists. Think of the very well-known technique of systematic desensitization or the principles of working discrimination, reinforcement and modeling. In this regard, Luigi Peresson wrote in his article[12]:

> "generally speaking, all the guided imaginative and visualization techniques, so common in psychosynthesis, recall, in certain respects, the procedures of *behavior therapy* including the latest indications offered by Bandura and colleagues with the *modeling* techniques."

I will later discuss the importance that Psychosynthesis attributes to the systematic use of various active techniques. Here it is important to emphasize how it considers them useful and effective in eliminating a number of symptoms and allowing the patient to discover and use their own resources. However, it finds them unsuitable for identifying the true cause or origin of the disturbance. For this reason, Assagioli proposed a psychological practice that integrates existential methods with the active approach and which completes the "two dimensional" vision proposed by the behavioral theory with the "three dimensional" vision of depth psychology.

---

11   Ibid, p. 34.

12   L. Peresson, op. cit., p. 31.

CHAPTER II

THE SECOND FORCE: PSYCHOANALYSIS

1. The antecedents

Psychoanalysis, the other dominant school of 20th century psychology, did not originate with psychology. It is grounded in psychiatry which was firmly established as a branch of medicine in the nineteenth century.

Between the eighteenth and nineteenth centuries, the problem of the specificity of mental illness was repeatedly raised in relation to other afflictions of the human body, and towards the mid-nineteenth century, particularly in Germany, a new psychiatry was developed which based its beliefs on a fundamental assumption: the adaptation of pathology to organic causes. This orientation had a promising start but failed to detect a specific organic base for psychoneurosis and other mental disorders.

And so some psychologists and psychiatrists, especially French (Pierre Janet, Liébault, Hippolyte Bernheim and Jean-Martin Charcot), realized that the rigid deterministic conception of the pathological symptom did not hold up and began to look for different approaches to mental illness. The use of the "dynamic" adjective was then disseminated so as to distinguish psychic nervous disorders from the organic diseases of the nervous system. The constant attention paid to the patient in his tangible humanity and the interpersonal relationship he had with the physician was of utmost importance.

In essence, a psychodynamic perspective was developed based on the idea of a psychological genesis of mental illness and on psychotherapeutic intervention. The pathology found its therapeutic direction in an interpersonal relationship because, as it started to be suspected and was later demonstrated by Sigmund Freud (1856-1939), it was indeed an altered interpersonal relationship that had caused the disease itself.[13]

2. The origins of psychoanalysis

Freudian thought was developed in the environment of the "grand Vienna", the capital of the Austro-Hungarian empire on the threshold of its decadence. Freud studied at the University with the German physician Ernst Wilhelm von Brücke (1819-1892), the principal exponent of the Physics School of Berlin and

---

13   L. Mecaci, op. cit., pp. 95-101.

Theodor Meynert (1833-1892), a psychiatrist who took inspiration from the ideas of philosopher Johann Herbart (1776 -1841).

Berlin's *Physics School* proposed to abolish all non-scientific thought by referring to a single basic discipline: physics. Representatives regarded the individual as a machine and tried to explain psychic phenomena according to this theoretical model.

In contrast to the Berlin school, *Herbartian psychology* supported by Meynert upheld the supremacy of psychology over physiology and attributed great importance to unconscious mechanisms in the determination of psychic processes.

When, towards the end of the century, the crisis of natural sciences emerged, the future father of psychoanalysis, perhaps following the suggestions received by his teachers, was among those who began to doubt that all phenomena was of a physical origin. Charcot had successfully used hypnosis to treat hysteria, definitively placing under discussion the organicist orientation of psychiatry and Freud. In 1885 Freud went to Paris to attend Charcot's demonstrations, and returned to Vienna deeply impressed by what he had experienced during his stay in the French capital.

In collaboration with Josef Breuer (1842-1925), he began using hypnosis to treat neurotic patients. But later, Breuer and Freud, unhappy with the results of hypnosis, experimented with another method termed "catharsis" that no longer aimed at eliminating the symptoms directly, but at overcoming the resistance that the patient put up when he/she was led to remember the events that were believed to be the cause of the pathology.

Freud and Breuer soon disagreed on the causes of this sort of amnesia and Freud continued his own investigations by abandoning the use of hypnosis in favor of the method of free associations that would become the cornerstone of psychoanalytic therapy.

3. The extraordinary contribution of Freud's work

Freud's contribution was truly extraordinary, given the state of psychiatry of the period. Practically singlehandedly, he discovered the unconscious and its dynamics. While behaviorists refused to consider the existence of unconscious psychic phenomena, Freud saw them as the essential source of behavior.

> "If objectivist psychologies—because of the fact that what is happening inside can be considered as inessential and negligible, and only the external aspects of behavior are scientifically observable—can be qualified as 'superficial psychologies', psychoanalysis can be called 'psychology of the substratum, in that it assumes as essential in psychic life, and important towards understanding its meaning and establish its laws, what lies below: in the hidden depths of the unconscious."[14]

---

14   C. Musatti, Freud, Bollati Boringhieri, 1970, p. 29.

In psychoanalytic theory, understanding the dynamics of the unconscious is essential to understanding the therapeutic process. The father of psychoanalysis dynamically approached psychiatry by studying the forces that led to the development of psychic disorders and underlining the importance of infantile experiences in the future development of the individual.

The background image is that of impulses that want to be discharged and of various antagonistic forces that inhibit them and, as a consequence, deform them. The job of a good analyst will be to eliminate obstacles preventing the expression of primary forces. Freud identified in the libido, or sexual drive, the primary of these psychological forces. He then considerably extended the concept of human sexuality introducing the idea of infantile sexuality and outlined the main phases of psycho-sexual development in childhood by tracing neuroses to traumatic experiences during this development.

Another of Freud's fundamental discoveries was the interpretation of dreams, considered the hallucinatory fulfillment of infantile desire. The analysis of dreams, with the method of free association, became the cornerstone of psychoanalytic interpretation, the highroad towards discovery of the unconscious.

Many other themes elaborated by Freud merit a more detailed discussion, but that is not the intent of this chapter. I will just recall some other equally important moments of Freudian thought, like the theory of the Oedipus complex and its influence in childhood and adult life, the theory of an instinct of life and an instinct of death, the topic of narcissism, the comparison of the principles of pleasure versus reality, the extension of psychoanalytic investigation into artistic creativity, religion and social sciences.

4. The image of the individual in psychoanalysis

For Freud, mental contents can be divided in two different ways, called topographies (from Greek *topós* = place). The first distinguishes unconscious, preconscious and conscious. The *unconscious* is considered to be the seat of forgotten or removed desires, impulses and memories that have never reached the consciousness. It drives impulses to satisfy those desires according to what is called the "pleasure principle". Even the *preconscious* contains memories of the individual's past experience. What distinguishes it from the unconscious is that its contents can become conscious with a concerted effort. The last state of mind is *conscious* whose contents are immediately accessible to the subject. It is based on the "principle of reality".

After 1920 Freud formulated a new theory of the personality, an alternative to the first topography, based on three distinct structures called Id, Ego and Super-ego. This period was also marked by significant changes in the understanding of therapeutic processes, especially by the discovery of *translational neurosis* or *transference*. According to this second topographic issue, the *Id* is the site of the removed psychic contents, a territory of conflicting impulses and continuous pressures that are constantly in need of satisfying pleasure and selfish needs. The *Super-ego* is an almost unconscious structure, which originates from the internalization and exacerbation of codes of conduct, moral prohibitions, commands, and the rules imposed by parental figures. Its job is to prevent the Id from freely acting on its own impulses. The *Ego* is the organizing personality structure and its main task is to act as mediator between the demands of the Id, the requirements of reality and the prohibitions imposed by the Super-ego. This consideration brings Freud to affirm that the Ego is "the servant of three tyrants" and that is why it is very weak and unstable, constantly engaged in a struggle for existence.

Therefore, Freudian psychology is basically a psychology of conflicts where there is no room for the development and the qualitative improvement of the Ego, since its expansion can only be at the expense of the Id or the Super-ego.

The reference to the unconscious and irrational sources of psychic processes has linked Freudian thought to the philosophies that, between the nineteenth and twentieth centuries, were marked by the refusal of rational and scientific explanation. In reality, for Freud, digging into the unconscious did not mean at all to favor the abandonment of the Ego to the world of irrationality, but rather to promote the critical awareness of the determination of one's psychic life.

Freud always tried to make his creation a scientific discipline by repeatedly emphasizing the derivation of psychoanalysis from the natural sciences, especially from physics and medicine. This intention is also clearly perceived in the choice of using the basic representations of classical physics to express his theories and thus to establish a conceptual relationship between psychoanalysis and Newtonian physics. In this regard, the Austrian physician and essayist Fritjof Capra[15] maintains that:

> "as Newton founded the absolute Euclidean space as a reference system in which material objects are located and measured, so Freud established the psychological space as a reference system for the structures of the mental apparatus. The psychological structures on which Freud founded his theory of human personality (Id - Ego - Super-ego) are seen as forms of "interior" objects, situated and extending in the psychological space."

And as in Newtonian physics, also in psychoanalytic theory, the mechanistic conception of reality led to strict determinism: every psychological event has a defined cause that gives rise to a defined effect, and the whole psychological state of an individual is determined solely by the initial conditions of early childhood. The "genetic" approach of psychoanalysis thus consists in attributing the symptoms and behavior of a patient to early developmental stages along a linear chain of cause and effect relationships.[16]

---

15   F. Capra, *Il punto di svolta*, Ed. Mondadori, 1995, p.150.

16   Ibid, p. 152.

These, together with other positions, will trigger the criticisms and disagreements that led first to the "schisms" of Alfred Adler (1870-1937), Carl Gustav Jung (1875-1961), Wilhelm Reich (1897-1957) and Otto Rank (1884-1939) and, soon after, the birth of the "third force" of psychology or humanistic psychology. It will be precisely these positions that will push Assagioli to move away from psychoanalysis to found Psychosynthesis.

5. Psychosynthesis and "depth" psychology

If it is not conceivable to see in Assagioli a forerunner of psychoanalysis, it is justified to consider him as one of its very first scholars. From Freud - Jung correspondence, we know that the creator of psychoanalysis had many hopes in the young Italian psychiatrist as a vehicle for disseminating his theories in Italy. Assagioli, however, soon departed from the psychoanalytic line to create his own orientation, and the underlying reason that led him to take his course was the different conception of the individual he had come to create.

From the time his first articles appeared in several journals[17] at the beginning of the last century, alongside the praises addressed to the "bold innovator" for the "extraordinary practical importance of the original and ingenious methods for exploring the subconscious and for studying sexuality" and for "the very important result" of the discovery of infantile sexuality with the related educational implications, he voiced some criticisms.

First of all, he did not share the exceptional prominence Freud gave to the inferior and instinctive side of sexuality at the expense of the higher manifestations of love. Secondly, he did not agree with the unjustified generalization of healthy persons by facts and laws discovered by studying sick subjects. He criticized the fact that Freud excessively ignored the psychopathogenic action of other instincts, emotions and passions, assimilating tendencies to the sexual instinct that are clearly distinguished by essential differences. Finally, he did not approve of the little emphasis Freud placed on the difference between the suppression and conscious domination of the instincts and the importance of the sublimation process.

Assagioli could not accept the psychoanalytic view that human beings are obsessed with the constant and unconscious thought of having to decide whether to satisfy their instincts, to suppress it or to give it up temporarily. The life of such a

---

17   R. Assagioli, *Gli effetti del riso e le loro applicazioni pedagogiche*, "Rivista di psicologia applicata alla Pedagogia e alla Psicopatologia", 1906; *Seconda riunione psicoanalitica*, "Rivista di Psicologia Applicata", a. VI, n. 3, 1910; *Die Freudschen Lehren in Italien*, "Jahrbuch der Psychoanalytische und Psychopatologischen Forschungen", a. 1910; *Le idee di Sigmund Freud sulla sessualità*, "La Voce", 1910; *Le idee di Sigmund Freud sulla sessualità*, *Corso di lezioni sulla psicosintesi*, manuscript.

person and their works is ultimately nothing more than an attempt, more or less successful, to satisfy their sexuality. And above all, Assagioli could not accept that great mystics, saints, artists and scientists were dismissed as hysterical, neurotic or psychotic. Regarding this he wrote[18]:

> "A 'pathology' has arisen in the field of psychology, which shows a great misunderstanding of spiritual values and tends to 'explain' the highest manifestations of the human soul as simple derivations or transformations of instincts and inferior tendencies. But what is superior cannot be 'explained' with something that is inferior!"

5.1. Eros and sexuality in Psychosynthesis

Concerning the topic of sexuality, the first requirement for psychosynthesis is to forego a reductive view of sex and propose a definition that concurs with the breadth of the image of the individual it carries. Psychosynthesist Mariella Lancia[19] has dedicated an entire book to the subject; in it she writes that Psychosynthesis, in line with the "third" and the "fourth" forces of psychology, sees error in the Freudian conception that love is a derivative of sex, a product of repression and the taboo of incest, as well as its tendency to confuse love and sexuality. For Assagioli, sexuality is one of the many expressions that love generates. Among these are love for oneself, maternal and paternal love, fraternal love, love for friends, love for an ideal, love for nature and animals, for art, poetry and music, love for God, love for life and its creation.

The psychosynthetic view, contrary to Freud's position, sees eros as a primordial vital impulse. It is the eros that gives rise to fundamental instincts, and sexuality is just one of its applications together with the tendencies of conservation and aggression, which are also necessary for the preservation of life.[20] We can say that Assagioli relies on Hellenic and Platonic visions of eros, seen as nostalgia and research, carried out through the process of synthesis of opposites, of lost unity, of the One.[21] The eros therefore guarantees not only the survival of the species, but, above all, the advancing of the individual towards union with the other within theirself, with others and with the transcendent, the Other with a capital "O". Therefore, according to Psychosynthesis, sexuality can be defined as[22]:

> "one of the manifestations of the energy of the Eros that functions through the psycho-sexual polarities of men and women, which in turn are the expression in the human world of that universal principle of bipolarity that is indispensable to the production of energy."

---

18   R. Assagioli, *Psicosinetsi - Armonia della vita*, op. cit., p. 80.

19   M. Lancia, *La sessualità nel processo educativo*, ed. Istituto di Psicosintesi, 1992, p. 21.

20   Ibid, p.16.

21   P. M. Bonacina, *L'uomo stellare*, Ed. Giampiero Pagnini, 1998, p. 163.

22   M. Lancia, op.cit., p. 16.

Therefore, sexuality is seen as an activity that affects the totality of the person, involving all the areas of their biopsychic make-up: lower, middle and higher unconscious, personal self and Transpersonal Self, expressing itself through all its psychological functions (sensation, impulse-desire, emotion-feeling, thought, imagination, intuition and will) and covering every area of human experience[23]:

- *intrapersonal* experience: in Psychosynthesis, intrapersonal sexuality is the basis to access proper interpersonal sexuality; Novalis said: "only a person who is happily married to himself/herself is ready to marry another";
- *interpersonal* experience: the most obvious and studied aspect of sexuality, the one that receives more attention from individuals, public opinion and specialists; of course, Psychosynthesis does not assign importance solely to coitus and orgasm, but looks at the relationship with the other, with the companion, to contact in their bio-psycho-spiritual entirety;
- *social* experience: human sexuality is not only a biological function linked to reproduction, but an unbreakable force towards the other, towards interrelation and communication; the experience of the couple and the energy created in the two-person relationship tends to radiate in all directions becoming an acquisition for the whole community;
- *transpersonal* experience: if the individual defines theirself as a being that is constantly transcended, this natural tendency to go beyond cannot avoid investing in the field of sexuality; in many religious, philosophical and spiritual traditions, the conjugal union is symbolically linked to the divine, and many are the practices that aim to use sexual energy to elevate that union to the pinnacles of illumination; it seems therefore that the individual has always felt that sexuality embodies a secret that connects it closely to the transpersonal dimension.

Having said all this, it seems obvious that, for Psychosynthesis, the purpose of sexuality cannot be reduced to the sole purpose of generating other human beings in order to guarantee the continuation of the species; instead it is seen as the instinct that leads to bringing individuals closer together in order to give life to new forms, even on levels other than that of the physical-biological: on the emotional level creating bonds, affection, friendships, couples, families and groups of various kinds; on the mental level by generating participatory awareness, shared ideas, cooperative intelligence, convergence of thought; on the spiritual level, creating spiritual communion, spirit of brotherhood, collective values, universal ethics.

---

23   Ibid pp. 28-36.

5.2. The three aspects of psychoanalysis

In a very interesting writing, Assagioli[24] clearly distinguishes the three aspects of psychoanalysis that, according to him, are usually confused. Psychoanalysis can indeed be defined as:

1. a *group of psychological methods* for exploring the subconscious or unconscious and bring their content to light;
2. a *method of care* for many neuro-psychic maladies as well as numerous physical symptoms having psychic origins (psychosomatic disturbances);
3. a system of *doctrines, hypotheses* and *interpretations* not only of psychopathological symptoms but also various manifestations of human life: literature, art and even religion.

Assagioli considers *psychoanalytical methods* of investigation into the unconscious to be unquestionable acquisitions of psychology that have led to discoveries of great importance and utility. As for the more general use of psychoanalysis as a *therapeutic method*, he is cautious: it can give good results in the right cases, but if it is indiscriminately used to treat any disorder, it can produce serious difficulties. Finally, the *doctrines* and *interpretations* of Freud and his followers should be subjected to attentive questioning, according to our author.

As in the case of behaviorism, with regard to psychoanalysis the father of Psychosynthesis, while not sharing the theoretical postulates, recognized the great contributions and perceived the practical importance of the discoveries to a point where he included psychoanalytic techniques in those of Psychosynthesis. From this is derived the inclusion of Psychosynthesis in that cultural context which is not merely a response to Freudian teaching, but which, while assuming some basic assumptions, tends to exceed it, to complete it. Assagioli never underestimated the merits of psychoanalysis in having discovered the unconscious and affirmed[25] that "with this, a third dimension was added to psychology, which was first 'superficial', meaning, it was occupied only with the psychological manifestations that appeared on the surface of waking consciousness, ignoring all that takes place in the 'depths'". Psychoanalysis as a method of exploration of the unconscious has never been challenged by Assagioli, on the contrary, he considered it the first fundamental phase of any therapeutic process. Indeed he stated[26]:

---

24   R. Assagioli, *Psicoanalisi e psicosintesi*, in *Corso di lezioni sulla psicosintesi*, manuscript, 1963.

25   R. Assagioli, cit. in L. Peresson, op. cit., p. 27.

26   R. Assagioli, *Principi e metodi della psicosintesi terapeutica*, Ed. Astrolabio, 1973, pp. 27-28.

"First of all we must venture audaciously into the depths and abysses of the unconscious to discover the obscure forces that threaten us; the ghosts and images that obsess and slyly dominate us; the fears that paralyze us; the conflicts which deplete our energy. (...) This can be done thanks to psychoanalysis, through dream analysis, free association, word association, spontaneous drawing, analysis of imaginative activity, of psychological disorders, of errors and of forgetting, etc."

To then state, as Assagioli does, that psychosynthesis begins where psychoanalysis ends, means explicitly declaring the role that Psychosynthesis proposed since the beginning. In this perspective, it is fully entitled to enter into that broader psychological current that we can call "humanist-existential"[27].

---

27   L. Peresson, op. cit., p. 28.

CHAPTER III

THE THIRD FORCE:
EXISTENTIAL-HUMANISTIC PSYCHOLOGY

In the first half of the 21st century, in North American psychology, there were two separate and antagonistic schools. *Behaviorism* was the most popular model in the academic field and *psychoanalysis* served as a basis for the practice of psychotherapy.

Then, in the late '50s and early '60s, clinical psychologists developed theoretical models of the psyche and of behavior and therapeutic orientations that differed notably from those previous. This current was called the "third force" of psychology, or *existential-humanistic psychology*. In it, many of the teachings of non-orthodox psychoanalytic schools and some of the topics of the phenomenological-existential orientation in psychiatry came together. American psychologist Abraham Maslow (1908-1970), traditionally considered one of the founding fathers of the movement in question, wrote in 1962[28]:

> "This group includes Adlerians, Rankians and Jungians, as well as all neo-Freudians (or neo-Adlerians) and post-Freudian (psychoanalytic psychologists of the 'I', as well as writers such as Marcuse, Wheelis, Marmor, Szasz, N. Brown, H. Lynd and Schachtel, who recall Talmudic psychoanalysts). In addition, the influence of Kurt Goldstein and his organizational psychology is growing more and more. This is also the case for Gestalt therapy, Gestalt and Lewinian psychologists, general semanticists and psychologists of the personality such as G. Allport, G. Murphy, J. Moreno and H. A. Murray. A new and powerful influence is constituted by existential psychology and psychiatry. Dozens of other important scholars can be grouped as psychologists of the self, phenomenological psychologists, growth psychologists, Rogerian psychologists, humanistic psychologists, etc. etc. etc. It is impossible to provide a complete list."

1. The antecedents

Although we cannot refer to phenomenological and existential psychology as a body of conclusive doctrines, it is nevertheless possible to find an undeniable fundamental unit, a point of common origin, which constantly recalls the thinking of Edmund Husserl and Martin Heidegger, and that, in more general terms, can

---

28   A. Maslow, *Verso una psicologia dell'essere*, Ed. Astrolabio, 1971, p. 11.

be framed in the vast reaction to positivism that has enlivened European culture in many of its manifestations since the end of the last century.[29]

1.1. Phenomenology, existentialism and Gestalt psychology

At the start of the twentieth century, and following the catastrophic experience of the First World War, various philosophical and cultural movements highlighted the limits of positivism, considering it a schematic and abstract science that, with its utmost confidence in technology, capitalism and rational organization of society, had little to say about the most profound human issues. The phenomenological movement before, and existentialism after, were the philosophical currents that tried to end this impasse.

The scholar who laid the foundations of this renewal was Austrian philosopher and psychologist Franz Brentano (1838-1917). He reintroduced the concept of *intentionality* in contemporary philosophy, that is, the idea that every mental phenomenon, every psychological act, is directed at something, has an object: every belief has a "believed", every desire has a "desired".
The concept of intentionality implies the idea of the impossibility of objectively investigating psychological reality outside of the relationship it has with the subject that experiences it. Therefore, according to Brentano, psychic phenomena can only be acquired through the phenomenological method, consisting of the investigation of immediate internal experience.

According to Edmund Husserl (1859-1938), Brentano's direct student and founder of phenomenology as a philosophical theory, such *phenomenology* is an approach to the theory of awareness that "offers to describe the phenomena as they appear, to grasp its pure form, or essence"[30]. The phenomenological process therefore requires the suspension of every judgment and of every theory, putting in parentheses everything that is already known, to allow the emergence of phenomena as they are "genuinely, essentially given"[31]. In fact, according to Husserl, in the naturalistic psychology of the time, the error of science starting with Galileo was repeated:

"This science has nothing to say to us. It basically excludes those problems that are the most burning for man who, in our tormented times, feels to be at the mercy of destiny; the problems of the sense or the non-sense of human existence as a whole. (...) Ultimately they concern (...) the man who must freely choose, the man who is

---

29   M. Rossi Monti, S. Vitale, *Dall'analisi esistenziale alla teoria dei sistemi*, ed. Feltrinelli, 1980, p. 6.

30   U. Galimberti, *Filosofia*, Ed. Garzanti, 1993, p. 370.

31   Ibid, p. 370.

free to rationally mold himself and the world around him. (...) Obviously the fact is, mere science has nothing to say about it. It stems from any subject."[32]

Husserl's point of view was further developed by philosophers such as Maurice Merleau-Ponty, Jan Patočka, Hannah Arendt, Dietrich von Hildebrand and Emmanuel Levinas. Moreover, phenomenology has had a profound influence on today's cognitive sciences and analytical philosophy.

The maximum expression of phenomenology in psychology would be *Gestalt psychology*, or the psychology of form. This psychological current, which concerns the study of perception and experience, was initiated and developed at the beginning of the 20th century in Germany, and then continued its progress in the U.S.A. where its main exponents, Czech psychologist Max Wertheimer (1880-1943) and German psychologists Wolfgang Köhler (1887-1967), Kurt Koffka (1886-1941) and Kurt Lewin (1890-1947), emigrated in the period of Nazi persecution. The main idea of the founders of Gestalt psychology was that the whole being was something other than the sum of the individual parts. In this way, they opposed the model of structuralism, disseminated at the end of the 1800s, and its fundamental principles, such as elementalism. Their studies focused above all on perceptual aspects and reasoning, and contributed to the development of research on learning, problem-solving, memory, thinking, and social psychology.

Starting in the 1920s, the phenomenological perspective received the contributions of the budding *existentialism*. In opposition to idealism and rationalism, it stresses the specific value of individual human existence and its precarious character. The most important representative of existentialism on a phenomenological basis was German philosopher Martin Heidegger (1889-1976). Heidegger attempts to exceed phenomenology, effectively aiming to surpass all western rationalist metaphysics, which he claimed had lost its objectivity, degenerating into scientific and technical knowledge, identifying itself with logic, considering a human being as a "simple presence" (evidence), while the real need is to base philosophy on the dramatic state of existence.

Existentialism has not only been expressed in philosophy, but has also found significant space in literature, art and psychology. The most famous works in this field are the writings of French philosophers Jean-Paul Sartre and Maurice Merleau-Ponty.

Actually, the theories of all these authors have had little influence on the evolution of scientific psychology of the early twentieth century. However, they will be examined with renewed interest precisely by a certain phenomenological psychiatry and, subsequently, by a budding humanistic psychology.

---

32   E. Husserl, cit. in L. Mecacci, op. cit., p. 92.

1.2. Comprehensive psychology, phenomenological psychiatry and existential analysis

I have already pointed out in the previous chapter that, although psychoanalysis delivered the final blow to nineteenth-century somatic psychiatry, Freud's work reflects a conception of humankind and nature that has undeniable background references in nineteenth-century reductionist and determinist positivism. However, since the beginning of the last century, other psychiatrists have stood against reductionist psychiatry; they developed their criticism from a perspective completely different from the psychoanalytic because their theoretical references do not delve into the positivist philosophy, but rather into those orientations: phenomenology first and existentialism after, that depart from a radical reversal of the positivist philosophy itself.[33] To illustrate this reversal of perspective we can compare the positions of two well-known scholars regarding the difference between "explaining" and "understanding". For Hans Eysenck, well-known behavioral psychologist and influential advocate of the inheritance of intelligence:

"the term 'explanation' must be used in psychology with exactly the same connotations used in the exact sciences. This essentially means that the description, quantitative if possible, is the more appropriate synonym than the comprehension; understanding, in a certain non-scientific sense, is the function of many things, including the actual levels of arbitrary beliefs and superstitions, and cannot be verified with reality."[34]

By contrast, according to German psychologist and philosopher Wilhelm Dhiltey, whose work outlined the differences in the object of the investigation of the sciences of the spirit, or of human sciences, compared to that of natural sciences:

"the sciences of the spirit differ from the natural sciences in that the latter have as their object the facts that appear to the consciousness from the outside, that is, as phenomena given singularly, whereas in the former, the facts arise originally from within as a living connection", so "we explain nature, but understand psychic life."[35]

Precisely on the distinction introduced by Dilthey between the explanation (*erklären*) of the natural sciences and the understanding (*verstehen*), of the very sciences of the spirit, *comprehensive psychology* was developed by German philosopher and psychiatrist Karl Jaspers (1883-1969). According to Galimberti[36], "this methodological correction has emancipated psychology from the methodology of the natural sciences, replacing that interpretive instrument which is universal

---

33   L. Mecacci, op. cit., p. 162.

34   H. Eysenck, cit. in U. Galimberti, Psicologia, Ed. Garzanti, 1999, p. 218.

35   W. Dhiltey, cit. in U. Galimberti, op. cit., p. 821.

36   U. Galimeberti, op. cit., p. 821.

law with that other instrument, more psychological than the meaning expressed by the individual case."

The therapist's task at this point is no longer to form a diagnosis by classifying the patient's pathology, but rather to empathetically participate in his existential situation. This involves an investigative orientation very different from the objective detachment advocated both by behaviorism and psychoanalysis, in favor of open participation simultaneously towards the other and towards their own potential to understand it.

These topics were further elaborated by Swiss psychiatrist and psychologist Ludwig Binswanger (1881-1966), the leading exponent of *phenomenological psychiatry* and *existential analysis*, also called anthropoanalysis. For this scientist, the peculiarity of human beings is not that they are an abstract subject or a natural object, but concrete beings who are orienting and designing their existence within the world. Anthropoanalysis sees humankind not only as a mechanical necessity and an organization; in other words, the individual is not just "world" or "in the world", but his/her presence means a "being in the world" as a project and opening of worlds.[37]

Binswanger's criticism of psychology and naturalistic psychiatry also involves Freud and psychoanalysis. I have extended some of the observations regarding Freud to enable me to adequately highlight the main points of dissent raised in the same years by Roberto Assagioli, points that humanistic psychology will raise some time after.

Firstly, for the father of anthropoanalysis, it is not possible to accept the Freudian belief that "the deepest essence of man is in the instinctive impulses of elemental nature, which are similar to all men" and that "the quality differences of the products are reduced to quantitative changes in the ratio of those elements."[38] He believed that by attributing to the body and the needs a sovereign power over the whole human condition, the image of the individual becomes 'unilateralized' and falsified in an ontological sense.

According to Binswanger, the individual can only be interpreted as an individual, not as nature, life, will, or spirit. Consequently, the Freudian idea of "homo natura" is a scientific construct possible only through the destruction of the globality of human experience, that is, of anthropological experience. Only after destroying the individual "as he/she really is" can one agree to reconstructing him or her according to a particular idea, for example according to the Freudian principle of pleasure. Only in this way can desire become the only perspective in which the "homo natura" of psychoanalysis is seen. Binswanger writes[39]:

"Between instinct and illusion we can imagine seeing only one being who can do nothing but desire. And on the contrary, it is only by constructing a similar

---

37   L. Mecacci, op. cit., pp. 165-166.

38   L. Biswanger, Essere nel mondo, Ed. Astrolabio, 1973, pp. 160-164.

39   Ibid, p. 169.

being that primary modes of human existence, such as religion, morals, and art, be explained as illusions or reduced to the need for illusion."

In the psychoanalytic view of humankind, need replaces freedom and mechanism replaces reflection and decision. This means that Freud has been able to prove that the domain of the mechanism extends to the apparently freer regions of the human spirit and thus offers the possibility of "repairing" this spirit in a so-called "mechanical" manner through psychoanalytic techniques. But, says Binswanger, "in psychoanalysis we talk of 'our' mental apparatus, 'our' mind, 'our' thoughts 'our' needs. In all these possessives we speak of a being that is obvious and obviously becomes omitted: we speak, that is, about presence as 'our' presence."[40] He concludes:

"If we omit this 'mine', this 'ours', this 'I' or 'he' or 'us', we get a psychology that becomes indeed 'impersonal' and 'objective', but at the same time loses its scientific character of an authentic psychology, and becomes a natural science", and "by now we know that natural science does not exhaust the whole of man's human experience."[41]

The task of anthropology is properly that of disassembling the special ideas of humankind, to reinsert them into the totality of human existence. The horizon of psychological investigation is then identified in the "presence", in the way that the single existences decline their original way of being open to Being.

2. The third revolution in psychology

At the end of the '50s in the United States, we saw the dissemination of a conception of psychology based on the tenets of existentialism, phenomenology and pragmatism. A symposium on existential psychology was held in 1959, and in 1963 another was conducted on behaviorism and phenomenology. The phenomenological and existential currents then came together in the "third force", *humanistic psychology*. The character of the new association is well summarized in the statute of the *American Association for Humanistic Psychology* that reads:

"As the 'third force' of contemporary psychology, (humanistic psychology) is concerned with topics that have had limited space in existing theories and systems: for example, love, creativity, self, growth, organism, the fundamental need of gratification, self-realization, higher values, being, becoming, spontaneity, play, humor, affection, naturalness, warmth, self-transcendence, objectivity, autonomy, responsibility, meaning, fair play, transcendental experience, culminating experience, courage and related concepts."[42]

---

40   Ibidem.

41   Ibid, pp. 175-176.

42   Cit. in L. Mecacci, op. cit., pp. 93-94.

Humanistic psychology is not configured as a precise theoretical system or a school of thought, but is found at the convergence of different thought lines. In it, some of the positions of non-orthodox psychoanalytical schools converge with the themes of the phenomenological-existential direction in psychiatry.

Among the objectives of this movement's program is the intention to react to the typical orientation of the two previous revolutions in psychology: behaviorism and Freudian psychoanalysis.

According to the psychologists of the "third force", *behaviorism* is characterized by a substantial lack of respect for the human person, reducing him/her to the rank of "organic machine", a simple subject of research. The vision of the individual as a machine, or thing, could only be translated into the observation of behavior in its objective manifestations, apart from any subjective, individual, and inner characteristic. Humanistic psychology refused to see humans simply as complex animals that blindly respond to environmental stimuli; it underlined the problematic nature and the limited value of the great confidence that behaviorists had in experiments on animals. It recognized the utility of that approach in some areas of psychological research, but firmly indicated its inadequacy to understand specifically human abilities such as consciousness, guilt, creativity, humor, play and so on. Humanist psychologists, rather than studying the behavior of rats, pigeons, or monkeys, focused on human experience and maintained that in a comprehensive theory of human behavior, feelings, desires and hopes were equally important to external influences.

Psychoanalysis, on the other hand, presents an image of the individual who appears to be a helpless victim of powerful inner forces that dominate and move him/her to their liking. Humanistic psychology criticized Freud for having derived his theories about human behavior from the study of neurotic and psychotic individuals. It was thought that conclusions based on the observation of the worst aspects of the human being inevitably provided a deformed vision of human nature. Abraham Maslow[43], the leading exponent of the new "force", wrote that Freud had provided the unhealthy half of psychology and that the task of humanistic psychology was to complete it with the healthy half.

In the new vision into the depths of the human being there is not only a threatening intertwining of sexual and aggressive instincts, but also a natural tendency toward creativity, love and self-realization. Humanist psychologists stressed the need to study humans as integral organisms and focused not only on stricken individuals, but also on healthy people and on the positive aspects of their behavior. As pointed out by American psychologist Rollo May[44] (1909-1994):

> "It is not meant to deny the existence of certain mechanisms, but rather to reiterate that they assume their true meaning only if they are transposed into the context

---

43   A. Maslow, op. cit., p. 17.

44   R. May, *Psicologia esistenziale*, Ed. Astrolabio, 1970, p. 64.

of the 'existing and living' human being, or better 'in an ontological context'; they remain useless abstractions when considered separate from the totality of the person."

3. The principles of humanistic psychology

Humanistic theories are all inspired by the concept of *personality as an organic and integrated unity* that had been highlighted by certain psychologists and psychiatrists of the early twentieth century.[45] In particular, in the 1930s, the American neuropsychiatrist of German origin Kurt Goldstein (1878-1965) presented his organismic theory, inspired by Gestalt theory. In it, he claimed that humans show a dynamic organization of psychic functions that cannot be studied individually but only in their constant interaction-integration into the process of adjustment to the environment. Self-realization is the motivational force that drives this continuous process of integration and growth of one's personality, seen as the fruit of psychic organization. Similar concepts will be resumed and developed by various scholars, including Andras Angyal (1909-1960), Gardner Murphy (1895-1979) and, above all, Abraham Maslow and Carl Rogers (1902-1987).

3.1. Inadequacies of orthodox scientific methods

In humanistic psychology the need to go back to a view which takes in the person as a whole joins with an openly critical attitude towards the orthodox scientism of the positivist. Maslow wrote:

> "Science, which is commonly conceived by the orthodox scientist, is completely inadequate to these tasks but I am sure that it is not necessary that science limits itself to orthodox methods. It is not necessary for it to relinquish the problems of love, creativity, value, beauty, fantasy, ethics, and joy, leaving them all to non-scientists, poets, prophets, priests, dramatists, artists, diplomats. (…)
>
> For science to help man toward his full and positive realization, all that is needed is a widening and a deepening of the conception of its nature, its purposes and its methods."[46]

Humanistic psychology does not at all reject the scientific approach to the problems that it considers; indeed, it is "the only way we have to show the truth", the only one that "can overcome the character differences between seeing and believing"[47]. However, it is necessary to employ methods of study that are more

---

45   L. Mecacci, op. cit., p. 173.

46   A. Maslow, op. cit., p. 10.

47   Ibid, p. 10.

consistent with the subjects under investigation, promoting a qualitative approach to research. The existential orientation in psychology enables notable emphasis on the need to start from experimental knowledge rather than from conceptual systems, abstract categories or *a priori* positions. Humanistic psychology requires a personal, subjective experience as a foundation on which to build theoretical knowledge.

3.2. Renewing the image of the human being

For humanistic psychology it is a priority to renew the anthropological principles that underlie the image of the human being since, as Austrian psychiatrist Viktor Frankl (1905-1997), founder of *logotherapy*, writes:

> "The anthropology of psychotherapy does not yet present the image of the true man, but only the image of a man it conceives as the result of a play of forces called Ego, Id, and Super-Ego, or as a product whose factors would be the impulses, heredity, and the surrounding world."[48]

This renewal must take place through two fundamental steps. First, through the clarification of the anthropological concept implicit in the natural sciences and psychoanalysis that substitution of the primordial orientation of human beings toward a meaning with its apparent state of impulsivity and eliminating its aspiration towards the values that actually characterize the individual makes it recognizable only as an aspiration to pleasure. Second, by reformulating the underlying foundations in favor of a new vision that sees the search for meaning, values and authentic content as fundamental.[49]

The new anthropological perspective will therefore have to consider human beings in their entirety, seen "in perpetual motion and looking toward the fulfillment of a personal task that is original and unrepeatable, the fruit of true freedom that no one can trample despite all the conditioning they are subject to"[50]. It is necessary for the new vision to regard the individual as free, not so much *from* something, but *facing* responsibility for his/her attitude toward life and experience. The new orientation sees the individual as yearning towards the infinite and the future, and does not refer only to the past. It doesn't concentrate attention only on the suffering aspects of the person, it also looks at their healthy part.

Humanistic psychology is strongly critical of a dehumanized and dehumanizing society it blames for the collapse of values, the spread of a climate of anguish and despair, of "rampant conformism and totalitarianism", and of "nihilistic and

---

48   V. Frankl, *Alla ricerca di un significato della vita*, Mursia ed., 1952, p. 111.

49   Ibid, pp. 5 e 98.

50   Ibid, p. 5.

reductive indoctrinations"[51]. According to this perspective, it is no wonder that the human being is plunged into profound existential frustration. According to Frankl, the individual faces three possibilities: pander to conformism, submit to totalitarianism, or become neurotic. Such neurosis cannot, however, be traced back to complexities and conflicts in the classical sense. It is indeed symptomatic of the frustration of that aspiration which is the basis for a motivational theory that has usually been referred to as "the will of meaning" or "the need for self-realization". Such neurosis is a disorder of motivation linked to the failure to realize the healthy and natural human aspiration towards a life as significant as possible.

Therefore it is important to point out that, in a society that has lost all reference values, existential crises at the base of a neurosis defined as noogenic, that is, rooted in the spiritual or mental sphere, do not represent a state of illness in itself. Quite the contrary. According to humanist psychologists, the yearning of the human being for a life as meaningful as possible is so scarcely pathological that it can, and must, be put in motion by the same therapeutic action. But if it would be false to think that existential frustration, in itself, already represents a pathological phenomenon, it is just as likely that it becomes actually pathogenic, leading to a neurosis. Obviously, a psychological approach that has not itself reviewed the nihilistic anthropological assumptions upon which it is based cannot properly address contemporary existential frustration.

3.3. Redefinition of the concepts of "health" and "illness"

It then becomes fundamental to redefine the terms "health" and "illness". Maslow strongly rejects the distinction between health and illness, at least in the sense that being ill means having particular symptoms, while a healthy subject does not have them. He states that "personality problems can sometimes consist of heavy protest against the psychological crushing of our bones, that is of our intimate nature", and in this case "it would be unhealthy not to react while the crime is perpetrated." He writes provocatively[52]:

"Being ill means you may have symptoms? Well, I claim that illness may consist in not feeling any symptoms even when I should. And health...does it mean that you have no symptoms? I deny it. Which of the Nazis in Auschwitz or Dachau was in good health? Those with tormented consciences, or those whose consciences seemed clear, limpid, and serene? In that condition, was it possible for a profoundly human person not to feel conflict, suffering, depression, rage, and so forth? In a word, if you tell me you have a personality problem, until I know you better I can't be sure if I have to tell you 'good!' or 'I'm sorry'."

---

51   Ibid.

52   A. Maslow, op. cit., p. 19.

From this perspective, humanistic psychology believes that a much better term for "psychological health" and "psychological illness" is "self-realization" because it "emphasizes total humanity"[53] and aims not only at achieving a state of non-illness, but also at uncovering the highest human potentialities.

3.4. Self-realization and metamotivation

Umberto Galimberti[54] writes that in humanistic psychology motivations for the subject's action cannot be immediately traced back to underlying impulses, but are fostered by unquantifiable values such as the need for exploration, creativity, the vision of the world in which the subject searches for their place, the quality of relationship with others, and above all, the self-realization that is the basis of the humanistic interpretations of need, motivation, and personality. The *theory of self- realization* places the emergence of motivation in the self-realization project. The assumption is that human beings, unlike animals, propose to do something without being simply forced or urged. At this level, motivation is identified in the concept of volition and is considered relatively independent of the organic state and the condition of need.

It should be pointed out that, for humanist psychologists, self-realization is an ideal goal that is expressed as a process and as a tendency rather than as a truly achievable stage. Maslow[55], aware of the fundamental difficulty associated with this concept, does very much to redefine the term by clarifying that self-realization is not a definitive or final situation, or a distant goal, but rather a dynamic, active process that lasts all through a person's existence. He shifts his thinking from the consideration that motivation is the distinctive trait of identity. In his studies of people who achieve some degree of self-realization, he found that their motivational life was different from the norm, paradoxically unmotivated or metamotivated, irregardless of the effort. He then proposed a scheme, the famous pyramid shown on the next page, which, in addition to the hierarchical order of needs, provided for the distinction between motivations dependent on a state of deficiency (D-needs) and motives of growth or being, independent of a state of deficiency (B needs).

According to this theory, the motives for growth or being come into play when those "of deficiency" are satisfied:

> "And so, growth exists not only as the progressive gratification of the fundamental needs, to the point where they disappear, but also in their form of specific growth motivators above and beyond these fundamental principles."[56]

---

53   Ibid, p. 8.

54   U. Galimberti, op. cit., p. 861.

55   A. Maslow, op. cit., p. 36.

56   Ibid, p. 41.

Finally, according to Maslow, motivation based on deficiency is episodic, whereas accretive is continuous and thus represents the natural tendency toward development and self-improvement that distinguishes every healthy individual.

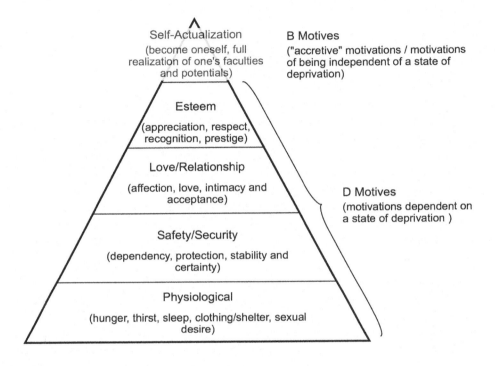

3.5. "Peak experiences" and perception of identity

This tendency toward growth and self-realization seems to occur through unique and unrepeatable events that Maslow calls *peak experiences*, whose development comes from material collected in about eighty interviews with people who had been able to achieve a significant degree of self-realization and, in particular, to love.

These individuals refer to the peak experience as the fundamental characteristic, precisely that acute experience of one's own identity. During "peak experiences", they perceive that they are closer to what they consider to be their real self, to have reached their highest degree of identity.

For humanistic psychology, the concept of identity or, better, the experience of identity plays a central role and is considered an indispensable condition of human nature. Maslow, aware that the term "identity" acquires very different meanings according to the author and the scientific orientation, proposes a formulation based on the experiential data that emerged during these interviews and not on some particular theory. Subjects described the acute experience of their identity as follows[57]. During the "peak experience":

- they feel more integrated than at other times and more integrated in multiple ways;
- becoming more concretely themselves, they are more capable of merging with the world, as much as with the prior non-self; meaning, the greatest thing identity can obtain is simultaneously transcending oneself;
- they feel at the maximum of their potentialities, and feel they use their skills in the best and fullest way, feel more intelligent, perceptive, spiritual, strong, and graceful;
- they require less effort and function more easily;
- they see themselves, more than on other occasions, as the active center, in control and creative, in both their activities and perceptions;
- they feel extremely free from inhibitions, cautions, fears, doubts, controls, reservations, self-criticism and restraints, and therefore more spontaneous, more expressive, behaving more innocently and naturally;
- they feel more creative, inventive, unhindered by excessive desires or needs, exerting less effort, free of motivation, and tendencies, and feel they have transcended ordinary needs and impulses;
- they are clearly aware of the uniqueness of each individual person, where the interchangeability of roles disappears;
- they feel more concrete, more established in the experience;
- expression and communication tend to become poetic, mythical and elated as if it were the natural language for communicating;
- playfulness and humor are a characteristic of the peak experience along with wonder and amazement.

Peak experiences have very interesting beneficial effects and therapeutic value. They may actually cause the definitive elimination of various types of symptoms and change in a positive way the conception that a person has of theirself, of others and of the world. They can free the individual, leading one towards ways of being more creative, expressive, and spontaneous. Those who have had a "peak experience" remember it as an extremely important and desirable event; they try to repeat it and are more inclined to feel that life is worth living.[58]

For these reasons, humanistic psychology considers it important to study such episodes more profoundly and build a new image of the human being that understands them without reducing them to neurotic or regressive symptoms.

---

57   Ibid, pp. 110-119.

58   Ibid, p. 107.

4. Implications in the therapeutic environment

More than a defined school, humanistic-existential psychotherapy is an attitude that unites all psychologists of the "third force". The humanistic orientation in psychotherapy encourages therapists to move away from a reductive vision, which is reflected in a subtle and significant change in the terminology employed. Instead of treating "patients", therapists deal with "clients" and the interaction between the therapist and the client, rather than being dominated and manipulated by the former, is seen as a human encounter between equals.

The main innovator of this therapeutic development was American psychologist Carl Rogers (1902-1987), who developed non-directive psychotherapy, or *client-centered therapy*, the purpose of which is not to help the individual solve a problem, but to facilitate their innate capabilities of self-regulation and self-realization. His method is based on empathy and non-directivity, and the theoretical assumption is the motivational optimism for which the individual naturally pursues his or her own development. The essence of the humanistic approach consists in seeing the patient/client as a person capable of growth, recognizing the innate potentialities in all human beings. Writes Viktor Frankl:

> "It has been repeated enough that the methods and techniques of psychotherapy are the ones that are the least effective of all. The human encounter between a physician and an ill person is rather decisive. (...) In my opinion the sun has set on the dream of a half-century: the dream of being able to count on a mechanism of the soul and on a technique of psychotherapy(...)"[59]

Carl Rogers has identified within this approach three fundamental conditions that the psychotherapist has to follow: spontaneity/genuineness, accurate empathic understanding and an unconditionally positive attitude. The most important condition is the first, that is, the spontaneity and genuineness of the therapist, since this condition is based on the possibility of establishing human contact, from person to person, with the patient/client. Only by establishing an empathetic relationship of mutual trust and esteem with the client will it be possible to free up their most authentic potential by directing them to the attainment of ever-increasing integration. In the therapeutic process, the client must not be guided and interpreted, but oriented towards personal growth, towards better knowledge and realization of self.

And so, according to Rollo May, in the sort of artistic process that psychotherapy is, it is necessary to sacrifice, difficult as it might be, the stereotypical technique, the "facade" or "professional mask", that serves more than anything to relieve the anxiety of the therapist:

---

59   V. Frankl, op. cit., p. 44.

"This is where phenomenology, the first stage of the existential psychotherapeutic movement, has been useful to many of us. Phenomenology is the attempt to take the phenomena as they appear. It is the disciplined attempt to liberate one's mind from the assumptions that so often make us see in the patient only our theories or the dogmas of our systems."[60]

4.1. The new social orientations

While humanistic psychologists criticized Freud's view, considering it excessively focused on the study of sick individuals, another group of psychologists and psychiatrists, including Harry Stack Sullivan (1892-1949), Karen Horney (1885-1952), and Erich Fromm 1900-1980), saw the main deficiency of psychoanalysis in the absence of social considerations. They emphasized that Freudian theory cannot deal with interpersonal relationships or wider social dynamics because it lacks a conceptual framework that leads to a fuller understanding of the interpersonal experiences shared by humans.

The inclusion of social orientations created new therapeutic approaches that focus on the family and other social groups. The *family therapy* movement, which began in the 1950s and developed new concepts and practices on the meaning of disturbances and psychic symptoms expressed by individuals, still today represents one of the most innovative and effective therapeutic approaches. It has explicitly incorporated some of the new systemic concepts of health and illness.

Group therapy had been practiced for many decades in various forms but had always been limited to verbal interactions until humanist psychologists applied non-verbal, cathartic, and body-expression techniques to the group process. The purpose of these groups is no longer limited to therapy alone, but has an explicit objective in self-exploration and personal growth.[61]

A holistic vision does not divide the healthy part from the ill part of the human being. In it, the individual is not only seen through the deforming lens of the pathology, but as a totality that is constantly growing and projected towards the future. And so, the concept of therapy expands to reach the areas of education and self-training, in which the task of the therapist is no longer to reach an illness-free stage. Indeed, this becomes only the first stage of a process in which the growth of the person goes further, towards fullness and maturity. There is no longer the idea of seeing the human being "only" as an organism to heal, but also as someone to educate and to provide the tools that enable them to assume responsibility for future growth. Here, then, is the need for education in taking responsibility for their attitudes, the liberation of their potential, for their conquest of freedom.

---

60   R. May, op. cit., p. 24.

61   F. Capra, op. cit., p. 303.

5. Psychosynthesis and humanistic psychology

Many themes of existential-humanistic psychology are found in Roberto Assagioli's work. It's enough to think of the importance that he assigns to the experiences of identity and self-consciousness considered as self-awareness; to the significance given to the theme of will and, with it, its corollaries of freedom, responsibility, choice and self-determination; the priority given to understanding over interpretation, to the constructive approach over that of simplification; to the emphasis on the meaning that each individual gives to life or searches for in their life; to the conception of synthesis in terms of harmony, above all between the individual and theirself, between the individual and nature, between the individual and his/her fellow beings; to recognizing the great influence that values have in determining the life of an individual; to the emphasis on the present and the future related to the past, and so on.

But the most obvious contribution provided by Psychosynthesis to existential-humanistic orientation is that derived from its way of understanding the therapeutic framework. Indeed Assagioli[62] asserts that psychosynthetic treatment "transcends its immediate medical usefulness" adding that "it generates a dynamic conception of psychic life in the subject with its limitless possibilities of development and self-realization".

5.1. Assagioli: pioneer of the third force of psychology

Assagioli was perfectly aware of the role he had as precursor of the third force of psychology, as he wrote in this passage:

"Here I feel legitimized, I would almost say obliged, to recall the independent contribution that has been given in Italy to the development of this humanistic psychology. As far back as 1909 I had outlined some essential points in a study on *The Psychology of Force-Ideas and Psychagogy*."[63]

Thus Psychosynthesis preceded by many decades the birth of humanistic psychology. Already in the 1909 article on psychagogy (see Part 1, Chapter I, Para. 4.2.), he wished for a synthesis between clinical psychology and studies of spiritual experiences, and stated that "from the amazing psychic life one begins to recognize the enormous complexity, the incessant dynamism, the vast unexplored regions, the unsuspected extraordinary energies." "It has been seen," he said, "that the psyche is not something rigid and independent that can only be observed and described like a piece of quartz or an onion, or that lends itself to experiments like a frog or a turtle; it is wonderfully flexible and can be profoundly

---

62   R. Assagioli, cit. in L. Peresson, op. cit., pp. 28-29.

63   R. Assagioli, *Le nuove dimensioni della psicologia*, in *Corso di lezioni sulla psicosintesi*, 1973, p. 11.

modified in various ways."[64] He continued by noting that, although the psyche is profoundly modifiable, its own flexibility helps it to continually escape from those who are trying to mold it. Assagioli therefore hoped for an accurate study of the psyche's nature and the laws that govern it, in order to form a series of practical and effective methods independent of any special philosophical doctrine.

To indicate the uniting of all of these methods, Assagioli then proposed to resume the ancient Platonic denomination of *psychagogy*. With this term, however, he did not intend to refer either to a new theory or to a particular technique, nor to a more or less creative fusion of psychological theories with the pedagogical. Instead he referred "on the one hand to the practical and active character of the discipline, and on the other the fact that it is not about the education of separate faculties, but the whole culture of the entire psyche"[65]. The goal of psychagogy was therefore not to add one or another theory to some interpretations, nor even to form mental schemes or ideas regarding human psychology. The goal of psychagogy was to touch those "essential" points of human development, employing specific techniques, focusing on the development of what is implicit and potentially present in human nature.[66]

Faced with the new discoveries of the third force, which demonstrated that the character, far from being rigid and immutable, continually changes due to the action of innumerable influences, Assagioli was excited: the individual had no excuse for not taking full responsibility for what he/she was. Here, then, is a theme, dear to both existentialists and the humanists, which bursts loudly onto the scene: the theme of the innate freedom of the human being, one's ability to decide for oneself. In other words, our author highlighted the central function of the will. Consequently, the inevitable transformations the individual is constantly subjected to, instead of being slow, chaotic, and unconscious, may become conscious and intentional. Among the methods used to facilitate this process, Assagioli indicated introspection; however, it should not remain a pure intellectual exercise but become operative, transforming into decision, into actual change.

With these proposals, formulated in Italy at the beginning of the last century, the future father of Psychosynthesis laid the foundations for a new and different application of psychology in education, broadly understood as a component of a complex learning process for all ages. With the introduction of psychagogy, the scientific interest in the "motivation towards growth" was proposed, ranging beyond a mechanistic discussion. This concept would be developed by Maslow and the entire field of humanistic psychology fifty years later.

---

64 R. Assagioli, *La psicologia delle idee forza e la psicagogia*, op. cit.

65 R. Assagioli, *La psicologia e l'esistenza umana*, in *Corso di lezioni sulla psicosintesi*, 1971, pp. 7-8.

66 S. Tilli, *Concetti della psicologia umanistica di Roberto Assagioli*, Ed. Istituto di Psicosintesi, Firenze, 1980, p. 51.

5.2. The positive existentialism of Psychosynthesis

I have already spoken of how psychiatrists and "existentialist" psychologists propose to understand the individual, not as a set of mechanisms or static schemes, but as a being that is always on the verge of emerging, becoming. The corollaries of existential psychotherapy that we find largely in Psychosynthesis derive from this approach: the concept that the human being is in constant development; the central aspect of psychotherapy intended as the help offered to the patient to recognize and experience their own existence; the role of the therapist as "an existence that communicates with another"; the importance attached to the focus in therapy so that "truth exists for the individual only if produced in actions".[67]

This concept of a "call to action" is a constant in Psychosynthesis thought. As psychiatrist and psychotherapist Bruno Caldironi[68] wrote in an interesting article regarding Assagioli's relationship with existentialism:

"Existentialism is not just a philosophical doctrine: it is not developed only by philosophers who work to clarify its reasoning. The importance and significance of their work lies in the fact that they only express and reveal an attitude that is imposed on man by the concrete tasks that await him in the world: that is, to be pragmatic."

According to existentialism and the mindset of Psychosynthesis, the being which the individual is seeking in his/her existence is not an object the nature of which he/she must be limited to investigating and recognizing. It presents a choice on which he/she must decide: it is ultimately the decision on being, which we find in the Assagiolian conception of the act of will. With the theorization on the will, the founder of Psychosynthesis offered perhaps his most original contribution. In Psychosynthesis the will takes on a central position as the essential function of the 'I' and the source of all choices, decisions and commitments.

Therefore, in common with the principles of existentialism, Psychosynthesis has the interests of the human being, the search for the meaning of existence, the goal of succeeding in pursuing one's course even among the obstacles represented by the existence of the world itself in its extreme complexity and natural conflictuality. But, says Caldironi:

"Psychosynthesis thought goes further: it can rightly represent the fullest amalgamation of the studies of existence; not limiting itself to desperately and helplessly accept human finiteness, nor even to avoid acknowledging this reality by creating a false positive view, denying the problem in its essence. Assagioli takes

---

67   L. Peresson, op. cit., p. 30.

68   B. Caldironi, *L'esistenzialismo positivo e Roberto Assagioli*, in "Rivista di Psicosintesi Terapeutica", Anno II, n. 2, p. 15.

into account the finiteness, precariousness and even vulnerability of the human being, but aims to lead him/her towards integration and self-realization (...). Through psychosynthesis, everyone can use the series of individual characteristics and potential not only to reflect personally and individually on the meaning of existence (...), but also by personally going through the unrepeatable experience, the challenge and the adventure of being, in a full and creative manner."[69]

5.3. The rediscovered Self

One of the authors that expanded, and continues to expand Assagioli's ideas in a humanistic-existentialistic context is a psychiatrist from Florence, Alberto Alberti, one of Assagioli's direct students.

In Psychosynthesis, the concept of the *Transpersonal Self* is of fundamental importance (see Part 4, Chapter III, Para. 4), but it is more correct to say "the existential experience of the Self", because in reality it is actually impossible to give a conclusive definition of what the Self is. In fact, according to Assagioli, the sole intellectual concept has no value if it does not produce a real transformation in the person, unless it becomes a direct, existential experience, an "immediate fact of conscience" which itself has its own evidence and proof.[70] Alberti writes[71]:

"Psychosynthesis ideally strives to understand the totality of the psychological elements that comprise the human being, and for this to happen, it has to pivot on a unifying center that is as wide and inclusive as possible. This unifying center is the Self, which is the essence and soul of man, his true identity, his highest and deepest nature. The Self expresses the highest degree of consciousness, love, and will. The Self can be considered as a center of synthesis that integrates and unites the whole of man. Freedom may perhaps be considered its fundamental quality, so it could be defined, from this point of view, as the freedom of the soul, which knows, loves and desires."

The Self in Psychosynthesis thus constitutes the guarantee of permanence and unity facing the flow of the multiplicity of psychic life. Alberti defines it as an experience of harmony and synthesis, a very intimate, profound and, at the same time, peaceful experience that does not exalt the personality of the subject or destroy it. This is a very significant life experience, where the meaning and value of life is revealed to those who live it, and with it, that of their own personal existence.

As we will see in more detail later on, the orientation of Psychosynthesis makes a distinction between what is "part" and what is "totality", and also between what separates totality by dividing it into parts (non-self), and what instead unites

---

69   Ibid, p. 18.

70   A. Alberti, *Il Sé ritrovato*, Giampiero Pagnini ed., 1994, p. 27.

71   Ibid, p. 20.

the parts and maintains the whole, and emanates from it (Self)[72]. Therefore the conflict between multiplicity and unity, or, as Assagioli said, between "vaguely understanding it as one and then finding it multiple" becomes one of the fundamental problems of life, a dilemma that rests on the specific human condition of liberty. So our conscious self finds itself in a specific intermediate existential position between Self and non-Self, between a tendency toward growth and a tendency toward regression, between a tendency toward synthesis and one toward disintegration, between the past and the future, between multiplicity and the unit.

Again according to Alberti, the path towards the Self, the orientation towards one's own essence, is experienced as a yearning, an aspiration, a thrust filled with the joy of life. But it is possible that the individual, being free, decides to go the other way, towards the non-Self. In this way he/she follows a path that could be called "antiexistential", a journey of departure from his own essence, from himself. In short, one can choose the will of life, or decide to be passively overcome by an against-the-will or death instinct. One can say *Yes to Life* or *No to Life*. Alberti[73] represented this fundamental dilemma qualifying human existence in the following scheme:

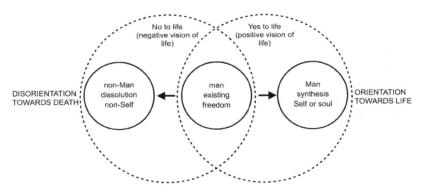

By choosing and following the path towards the Self, the individual enters into movement towards existence and does it through presence, that is, through acceptance and the total and free expression of theirself. In Psychosynthesis, presence implies the individual not as an abstract entity, but as a living being solidly immersed in their existential experience. It is therefore *a total presence* that is expressed and implemented in the completeness of all levels of the individual: physical-biological, psychic and spiritual, and in the totality of its intra-personal, inter-personal, social, and cosmic relationships. It is a presence that also means *freedom*, that is, in the freedom to be oneself; *knowing*, that one is aware; *a Willer*, able to act on existential situations, both in the sense of accepting them and in

---

72   Ibid, p. 9.

73   Ibid, p. 46.

the sense of change; *presence with love and joy*, since relationality and joy are an ontological fact; and finally *being present*, the total presence moving towards Being, which in turn takes place, manifests itself, reveals itself, and draws the existence of the individual to itself.[74] This decomposition of self naturally recaptures the existential dichotomy of the human being, placing it as an element of synthesis between the inflation of "being everything" and the deflation of "being nothing", precisely the simplicity of "Being".

5.4. The existential meaning of psychic suffering and its treatment

According to this point of view, psychopathological syndromes will have a different meaning, depending on whether they arise along the path to the Self or along the path leading away from the Self. Psychic disturbances can then be divided into two categories: first, *physiological disorders* due to growth, which do not constitute a true pathology but rather have evolutionary significance; second, *pathological disorders* that have involuted significance and are regressive. However, given the fundamental multiplicity of the human soul, often a mixed, partly existential, partly anti-existential pathology can arise.

For Alberti, solitude, or rather the subjective illusion of solitude, can be considered the pivot around which pathology rotates, the fundamental disease of existence. Indeed, since the essence of the individual is relational, any push toward isolation, toward separation, can only lead to a loss of vital momentum, a fracture in existence. For Psychosynthesis, authentic self-realization goes hand in hand with the overcoming of solitude. Alberti writes:

> "It is also fascinating that Assagioli, who has devoted his whole life to self-realization and the teaching of methods to implement it, gave his last lecture on this theme (*La solitudine e il suo superamento mediante la comunicazione e la comprensione - Overcoming Solitude with Communication and Understanding*, Florence, 1974) almost to reiterate, before dying, the inseparability of the two processes."

The only possible treatment is then constituted by the experience of the Self, the finding of the Self (the "I'm here again") or in any case by the experience of reconciliation with life, which constitutes the thread of Ariadne that reconnects the individual to his/her own essence. In this sense, Psychosynthesis recognizes one's Transpersonal Self, one's soul, as the only true guide for the patient: "It is our soul that drives us toward the soul"[75]. The therapist's job is to be a living example, to invoke and catalyze inner guidance of those who are suffering. For

---

74   Ibid, pp. 29-30.

75   Ibid, p. 37.

Alberti, "whoever really wants to help must be a 'guide towards self-guidance'"[76]. This process can be favored by creating a therapeutic climate around the suffering person consisting of synthetic elements, that is to say aggregating and cohesive, such as feelings (respect, love, trust, courage, hope, joy) that come from the soul of the individual and relate to the soul of the individual: therein lies their healing and anagogic power.

5.5. Similarities and differences between Psychosynthesis and the "third force"

Undoubtedly, Assagioli greeted the rise of the "third force" in psychology with joy. We can imagine that after decades of solitary hardships, he felt encouraged by the new ideas that came from America. And the fact that more scholars had come independently to the same conclusions would have given him further reason, if ever he needed it, to believe that his insights had an impact on the reality of the individual's psychic life. But the father of Psychosynthesis had already gone beyond, and had developed some concepts in a manner more precise and definitive than that of his overseas colleagues.

In this regard, it may be useful to note the similarities and differences between the theorizations of Roberto Assagioli and those of humanistic psychology.

First of all, it is clear that both approaches emphasize the importance of not just studying the sick by limiting the psychological analysis to the investigation of the Freudian unconscious. Introducing concepts such as "superconscious", "Transpersonal Self" (Psychosynthesis), "meta needs" and "superior tendencies of the psyche" (Maslow et al.), the horizons of research are broadened by attributing crucial importance to already existing qualities and abilities in a person, to their strengths and potential for creation, inspiration and transcendence.

Certainly both Psychosynthesis and humanistic psychology recognize the unquestionable importance of Freud's work, but they also identify its limits. For Assagioli as well as for many of the exponents of the third force, many psychosomatic disorders are caused not by the removal of the contents of the lower unconscious, but rather to the repression of elements from the superconscious, that is, to the failure to realize their highest potentials, to the betrayal of their existential task.

In addition, both Assagioli and scholars of humanistic psychology share the belief that psychotherapy and education are two aspects of the same process: the development and growth of the human being doesn't stop with the removal of emotional blocks and serious symptoms, but goes beyond the person.

Finally, both humanistic psychology and Psychosynthesis are orientations that suggest action, which want to contribute to the formation of a new way to live and not just to describe, to theorize, or to dabble in sterile academics. They hold

---

76   Ibid.

to the opinion that the time when science must be neutral is over and highlight the need to talk about values in a scientific way.[77]

But, as mentioned, Assagioli went beyond in this thinking, preceding those evolutions in humanistic psychology that would lead to the rising of the fourth force, Transpersonal Psychology.

First of all, he felt it important to distinguish *personal psychosynthesis*, which concerns the harmonious organization of the bio-psychic elements residing in the lower and middle unconscious around the personal self, from *transpersonal psychosynthesis*, which deals instead with the organization of the bio-psychic elements from the lower, middle, and superior unconscious around the Transpersonal Self.

He also attached great importance to the difference between *transpersonal experience*, which consists of becoming conscious of the contents of the higher unconscious, and the *realization of the Transpersonal Self*, considered a reality of which one can have direct experience. We will have a look at these important topics further on in the text. For now it is important to note that these necessary and lucid clarifications are less present and clear from the psychologists of the third force than they are in the writings of the father of Psychosynthesis.

---

77   P. Ferrucci, *Psicologia umanistica e transpersonale - Maslow e la psicosintesi*, in *Corso di lezioni sulla psicosintesi*, manuscript, 1971.

CHAPTER IV

THE FOURTH FORCE: TRANSPERSONAL PSYCHOLOGY

1. From humanistic psychology to transpersonal psychology

One of the central themes of humanistic psychology was self-realization. During the subsequent rapid development of this branch of knowledge, it became increasingly clear that the humanist orientation was becoming open to dialogue with new discoveries of science and the lessons of the great spiritual systems. This movement was specifically concerned with the transcendental, spiritual aspects of self-realization.

Probably this new focus stemmed in part from the need to respond to some of the criticisms of humanistic psychology. It was believed that the emphasis on self-realization led to excessive concern for oneself by neglecting ties with other people and society, implicitly emphasizing affirmation of self at the expense of the transcendence of the 'I', or personal self.[78] We have already seen how much care Abraham Maslow took in defining the term "self-realization" correctly, and even Viktor Frankl[79] strove to point out:

"If it is true that gratification and self-realization have their place in human life, they cannot be achieved unless they are 'per effectum', and not 'per intentionem'. Only insofar as we give, we offer, we be at the service of the world, for the tasks and the needs that call to us in our lives, (...) to this extent only we will be gratified and fulfilled. In a word, the essence of human existence lies in its self-transcendence."

For *Transpersonal Psychology*, as is already the case for humanistic psychology, self-realization is not therefore understood as the realization of self on an ego-centric level, but as the transcendence of the self towards the Other in all its multiple dimensions: others, the world, the spiritual dimension, the Absolute. It will therefore focus its attention and efforts on everything that can facilitate this process by addressing the recognition, understanding and creation of non-ordinary states of conscience and the psychological conditions that are barriers to such achievements.

In the first issue of the "Journal of Transpersonal Psychology", introduced

---

78   A. Maslow, op. cit., p. 8.

79   V. Frankl, op. cit., pp. 71-72.

in 1969, Anthony Sutich[80] (1907-1976), a student of Maslow, identified the new topics of the "fourth force":

> "Transpersonal Psychology is the title given to an emerging force in the psychology field by a group of psychologists and professional men and women from other fields who are interested in those *ultimate* human capacities that have no systematic place in positivistic or behavioristic theory ("first force"), classical psychoanalytic theory ("second force"), or humanistic psychology ("third force"). The emerging Transpersonal psychology ("fourth force") is concerned specifically with the *empirical*, scientific study of, and responsible implementation of the findings relevant to becoming, individual and species-wide meta-needs, ultimate values, unitive consciousness, peak experiences, B-values, ecstasy, mystical experience, awe, being, self-actualization, essence, bliss, wonder, ultimate meaning, transcendence of self, spirit, oneness, cosmic awareness, individual and species-wide synergy, maximal interpersonal encounter, sacralization of everyday life, transcendental phenomena, cosmic self-humor and playfulness, maximal sensory awareness, responsiveness and expression, and related concepts, experiences and activities."

2. Non-ordinary states of consciousness and a new view of the unconscious

Continuing the research with which psychoanalysis investigated the "deep" level of the psyche and developing the contributions of humanistic psychology that emphasized the area of the self, Transpersonal Psychology deals with the "high" level of the psyche, the seat of human potential. The interest in such studies derives from the fact that "peak experiences" such as creative expression, motivation to altruistic action and states of enlightenment often occur in people with excellent psychological health quotients.[81]

2.1. Non-ordinary states of consciousness

Filling the cultural and epistemological vacuum on the nature and characteristics of *non-ordinary states of consciousness* is one of the objectives of Transpersonal Psychology and is certainly the research area that has yielded its most fertile fruits.[82] Evidently, this program objective is strongly influenced by Maslow's pioneering research on "peak experiences".

In the mechanistic paradigm, the only normal state of consciousness is that of ordinary wakefulness, and apart from the states of sleep and dream, every other condition is considered pathological. Reacting to this reductive approach

---

80   A. Sutich, in "Journal of Transpersonal Psychology", n. 1, 1969.

81   L. Boggio Gilot, *Crescere oltre l'io,* Cittadella ed., 1997, pp. 6-7.

82   Ibid, p. 69.

and following Maslow's footsteps, a group of American psychiatrists and psychologists, including Claudio Naranjo, Ralph Metzner, Stanislav Grof and Charles Tart, carried out in-depth research on the subject. For these scholars, a *state of consciousness* can be defined as a pattern and a mode of mental functioning to which attention, awareness, will, thought and feeling belong. Obviously, this model can show a variety of specific features even within the same global scheme, but when the experiential sensation of a state of consciousness differs decisively from that of another, it is referred to as a *non-ordinary state of consciousness* that consists of a radical alteration of the mode of perception, such that the one who experiences it attests to the presence of different laws to which their behavior is subjected and the need to submit their experience to a new global model.[83]

According to the transpersonal approach, any state of consciousness is an arbitrary way of processing information coming in from one's surroundings, to selectively store some of them and discard others, to attribute importance to them according to a particular scale of values and, as a consequence, to act and experience things in certain particular ways. Following this vision, transpersonal psychologists broaden their field of investigation including experiences generated by hypnosis, or by the administration of drugs, or through various types of trance and, above all, by states generated through the practice of certain meditative techniques. In this regard, Charles Tart[84] states that:

"One of the most important statements of spiritual psychologists is that some non-ordinary states of consciousness are more authentic and useful in understanding certain kinds of problems, such as the relationship of man with the totality of existence, compared to our common state of wakefulness."

And so, interest in non-ordinary states of consciousness and in "peak experiences" naturally lead the exponents of the "fourth force" to examine the traditions that have studied such human mental processes through the ages.

2.2. The dialogue between Eastern and Western spiritual traditions

Studies on non-ordinary states of consciousness and "peak experiences" showed that such experiences were also present in other cultures, and indeed, various psychologies, philosophies and oriental religions even described whole categories of experiences of this type. In addition, contrary to those studied by Maslow for whom "peak experiences" were usually spontaneous, the respondents declared to be able to induce them at will.[85] By doing so, transpersonal psychologists found themselves in a radically different position from that of most of the major schools

---

83   C. Tart, *Psicologie transpersonali*, Ed. Crisalide, 1994.

84   Ibid, p. 32.

85   R. Walsh, *I confini della psicologia*, in *I nuovi paradigmi della psicologia*, op. cit., p. 66.

of Western psychology, which have always shown a tendency to ignore all forms of religion or spirituality or to consider it rooted in primitive superstition, in pathological aberrations (Freud believed religion to be an obsessive-compulsive neurosis of humanity) or collective illusions about reality inculcated by culture and the family environment.[86]

Moved by the awareness that age-old systems established in other cultures had much to teach, the newborn Transpersonal Psychology opened up a fruitful exchange with these spiritual traditions. The attitude taken by the "fourth force" is not to embrace such systems in an unquestioning way, nor to reject them without reflection. It intends to see them as privileged interlocutors, as sources of inspiration, studying the diverse symbologies, the diverse visions of the cosmos and humankind, the diverse technologies of the self.

According to transpersonal psychologists, Buddhism, Hinduism and Sufism have their own psychology, as do Yoga, Christianity, Taoism, Alchemy, and the Kabbalah. These psychologies are living bodies of knowledge, and Transpersonal Psychology tries to translate traditional concepts into a "scientific" language, accessible to the contemporary Western mentality. The hypothesis that moves Transpersonal Psychology can be defined as follows:

"At the heart of the great religions lies a core of wisdom known in terms of eternal wisdom, perennial philosophy, transcendent unity of religions or disciplines of conscience. This perennial wisdom, to be understood, practiced, and experienced in the right way, seems to require a new affirmation and a new interpretation in the language and the concepts of every culture and age. One of the predominant concept systems in modern Western culture and one of the most important to treat transpersonal development is psychology. (...)

In other words, contemporary psychology, and especially those schools such as Psychosynthesis and Transpersonal Psychology, can thus offer a way in which eternal wisdom can again make its entrance into instilling and perhaps transforming Western culture."[87]

2.3. A new view of the unconscious

Examining spiritual states entails a new view of the unconscious that, in turn, requires a new view of the concepts of development, maturity, health and illness.

Transpersonal theory refuses to consider the self as the ultimate reference, since it considers it to belong to an All who hosts it as its part. The transpersonal model, widening the vision of the human being and consciousness to include the

---

86   F. Capra, op. cit., p. 303.

87   R. Walsh, op. cit., pp. 76-77.

spiritual dimension, naturally leads to a revision of assumptions about the nature of the unconscious. In fact, according to this vision, the unconscious possesses not only potentials of instinctual, emotional and mental types, but also of intuitive, archetypal and spiritual types.

Carl Gustav Jung had already discussed unconscious religiosity, a theme that was resumed by humanistic psychologists. In this context, a fundamental turning point is provided in particular by the proposal of Roberto Assagioli (see Part 3, Chapter II). So then, if the archaic unconscious can be considered the past of humanity, the "emerging" or "superior" unconscious is the future. From the transpersonal perspective, the potentialities of the unconscious appear as abilities and talents that, in favorable conditions, tend to get actuated spontaneously.

Consistent with this vision, many psychological ailments are derived from the removal of the potentialities that allow the individual, without denying it, to go beyond his/her self, and to thereby satisfy the need for transcendence.[88] Resistance to the integration of the emerging unconscious can be attributed to rationalizations that are opposed to transcendence, and to the fear of death, de-sacralization and the repression of the sublime.

3. The theory of transpersonal development and the concept of maturity

The theory of transpersonal development envisions human growth "as the progressive integration, in the field of awareness, of latent potentiality".[89]

Traditional psychology has investigated the process of evolution from childhood to adulthood. According to one of the foremost exponents of Transpersonal Psychology, American philosopher and essayist Ken Wilber[90], connecting the evolutionary stages outlined by evolutionary psychology with those illustrated by perennial philosophy a *circular pattern of life* is obtained, ranging from an instinctive, subconscious, pre-egoic and pre-personal level, passing through a mental, self-conscious, self-centered and personal stage to a spiritual, super-conscious, trans-egoic transpersonal level.

Therefore, the entire cycle of development shown on the next page can be divided into two arcs:

- that of *personal development*
- that of *transpersonal development*

---

88   U. Galimberti, *Psicologia*, op. cit., p. 860.

89   L. Boggio Gilot, op. cit., p. 98.

90   K. Wilber, cit. in L. Boggio Gilot, op. cit., p. 98.

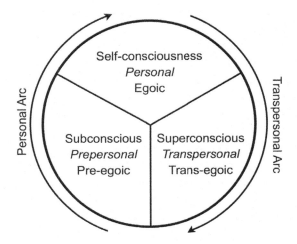

The first arc develops from pre-logic subconsciousness, determined by the impulses and primitive emotions in which the human being lives under the dominion of a female-maternal principle, to logical self-consciousness, in which a principle of male-paternal determination, aimed at having a role in the world, controls instincts and emotions. The second arc goes from the self-conscious domain of a personal self focused on fulfilling its own needs in the world, to a superconscious, in which the self is under the influence of the Transpersonal Self: in this phase male and female merge into the androgenic transpersonal whole. The first arc is exterior, characterized by the gratification of needs of security and self-assertion, and has self-realization as its objective; the second is interior, characterized by the needs of growth and knowledge, and has the goal of self-transcendence.[91]

According to this briefly outlined point of view, the degree of maturity lies along a *continuum* of development and, paraphrasing the psychologist and psychotherapist Laura Boggio Gilot[92], is evaluated on the basis of:

1. *sense of identity*;
2. *perception of reality* and *cognitive attitude*;
3. *type of sentiment*;
4. *nature* and *form of interpersonal relationships*;
5. *needs* and *motivations*
6. *values*
7. *behavior*

---

91   L. Boggio Gilot, op. cit., p. 99.

92   Ibid, pp. 113-116.

The arc of personal maturity, or self-realization develops:

1. from the *sense of self* connected to processes of identification which derive from the judgments of parents and surroundings, to the sense of self reflecting one's own real potentialities

2. from the sensory and pre-reflective *cognitive functions* to the analytical and synthetic; in other words, from pre-logic perception, in which the object is assailed by projections due to needs and fears, to the logical perception, in which the unmasked object is recognized in its relative objectivity;

3. from the *feeling* determined by narcissistic and competitive aspects (anger, envy, hatred, jealousy) to the sentiment that takes into account others and respects their will (cooperation, responsibility);

4. from the *needs* resulting from deficiencies to needs of creativity and self-realization;

5. from dependent *interpersonal attitudes* to those independent;

6. from hedonistic *values* to humanitarian values;

7. from the pre-conventional to the post-conventional *ethic* which goes beyond adapting, beyond expectations and social conformism to be based on personal values.

The arc of transpersonal maturity or self-transcendence, evolves:

1. from the *sense of identity* contained within the body and qualified by mental content, to the sense of identity without boundaries that embraces the totality of creation;

2. from the *dualistic perception* of object/subject to the non-dualistic perception which recognizes the unity between the Transpersonal Self and the world;

3. from the logical and *cognitive predisposition* to the translogical which uncovers the archetypes;

4. from *sentiment* as a response to pleasure or displeasure to the balanced sentiment of unconditional love;

5. from the *need* of self-realization to the need for self-transcendence;

6. from *interpersonal relationships* governed by personal needs to interpersonal relationships based on the support of other human beings;

7. from personalistic moral *values* to values that follow universal principles;

8. from *dogmatic rigidity* to flexibility and tolerance which includes forgiveness.

It is very important in transpersonal psychology not to confuse the meaning of "stage" of human growth, which involves specific and stable experiences and acquisitions, with that of "state", which is indicative of a temporary expansion of consciousness. In fact, transient transpersonal experiences can also occur in psychologically fragile or disturbed personalities and, in the absence of a well-integrated structure, become psychological disorders of varying and sometimes even serious nature.

4. The emerging paradigm: the systemic view

The theory of development and the concept of maturity proposed by Ken Wilber allows us to introduce another fundamental theme of the "fourth force". Like the previous trends in dynamic psychology, the latter is also a product of the culture in which it is born and responds to the most obvious needs of the society in which it is disseminated. If psychoanalysis was born in the Victorian Europe of sexual repression while humanistic psychology emerged in the America of technological hyperdevelopment, transpersonal psychology arises from the crisis of materialistic culture and the eclipse of Cartesian rationalism. Laura Boggio Gilot states[93]:

"In recent decades the conception of the interconnected universe introduced by the explorations of the subatomic world and the developments of the sciences in general have undermined the conceptual basis of the mechanistic vision of the world, increasingly recognizing the inadequacy of this simplistic way of thinking about the universe, the human being, and the structure of knowledge in general."

From the various schools and psychological movements there is now emerging, although largely outside the academic institutions too closely linked to the Cartesian paradigm to appreciate the new ideas, a new psychology that is in-line with the systemic vision of life and which is harmonized with the conceptions of the spiritual traditions. This vision is ecological in the sense that it reconnects the life of the human being to the life of nature and the cosmos, and places the emphasis on the entirety and the intelligence of the universe.

The *theory of systems* has allowed us to formulate a new conception of the mind in a holistic and dynamic perspective. It conceives the individual as the result of the interrelationships between the parts that make it up as well as between these parts and the relational systems in which it is inserted, such as the family, the workplace and so on. It also states that the psyche's properties and functions cannot be understood by reducing them to isolated elements, just as the physical organism cannot be fully understood by analyzing it in its parts. The Austrian physicist Fritjof Capra[94] writes that "from this point of view, the Cartesian division between mind and body and the conceptual separation of individuals from their environment appear to be a collective mental illness shared by most western cultures."

In the past, several schools of psychology have proposed theories of the

---

93   Ibid, pp. 20-21.

94   F. Capra, op. cit., p. 304.

personality and systems of therapies that differ radically among themselves in the conception of the psychic functioning of the human being. These schools are typically limited to a narrow range of psychological phenomena: sexuality, birth trauma, existential problems, family dynamics, and so on.

A number of psychologists insist today that none of these approaches are wrong, but that each of them focuses on some part of an entire spectrum of consciousness, subsequently striving to generalize the understanding of that part in relation to the whole psyche. According to these researchers, there might be no theory capable of explaining the whole spectrum of psychological phenomena, but rather a network of interconnected models that use different languages to describe different aspects and levels of reality.[95] As Roger Walsh writes[96]:

> "For example, Freudian psychology and the object relations theory can present important topics on early development, while psychology and existential therapy have much to say about the universal themes affecting mature adults. Behavioral therapy can concentrate on the importance of identifying those specific environmental reinforcements that maintain proper or improper behavior, while cognitive therapies can help us appreciate the power of unrecognized beliefs and thoughts.
>
> Likewise, multidimensional schools such as Jungian psychology and Psychosynthesis emphasize, among other things, the possibility of transpersonal development and the therapeutic power of images and symbols. Asian systems, such as Buddhist psychology, Yoga, and Vedanta may be complementary to Western approaches, indicating, for example, the transpersonal and therapeutic power of ethics, meditation, meditative training, and attention."

According to this theoretical model, non-recognition of the limits of the empirical and rationalistic approach, and considering that which escapes this view as unrealistic, means transforming science into scientism. On the basis of this belief, Ken Wilber[97], referring to Hugh of San Vittore and Saint Bonaventure, spoke of an expanded epistemology and psychology with the use of three types of knowledge: sensory, mental-phenomenological and contemplative. Each of them is linked to a different "eye", which has access to a certain kind of reality:

1. the *eye of the flesh* (that is, of the senses), with which the external world—objects placed in space-time—is perceived, participates in the world of matter which is known through empirical sensory experience;

2. the *eye of reason*, through which knowledge of philosophy, logic and the mind is gained, participates in the world of ideas, images, concepts and symbols known through the phenomenological-interpretative experience;

---

95   Ibid, p. 305.

96   R. Walsh, op. cit., p. 70.

97   K. Wilber, *Eye to eye: The quest for the new paradigm*, Anchor/Doubleday, New York, 1983.

3. the *eye of contemplation*, by which knowledge of transcendent reality is gained and archetypal forms and qualities are perceived.

Each of these three "eyes" provides for a particular type of knowledge: sensory knowledge, the result of empirical research, whose data are things or objects; rational knowledge, the result of phenomenological research, whose data are thoughts, feelings and symbols; spiritual knowledge, the result of contemplative research, whose data are abstract and transcendent principles.[98]

The different psychological schools have traditionally used only one of these modes, one "eye", often denying the importance or validity of others. However, according to transpersonal psychologists, all three modes may be needed by a psychology that is aimed at including the full spectrum of human experience. Each degree of knowledge requires its own kind of research, observation and validation and is therefore the result of a specific science: empirical, phenomenological or contemplative. Whenever one of them is explained in terms of another, we come across reductivism.

5. The spectrum of consciousness

In the backbone of the systemic perspective we find Ken Wilber, who was inspired by the psychosynthetic vision proposed by Assagioli. Wilber arranged the intuitions of the great Italian pioneer in a theoretical model of personality that aids integration of scientific culture and spiritual tradition. As I have already mentioned, this model links childhood, adulthood and spiritual stages into a single *continuum* and suggests that the higher stages of personal and conventional psychological development may merge into the lower spiritual stages of transpersonal and transconventional development. Ken Wilber[99] writes in the preface of his book *No Boundary:*

"The number of (psychological) approaches available today is enormous (...). Moreover, many of these different schools of thought seem to contradict each other. They not only provide different diagnoses of cause and suffering but also prescribe different methods to alleviate it. (...)

To get out of this disconcerting diversity of views, I tried a synthesis that provides a global perspective. I have traced the different approaches to therapy, healing, and personal growth to a reference framework I called the 'spectrum of consciousness'. (...) We'll see how different therapies have addressed different levels of this spectrum."

---

98   L. Boggio Gilot, op. cit., p. 33.

99   K. Wilber, *Oltre i confini*, Cittadella ed., 1985, pp. 10-11.

The following graphic is proposed by the author[100]:

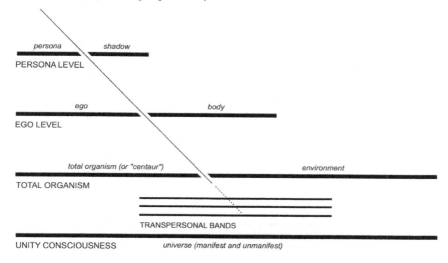

According to Wilber, the different *levels of consciousness* essentially coincide with the different ways in which we can answer the question "Who am I?". In other words, each level of the spectrum corresponds to a certain definition of identity. For the author, when an individual describes himself/herself it triggers mental processes that consist in tracing boundaries between what they consider to be "self" and what they consider to be "non-self". So answering the question "Who am I?" means answering the question "Where do I trace my border?"

The easiest borderline to recognize is that represented by the skin that covers the whole body, distinguishing it from the environment (*level of the total organism*). However, there is another type of border, more restrictive, provided by the identification of the individual with an aspect of the body called the mind, psyche, ego or personality at the expense of the body (*level of the ego*). In the end, the individual may even refuse to admit that certain aspects of his own psyche belong to him, further narrowing the boundary between the self and the non-self exclusively to certain areas of the ego and repressing other aspects that form the shadow (*level of the person*).

Instead, in the transpersonal bands, there is a process that goes beyond the individual. The common element at this level of consciousness is the expansion of the self/non-self boundary beyond the body's epidermal limit until it reaches the point where the subject identifies his/her true Self with Creation and feels one with the cosmos. Wilber defines this experience, which is promulgated and codified by all major religions, *"consciousness of unity"*.

It is important to emphasize that any borderline is also a potential battle line: the person versus the shadow, the ego versus the body, the total organism versus the environment.

---

100   Ibid, p. 22.

At this point, Wilber wonders whether the multitude of *therapeutic approaches* in circulation are all at the same level as the spectrum of conscience, or whether it is no longer correct to consider different orientations as being aimed at different levels of being of an individual. The answer, represented in the next graphic[101], is obviously affirmative.

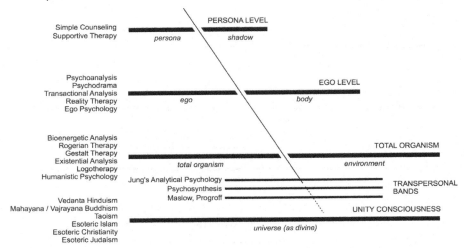

This diagram shows the main psychological schools in correspondence to the level of the spectrum with which they are connected. Wilber points out that the different levels easily blend into one another, so the proposed classification is in no way clear and rigid. Referring to the systemic view, therapy related to a given level will recognize and accept the potential existence of all the lower levels, but will negate the existence of the higher ones.

So simple *counseling* and *support therapies* tend to work exclusively at the level of the person. Instead, approaches such as *psychoanalysis*, *psychodrama*, and *transactional analysis* primarily address the ego level. *Existential-humanistic* approaches are directed to the total body. Finally, *transpersonal psychologies*, such as *Jungian psychology* and *Psychosynthesis*, embrace a vision that contemplates the consciousness of unity, which has then been conveyed by many religious traditions.

5.1. Health, illness and therapy from a transpersonal perspective

The transpersonal view has also led to a new definition of what is "normal" and what is "pathological": no longer based on the nature of the situations experienced by the person but on the way they are experienced and on the extent to which this person is able to integrate these experiences into his or her life. The new approach to psychology conceives mental illness as a multidimensional

---

101   Ibid, p. 23.

phenomenon involving interdependent physical, psychological and social aspects. Mental illness therefore involves an entire system, not just the person afflicted with it.

This new way of considering the pathology suggests that what we considered to be "normal" could be a form of arrested development, also called "pathology of the norm". Society could have a very powerful influence in driving people through social media, encouraging development to adhere to social standards and hindering it beyond these. Transpersonal Psychology therefore asks how the evolutionary level of a society can set a limit on the individual's level of evolution.[102]

As we have already pointed out, for Transpersonal Psychology, development takes place at stages, and each one corresponds to a specific structuring of identity and of consciousness (pre-personal, personal, transpersonal). And so, disturbances in the development of a particular stage differ from those of another.[103] Based on this important distinction, Wilber proposes to divide psychopathological disorders into three different bands:

Nomenclature	Relative Arc of Development	Type of disturbance
psychodynamic disturbances	the development from the subconscious to the self-conscious which arrives with the oedipal phase and concludes it	syndromes examined in psychoanalysis
cognitive-existential disturbances	the personal arc of the construction of the self up until full maturity	pathologies examined by humanistic-existential psychology
transpersonal disturbances	the arc of structuring from self-consciousness to superconsciousness, in which the development of personality passes the boundaries of the 'I' body-mind	pathologies of self-transcendence examined by transpersonal psychology

In any case, this encoding should be taken with a grain of salt: only rarely does mental suffering appear in such a distinct way; it's more typical to see a mixture of various pathologies.

6. Psychosynthesis and Transpersonal Psychology

As Laura Boggio Gilot[104] reminds us, the word "transpersonal" combines the Latin preposition "trans", which means "beyond, across", the term "personal" derived from the noun "person" whose etymological meaning is "the mask worn

---

102   R. Walsh, op. cit., p. 68.
103   L. Boggio Gilot, op. cit., p. 126.
104   Ibid p. 15.

by a character in a theatrical work". So Transpersonal Psychology is the psychology that is concerned with "what in man is beyond the ordinary personality"[105].

The term had already been used by Jung to designate that dimension of the human unconscious that is home to archetypal and collective forms, or rather, of the archaic and spiritual ancestral heritage of humanity. Roberto Assagioli would give it a more specific meaning, relegating it to the realm of a higher unconscious, from where the highest human potentials come, such as intuition, aspiration, artistic, philosophical, ethical, aesthetic and literary inspirations, altruistic love and illuminating experiences.

The father of Psychosynthesis had been interested in the spiritual dimensions of existence ever since he was young and never abandoned his vocation. As I have already mentioned in the previous chapter, he had hoped for a synthesis of clinical psychology and studies of spiritual experiences since his article on psychagogy in 1909. He firmly believed that each individual has the ability to go beyond the boundaries of his own personality, beyond thoughts and obsolete images of himself, beyond the pressure of social opinion, beyond the prejudices and his own little world to find another world, new and full of wonder.

It then seems natural to connect Psychosynthesis to Transpersonal Psychology, perhaps the field in which, more than any other scholar, Assagioli was a precursor and a pioneer. He collaborated, for example, with the "Journal of Transpersonal Psychology", and with Maslow, Watts and others of similar weight, he was among the founders of the *Transpersonal Institute*, where he is always remembered and cited as a master.

6.1. The first transpersonal model of the identity

The first *transpersonal model of identity* is precisely that which was elaborated by Roberto Assagioli. The father of Psychosynthesis sees the human being as a bio-psycho-spiritual unit composed of diverse interconnected levels. The unconscious, according to the psychosynthetic view, is composed of an individual dimension and a collective one: the individual unconscious is immersed in that of the collective, the homeland of the archetypes outlined by Jung. The individual unconscious in turn includes three levels: lower, middle, and superior.[106]

Of major importance, above all, is the relationship between the conscious self and the various levels of the unconscious. Regarding this Assagioli wrote[107]:

---

105   R. Assagioli, *Comprendere la psicosintesi*, a cura di M. L. Macchia Girelli, Astrolabio Ed., 1991, p. 130.

106   L. Boggio Gilot, op. cit., pp. 47-48.

107   R. Assagioli, *Psicoanalisi e psicosintesi*, op. cit., p. 6.

"Psychosynthesis aims to integrate the study of the conscious part of the personality and the lower and middle unconscious with that of the superconscious, the superimposed latent energies in each, and with the use of methods for their activation and integration in the human personality."

In fact, Psychosynthesis considers three different types of expansion of the consciousness, assigning them different meanings and functions[108]:

1. a *downward expansion*: exploration of the lower unconscious;

2. a *horizontal expansion*: participation and identification with other beings, nature and things;

3. an *upward expansion*: toward the levels of the super-conscious and transpersonal levels.

This upward expansion can come about in two different ways. The first is the elevation of the self, of the center of consciousness, towards the transpersonal levels; the second is the opening of the self to the influx of energies coming spontaneously from the higher unconscious. Assagioli was concerned with thoroughly studying the methods and techniques that can favor this osmosis between the conscious self and the higher unconscious, identifying the obstacles that prevent it, identifying the different paths that men travel to achieve such experiences and describing its characteristics and dangers.

I will deal more in detail with this transpersonal model of identity and its countless implications later (see Part 3, Chapter II). For now, it is sufficient to say that, for the first time in psychology, a *"superior" unconscious dimension* was introduced, the source of the highest human potential, which is not comparable to the Freudian instinctual unconscious and center of removal.

6.2. Dangers and clarifications

As I mentioned previously, the awareness of the risks inherent in transpersonal development and also in that orientation for psychology led Assagioli, prior to and more than other authors, to very clearly specify some of the crucial points of his thinking. Firstly, he asks the researchers dealing with the new frontiers of psychology to proceed cautiously, so as not to fall into the same mistakes made by their predecessors: they should not prematurely jump to conclusions and to undue generalizations. In this regard, he writes[109]:

"Some representatives of the new current have a tendency to return to the former conception of man as an already unified personality, which unfortunately is far

108   R. Assagioli, *Lo sviluppo transpersonale*, Casa Editrice Astrolabio, Roma, 1988, pp. 36-39.
109   R. Assagioli, *Principi e metodi della psicosintesi terapeutica*, op. cit., p. 41.

from being true. The push towards integration has been rightly described and highlighted as a fundamental and normal impulse of human personality; but this is very different from the illusion of a personality that functions from the beginning in an organic and harmonious way. (...) It is therefore evident that organic unity is a goal, not an existing reality, a goal that can be visualized, approached gradually, and to some extent, pursued."

In order to overcome these issues, Assagioli distinguishes two types of self-realization which, while having similar sides, are of different nature and have quite different manifestations: actualization of self and the realization of Self. The actualization of self, which corresponds to the *self-actualization* studied by Maslow, can be achieved under different conditions and does not necessarily include what is defined as the transpersonal level. On the other hand, an individual can have genuine transpersonal experiences without actually being integrated, that is, without developing a harmonic personality, with the consequent risk of being unbalanced, exalting and incorrectly interpreting the experience.

That is why Psychosynthesis strives to distinguish a *personal psychosynthesis* from a *transpersonal psychosynthesis*, assigning different and precise tasks to each. In fact, personal psychosynthesis consists of the organization of biopsychic elements around the personal self, in the development and harmonization of the functions and human potentials at all levels of the lower and middle zones of the individual, in the coordination of the various parts of the self towards a fuller and richer life. Transpersonal psychosynthesis, on the other hand, includes the manifestation of superconscious forces, the organization of the biopsychic elements around the Transpersonal Self, and one of the purposes it tends toward is that the will of the Self becomes conscious[110]. As we have seen, confusing the two approaches can lead to serious mistakes both from a diagnostic point of view and also from a therapeutic, educational and self-training perspective.

Finally, another source of error Assagioli pointed out was the confusing of the *superconscious* with the Self. According to Assagioli[111]:

"The superconscious is different from the Self (...). Developing or becoming aware of the Self means a more or less temporary identification or fusion of the consciousness of the 'I' with the Self (...). In this case, all the contents (sensations, thoughts, feelings, etc.) of the personality are temporarily eliminated, both on the normal and superconscious levels. Only the pure and intense experience of the Self remains."

According to Psychosynthesis, the experiences associated with awareness of the contents of the superconscious may or may not include the Transpersonal Self. A

---

110   R. Assagioli, *Comprendere la psicosintesi,* op. cit., pp. 102-103.

111   R. Assagioli, *Principi e metodi della psicosintesi terapeutica,* op. cit., p. 166-1677.

paradoxical phenomenon may also occur: the ascension to superconscious levels and their exploration, while approaching the consciousness of the Transpersonal Self, can sometimes be an obstacle to its development. This is because you can be so fascinated by the wonders of the superconscious kingdom, you can identify with it and, in some aspects and manifestations, so much so that you lose contact with the impulse to "reach" the Self.

6.3. The neutrality of Psychosynthesis

Assagioli maintained that the term "spiritual" was used in an overly superficial and vague way, opening the way to inappropriate confusion and erroneous interpretations due to its association with religion and philosophy. He stated[112]:

> "While the spiritual achievements of the past were expressed through precise forms, or religious or philosophical concepts, and the methods of achievement were closely related to associated doctrines, beliefs and systems, one now realizes that these relationships are not necessary; the investigation of super-conscious levels of spiritual reality can be carried out with an open mind or scientific attitude, that is, with a universal spirit."

The founder of Psychosynthesis, therefore, considered that the "transpersonal" expression lends itself better to the more precise and neutral requirements of a scientific approach, being purely indicative of a level higher than that of the "normal" human being, able to account for many superconscious experiences that also have non-religious qualities, such as artistic creation, scientific insights, and motiviation to altruistic action, and to avoid confusion with many pseudo-transpersonal or parapsychological phenomena.

This distinction made by Psychosynthesis between superconscious phenomena and parapsychology is extremely important because research has often confused the two domains. Psychosynthesis feels that parapsychological skills are not necessarily an indicator of contact with the superconscious; indeed, they can sometimes represent the opposite, that is, an indiscriminate openness to the lower levels of the personal or collective unconscious.

Assagioli wanted to make it very clear that although Psychosynthesis deals with the higher aspects of the psyche, including religious experiences, it does not present a new philosophy or a new religious conception. As we have already said elsewhere—but it is good to repeat it because too often Psychosynthesis is accused of being a metaphysical speculation—it does not directly probe into the final problems, does not try to answer philosophical and religious questions such as "What is the Spirit?", "Does God exist?" As the founder liked to say, it merely

---

112 R. Assagioli, *La psicologia nell'avvenire*, manuscript, 1968, p. 3.

leads the individual to the threshold of the mystery and then leaves him or her free to find his/her own answers.

> "(Psychosynthesis) is not a philosophical, theological or metaphysical position; rather, it is the acknowledgment that all manifestations of the human psyche, such as creative imagination, intuition, genius, superior feelings, impulses to altruistic and heroic actions are facts; facts no less real than the instinctive impulses, spontaneous or conditioned reflexes, and that they lend themselves to scientific study and to be activated, developed and utilized."[113]

And so, the experiences that can be called "existential", that is, internal illumination, are one thing, and the consequences, doctrines or beliefs that men derive from it are quite another. Psychosynthesis studies the former but does not deal with the latter, and takes a substantially pragmatic, open and inclusive attitude towards such experiences. It affirms the reality of transpersonal experience, the existence of higher values, and is neutral with regard to doctrinal formulations and institutions. Its purpose is to help those who feel the aspiration to attain the direct experience of superconscious reality and the Self.

Assagioli believed that this secular approach would have allowed the non-religious, those who have no clear philosophical conviction and the agnostics to approach the exploration of the inner world while helping, on the other hand, those who already belong to a religion or a definite philosophy, to have an open mind toward formulations and symbologies differing from their own.

6.4. Scientific investigation of transpersonal phenomena

For Assagioli it was paradoxical that an abundance of accounts of transpersonal experiences of men and women from every time and place did not correspond to adequate scientific research or to an equally appropriate experimental investigation. He therefore precedes the members of the "fourth force" by asking, indeed, underlining the "necessity and urgency of a study and scientific experimentation of that field, independent of any doctrine, system or personal authority."[114]

Psychosynthesis maintains that transpersonal phenomena, being human psychological experiences, can and should be scientifically studied and included in an integral conception of the human psyche. Assagioli[115] suggested orienting this study to distinguish different aspects, or stages:

1. First of all, the study of *phenomenology*- the collection of experiences, of observed

---

113 R. Assagioli, *Principi e metodi della psicosintesi terapeutica*, op. cit, p. 163.

114 R. Assagioli, *Lo sviluppo transpersonale*, op. cit., p. 55.

115 Ibid, pp. 23 e 56.

facts, as described by many people from every time and place (through biographies, autobiographies, letters, interviews and questionnaires).

  - The *examination, classification, interpretation* and *evaluation* of the collected data.

  - The *experimentation* of *psychological methods*, both those that facilitate the descent of superconscious elements into the field of consciousness, and those that promote the rise of the center of consciousness into the luminous upper regions.

2. The study of the *modes of transition* between the superconscious and the conscious.

3. The study of *techniques* used to facilitate this passage. They include the various practices, both external and internal, of various religions; and the various exercises that are employed in different ways but which can be called by the generic name of yoga.

4. The *verification of the immediate results*, and their subsequent effects.

5. The study of *methods to prevent dangers* and to avoid the damage that can be caused by the "descent" or break-out of transpersonal energies

6. The study of the *modes* and *most useful applications* of those achievements and energies.

"To do this, we need the courage to forget everything we know, to come into contact with the new, and to be truly capable of wonder"[116]

---

116 P. Ferrucci, *Introduzione alla psicosintesi*, Ed. Mediterranee, 1993, p. 231.

CHAPTER V

"PSYCHOENERGETICS" AND THE INTEGRATIVE VIEWPOINT IN PSYCHOSYNTHESIS

Assagioli was always very attentive to the development of sciences, but there was one he was especially passionate about: *physics*. Throughout his life he kept constantly informed of the new developments in this science and he fully appreciated the revolutionary push to the frontiers opened by scholars such as Albert Einstein, Max Planck, Wolfgang Pauli, Niels Bohr, Werner Heisenberg and others. For our author, science and physics opened the doors to new models of reality, to new categories of thought. Scientific discoveries, postulating the existence of a correlating energy, with the consequence that distinguishing and separating the material from the intangible is an outmoded way of thinking, forced the reformulation of ideas not only regarding physical but also psychological phenomena. The father of Psychosynthesis was convinced he was witnessing a revolution, perhaps more significant than the Copernican, which would have impacted all human knowledge.

As in the case of Jung, who we can consider the scholar closest to the Assagiolian conception, it is a shame that the language of the modern theory of systems was also not yet available to Assagioli. In fact, the great Swiss psychiatrist wrote[117]:

"Sooner or later, nuclear physics and the psychology of the unconscious will approach one another, since both, independently of one another and starting from opposite directions, move forward into a transcendental territory ... The psyche cannot be totally different from matter, since in that case how could matter move? And matter cannot be alien to the psyche, because otherwise how could matter produce the psyche? Mind and matter exist in the same world, and each one is part of the other, otherwise any mutual action would be impossible. If only research could advance abundantly, we should therefore come to an ultimate agreement between physical and psychological concepts. Our present efforts may be daring, but I believe they are in the right direction."

1. Psychoenergetics: an ecological and interdependent perspective of life

In this regard, Assagioli put forth the hypothesis of a future "fifth force" of psychology based on the emerging scientific paradigm and its relationships

---

117   C. G. Jung, *Aion: ricerche sulla storia del simbolo*, in Opere, vol. IX, parte II, 1951.

between mind, energy and matter; he called it *psychoenergetics*. It investigates all existing forces in the universe and their relationships, namely[118]:

1. *physical energies* (starting at the subatomic level and ranging up to the astronomic);
2. *biological energies*, organizers of all living matter;
3. specifically *psychic energies*;
4. *transpersonal energies*.

Assagioli felt a strong sense of living in an era where the need to harmonize, coordinate and synthesize fields of knowledge and different experiences was increasing, and he considered psychoenergetics one of the potential examples of the fertility of these syntheses. Psychoenergetics therefore appeals to scholars of the natural sciences, as well as those of historical and humanistic sciences.

In Psychosynthesis, the individual is considered a living subject that finds itself at the center of various types and levels of energy (physical-biological, psychic and transpersonal, conscious and unconscious). These energies interact dynamically with each other, and the individual struggles to coordinate such multiplicity into an organic and harmonic unit. So the image proposed by Psychosynthesis is not just a series of dynamic relationships between psychic energies ("psychodynamics" in the strict sense), but rather a total, holistic view of humankind and human life, a "psychoenergetic" vision.

Psychoenergetics can be considered as the science that investigates the interactions and transformations between all kinds of energies, both microcosmic and macrocosmic. Therefore, the object of study is no longer the individual separated from their relational context but, according to an ecological and interdependent perspective of life, the individual as being in a relationship, not only with their own self and with others in the family group, but with society and all humanity, as well as with all the energies of the planet and of the cosmos.[119] The concept of collective unconscious, accepted by Psychosynthesis, actually implies the existence of a bond between the individual, humanity, and the planet that supports it, conceived as an interdependent whole. This bond is not to be seen within a mechanistic framework, but is in close agreement with the systemic view of the mind.[120]

---

118 R. Assagioli, *Le nuove dimensioni della psicologia*, op. cit., p. 18.
119 M. Rosselli, A. Alberti, *Psicosintesi e nuovi paradigmi in psicoterapia*, in "Rivista di Psicosintesi Terapeutica", Anno I, n. 1, p. 58.
120 F. Capra, *Il punto di svolta*, op. cit., p. 299.

1.1. The unity of all things[121]

It is important to emphasize that, for many scholars, the new vision of the universe designed by quantum physics is perfectly matched with the theories developed over time by great mystics and esotericists. Quantum mechanics, in fact, reveals the essential interconnection of the universe and makes us realize that we cannot break the world into elementary units having independent existences. The fundamental uniqueness of the universe, the awareness of unity and mutual interplay of all things and events is therefore not only one of the most important revelations in modern physics but also the main characteristic of mystical or transpersonal experience. Though spiritual traditions differ in many details, the conception of the world they envision is essentially the same: everything is seen as an interdependent and inseparable part of a cosmic whole, a different manifestation of the same ultimate reality, whether it is called Brahman, Dharmakaya, Tao, Tathātā, God or absolute Essence.

In this regard, it may be interesting to place two quotations side-by-side, as Fritjof Capra did in *The Tao of Physics*: the first is attributed to the great Buddhist monk and mystic Nagarjuna (2nd century A.D.), the second is from German physicist Werner Heisenberg (1901-1976). Note the substantial similarity of the terms used:

"Things derive their being and nature by mutual dependence and are nothing in themselves."[122]

"The world thus appears as a complicated tissue of events, in which connections of different kinds alternate or overlap or continue and thereby determine the texture of the whole."[123]

The image of a cosmic network of reciprocal connections, emerging from modern atomic physics, has been widely used in the East to convey the mystical experience of nature. For the Hindus, Brahman is the unifying thread of the cosmic network, the ultimate base of all being. In Buddhism the image of the network has an even greater function. It is said that in the sky of Indra there is a network of pearls arranged so that if one is observed, the reflections of all the others are seen. Similarly, every object in the world is not just itself, but it implies every other object and, in fact, is everything else.

These ideas greatly fascinated Assagioli, who was one of the first to discover the similarities between the revelations of quantum physics and the theories of different spiritual traditions, trying to glean direction for psychology and gestating the

---

121   F. Capra, *Il Tao della fisica*, Adelphi, 1989, pp. 147-163.

122   Nagarjuna, cit. in F. Capra, op. cit., p. 158.

123   W. Heisenberg, cit. in F. Capra, op. cit., p. 158.

birth of "psychoenergetics". Psychiatrist and psychologist Pier Maria Bonacina writes[124]:

"To state that matter is energy and that everything is interrelated means to feel the need to look around with new eyes, with new minds, with new awe, wonder and enthusiasm. It means to observe with new interest, new freedom and new interpretative models the processes of thought, psychological functions, personality, identity (...)"

2. Conclusions: the integrative view in Psychosynthesis

It's not possible to understand Psychosynthesis if the intrinsic value of the open attitude and sensibility with which Assagioli turned to all that humankind produces is not clear.[125] According to the psychologist and psychoanalyst Sebastiano Tilli[126], the position of the father of Psychosynthesis in Italian culture can be termed very unusual. He points out that in all the various forms of theorization, or in the various movements in Italy that are concerned with the field of culture, the overcoming of the status quo almost always occurs by way of opposition.

Bearing in mind this picture, we cannot help but notice that Assagioli seemed to stand out, differing significantly from such uniformity of attitudes, seeming almost not to belong to the same cultural background. The father of Psychosynthesis always cultivated an active approach, proceeding not in opposition, but positively. It is evident throughout his work how he had always consciously avoided emphasizing the negative sides or the weaknesses of a theory or movement, choosing rather to highlight the good, the positive aspects, even if he was moving past them.

This attitude, according to Tilli, is interesting from a psychological point of view. Indeed, the position of a person towards life, and hence to both self and others, changes according to the type of approach that is being made; the cultural orientation that through its thoughts is transmitted to others also changes. This is even more important in the case of founders and leaders, who are capable of giving a precise imprint on a whole research movement and the associated interpretation of reality.

Assagioli was a profound believer in the intelligent line of understanding and dialogue, without the counterproductive and argumentative attitude with which the various productions of the human being are taken into consideration. In his words[127]:

---

124   P. M. Bonacina, *L'uomo stellare*, Giampiero Pagnini ed., 1998, p. 306.

125   S. Tilli, op. cit., p. 39.

126   Ibid, p. 36.

127   R. Assagioli, *Sintesi nella psicoterapia*, presentation at the VI International Congress of Psychotherapy, London, 1964, p. 5.

"In any case, the first thing (...) would be to establish relationships of appropriate cooperation. This means first of all admitting that any point of view or partial system is valid since it offers something positive, and is invalid to the point it excludes and denies. We must admit that every school, movement, point of view or technique has its merits and limitations; therefore it is important to know, appreciate and use as many of them as possible. This would make a fruitful collaboration possible (...)"

Therefore, Psychosynthesis does not consider the different psychological schools to be in contrast with each other. It is not a matter of making a definitive choice between them. Each is valid within its defined range or scope. Psychosynthesis is an open system, in continuous interaction with all humanities and their historical evolution. We could compare it to a dynamic process which stretches horizontally, interacting with all the sciences that deal with humankind, and continually renews itself vertically in relation to its evolution, both with respect to the individual in their maturing phases and with respect to the evolution of humanity as a whole, also understood as scientific progress.[128]

Psychosynthesis is a psychology that opens in all directions with an inclusive, integral attitude, free of hermeticism and, above all, synthetic in the deep sense of the term. It offers a holistic view of humankind[129]. It accepts the contributions and assumptions of various branches of psychology, be they existential-humanistic, phenomenological, psychoanalytical, experimental, and others; but it does not do so in an indiscriminate way. These contributions are rather structured within a new and autonomous system, which constitutes the true doctrinal system of Psychosynthesis.[130]

Probably from here the accusations often arise that Psychosynthesis is a sort of "heterogeneous eclecticism" without realizing that the supposed "eclecticism" is, if anything, "systematic", since it is based on clear and stated assumptions that we can summarize:

"Psychosynthesis can be defined as recognition and activation of synthesis in all fields.
First of all, the conception of man as a bio-psycho-spiritual being.
In the cultural field as a synthesis of all the positive, constructive elements existing in each school or psychological movement, with the intent of integrating American, European and Eastern psychologies.
Finally, the integration of psychology into the whole sphere of knowledge and human activities, with other sciences, with philosophy, with religion and with art. But as in every true synthesis, without loss of the particular identity, the methods and fields of activity of each component."[131]

---

128   M. Rosselli, A. Alberti, op. cit., p. 54.

129   P. M. Bonacina, op. cit., p. 9.

130   B. Caldironi, *Seminari di psicopatologia e psicoterapia*, Claudio Nanni ed, 1992, p. 311.

131   R. Assagioli, *Psicoanalisi e psicosintesi*, op. cit., pp. 6-7.

"Both/and" instead of "this or that": herein is the guiding principle of Psychosynthesis. And this principle connects the systemic vision. Psychosynthetic theory states that every hypothesis on the human phenomenon should be inserted in a vast context and in a myriad of connected systems.

In his writings Assagioli puts the individual in a dynamic relationship directed both downward, towards the biological dimension, and upward, towards the transpersonal dimension. As I have already pointed out several times, the psychosynthetic model takes into account both sides of this relationship with the intention of their integrating. The individual becomes the hinge, the point of synthesis in which the systems of earth and sky unite.

But the psychosynthesis of the individual is just a starting point, because the fields of application of psychosynthetic practice are actually many (see Part 3, Chapter VI). It also inevitably includes just and harmonious relationships, both interpersonal and between groups. For this reason, Assagioli wrote in 1961 that often it is not enough to care for the individual alone, but also to be concerned with the environment in which they live, their family, their social group.

As a result, in addition to individual psychosynthesis (therapeutic, educational and self-developmental), Assagioli set as many fields of action as are the systems in which the human being is immersed:

- *psychosynthesis of the couple*: mutual integration based on the difference and the complementarity of the qualities;
- *interpersonal psychosynthesis*: which studies the relationships and syntheses among people, the psychological problems that exist and the appropriate methods to proceed towards harmonization;
- *psychosynthesis of ages*: with the aim of keeping the best aspects of each age alive, conscious and functioning, both internally and through intergenerational dialogue;
- *social psychosynthesis*: a study of the integration and harmonization of increasingly large groups of humans, from the couple to the whole of humanity;
- a *psychosynthesis of nations* and a *planetary psychosynthesis*: based on the fundamental principle of the interdependence of peoples.

Psychiatrists and psychosynthesists Massimo Rosselli and Alberto Alberti[132], two direct students of Assagioli, rightly emphasize that the theoretical assumptions of Psychosynthesis appear today as modern and fertile, almost as if integrating with the advancement of psychological science to better reveal their value and their practical utility. In fact, in that same Assagiolian metapsychology,

---

132   M. Rosselli, A. Alberti, op. cit., p. 54.

aspects emerge that, especially in the recent years, are found as innovative trends in psychological and therapeutic fields: on one hand, the expansion of the study of the individual in a multidimensional horizon, on the other the study of evolutionary development, no longer focused mainly on childhood and adolescence, but the entire life cycle.

Assagioli strongly supported the theoretical and pragmatic value of *synthesis*: synthesis between personal and transpersonal dimensions; synthesis between mind and body (psychosomatic concept); synthesis of opposites; interpersonal and group synthesis; synthesis in therapeutic approaches; synthesis between the various branches of science and so on. Time has proven him right. Now this trend has become a necessary movement in modern psychotherapy, leading to the broadening of horizons of different schools, to discovering greater common ground, to creation of a technical and methodological inclusivity, and the development of an increasingly targeted and individualized approach to the needs of the patient.

To emphasize, as I have done in this second part of the text, the common elements of Psychosynthesis with other movements means enhancing its intrinsic dynamic and open system characteristics, while at the same time, as I will better outline in the display of its core principles, recognizing its specific physiognomy and the strong nucleus that distinguishes it from other schools.

In the later part of his life, in an interview with American writer and philosopher Sam Keen[133] for *Psychology Today*, Assagioli answered this question in the following way:

S.K.: "What are the limits of Psychosynthesis? If you were a critic of your own system, what would you criticize?"

R.A.: "That should be your job but I will do it. It is fun. I will answer paradoxically. The limit of Psychosynthesis is that it has no limits. It is too extensive, too comprehensive. Its weakness is that it accepts too much. It sees too many sides at the same time and that is a drawback."

---

133   R. Assagioli, *Intervista con Sam Keen*, Centro Studi di Psicosintesi "R. Assagioli", Firenze, p. 19.

PART THREE

THE FRAMEWORK
OF PSYCHOSYNTHESIS

Setting and Stages of the Journey

After having placed Psychosynthesis in its position among the other major forces of psychology, in this third part I will now attempt to formulate a definition.

To this end, I will refer to the writings of both Roberto Assagioli and his students, as well as the descriptions, finally available in Italy, in the encyclopedias and in dictionaries devoted to psychological and humanistic sciences. It does not seem strange that, to a conception that is multidimensional and open to change such as the psychosynthetic, one can approach a myriad of definitions that find their common thread in the principle of synthesis.

In carrying out this task it will be impossible not to mention the *image of the individual* that drives Psychosynthesis, exemplified in the well-known Assagiolian *Egg Diagram* and the *Star Diagram of psychological functions*. I will continue by illustrating what are generally considered the *phases of the path* of Psychosynthesis that develop, starting with the delphic imperative "Know thyself!", through the phases of guidance, or mastery, and transformation of oneself. Finally, I will deal with the principal *techniques used* in Psychosynthesis and its many *fields of application*: therapeutic, self-training, social, educational, and interpersonal.

CHAPTER I

THE DEFINITIONS OF PSYCHOSYNTHESIS

1. The antecedents

Assagioli was certainly not the first to use the term *psychosynthesis*; it had also been adopted by other authors, usually indicating an approach to psychotherapy that, after correcting defense mechanisms and resistances through analytical methods, aims at the reconstruction of the personality. Freud in particular judged Psychosynthesis superfluous, maintaining that it appears by itself, as soon as the neurotic conflicts were resolved. Instead Jung highlighted it "to emphasize the constructive and prospective character of his investigative method compared to the causal procedure adopted by the Viennese master"[1].

In this sense we can say that from the beginning this term has been linked to a new image of the individual and a new methodological approach to therapy, education and self-training. For this approach, "the unconscious material cannot only be reduced, in the sense of 'redirected' to the archaic and infantile conditions of the individual as the reductive method proposes, but can also be read in a finalistic way in the sense that it anticipates possible personality developments"[2]. Adhering to this new approach were those who, among psychiatrists and therapists, began to recognize, besides the symptomatic dimension, the importance of the symbolic. Alongside the past, the importance of the future, alongside the pathology, that of health, besides limitations, impotence and conditioning, also the infinite possibility of growth and maturity, the importance of responsibility and creativity of the human being.

For his part, Assagioli began to use the word "psychosynthesis" publicly in 1926, when he wrote the book *Psychosynthesis: A New Method of Healing*. But he had already outlined the guiding lines of his thought twenty years earlier, with his articles on psychagogy. He defined his psychological system, and its therapeutic-educational-developmental practice, "Psychosynthesis" precisely to emphasize the characteristics of a holistic, integral vision. As a way of introducing the book *Principi e metodi della psicosintesi terapeutica* (*Principles and Methods of Therapeutic Psychosynthesis*) he wrote[3]:

---

1   U. Galimberti, *Psicologia*, op. cit., p. 868.

2   Ibid, p. 258.

3   R. Assagioli, *Principi e Metodi della psicosintesi terapeutica*, op. cit., p. 10.

"The word 'psychosynthesis', and expressions such as 'mental synthesis' and the like, have been used by various psychologists and psychiatrists. Limiting ourselves to the field of psychotherapy, we find Janet (1908), Neutra (1923), Bjerre (1920), De Jonge (1937), and Trüb (1935).

Freud mentioned the synthesizing function of the 'I'. But they used the word mainly in the sense of 'treatment of functional dissociation', meaning to restore the condition existing before dissociation produced by traumatic experiences or strong conflicts.

Others, like Jung who mentioned synthesis as a 'transcendental function'; Maeder (1918-1927), Caruso (1952), Stocker (1957), and Kretschmer Jr. (1958) used the terms synthesis, psychosynthesis, synthesis of the existence, synthetic psychotherapy in a broader sense, like the development of an integrated and harmonious personality that also includes the unconscious aspects of the psyche. Recently, the word 'psychosynthesis' was adopted by Lepp (1957) and Crawford (1956), as well as by R. and H. Hauser (1962).

The conception and practice of Psychosynthesis, as I conceived it, developed and practiced it for more than 50 years, while it includes those mentioned above, is in part different: wider yet at the same time more defined and more technical."

Assagioli believed that the authors who had used the term before him had done so randomly, without fully grasping the innovative potential and without fully digesting all the ideas he had developed. That's why his intention was to create a truly systematic treatise, followed afterward by a methodical application.

2. An attitude, a movement, a trend, a destination

> "Above all, Psychosynthesis (...) can be indicated
> above all as an attitude and a slow conquest towards
> integration and synthesis in every field (...).
> It could be called a movement, a trend, a
> destination."[4]

Psychosynthesis, consistent with its profoundly humanistic approach, likes to define itself as an *attitude* rather than a school or philosophy. Borrowing the words of the existential psychologist Rollo May[5] (1909-1994), we can state that it is "not a therapeutic method but an attitude towards therapy" and that "it is not in itself a complex of new techniques but an attempt to understand the structure of the human being and his experience on which all techniques must be based."

So, first of all, Psychosynthesis is a trend towards integration and synthesis innate to the psyche itself. Sebastiano Tilli writes that "in this sense it can employ

---

4   R, Assagioli, cit. in A. Alberti, *L'uomo che cura, l'uomo che soffre*, Giampiero Pagnini ed., 1997, p. 24.

5   R. May, op. cit., p. 20.

a number of techniques and methods to promote such inner movement, and has a specific orientation and a precise direction, but cannot be considered identifiable in any formally structured organization that determines orthodoxy *a priori*."[6]

Keeping this premise in mind, I will try to provide more detail and more exacting definitions.

2.1. The bio-psycho-spiritual concept

Psychosynthesis is also a conception of the individual as being bio-psycho-spiritual.[7] It is important to emphasize, as I have already pointed out elsewhere, that the term "psychosynthesis" should always be understood as an abbreviation of the more appropriate term "bio-psychosynthesis". As Assagioli[8] explained in a report to the International Conference on Psychosomatic Medicine in 1967 (see Part 1, Chapter III, Para. 2):

> "...the real name for psychosynthesis is bio-psychosynthesis. Practically speaking, it's often easier to use the word psychosynthesis, but remember that it must include the body, the "bio", and so it will always be bio-psychosynthesis."

Our author believed that it was not possible to talk about harmonious integration of personality forgetting the body. The psychosynthetic approach thus gives full recognition, both theoretically and practically, to the reciprocal relationship between body and psyche and their use in therapeutic and developmental practice.

2.2. A dynamic conception of psychic life

It has often been repeated that Assagioli's work is, in its essence, a dynamic conception of mental life, articulated around a central axis: the idea of a drive towards growth, development and transformation, understood as a propulsive element internal to the psyche. Furthermore, it is possible not only to awaken it, but also to cultivate and educate it with the appropriate means.[9] Assagioli gradually moves his interest from the logic between the unconscious and the conscious toward that between unity and multiplicity, arriving at identification of the central problem of the individual, especially in the absence of harmony, synthesis and integration.[10] Consequently, he wrote[11]:

---

6   S. Tilli, op. cit., p. 113.

7   R. Assagioli, *Psicoanalisi e psicosintesi*, op. cit., p. 7.

8   R. Assagioli, *Medicina psicosomatica e bio-psicosintesi*, Acta Medica Psychosomatica, 1967, p. 3.

9   S. Tilli, op. cit., p. 6.

10   A. Alberti, *Il Sé ritrovato*, op. cit., p. 19.

11   R. Assagioli, *Principi e metodi della psicosintesi terapeutica*, op. cit., p. 36.

"Psychosynthesis is not a particular psychological doctrine, nor a specific technical process. It is first and foremost a *dynamic*, and, it could be said, dramatic, conception of *psychic life*, a struggle between a multiplicity of rebellious, conflicting forces and a unifying center that tends to dominate them, to bring them into harmony, to use them in the most useful and creative ways.

Psychosynthesis is a *set of techniques and methods of psychological action* coordinated and aimed at promoting and helping the integration and the harmonious development of human personality. Thus, depending on its different fields of action, it is, or may become:

1. A *method of self-training and psycho-spiritual realization* for all those who refuse to be slaves of their inner ghosts and external influences, refuse to passively let the psychic forces play inside them, but want to become "lords" of their own inner realm.

2. A *method of cure for neuropsychological and psychosomatic illnesses and disorders*, the most effective when the profound cause of these ills is the struggle between conscious and unconscious psychic forces; or in one of those complex and tormenting crises that often precede spiritual awakening or some other important step in spiritual development.

3. A *method of integral education*, which aims not only to promote the development of the various attitudes of the child and the adolescent, but helps them to discover and to confirm their true spiritual nature and, under the guidance of this, to form an autonomous, harmonic, and efficient personality.

In addition, Psychosynthesis can be considered an individual expression of a wider principle, of a general law of interpersonal and cosmic synthesis."

This definition is in harmony with the fields of application Assagioli conceived for Psychosynthesis: therapeutic, self-training, inter-individual, social, and educational (see Part 3, Chapter VI). He had therefore formulated psychological, pedagogical and therapeutic theories, and Psychosynthesis can consequently be defined more or less comprehensively, depending on how much of the Assagiolian work is included within it.

2.3. A trend in modern psychology

Finally, Psychosynthesis can be termed "a trend in modern psychology that has an original theoretical systematization, a peculiar metapsychological corpus, and a corresponding and equally peculiar way of conducting therapy"[12]. Psychiatrist and psychosynthesist Bruno Caldironi[13] believes it is right to speak of "original theoretical systematization": Psychosynthesis welcomes the contributions of many

---

12   B. Caldironi, *Seminari di psicopatologia e psicoterapia*, Claudio Nanni Editore, Ravenna, 1992, p. 311.

13   Ibid.

schools of psychology and philosophy, but integrates them into a specific and absolutely original vision of humankind and life. Reflecting on an analogy coming from the psychology of perception, he states that the various contributions (the contributions of existential, phenomenological, psychoanalytical, transpersonal, and experimental psychologies) are structured to form a new *Gestalt*, an original and independent system.

The psychosynthetic metapsychological *corpus* also appears to be quite special. In fact, while accepting many of the tenets of other currents, it independently constitutes a new and different interpretation of many psychic phenomena, a particular psychodynamic view and, above all, its own personality theory illustrated in the Egg Diagram and in the Star Diagram of the psychological functions.

CHAPTER II

THE EGG DIAGRAM:
THE GEOGRAPHY OF THE PSYCHE AND ITS MEANINGS

> *In alchemy the egg indicates chaos understood and grasped by the maker, the primal matter containing the soul of the world to which it is chained.*
> *From the egg, symbolized as the round cauldron, the eagle rises, or the phoenix, the soul finally liberated (...)"[14]*

The arising, in the human mind, of the question "but who am I, really?" indicates the activation of an inner process that stimulates the individual to go in search of an answer. Psychosynthesis suggests, as a point of reference from which to start the journey of knowing oneself, a framework, "a mandala that intuitively illustrates the vision of the man it proposes"[15].

1. The limits of the diagram

Starting from a generic analogy, the psychic aspects of the human being can be considered places. This analogy was also used by Freud in his metapsychology in which he spoke of a "topography" (from the Greek *topos* = place), distinguishing three fundamental aspects: the *Ego*, the *Id* and the *Super-ego*. The psychosynthetic representation can be partially understood in this metaphorical context.

Assagioli's aim was to represent, through the graphic scheme he developed, "a multidimensional conception of human personality, certainly not perfect and definitive, but wider and more responsive to the multiform reality of what has been formulated so far."[16] He was perfectly aware of the approximation and over-simplification in this representation. But he felt that in the study of such a complex and elusive reality as psychic life, it was useful to clearly lay down some fundamental structural distinctions. Assagioli considered this scheme to be an essentially didactic tool that would provide for a clear vision of the whole, the interconnections of the various parts and their different meaning and value.

---

14   C. G. Jung, *Psicologia e alchimia*, Boringhieri, 1981, p. 206.

15   B. Caldironi, op. cit., p. 312.

16   R. Assagioli, *Principi e metodi della psicosintesi terapeutica*, op. cit., p. 22.

So, in Psychosynthesis, before presenting the Egg Diagram, one never tires of observing its intrinsic limitations and risks. First of all, by saying beforehand that any pattern with which you try to depict such a subtle and dynamic reality as psychic life can only be incomplete and inadequate. Secondly, emphasizing, as in semantics, that our words, symbols and signs are only maps, and not the territory. It is important to highlight the risk of confusing the model with reality, and of believing that the regions that it depicts have been explored only because one has intellectually studied every detail.

2. Its potential

Although Psychosynthesis openly states that the Assagiolian scheme does not do justice to the dynamic aspect of the psyche, we must add a reflection. While it is true that the "topographic" representation of psychic life offers a predominantly static, anatomical view, it is worth noting that Psychosynthesis is able to convey a dynamic image of the individual as well. This is seen in constant development, stretched between the past (the lower consciousness) and the future (the upper unconscious), moving towards the Transpersonal Self along an existential path represented by the dotted line linking the 'I' or personal self to the Transpersonal Self.[17] We can therefore maintain that the scheme proposed by Assagioli recognizes both a temporal connection between past and future, and a spatial connection between multiplicity and unity. The first generates problems solvable through a process of maturation, the second generates conflicts resolved through synthesis, unification and self-realization.[18]

That said, I think I can now put forward that the Psychosynthesis "topography", for its continuous uncovering of new senses and meanings, besides being a schematic can be considered a metaphor, a symbol. I will return to this point in the last paragraph of this chapter.

3. The Assagiolian "topography" [19]

---

17   U. Galimberti, op. cit., (p. 868) and R. Harré, R. Lamb, L. Mecacci, Psicologia - *Dizionario enciclopedico*, Ed. Laterza, 1986.

18   U. Galimberti, op. cit., p. 868.

19   The following texts have been used in the composition of this paragraph: R. Assagioli, *Principi e metodi della psicosintesi terapeutica*, op. cit. (pp. 23-26); R. Assagioli, *Lo sviluppo transpersonale*, op. cit. (pp. 26-27); B. Caldironi, *Seminari di psicopatologia e psicoterapia*, op. cit., (pp. 312-316); A. Alberti, *L'uomo che cura, l'uomo che soffre*, op. cit. (pp. 27-32) and *Psicosintesi - Una cura per l'anima*, l'Uomo Ed., Firenze, 2008 (p. 43); P. Ferrucci, *Introduzione alla psicosintesi*, op. cit. (pp. 12-16); P. M. Bonacina, *L'uomo stellare*, op. cit. (pp. 19-32); D. De Paolis, *L'io e le sue maschere*, Ed. Istituto di Psicosintesi, 1996 (pp. 13-16); S. Tilli, *Concetti della psicologia umanistica di Roberto Assagioli*, op. cit. (pp.121-123); U. Galimberti, *Psicologia*, op. cit. (p. 868); Harré, Lamb, Mecacci, *Psicologia - Dizionario enciclopedico*, op. cit.; M. L. Girelli, *Psicosintesi e*

"One can truly say that each of us, in different amounts, has developed and activated all the instincts and passions, all the vices and virtues, all the tendencies and aspirations, all the faculties and talents of humanity."[20]

I have already said that Psychosynthesis is based on an integral, complete, and multi-dimensional image of the individual, seen as a bio-psycho-spiritual being. This means that the individual is seen as a being that moves in various dimensions, always seeking the totality and completeness of theirself at all levels, from the physical-biological through the psychological, to the spiritual.[21] To illustrate this multiform reality, Assagioli proposed the following graphic:

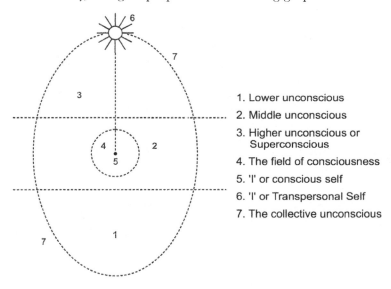

1. Lower unconscious
2. Middle unconscious
3. Higher unconscious or Superconscious
4. The field of consciousness
5. 'I' or conscious self
6. 'I' or Transpersonal Self
7. The collective unconscious

The outer ovoid includes the total biophysical individual. All lines are dotted to indicate that there is a continuous exchange of elements between consciousness and unconscious and between the various levels of the unconscious, that can be defined as *psychic osmosis*. The distinction between the various levels of the unconscious is very clear in Psychosynthesis and Assagioli proposed it in 1911 when he presented his paper *Il subcosciente (The Subconscious)*[22] at the *International Convention of Philosophy* in Bologna.

concezione dell'uomo, in *I nuovi paradigmi della psicologia*, op. cit. (pp. 172-5); Claudio Widmann, *Le terapie immaginative*, Ed. Magi, Roma, 2004.

20   H. Keyserling, cit. in R. Assagioli, *Psicosintesi - Armonia della vita*, op. cit., p. 17.

21   A. Alberti, *L'uomo che soffre, l'uomo che cura*, Giampiero Pagnini ed., 1997, p. 2

22   R. Assagioli, *Il subcosciente*, Biblioteca Filosofica, Firenze, 1911.

3.1. The Lower Unconscious

The *lower unconscious* corresponds in part to the Freudian unconscious and can be considered biopsychic. It contains the intelligent psychic activities that preside over organic life, basic instincts or impulses such as sexuality and aggressive behavior inherited from animals, unconscious habits and automatic behavior, primitive and non-dominant parapsychological sensitivity, elementary dreams and imaginative activities and the psychic past of the individual. There are also the removed conflicts, psychic complexes with strong emotional tones produced by individual and hereditary experiences and traumas of the near and remote past, and the the roots and causes of various pathological manifestations (phobias, obsessions, deliria, impulsiveness, depression and mania). Hence, if conflicts and incomprehensible complexes of the conscious personality disturb and render our lives dysfunctional, the importance of exploring its abysses.

It is important to emphasize that the term "lower" does not have a negative meaning; it is not supported by disparaging judgments about what this level of the unconscious holds, but only indicates that it is the *foundation of the entire psychological structure* and its supporting role allows for the further development of the psychic dwelling.[23]

3.2. The Middle Unconscious

The *middle unconscious* corresponds to Freudian preconscious. It encompasses the psychic present of the individual and contents of a nature similar to those of wakeful consciousness which, for the general economy of psychic functioning, one should not be constantly aware of (or contents from the "past" but easily accessible by the memory, or even "future" but as potentially viable and near in time). The middle unconscious can also be considered as the *great archive of the memory*. The material stored in it, unlike that which has been removed, resurfaces easily. At this level of the unconscious we find the elaboration of experiences made, the preparation of future activities, much of the intellectual, theoretical and practical work, as well as imaginative and psychic creation of different degrees and values.

It is necessary to clarify that the term "unconscious" is not meant to be a noun but an adjective: indeed it refers to a transient condition of certain psychic contents that are temporarily outside the field of consciousness, but at another moment, may become "conscious".

3.3. The Higher Unconscious

The *higher unconscious* is one of the most exquisitely psychosynthetic notions. It is the spiritual, *transpersonal dimension* of the individual. It encompasses the psychic future, the virtues, talents and qualities that have not yet been actuated, the

---

23   R. Harré, R. Lamb, L. Mecacci, op. cit.

potential of the individual, all the faculties of value and higher level, the broader insights, the inspirations, the impulses to altruistic action, the creativity, feelings of a unifying and synthetic nature like faith, love, courage and joy. In addition there are the ethical, aesthetic and spiritual senses, the states of enlightenment and ecstasy, noble ideals, and the higher parapsychology faculties. Hence the importance of opening up to this dimension and making contact with superconscious energies to renew and enrich our life's project and regenerate our personality.

It is perhaps appropriate to distinguish the higher unconscious from *transpersonal consciousness*. The higher unconscious refers to a dimension of which the individual is unaware here and now. Transpersonal consciousness is characterized by the persistence of a transcendent dimension for a certain amount of time in the field of consciousness.

3.4. The Field of Consciousness

Field of consciousness, a term which is not exact but is clear and comprehensible, refers to that part of psychic content with which we are directly aware in any given moment. Perhaps it is more correct to say "field of awareness of the conscious 'I'".

Its area does not have constant dimensions; rather, it is variable in that it is comprised of psychic functions (sensations, emotions and feelings, impulses, thoughts, images and intuitions) that can be perceived, observed, analyzed and consciously evaluated in the here and now. The field of consciousness is therefore susceptible to significant transformations. For example, when we concentrate intensely on some practical activity, it "shrinks"; instead on other occasions it can expand to the point of including ever vaster zones of impressions and contents.

3.5. The 'I', or "personal self"

The 'I' is often confused with the conscious personality, but it is actually something different. Psychosynthesis considers the changing contents of consciousness (thoughts, emotions, sensations, desires, images, and intuitions), distinct from the self-conscious 'I' that contains them, perceives them and observes them. This difference could be metaphorically compared to "that existing between the illuminated area of a screen ('I') and the cinematographic images that are projected onto it (the contents)"[24]. The disidentification of the 'I' from the flow of such content is considered a fundamental experience in the process of a person's psychological maturity.

The most direct and immediate manifestation of the 'I' is the irrepressible sense of personal identity that persists throughout our existence despite the developments and transformations we meet.

---

24   R. Assagioli, *Principi e Metodi della psicosintesi terapeutica*, op. cit., p. 23.

The conscious 'I' is in fact understood as that part of the Transpersonal Self immersed in the psychic contents of the human personality and in the multiplicity of existential situations. So the 'I' is a reflection of the Self with which, though veiled and blurred, has its identity in nature. The 'I' and the Transpersonal Self are in fact only one reality experienced at different levels: our true essence beyond any mask and conditioning.

3.6. The Self, or "Transpersonal Self"

The idea of a *Transpersonal Self* is not merely theoretical and generic. In Psychosynthesis, one tries to identify a phenomenology that highlights the presence and the active role of the Self in an individual's life. Hence the Self is not intended as a simple transcendental function, but as a psycho-spiritual reality of which one can have conscious experience. It constitutes the authentic essence of the individual, their true identity, their deep being. It is an evolutionary destination in time, the only valid point of orientation, and the center of synthesis and cohesion in space. The Self enables the experience of the bio-psycho-spiritual whole, it is the unifying instance, but it cannot be assimilated by this whole. It is termed "Transpersonal" because it has a dual nature: individual and universal at the same time. Indeed, as seen in the diagram, it is partially located outside the ovoid, in relation to the collective transpersonal spaces, and partly within it. In this sense, it is possible to perceive the meaning of the Self as the "bridge builder" of human existence, as the link between the individual and universal aspects of humankind, between "to be" and "being".

3.7. The Collective Unconscious

The *collective unconscious* constitutes a vast and profound psychic territory corresponding to that described by Carl Gustav Jung, though with some differences. How we are able to see the limit between this and the personal unconscious is depicted in the diagram in a permeable way. From the interpretation that Jung has given to it, the concept of collective unconscious recalls the idea of a relative inseparability between living beings. Even though individuals sometimes perceive a sense of separation and solitude, they are not really isolated beings. They are part of continuous exchanges and passages of information with the environment in which they are immersed.

For Assagioli the collective unconscious is a wide world ranging from biological to transpersonal levels, in which it is therefore necessary to make distinctions of origin, nature, quality and value. He wrote[25]:

"I must observe that Jung often neglects these distinctions; he speaks of collective unconscious and mixes in what he calls 'archaic', that is, that which originates in the collective human experience over the millennia, with what is superior, we

---

25   R. Assagioli, *C. G. Jung e la psicosintesi*, in *Corso di lezioni sulla psicosintesi*, 1966, p. 8.

would say the superconscious (...). And so Jung speaks of 'archetypes' as 'images'; but sometimes he describes them as archaic images of the race, filled with strong emotional overtones accumulated over the centuries, while at other times he speaks of them as principles, as 'ideas', and he mentions their affinity with Platonic ideas (...). From the confusion between these two meanings there are various questionable and even unsuitable consequences in the practical field (...)".

Thus, in the psychosynthetic sense, some of the contents of the collective unconscious are of a primitive and archaic character, dating back to the past (lower collective unconscious); others, however, have a complementary, evolutionary and synthetic character and concern the future potentialities of humanity (the upper collective unconscious) while still others are of a middle value, belonging to the socio-cultural situation of the present (the middle collective unconscious) and more easily accessible to what we might call the field of collective consciousness.

Psychosynthesis also has another important distinction in the context of unconscious psychic spaces, that between a conditioned or *structured unconscious* and a *plastic unconscious*, the source of an undefined capability of learning, processing, creation and transformation. I will return to this important point in the next chapter when I will deal with the model of psychological functions (see Part 3, Chapter III, Para. 4.1).

4. A proposal for change

Assagioli always considered the Egg Diagram far from being perfect or definitively complete. Indeed, in the early 1990s, some American psychotherapists and psychosynthesists, including John Firman, Ann Gila, Molly Young Brown, and Tom Yeomans questioned two issues left open by the Egg Diagram. According to them, it does not seem able to describe in a sufficiently up-to-date manner neither the understanding of the human being that Assagioli himself had envisioned, nor the experiences recorded by many patients, students and therapists, and should therefore be amended. As stated by John Firman[26]:

"Assagioli's understanding of the Self and years of observing experiences suggest a change in the original Egg Diagram representing the personality. This change proposes that the Self is not represented as limited to the higher unconscious, but pervades all the levels of human experience. With this representation of the Self two points are clarified:

1. The self is intrinsically connected to the personality and not dualistically separated from it.
2. The realization of the Self is not a question of searching for particular experiences of unity or enlightenment, but to live the calling of one's own life, that is to say dharma, the transpersonal will, in relationship to other people and the world."

---

26   J. Firman, *A Suggested Change in the Egg Diagram*, in "*Revista dell'Istituto di Psicosinte-si*", anno XII, n. 2, October, 1995

Regarding the first point, the main problem identified by Firman consists in the possible *misunderstanding of the personal self* seen as intrinsically disconnected and separated from the personality and the world. This misunderstanding, conveyed partly by the disidentification exercise, far from leading to the true liberation of the self could instead encourage devaluation of the individual's connection to and roots in the world, resulting in feelings of disorientation and alienation. However, it should be remembered that the objective of disidentification is to promote a greater awareness of the various contents of consciousness (expansion and integration oif the conscious) and not their removal (dissociation of the unconscious). The self is therefore to be considered transcendent-imminent, distinct from the contents of the consciousness and at the same time in relation with them. "In other words, while there is transcendence—the understanding that I am distinct from a particular identification —there is also immanence, an opening to many more experiences beyond that single limited identification"[27].

Secondly, the original diagram does not sufficiently underline Assagioli's intuition that *the Self is transcendent compared to all the contents and bio-psycho-spiritual processes*, even compared to the transpersonal qualities of the higher unconscious. The graphic representation of the Self, placed at the summit of the ovoid, seems to associate it only with the sublime energies of the superconscious, favoring the misunderstanding that, in order to contact the Self, we should distance ourselves from the plains of the middle unconscious and from the depths of the lower unconscious.

Contrary to this simplistic concept of the Self, many people have said they perceived its presence even in daily life, in everyday relationships, or even in the depths of despair and disintegration, lost in compulsion and dependence. These experiences reveal that the Self is such a vast presence that it cannot be limited to only the higher unconscious. In consequence it seems that the Self pervades all areas of personality (lower, middle and higher unconscious) and therefore it can also be experienced by working on the wounds of childhood, or simply by fulfilling daily tasks, and not only at the peaks of the superconscious.

Therefore, according to Firman[28], Self-realization is not to be seen as an ascent from the past of the lower unconscious to the future of the higher unconscious, but rather as a tendency towards an ever-increasing ability to take on a range of experiences that include both of these areas of personality, or rather, as an expansion of the middle unconscious.

Finally, the Egg Diagram tends to favor the confusion between *transpersonal psychosynthesis* and *Self-realization*. The first concerns the assimilation and integration of the material of the higher unconscious with the preexisting aspects of the

---

27   Ibid, p. 40

28   Ibid, p. 38.

conscious personality. The realization of the Self regards the constant relationship between the personal 'I' and the Transpersonal Self, and, depending on the path of each one, can involve work with the material of the middle and lower unconscious (personal psychosynthesis) or that of the higher unconscious (transpersonal psychosynthesis), or work on both levels simultaneously.

For Firman, the difference between transpersonal psychosynthesis and Self-realization can be metaphorically represented by the difference between falling in love and marriage. The first concerns only one aspect of the relationship, the exciting, bright and happy initial period; the second is characterized by a relationship engaged in every moment of every day of one's life, and can alternate between moments of ecstasy and unity and times of solitude and suffering. I have attempted to summarize the proposed distinctions in the following diagram:

Personal psychosynthesis	Concerns the assimilation and integration of the material of the lower and middle unconscious with the preexisting aspects of the conscious personality
Transpersonal psychosynthesis	Concerns the assimilation and integration of the material of the higher unconscious with the preexisting aspects of the conscious personality
Realization of the Transpersonal Self	Concerns the constant relationship between the personal self and the Transpersonal Self and may involve an effort of personal psychosynthesis, transpersonal psychosynthesis, or both simultaneously

5. A development proposal

At the end of the '90s, psychiatrist and psychotherapist Alberto Alberti[29], a direct student of Roberto Assagioli, suggested further elaboration of the schematic that I think is interesting to relate, not just for the suggestivity of the proposal, but also to show how the psychosynthetic ovoid is rich in stimuli and lends itself to new developments.

Alberti proposed the distinction of five directions along which the transpersonal movement of the 'I' can take place since, as he writes, "authentic spirituality is not something that really transcends man, but coincides with human totality (the Self), and is the harmonious and fruitful synthesis of the spirit with matter (body), of the mind with the heart (…)"[30]. We can therefore recognize:

1. *a descending direction*: characterized by a "deepening" movement, whereby the individual descends into their "roots", accepting their dependence on the

---

29   A. Alberti, op. cit., pp. 37-43.

30   Ibid, p. 37.

human condition and their bonds with biological matter and instincts. The feeling that accompanies this direction is the *faith* that allows us to root into human reality by opening a positive vision of life;

2. *a central direction*: characterized by a "centering" movement, which goes from the periphery to the center. With this movement, the individual is centered on theirself, discovers and becomes aware of their own identity and individual will, defines their own boundaries and places theirself in the center to guide their personality. The characteristic sentiment of this direction is *courage*, which transforms a simple person into a warrior, that is, into a human being who struggles for the significance of their existence. In doing so, they must first take possession of their own life, to distinguish it from that of others and assume full responsibility, that is, to know and recognize theirself, abandoning dependence on parents or on their expectations;

3. *a horizontal direction*: this direction is characterized by an expanding and "enlarging" movement, going from the inside to the outside, from the individual to the other. Individuals extend outwardly, seeking self-completion through union with another person and in general with other human beings. This "relational" direction could be defined both in an emotional sense and in the sense of language and communication. *Love* is the feeling that marks the enlarging movement. It transforms a simple person into a lover, i.e. into an individual who aspires to complete theirself through union with another. This finds its highest form of expression in altruistic love (*agapè*) because authentic love is not only an emotional experience but also includes a cognitive aspect; it is not only union but also empathy, listening, deep understanding, language and communication;

4. *a vertical direction*: characterized by an "ascending" movement towards the upper regions of the superconscious and Transpersonal Self. *Humility* is the feeling connected to this direction. The word humility comes from the Latin "humus", meaning earth. It pushes the roots of the individual down into the earth, and at the same time allows them to grow upward and stretch out to the heavens. Humility is to descend in order to ascend; it is not to be understood as a "means" for elevation; it is the existential reality in which one lives. If an individual establishes theirself in their reality, that is, if they have the courage to be simply "what they are" then one spontaneously grows and develops. According to Alberti the process can only be indirect;

5. *a circular direction (or of totality)*: characterized by the movement of development and irradiation of the Self, of its rhythmic and harmonic flow, which constantly vibrates and expands in relation to interdependence with the whole of life. *Beauty* is the element that allows the individual to grasp the harmony in all things. With beauty he/she penetrates into the poetic dimension of life.

And so Alberti suggests integrating and developing the Egg Diagram in this way[31]:

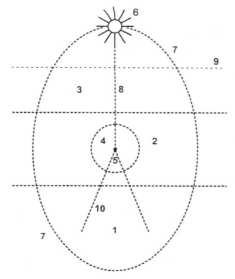

1. Lower Unconscious
2. Middle Unconscious
3. Higher Unconscious or Superconscious
4. Field of Consciousness (centrality: *courage*)
5. Conscious 'I'
6. Transpersonal Self
7. Collective Unconscious
8. "I - Self" connecting line: vertical branch of *humility*
9. "I - Others" connecting line: horizontal branch of *love*
10. Projection line of the Lower Unconscious: roots (faith, trust)

1. adding a transversal branch in the area of the superconscious representing the horizontal widening toward the other through love and language;
2. indicating the central point, which represents the 'I', as the move towards further understanding of the centrality (establishing oneself at the center of the identity), with a corresponding sentiment of courage;
3. redefining the vertical branch as an ascending movement of the 'I' towards the Self (which is also a descent of the Self towards the 'I') through the sentiment of humility;
4. adding two projections of the 'I' in the lower unconscious, meant as roots, which correspond to the sentiment of faith or trust;
5. indicating the dotted lines as "bio-psychic borders of the personality";
6. and finally, recognizing the Self as a "Moment of Synthesis", the experience of accepting a moment of intimacy and poetry in harmony with the poetry of life and the universe.

The intersection of the horizontal and vertical lines is to be considered as an experience of the Self, the best possible experience of "totality" in relation to the evolutionary phase of a given moment: spirituality is not transcendence or immanence, but simply *totality*.

---

31   Ibid, pp. 42-43.

This way of considering the Egg Diagram agrees with a vision of development structured according to diverse phases of identity definition.[32] The favorable resolution of each phase brings the development of the corresponding sentiment.

Stage of identity	Period of life*	Type of relationship	Statement	Sentiment
Unconscious, omnipotent, symbiotic	In the womb and first three months	Unconscious Self (with the totality of life)	All is, because I am	Silence, (perception of one's unlimited potential)
Dependent	Infancy	I-You (with the parents)	I am, because you are here for me	Faith, trust
Independent	Adolescence	I (with oneself)	I am here for myself	Courage
Interdependent	Adulthood	You, I-You, We (with others)	I am, because we are	Love (respect, friendship and love within the couple, compassion, fraternity)
Transdependent	Advanced age	Conscious Self (with the Other, Life, universal Reality)	I am, you are, we are, in an existing universe	Humility (harmony, synthesis, peace, joy)

* The periods of life indicate not so much a physical age, as an interior age

As is evident from the scheme in which I tried to summarize Alberti's formulations, in the stage of *omnipotent identity* (life in the womb and the first three months after birth), which corresponds to the unlimited perception of its potential, the Self is unconscious, and "expresses" itself as silence. At the stage of *dependent identity* (infancy), which corresponds to the feeling of trust, the Self expresses itself in the relationship of support and dependence on parents. At the stage of *independent identity* (adolescence and early youth), which corresponds to the sentiment of courage, the Self is established in the relationship with itself and has the need to separate from others, to become aware of its own borders, to experience its own strengths, its will and freedom to question the meaning of life in general. In the phase of *interdependent identity* (adulthood), characterized by the feeling of love and the overcoming of self-centeredness, the Self manifests itself in relationships with others, intended as adult relationships between people who each possess their own already-established identity. In the phase of *transdependent*

---

32   A. Alberti, *Psicosintesi, una cura per l'anima*, op.cit., p. 69, and A. Alberti, *Psicosintesi e oltre*, L'uomo ed., 2007, pp. 99-106.

identity, which is connected to the sentiment of humility, the Self becomes part and partaker of a larger and universal reality, of an even broader and complete entity that gives joy and meaning to the entire existence.

6. In conclusion: diagram, symbol or metaphor?

The experience of the Self is an ancient search, as ancient as humankind. Religions, philosophies and mythologies from every epoch and from every part of the planet testify to it. This search was then taken up, with different inflections, from the existential psychology of the twentieth century, from Jung's depth analysis and from the humanistic orientation; in other words, from all those who preferred to elevate themselves beyond the observing of those schemes that forced human psychology into a deforming vice. Psychology then began to open up to new horizons and to use the yardstick of symbolism to express things that otherwise could not be grasped.[33]

Even Psychosynthesis considers the symbol a superior means of knowledge as it is capable of linking thought to the imagination, which in turn is considered a fundamental function of the psyche. I believe that the profound meaning of the scheme suggested by Assagioli can be better understood in light of these reflections.

Many authors, speaking of the Assagioli's Egg Diagram, have called it a *mandala*. This definition seems to be appropriate to me since, just like a mandala, it is also a psychagogic image capable of guiding the person who meditates through the inner worlds, towards the awareness of the relationships between the different planes of reality and the experience of psychic totality. Jung turned to the image of the mandala to trace "a symbolic representation of the psyche, whose essence is unknown to us"[34]. And so did Assagioli.

6.1. The Alchemic Egg

Looking with this view at the diagram proposed by the father of Psychosynthesis, we see that the shape used to represent the entire bio-psychic essence of the individual, an ovoid, is rich with hidden meaning.

As historian of religion Mircea Eliade[35] (1907-1986) noted, in the structure of all cosmogonies, the egg is the image and model of totality. In Oriental thought

---

33   S. Tilli, op. cit., p. 68.

34   C. G. Jung, cit. in J. Chevalier, A. Gheerbrant, *Dizionario dei simboli*, Rizzoli, 1986, vol. 2, p. 58.

35   35 M. Eliade, *La naissance du monde*, Parigi, 1959, cit. in J. Chevalier, A. Gheerbrant, op. cit., p. 522.

(Hindu, Buddhist, Taoist), the theme of the Primordial Egg is closely related to the idea of the Great One, whose definition of principle is neutrality in the face of the innate duality of life, faced with Non-Becoming and Becoming, since it is a synthesis of both things simultaneously.

But if, on the one hand, the Egg symbolizes the One beyond the dichotomy Being/Not-Being, on the other hand, it is also genesis, revelation.[36] The Cosmic and Primordial Egg is One, but it encloses Heaven and Earth, the lower waters and the upper waters, the yin and the yang. In its entirety it contains the seed of all the possibilities of existence, the multiplicity of all beings. In fact, the Egg, in symbolic thought, is linked to the idea of the germinating wealth of Chaos. It is what happens to chaos as the first principle of organization, from which all differences derive. Here is why the "origins" and "principles", which the symbolic Egg accounts for, describe the transition from the One to the Multiple, from Chaos to Order, from non-existence to life. At the same time, it also symbolizes the memory of the primordial state, the return to the "matrix" of things.

Applied to alchemy, the analogical symbolism of the egg concerns the vessel in which transmutation takes place. The *athanor*, the furnace of the alchemists, was traditionally compared to the Cosmic Egg because of its shape and, above all, its role as a matrix. It represents the seat, the place of all the transmutations. C. G. Jung[37] provided an excellent summary of the symbolic relationships between the Egg and the Alchemical Work:

> "In alchemy, the egg signifies chaos, understood and grasped by the maker, the primal matter containing the soul of the world to which it is chained. From the egg, symbolized as the round cauldron, the eagle, or the phoenix rises, the soul finally liberated (...)".

As in the cosmogenies, the psychic egg contains Heaven and Earth, all the seeds of good and evil, the laws of rebirth and development of the personality.[38]

It is often told that the first Man was born from the Cosmic Egg. In many stories about the origins, he is entrusted the task of shoring up the heavens and the earth constantly threatened with disintegration. The man born from the Primordial Egg is therefore the principle of unity and synthesis; he is entrusted with the task of harmonizing the various elements that make up the cosmos.

6.2. The Tree of Life

Other authors suggest a further and evocative key to the psychosynthetic diagram overlaying the symbol of a tree, especially the Kabbalistic Tree of Life[39].

---

36   C. Amariu, *L'uovo*, Ed. Mediterranee, 1988, p. 8.

37   C. G. Jung, *Psicologia e alchimia*, op. cit., p. 206.

38   J. Chevalier, A. Gheerbrant, op. cit., p. 523.

39   P. M. Bonacina, *Appunti di un geografo su una rappresentazione dell'essere umano della*

Let's not forget that Assagioli was Jewish and that during his life he cultivated numerous friendships with the exponents of progressive Jewish thought and at the same time applied himself passionately to the study of the most diverse esoteric traditions, among which we can in no way exclude that of the Kabbalah. For this reason, it is not surprising that he himself affirmed in one of his writings to have long contemplated and derived inspiration from the psychospiritual conception of the human being borrowed from Jewish tradition.

The Kabbalah makes the tree the image of the individual. But the tradition of symbolizing the individual with a tree is universal: the plant that is born, grows and dies is assumed as the symbol *par excellence* of the human being. All the main interpretations of this symbolic theme are articulated around the central idea of a living cosmos in continuous regeneration. Therefore, the tree symbolizes life in its dynamic sense. It goes from the depths to the heavens as a means of living communication that connects the three levels of the cosmos: the underground level, by the roots that dig into the depths of the earth; the surface of the earth, by the trunk and the lowest branches; and the skies, by the upper branches, and the sun-kissed crown. The birds of the sky resting on its branches are the upper states of being. How could the analogy with the psychosynthetic schematic be anything but clear?

The tree, like the individual, is a symbol of the relationships that one can establish between heaven and earth and it is also symbol of the union between the continuous and the discontinuous: leaves, branches, roots, trunk, flowers, fruits are all connected and the tree is their unity. As on the path to self-realization, which is to coordinate multiplicity in unity, the tree represents an orderly, dynamic progression, the potential of development. Jung interpreted it as "a symbol of Self in cross-section (...), the Self represented as a process of growth"[40]. For the alchemists it symbolized the alchemical process itself, in the form of that *arbor philosophica* that the adept may have "seen" while contemplating the smoke of his alembic.

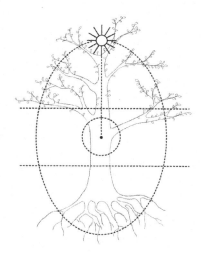

There is a very interesting tradition, confirmed by Vedic texts and by Kabbalistic and Islamic esotericism: that of the inverted tree. It seems to arrive from a specific conception of the role of sunlight in the growth of living beings who would absorb life from above, making it penetrate downward. This results in

psicosintesi, unedited manuscript, e W. Parfitt, *The Qabalist*, in "Rivista dell'Istituto di psicosintesi", anno XIV, n. 1, aprile 1997.

40   C. G. Jung, cit. in R. Cook, *L'albero della vita*, Ed. RED, 1987, p. 84.

a reversal of particularly significant images: roots penetrate into the sky, towards the sun, but have the role of the leaves while the branches stretch out towards the ground and act as roots. This inverted, unusual tree shows a cyclical movement in these descending and ascending communications and is a sign of coexistence, in the tree archetype, of the pattern of cyclical reciprocity that recalls that process of reciprocal evolution of the 'I' towards the Self and the Self towards the 'I', well described by Alberto Alberti (see Part 4, Chapter III, Para. 3). This point is also represented by the ambivalence of the symbolism of the tree that is together both phallus and womb.

In conclusion, after having noted the many symbolic values potentially implicit in the Egg Diagram, we can certainly consider it not only as a simplistic and static scheme, a "topographic", but also a true mandala, a symbol from the psychagogic function that can allude to and refer to a multitude of meanings and interpretative schemes. All this can only re-emphasize the extreme versatility, openness and dynamism of the psychosynthetic orientation.

CHAPTER III

THE STAR DIAGRAM OF THE PSYCHOLOGICAL FUNCTIONS AND THE LAWS OF PSYCHODYNAMICS

As a complement to the Egg, Psychosynthesis proposes another diagram, or rather, another mandala: the *Star Diagram of Psychological Functions*. This schematic realizes the incredibly flexible and dynamic aspect of the biopsychic constitution of the human being.

1. A comparison: the psychological functions according to Jung and according to Psychosynthesis

In dealing with the psychic functions of the individual, Psychosynthesis is very close to the Jungian conception, but it differs clearly and precisely in at least three points: imagination, instincts, and will. Assagioli gave much credit to Jung's admitting to the existence of intuition, but he also wrote:

"According to Psychosynthesis, the four fundamental functions of Jung (sensations, sentiment, thought, intuition) do not fully describe psychic life; there are other equally fundamental functions that merit emphasis. The first is the imagination; I would say that it is strange that Jung would fail to recognize the imaginative function, when instead he assigned great importance to images and symbols. The explanation lies in the fact that in his view the activity of imagination can be manifested in all other functions. But (...) I do not see how fantasy, how imagination can manifest itself in the function of sensation which is a perception, through the senses, of so-called external reality, that is through vibrations coming from the outside world.

Another group that must be taken with equal consideration are dynamic functions; this group includes instincts, tendencies, impulses, desires; in short everything that drives action. I have included desire in these dynamic activities since, when it comes to desire, only the purely subjective aspect is considered. Desire is something that one feels, an emotion that one has; (...) in reality, desire is a dynamic force that drives one to act. It has been said that it is a primordial tendency, the impetus of attraction to the non-self; in fact, in a good psychological and psychoanalytical dictionary that is compiled with objectivity (*A Comprehensive Dictionary of Psychological and Psychoanalytical Terms*), desire is considered to be something active that is also called "wanting", "craving" (wanting to possess something). (...)

Perhaps it was amazing that among these active trends he has not mentioned the will. Well, there is a fundamental difference between instincts, impulses, desires on the one hand, and will on the other (...). Will, in a sense, is something mysterious (...). I quote in this regard the English dictionary of psychological terms that I have just mentioned. Under the heading 'will' and 'voluntary activities' it says: 'Scientific psychology has not yet reached the point where it is possible to define how these terms should be used; and yet it seems impossible to do without the concept of a process of behaviors that must be called voluntary, that differ from other behaviors in various, poorly-defined ways.'...

One of the reasons for this mystery about will is that it is intimately linked to the 'I', to the center of consciousness (...); therefore, if, as we shall see, in general there is a very vague sense of oneself, of self-awareness, it is natural that there is an equally vague and indistinct sense of its fundamental function: the will."[41]

2. The Star Diagram

To represent this psychic structure Assagioli proposed the following scheme in which each of the six sides indicates "the biological structure and psychic processes of a single function"[42].

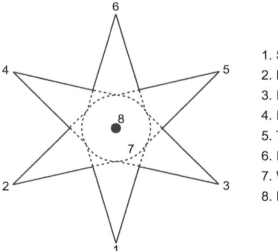

1. Sensation
2. Emotion
3. Impulse/Desire
4. Imagination
5. Thought
6. Intuition
7. Will
8. Personal self, or 'I'

1. *Sensation*: information, messages received through the senses; sensory perception of external reality, that is, of some of the impressions that come from the outside world. Its mechanism is: stimuli - sensations - perception - apperception - mental reconstruction of sensed data. Perceptions induce emotional

41   R. Assagioli, *C. G. Jung e la psicosintesi*, op. cit., pp. 3-5.
42   P. M. Bonacina, *L'uomo stellare*, op. cit., p. 44.

reactions that often alter their accuracy even to the point of misinterpreting the perceived object. Therefore, the will intervenes in managing, adjusting, and using the sensory functions to get the greatest benefit possible.[43]

2. *Impulse/Desire*: a spontaneous tendency that moves us or tends to do so; the impulses and desires are the springs that are found behind every human action. Of very different origins, nature, value and effects, there is often a contrast between the various impulses, and between them and the will, so the impulse must be recognized and examined with the greatest objectivity possible. All people are moved by a desire of some kind, from those regarding sensual pleasures to the most idealistic aspirations.[44]

3. *Emotions/Feelings*: in general one can say that the emotional elements provide energy, give life. The series of emotions include: passion, personal sentiments, aesthetic and moral sentiments, universal sentiments.[45]

4. *Thought*: ability to reason, to focus the mind's attention; it is less common and less developed than you think. Emotions, desires and imagination continually tend to pull it off course. When guided by the will and enlivened by sentiment, thought is creative.[46]

5. *Imagination*: with this function we can vividly bring objects and perceptions to the mind. Evocator and creator of visual images, but also auditory, olfactory, tactile and taste impressions. Creative imagination, based on the psychological law for which each image contains a driving element that tends to translate into action, has great importance, though not yet sufficiently recognized and used.[47]

6. *Intuition*: etymologically linked to vision and means looking internally. In its highest form it can be considered a supra-rational understanding of reality. It does not work piecemeal as does the analytical mind, but perceives a totality directly in its essence. A complete cognitive process involves the intelligent understanding of intuition, its interpretation and inclusion in the body of preexisting knowledge.[48]

The six functions crown the *will* to which the central position is attributed as the specific and privileged function of the 'I' or personal self. The close connection between will and center of self-awareness is a cardinal point of psychosynthetic theory. Assagioli wrote[49]:

---

43   R. Assagioli, *Comprendere la psicosintesi,* op.cit., p. 114.

44   Ibid, pp. 45 e 63.

45   Ibid, p. 51.

46   Ibid, p. 90.

47   Ibid, p. 62.

48   Ibid, p. 68.

49   R. Assagioli, cit. in P. M. Bonacina, op. cit., p. 44.

"At the center of the 'I' there is an active element and a passive element, an agent or actor, and a spectator. Self-awareness implies that we act as observers or witnesses of what is happening inside or outside. In this sense, the 'I' possesses no dynamics in itself, but is rather a point of observation, a spectator, an observer looking at the flow, the course of events: that is, the center of consciousness. Simultaneously, the will actively intervenes to orchestrate the various functions, forces and energies of personality, to create commitment and to solicit action in the external world."

In the center of the personality, therefore, there is a unit of observation and action, actor and spectator. According to the psychosynthetic approach, the self-regulated and finalized use of functions is possible to the extent that the 'I' has claimed a space of freedom from identification with the contents of the field of consciousness, and retaken command of the quality that more belongs to it: the will. Through it the 'I' directs, balances and regulates all other functions. The will does not directly effect the actions, but coordinates them by harmonizing feelings, emotions, impulses, thoughts, images and intuitions towards the prede-termined goal. It is important to understand this point: in Psychosynthesis, the *will* is meant as a *regulatory function independent* of other psychic elements, so that it is defined as a meta-function.

I will dedicate a whole chapter to the central theme of the will (see Part 4, Chapter IV). For now, it is enough to emphasize that this notion has nothing to do with "voluntarism".

3. The stellar individual

In his text entirely devoted to the study of this subject, psychiatrist and psycho-synthesist Pier Maria Bonacina[50] writes that in the "ideal" adult, all psychological functions would be adequately developed. In fact, the "stellar individual" knows and acts in a situation with the thought that contacts him or her, with the emotion with which he/she identifies, with the sensory perception he/she experiences, with the imagination that vitalizes him or her and with the intuition that perceives the essence that animates him or her. But it should be pointed out that if, in the-ory, the goal of harmoniously and equally developed functions is conceivable, in practice it can only be reached by approximation.

The rays of the Star are shown in the diagram as equal in dimension in order to emphasize that the functions are similar in terms of quality and quantity, significance and importance. But in truth each person has to manage non-harmonic functions. Each person has a personal development related to age, genetic factors, environmental factors, personal typology and the existential situation of a given time. The Star is therefore personalized.

---

50   P. M. Bonacina, *L'uomo stellare*, op. cit., pp. 45-46.

Again Bonacina[51] proposes to overturn the viewpoint according to which the Assagiolian ovoid is made up of the structures and processes of the individual functions. He suggests instead representing each function with its own ovoid which, by merging with the others, forms the global ovoid (see the figure below).

According to this hypothesis, the lower, middle, higher and collective unconscious and the field of consciousness are present in five of the seven psychological functions. Exceptions are Intuition and Will. Some contents occupy the field of consciousness and feed the incessant stream of what is flowing in front of the attention, while others, the majority, remain unconscious. For example, in the ovoid of the emotive function, state of mind and daily feelings cram into the field of consciousness; due to their conflicts other emotions are relegated to the lower unconscious; easily accessible feelings lie in the middle unconscious; others of higher quality reside in the upper regions; while the collective unconscious takes in the state of mind of a country, of nations and of the planet.

According to Psychosynthesis, harmonizing the functions and finalizing them towards a particular design is the goal of any psychological and educational procedure. The examination of individual functions is therefore considered indispensable in the phase dedicated to inventory of the personality. It is necessary to have an anamnesis summarizing their history and examining their meaning at all ages, their development in quality and quantity, and the chains of causes and effects.[52] All want to be educated. The initial focus is on those usually employed, followed by those that are partially experienced; later, those usually neglected will be considered; and lastly, we will turn to those which represent potential.

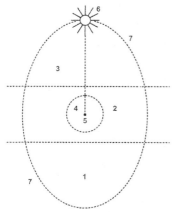

1. Emotions and sentiments which don't reach the field of consciousness, either because too primitive and archaic, or judged to be menacing and actively refused by the conscious part of the personality

2. Emotions and feelings, both positive and negative, which are easily accessible by the field of consciousness

3. Emotions and feelings of a higher, transpersonal nature, not yet accessible to the field of consciousness either through lack of maturity of an ordinary personality or because perceived to be menacing and actively refused

4. Emotions and feelings that are conscious in the here and now

5. The Personal "I"

6. The Transpersonal Self

7. Emotions and feelings of a collective origin, whether ethnic, national, or humanity in its entirety within which we find some of a primitive and archaic nature (lower collective unconscious), others linked to the socio-cultural situation of the moment (middle collective unconscious), others of a higher nature regarding the future potential of humanity (higher collective unconscious)

51   Ibid, p. 47.

52   Ibid, p. 93.

4. The Laws of Psychodynamics

From the Star Diagram shown earlier one can see that the functions are separated and distinct in each ray, while in the center part there is overlapping and blending of one into another. This emphasizes their deep connections. They do not stand alone, but cooperate constantly.

"Sensation has a movement component and movement has a sensory component, attention has an emotional foundation, emotions imply attention, thoughts have affection valence, and affections are preverbal thoughts. Functions are interrelated because the brain is a unique, indivisible phenomenon and works in syncretic and global ways. Nerve connections facilitate the reciprocal transmission of information and the mutual and constant influence."[53]

The *Laws of Psychodynamics* seen here below—formulated by Assagioli[54] in the early 1900s—find their justification in these connections and interactions. They state:

1. *Images or mental pictures and ideas tend to produce the physical conditions and the external acts that correspond to them.*

   This law reveals that every idea is an action in its latent state, and that each image has in itself a motor element. It is at the basis of all psychosomatic effects, both pathological and therapeutic, and explains the power that advertising and other subliminal persuasions exert. As we shall later see, the will can be consciously used by individuals to choose and evoke the images and ideas that will help them produce the actions they wish.

   To understand how an idea can become an action, just keep in mind some experiments conducted at Yale University, which demonstrate that imagining doing something, such as lifting a finger, requires the same mental effort as if it were actually done.[55] In both cases an electroencephalogram detects the same type of activity. This means that certain parts of our brain are activated in the same way, whether we do something, or just imagine doing it. It is therefore possible to imaginatively train to prepare for a certain activity[56]: for example, an examination, a sport, playing an instrument, having a relationship with others, dealing with a problem, and so on. All imaginative orientation techniques are an application of this law.

2. *Attitudes, movements and actions tend to evoke corresponding images and ideas; these in turn evoke or intensify corresponding emotions and feelings* (see Law 3).

---

53   Ibid.

54   R. Assagioli, *L'atto di volontà*, Astrolabio ed., 1977, pp. 43-54.

55   F. Guidi, *Iniziazione alla psicosintesi,* Ed. Mediterranee, 2005, p. 76.

56   P. Ferrucci, op, cit., p. 85.

This law reveals the meaning of behavior for the benefit of the mental states: through conscious and guided behaviors, the corresponding internal states can be developed. It is widely used, for example, by actors who evoke and intensify the atmosphere they want to create by assuming certain bodily postures and specific facial expressions. Also in yoga, Buddhism and other meditative disciplines, certain *mudra* (symbolic hand gestures) and specific *asanas* (body postures) are used to evoke certain inner states. The sacred dances of the Sufis, those of African tribes and the worship of saints are other examples of the use of certain body movements to create a certain kind of inner state. The "acting as if" technique, which consists in developing expressions, postures and attitudes that correspond to the way of being we want to evoke in ourselves, is an application of this law.

3. *Ideas and images tend to awaken emotions and feelings that correspond to them.*

The mental image is thus transformed into emotion. This law allows us to understand that being subjected to the influence of negative images and ideas means being subjected to real and true psychological smog, just as consciously cultivating images and positive ideas helps to develop the qualities that we ourselves choose to have. Wisely using this law, the will can mobilize the energy of emotions and feelings by means of appropriate ideas and images. The technique of evocative words is a systematic application of this law.

4. *Emotions and impressions tend to awaken and intensify ideas and images that correspond to or are associated with them.*

The third and fourth laws explain how commonly called "self-fulfilling prophecies" work. Based on these, retroactive function, or "feedback" is generated in emotions, which can be illustrated as follows (see also Law 1):

	Emotion/feeling	Thought/image	Physical condition
Vicious cycle	fear of illness	images and thoughts about illness	psychosomatic disturbance
Virtuous cycle	desire to get better	images and thoughts about getting better	beneficial effects on the organism

5. *Needs, urges, drives and desires tend to arouse corresponding images, ideas and emotions. Images and ideas, in turn prompt the corresponding actions* (See Law 1).

Inevitably we tend to translate what we want, more or less consciously, into thoughts, images and/or states of mind. As an example of how this law manifests itself, Assagioli points to rationalization, in which an impulse pushes the mind to find rational justifications to realize that impulse. This law is therefore very important in terms of motivation. It is also the basis of a tendency to think what is convenient for us to think: for example when we say we are not interested in something because, in reality, that thing frightens us.

6. *Attention, interest, affirmations, and repetitions reinforce the ideas, images, and psychological formations on which they are centered.*

This law is also much used by advertisers, but it can be turned to our benefit. Obviously, to obtain appreciable results, it is necessary to regularly use techniques that involve knowledge of the psychological laws. In addition, this law highlights the importance of the will that manifests itself in decision and choice: it can deliberately divert attention and interest in a negative idea-image and move them toward a positive idea-image.

7. *Repetition of actions intensifies the urge to further reiteration and renders their execution easier and better, until they come to be performed unconsciously.*

This law is connected to habits. This is important because when training and repetition bring elementary actions to an automatic level, knowledge is at the ready for more refined and creative uses. Assagioli cites the example of driving a car: initially all the driver's attention is absorbed by basic tasks such as pushing the clutch pedal to change gears and steering with the steering wheel; after a certain period of time, these functions become automatic and the driver's attention is free for other actions, such as talking to the traveling companion, thinking of what to cook when you get home or listening to something interesting on the radio.

But above all, this law is the basis for psychological habits. Indeed, the repetition, conscious or unconscious, of certain attitudes makes them habitual, that is, a constant characteristic of our personality. It is good, therefore, not to leave this process to coincidence or to external forces, and to use it wisely to develop positive habits.[57]

8. *All the various functions, and their manifold combinations in complexes and subpersonalities, adopt means of achieving their aims without our awareness, and independently of, and even against, our conscious will.*

According to this law, the mental image of the goal that is to be achieved starts an activity in the unconscious that is directed at achieving that goal. This law also reminds us that our unconscious is very powerful, and that is why our lives often take directions that are contrary to our conscious wishes.[58] That is why it is very important to cultivate an in-depth knowledge of one's inner multiplicity.

All imaginative techniques make use of this law.

---

57   F. Guidi, op. cit., p. 79.

58   Ibid, p. 74.

9. *Urges, drives, desires, and emotions tend and demand to be expressed.*

We know that the condemnation or repression of our impulses, desires and emotions is harmful and can cause various types of disturbances (psychic disturbances, muscle blockages, psychosomatic disorders). Moreover, we must not forget that every aspect of our personality, even those we do not like and which we consider to be negative, corresponds to an authentic need that has not yet found the right expression or the insufficiently developed quality. If, therefore, the expression of these instincts, impulses, and emotions is necessary, the question we have to answer is this: how can we express them in an appropriate and constructive way, or at least not in a harmful way?

10. *The psychological energies can find expression:*

- *directly*: immediately through an outburst, through a catharsis (like crying, screaming, laughing, exulting);
- *symbolically*: directing the energy, for example aggressive energy, toward an object (shaking a cushion instead of a person with whom we are very angry, or writing down anything that comes to our mind in a letter which we never send);
- *transforming and subliming*: giving the energy a higher impulse, for example transforming the sexual instinct into affectionate love and then into unconditional love; or using one's aggressive energies to fight for civil rights, or to insert more expression in one's creative activities, or to work harder on inner improvement.

As we have seen, relationships between the various functions are complex, but Assagioli[59] distinguished two fundamental types of interactions: those that occur spontaneously or mechanically, and those that can be influenced, governed, or directed by the will. Conscious use of these laws is considered fundamentally important by Psychosynthesis toward understanding transformative processes, but it should be emphasized that one must avoid the risk of it being put to the service of repression and negation of parts of oneself, or in the development of an illusory image of one's possibilities. The aim pursued is to structure ideas-images of synthesis and restoration, and certainly not to separate oneself from what one is, to take refuge in an illusory and idealized self-image. For this reason, the laws of psychodynamics are usually utilized only in the last part of the path, the phase of self-transformation, after acquiring a sufficient level of knowledge, acceptance and mastery.

4.1. "Everything is food": the plastic unconscious

The laws of psychodynamics are closely connected to another salient point of the psychosynthetic approach: the distinction, within the unconscious psychic

---

59   R. Assagioli, op. cit., p. 43.

spaces, between the conditioned, *"structured" unconscious* and the unstructured, *"plastic" unconscious*. Assagioli wrote[60]:

> "In classical psychoanalysis, the emphasis is on the first, (...) but there is a large portion of the unconscious which is *not* thus conditioned; it is plastic, and its susceptibility to being influenced makes it like an inexhaustible store of unexposed photographic film. The conditioned unconscious, on the other hand, can be compared to an accumulation of already exposed film. In this respect we are like motion-picture cameras functioning uninterruptedly, so that at every moment a new section of the sensitive film is receiving impressions of the images which happen to appear before the lens."

In support of this thesis, psychotherapist and psychosynthesist Piero Ferrucci[61] mentions the experiments conducted several years ago by neurophysiologist and Nobel Prize-winner Wilder Penfield. During brain surgery (performed without total anesthesia), he stimulated some brain cells: at each stimulation, the patient vividly remembered certain episodes of his life that were insignificant and, apparently, forgotten. It seems therefore that everything really is recorded.

The Hindus say: "*Sarvam annam*, everything is food"[62]. Food is not our only nutriment; we also feed on all kinds of impressions and influences: sound and visual vibrations, landscapes, architectural proportions, combinations of shapes and colors, odors, harmonies, musical rhythms and all the ideas, images and feelings with which we come in contact. All this, absorbed mechanically and without real attention, has made up our being and continues to shape it. Just as our body continuously absorbs vital elements, in the same way our unconscious absorbs elements from the psychological environment. It incessantly breathes and assimilates psychological 'substances' that, by their nature, will have beneficial or harmful effects on us.[63] We should then feel a little more responsible for the stimuli to which we expose ourselves.

The plastic unconscious is thus a wide area open to any kind of impression. It is a tremendous reserve of psychic energies, undifferentiated, hidden in everyone who provides the opportunity to absorb new stimuli, who transforms, learns, processes and creates. Psychosynthesis considers this infinite malleability of the psyche a wonderful resource, a precious treasure. In fact, the new impressions received by the unconscious do not remain static, but act in accordance with the laws of psychodynamics set forth earlier.

We can therefore learn to use these influences consciously and wisely, to construct in ourselves the attitudes and qualities that we choose to have. We can learn to cooperate with the plastic unconscious by using appropriate methods and by learning the rhythms and laws governing it.

---

60   Ibid, p. 44.

61   P. Ferrucci, op. cit., p. 41.

62   R. Assagioli, op. cit., p. 44.

63   Ibid.

CHAPTER IV

KNOW, MASTER, TRANSFORM YOURSELF: THE IMAGE OF THE INDIVIDUAL AND THE IDEAL STAGES OF THE PSYCHOSYNTHESIS PROCESS

1. The image of the individual

The Egg Diagram, the Star of Psychological Functions, and the Laws of Psychodynamics give life to a peculiar concept of the individual "as an incomplete being, driven by a feeling of emptiness, of insufficiencies, of separation and nostalgia for a lost unity"[64]. Assagioli[65] describes this situation with a beautiful image:

> "Every human being feels constantly driven to affirm themselves, to grow; everyone feels, except for short periods of fleeting and illusory fulfillment, perpetually dissatisfied. Man feels that he is missing something, that he is not what he should be; he is pervaded and flailed by the turmoil that was admirably expressed by Homer the blind seer, in the myth of Ulysses: a restless hero running throughout the world, 'chasing his soul turned into a siren.'"

The father of Psychosynthesis does not try to understand human beings by uprooting them from their world and the environment in which they are immersed, denying their opening or self-transcendence.[66] Psychosynthesis sees the individual as a being of a profound dynamism, or, as Assagioli himself says, of a profound dramatic nature: in constant struggle between the past and the future, between static, regressive tendencies and dynamic, progressive tendencies. This tension arises from the evolution of chaotic multiplicity toward unity, from separatism toward union, from the unconscious toward the conscious, from inertia toward activity, from oppression toward freedom.[67] A gradual process, it leads from initial disorganization, through increasingly broad and inclusive synthesis and integrative stages, to a continuous expansion of the boundaries of the sense of identity

---

64   U. Galimberti, op. cit., p. 868.

65   R. Assagioli, *Psicosintesi - Armonia della vita*, op. cit., p. 138.

66   L. Peresson, op. cit., p. 27.

67   A. Alberti, *Il Sé ritrovato*, op. cit., p. 20.

that ideally tends to comprehend the totality of the psychological elements that make up the individual. The psychosynthetic approach therefore proposes the image of a human being "on the road", oriented towards their self-realization, moving through time and space, in search of their own Self, which is a purpose and evolutionary goal in time, center of synthesis and cohesion in space.

Using another metaphor, we can say that the individual is a warrior, a mythical hero struggling in the search for the meaning of their life, finding it in the realization of the Self. And, as psychiatrist and psychosynthesist Alberto Alberti writes[68]:

> "The meaning of each single existence seems to be that of discovering (or rediscovering) and expressing the sense and the value of one's own individual task, placing it in harmonious relationships with others and all of humanity, and in tune with the sense of one's entire life."

Every single person takes a path to their deeper self that is simultaneously a path towards others. Each one, in order to find theirself, must become aware of their totality, which necessarily includes the awareness of their participation in the human totality. For this reason the individual, moving towards theirself, moves toward the other, toward others and all humankind, because "it is basically a relationship."[69]

This "being a relationship" brings one to discover that one's difficulties are similar to those of other human beings; one can free oneself of the erroneous, anguishing idea that one is abnormal and basically alone. Assagioli said[70]:

> "We all have the same fundamental problems, the same labors, the same tasks, the same path to walk, the same destination to reach. Feeling this solidarity and brotherhood is good: it tranquilizes, prevents us from feeling as if we're ill, eases excessive worrying and imparts a just sense of proportion."

The psychic function that the individual employs to walk this existential, sometimes easy, often arduous and tiring journey is the *will*. It is the fundamental experience of human life. It is that experience which allows the individual to make the crucial passage from a vision of oneself as an impotent object that passively experiences the events of life, to a view of oneself as a subject capable of self-determination, of choosing, of assuming responsibility, able to act freely and creatively to make changes and transformations.

The psychosynthetic approach considers this creative and positive approach as characteristic of the deeper essence of the human being. Assagioli maintained that from the repression of it derive frustration, depression, and anger. A fulfilled individual is indeed one who feels free in facing the tasks of life, free to participate creatively in one's own existence.

---

68   Ibid, p. 184.

69   Ibid.

70   R. Assagioli, op. cit., p. 105.

2. The keys to the psychosynthesis process

The individual with a psychosynthetic vision, like the mythical Ulysses, is afflicted with an unquenchable thirst for knowledge that "drives him to examine distant, immense worlds or even the simplest form of life swimming in a drop of water"[71]. This drive cannot leave one indifferent in the face of the unknown one harbors inside oneself, facing the central mystery of existence.

For this reason, Assagioli felt it strange and dangerous that modern individuals had studied the outside world as well as their own bodies with so much interest, courage and sacrifice, ignoring the exploration of the inner world, the knowledge of one's own nature as a human being; that humankind had come to know the mighty forces of nature while ignoring the forces that exist in and agitate the soul, so often letting these overwhelm and dominate the individual.[72]

The modern Ulysses, driven toward self-awareness, finds him or herself on an arduous voyage not just motivated by a thirst for knowledge and a fascination with mystery, but also for more personal, urgent reasons. The father of Psychosynthesis wrote[73]:

> "We try to bring light, order, harmony to ourselves. We try to recognize, amongst the innumerable thoughts, feelings, impulses, those that are the expression of our truest and deeper being, and those that come instead from external pressure or by instinctive tendencies, and we strive to suppress and eliminate those we recognize as not ours and not worthy of our attention. But we must acknowledge that such attempts are often unsatisfactory (...) For these practical reasons, therefore, it obliges not only a special class of scholars, but also all those who want to live in awareness, who want to be masters and not slaves in their own internal dwelling, the knowledge of themselves."

Assagioli believed this research was not just useful, but necessary. Firstly, to truly understand human nature, secondly to become "masters in our own house", and finally to modify and transform ourselves, to spark and encourage the process of change. These three purposes are summarized in the phrase that inspires all psychosynthetic work:

Know, Master, Transform Yourself

However, it is important to specify that in no way are these three stages to be considered in a strict chronological sequence. They constitute the ideal moments, distinct but not separated, of the path of Psychosynthesis. We could imagine this path in a circular way: know a part of yourself, master it, transform it and

---

71   Ibid, p. 85.

72   R. Assagioli, *La conoscenza di sé*, in *Corso di lezioni sulla psicosintesi*, manuscript, 1973, p. 1.

73   R. Assagioli, *Psicosintesi – Armonia della vita*, op. cit., p. 87.

then go on to another part of yourself, and so on. Assagioli loved saying that Psychosynthesis is a process that never ends. I have attempted to represent this process in the following diagram:

2.1 Know yourself: the double meaning of the Delphic imperative

"*Know yourself*" does not just mean "analyze your thoughts and feelings, examine your activities"; it means: "discover your most intimate Self, your true being, understand its wonderful potential"[74]. Assagioli's great credit was to try to harmonize the Greek interpretation of the above-mentioned imperative with the more transcendental Oriental meaning, which, since it has not yet suffered the "ego problem", relates "know yourself" to a Self uncontaminated by time, devoid of any historical dimension and ambiguity.[75] As always, Psychosynthesis is not so much about choosing between two possible ways of understanding the same process as referring to two distinct moments of one's journey towards self-knowledge.

But where to start? Assagioli proposes the general rule "from the known to the unknown", that is, from the surface of what appears phenomenologically to the mystery beyond such appearance. It is therefore considered appropriate to start from what is directly accessible to observation, from an examination of the conscious aspects of personality, and then to extend the investigation to the unconscious aspects. In order to truly know ourselves, it is not enough to know only the conscious aspects; a long exploration of the vast regions of the unconscious, in all its dimensions (lower, middle and high) is also indispensable.

The basic attitude that allows this exploration consists of taking the internal position of the observer or spectator; in other words, it is considered crucial to develop the ability to distance oneself cognitively from what is observed. This distancing leads to the discovery of the difference between the changing contents that move in the field of awareness and whoever is able to perceive and observe such a change. This "disidentification" of psychic content is, as we shall see, one

---

74   Ibid, p. 90.

75   D. Demetrio, *Manuale di educazione degli adulti*, Ed. Laterza, 1997, p. 204.

of the fundamental techniques of Psychosynthesis, an essential premise to gain access to the subsequent phases of mastery and self-transformation.

Cognitive distancing has the purpose of knowing oneself in all possible dimensions: the knowledge of one's own past history and of one's present existential situation, of the conscious and unconscious aspects of one's self and one's own potential and weaknesses, of one's abilities and deficiencies, of the innate multiplicity that characterizes us, and of the unity that comprises it. I will deal in detail with the numerous techniques that Psychosynthesis employs for this purpose in the next chapter.

2.2. Master yourself

What follows the work of exploration and discovery of our inner life are the tasks of taking possession of it, acquiring *mastery* of the various forces and the various elements that live and work inside us. This work is based on the following fundamental principle formulated by Assagioli[76]:

"We are dominated by all with which we identify ourselves.
We can manage and use all from which we disidentify ourselves."

If the phase of self-awareness leads to the discovery of the passive dimension of the self, considered a spectator of psychic life, the next stage of mastery involves the *activation* of its dynamic qualities and *of the will*. Instead of being manipulated by conscious and unconscious elements, the self, after being distanced from them and having known them better, can implement strategies for managing and mastering them.

The psychosynthetic approach considers mastery as the ability to strengthen or weaken, to momentarily and consciously assert or inhibit (not suppress!), to express or contain, develop or ignore the various aspects of ourselves depending on the moments and situations of life.[77]

Perhaps one can ask how the relationship between mastery and spontaneity is considered. It may seem paradoxical, but it is actually the ability to manage oneself which makes it possible to achieve a more authentic spontaneity. Indeed, for Psychosynthesis, true spontaneity is more than the worship of self-expression, an abandoning of any emotion, impulse, or whim: "it is the expression of our deeper and more true being"[78]. Rather than unknowingly or forcibly playing roles and putting on masks, we can choose the roles and masks that really represent us, inhabit them, animate them from within, eliminate them as the disguises we hide

---

76   R. Assagioli, *Principi e metodi della psicosintesi terapeutica,* op. cit., p. 28.

77   P. Ferrucci, op. cit., p. 71.

78   R. Assagioli, *Comprendere la psicosintesi,* op. cit., p. 121.

behind; we can instead make them modes of expression that we can use to reveal ourselves, our true face.

2.3. Transform yourself

Closely related to the ability to manage oneself is the magnitude of the change. In Psychosynthesis, *transformation* has great importance: all work in Psychosynthesis is aimed at this purpose. Some of the requirements considered indispensable to accessing one's transformative potential are: experience, comprehension, acceptance and learning to die.

Experience

First of all, Psychosynthesis maintains that only a real experience, a truth really experienced at all levels of existence that goes beyond the abstract idea, has the power to transform the individual. By paraphrasing Rollo May[79] we can state that there is no truth or reality for a living human except that determined by their participation, their awareness, and their relationships with it.

Comprehension

After experience comes comprehension. Assagioli wrote[80]:

"First of all we need to understand what we have found in ourselves. Comprehension has a transforming and liberating power that is generally not understood at all. Comprehension means realizing the true nature of a phenomenon; its origin, its function, its limits, its possibilities, the gifts it can give us, the dangers it carries. (...) Understanding an affection or a desire in a different way is to transform it."

Comprehension requires courage, honesty, as well as willingness to face one's emotional and sentimental illusions and the preconceptions and prejudices that may have been accepted without reflection.

Acceptance

Closely related to comprehension is acceptance, considered by Psychosynthesis as an indispensable condition for real growth. Psychologist and psychotherapist Daniele De Paolis[81] writes that the work of self-awareness and comprehension will serve very little if not followed by acceptance. True acceptance has enormous dynamic potential that can release much of the individual's creativity. Acceptance means an end to the struggle against oneself, an interruption of the mechanism of repression. Acceptance, rather than a technique, is understood as a gradual

---

79   R. May, op. cit., p. 19.

80   R. Assagioli, *Psicosintesi – Armonia della vita*, op. cit., p. 111.

81   D. De Paolis, op. cit., pp. 71- 75.

process of continuous progress that comes to show us our original face. The total acceptance of ourselves is an act of courage and humility that has the power to lead us to the experience of the totality of our essence. Alberti writes[82]:

"Knowing and accepting ourselves, showing ourselves as we really are allows us to design our identity (...). Providing a definition of ourselves, we open ourselves to the opportunity to change. In this way we truly enter life."

But we must be careful not to confuse acceptance with resignation: the latter is static and doesn't allow change; instead, the former is dynamic, an active movement that makes change possible. Here below is a summary of the differences:

RESIGNATION	ACCEPTANCE
Passive	Active
Static	Dynamic
Anchored to the past	Honors the past and present and looks toward the future
Generates feelings of impotence and frustration	Generates feelings of capability and satisfaction
Leads to a refusal of oneself	Leads to love for oneself
Effects: closes, hardens and fossilizes our being	Effects: opens, expands, softens and transforms our being

Acceptance not only has nothing to do with a passive attitude towards oneself and the world, but is rather the indispensable condition for change and growth. If we do not accept the reality of what we live and who we are, we forego the possibility of confronting ourselves with the parts of our being that require transformation. We are faced with a paradox: acceptance of what I am is the condition for change, while the negation of what I am leaves me stuck in my behavior.

Learning to die

Learning to die is perhaps the fundamental requirement of the transformative process. This means that we must find in ourselves the courage and the confidence to fully enter into pain, darkness and chaos. Symbolic and ritual death is a process that is found in many spiritual traditions and in many initiatory rites. Death always turns out to be the obligatory passage that allows the new, purified individual to experience rebirth, renewal of the entire psyche, emergence of new ideas and new attitudes, change and transformation.[83]

Techniques to help the transformation

---

82   A. Alberti, op. cit., pp. 90-92.

83   P. Ferrucci, op. cit., p. 103-104.

Psychosynthesis maintains that transformation is not just a spontaneous fact; it can be favored by the use of some specific techniques, for example by an act of creative imagination, in which a person creates a new image of theirself and chooses to conceive it in a concrete and persistent way. Where efforts, impositions, and good intentions achieve nothing, a simple act of imagination is decisive. Transformation can therefore be facilitated and directed, provided that:

1. we have the image of the final result, not the way to get there;
2. what we imagine must be compatible with our true nature.[84]

I will return to the use of these techniques both in the next chapter and in the fourth part of the book, entirely dedicated to the fundamental experiences of Psychosynthesis.

---

84   Ibid, p. 107.

CHAPTER V

PSYCHOSYNTHESIS TECHNIQUES

1. The differential approach: for a global vision

In Psychosynthesis it is highly important to be aware of the purpose and aim of the various techniques that we intend using. Indeed, these techniques are to be considered only tools, means to an end. As Assagioli wrote[85]:

> "Even though we employ the existing techniques in the best way possible, we must always keep in mind that they alone are not enough; as L.W. Dobb reminded us, 'the technicians have a tendency to be very fond of their psychological weapons, to the point of being corrupted by them.'"

According to our author this risk of corruption in Psychosynthesis is avoided in the following ways. First of all, the very number and variety of the techniques prevents us from assigning an excessive value to any one of them. Secondly, by continually focusing on the "spirit of synthesis", that is, on the constant commitment of each particular task toward the whole with which it is interacting. Finally, of particular importance is the emphasis on the core value of the human factor, of the dynamic and personal relationships between the individuals involved in the given therapeutic, educational or formative relationship.

> "We use a pragmatic approach and basically strive to respond to the direct needs of the patient, to meet them on the grounds of their more immediate and urgent issues (…). Practically speaking, we don't have a rigid system; it is a response to the real needs of the unique situation of each patient in each phase of their existence."[86]

And so, the answer to the question "*Which techniques are utilized in Psychosynthesis?*" the only answer can be: "*Those most suitable.*" In truth, this answer takes in a significant number of aspects. Bruno Caldironi[87] specifies that the techniques used must first be suitable for that particular person or group, and also suitable for the therapist or coach, and finally suitable for the moment. Psychosynthesis holds that every person, every situation in life and every interaction is unique and cannot be defined once and for all.

---

85   R. Assagioli, *Principi e metodi della psicosintesi terapeutica*, op. cit., p. 67.

86   R. Assagioli cit. in J. Firman e A. Gila, *La ferita primaria*, op. cit., p. 187.

87   B. Caldironi, op. cit., p. 320.

And it is well to be aware that the various phases of a therapeutic, educational or self-training project are also different, sometimes even contradictory, and therefore require different interventions. So a certain technique may prove to be useful in one case and not adequate, or even counterproductive, in other cases. It is therefore clear that each technical intervention needs to be carefully calibrated based on the characteristics that present themselves at a given time.

According to Psychosynthesis, *combining techniques* is extremely useful and is in no way difficult. Although Assagioli described them separately for instructional purposes, he proposed combinations of many of them for specific exercises. He made a precise distinction between techniques, exercises and methods. He considered a *technique* as a specific psychological process, applied to produce a certain effect on some aspect or some function of the psyche. An *exercise* consists instead of combining various techniques in order to produce a more general effect. Finally, a *method* is defined as a combination or an alternation of techniques and exercises used in a specific succession according to a defined program, with the aim of achieving the pre-established therapeutic, educational or formative goals.[88]

Among these purposes, the highest is gaining awareness of the Transpersonal Self; but first "it is necessary to help the subjects eliminate existing obstacles and conflicts, to integrate and harmonize the personality at all levels, and then, whenever possible, promote the union between the 'I' and the Self"[89]. I therefore reiterate that the general plan of intervention must always be kept in mind, to which every method, exercise or technique must be subordinate.

2. Classification of the techniques

In the attempt to classify the techniques used in Psychosynthesis one finds oneself in a truly embarrassing position. As I mentioned previously, we can say that all the techniques considered useful in a given situation are employed. In his book *Psychosynthesis, a Manual of Principles and Techniques* Assagioli listed over fifty that can be divided as follows[90]:

1. Inventory phase
2. Exploring the unconscious: the analytical techniques
3. Techniques for personal psychosynthesis
   Techniques of mastery
   Techniques of transformation

---

88   R. Assagioli, op. cit., p. 66-67.

89   Ibid.

90   R. Harré, R. Lamb, L. Mecacci, op. cit., M. Rosselli, *Introduzione alla psicosintesi*, Ed. Istituto di Psicosintesi, Firenze, pp. 29-30 and P. Guggisberg Nocelli, *Conosci, Possiedi, Trasforma te stesso - Una raccolta di strumenti pratici per l'armonia interiore, lo sviluppo del potenziale e la psicosintesi personale e transpersonale*, Ed. Xenia, 2016.

4. Techniques for transpersonal psychosynthesis

5. Other techniques

   Expressive and anchoring techniques
   Relational techniques
   Further techniques

2.1. Inventory phase

One of the prerequisites for the implementation of Psychosynthesis is to acquire as much knowledge as possible on the conscious and unconscious aspects of one's own personality. Assagioli recommended starting an inventory of conscious aspects, though their distinction from the unconscious is obviously only relative. The *inventory phase* aims to foster the *definition of a person's identity* with the consequent strengthening of the conscious personality, a premise for the proper assimilation of the unconscious aspects.

In this phase, inventory mainly refers to the patient's past, and the techniques used can be the following:

1. autobiography

2. biography

3. diary

4. inventory of the origins of the psychological characteristics:
   a) individual characteristics
   b) family influences
   c) collective, racial, national, class or social, group influences

5. inventory of polarities, ambivalences, and conflicts

6. inventory of the sub-personalities

7. inventory of the characteristics belonging to previous psychological ages

8. questionnaires

9. inventory of higher aspects (conception of the world, philosophy of life)

2.2. Exploration of the unconscious: analytical techniques

Analytical techniques are used to *evaluate blocks and potentials of the personality*, permitting the exploration of the unconscious, and getting to the roots of psychological complexes.[91] They are:

1. word association (Jungian method)

2. free association (Freudian method)

---

91   Ibid.

3. dream interpretation/analysis

4. projective and expressive techniques
   a) Rorschach
   b) Thematic Apperception Test (T.A.T.)
   c) modeling
   d) musical improvisation
   e) spontaneous movement, etc.

5. guided imaging (reve eveille)

6. free drawing

7. hypnosis

2.3. Personal psychosynthesis techniques

The full awareness and understanding of damaging images and complexes can help to dispel them but not necessarily bring about a positive, permanent change. According to Psychosynthesis, the cognitive work must be accompanied by a gradual and active exercise of all functions (sensation, impulse/desire, emotion/feelings, imagination, thought, intuition and will). The techniques employed are the following:

Techniques of mastery

In this phase particular attention is given to the *discovery of the personal self* and the importance of *cultivating the will* as a skillful agent capable of harmoniously coordinating the various aspects of the personality.[92] The techniques employed are:

1. catharsis
   a) recalling and "re-living" events
   b) verbal expression
   c) writing (symbolic satisfaction and outpouring)
   d) diary
   e) muscular discharging

2. critical analysis

3. disidentification and self-identification exercises

4. techniques for developing the will
   a) mobilizing energies
   b) performing useless actions
   c) exercising the will in daily life
   d) physical exercises for training the will

---

92   Ibid.

Techniques of Transformation

After comprehension and mastery we have the change and transformation step. This phase can bring about a reversal of values and other profound developments. In this stage, visualization is especially important in that it has the power to produce significant psychological and behavioral changes. The theoretical final goal is the *reconstruction of the personality* around a new and wider center of synthesis.

1. training and using the imagination
2. visualization (reproductive and creative)
3. evocative listening/hearing
4. imaginative summoning of other sensations
5. the psychosynthesis plan
6. the Ideal Model
7. use of symbols

2.4. Transpersonal psychosynthesis techniques

Assagioli considered attainment of personal psychosynthesis a satisfactory result, but he believed that for a number of people this level represented only a stage in their potential development. For these individuals, Psychosynthesis proposes a different solution, an even broader type of synthesis: transpersonal. This stage involves the *exploration of the higher unconscious* and, where feasible, the *realization of the Self*. The techniques suggested are in part the same used for personal psychosynthesis, but are used for different goals:

1. use of symbols
2. exercises for transpersonal psychosynthesis:
   a) exercise on the legend of the Holy Grail
   b) exercise based on Dante's Divine Comedy
   c) exercise on the blossoming of a rose
3. technique for the development and use of intuition
4. exercise to summon interior qualities and higher sentiments (serenity, love, joy, service...)
5. technique for imaginative evocation of interpersonal relationships
6. meditation techniques:
   a) reflexive meditation (concentration)
   b) receptive meditation (inner silence)
   c) creative meditation (creative use of the power of thought and imagination)
7. contemplation techniques
8. techniques for inspiration

2.5. Other techniques

Expressive and anchoring techniques[93]

Although transpersonal experiences can be beautiful and satisfying, Psychosynthesis considers anchoring these experiences to the plane of personality of primary importance. It also does not consider higher states of consciousness a guarantee of effective psychological functioning. Indeed, such experiences, if used and interpreted badly, can cause problems, and even real pathologies. The psychosynthetic approach therefore attempts to *harmonize* the *personal dimension with the transpersonal dimension* in the human being, thereby enabling effective translation of new acquisitions at all levels (physical, emotional, mental, relational).

Relational techniques[94]

Psychosynthesis considers interpersonal relationships the natural counterpart of individual growth. Individuals can learn to face the common obstacles in human relationships, and learn how to cultivate *interpersonal qualities* such as openness, love, and empathy, acquire new *communication skills*, and develop the awareness of belonging to a greater whole. Below is a list of some of the techniques used to facilitate these acquisitions:

1. group analysis
2. psychodrama
3. coordinated group activity
4. role playing
5. techniques for developing cooperation
6. techniques for eliminating prejudices

In addition, many techniques used in personal psychosynthesis can also be used in groups with the appropriate adaptations.

Further techniques

Here is a list of special techniques not previously mentioned:

1. acceptance technique
2. "acting as if" technique
3. bibliotherapy
4. body integration
5. development of concentration:
   a) internal
   b) in action

---

93   Ibid.

94   Ibid.

6. chromotherapy
7. music therapy:
   a) listening
   b) expression
8. play therapy
9. graphotherapy
10. logotherapy
11. technique for development of a sense of the right proportions
12. relaxation techniques (Autogenic Training, etc.)
13. substitution technique
14. suggestion and autosuggestion
15. technique for the synthesis of opposites
16. technique for transmutation and sublimation of aggressive sexual energies
17. humor technique

As can be seen in this chapter, the systematic use of numerous active techniques is a peculiar feature of Psychosynthesis. This approach also aims to be an answer to the emphasis placed by classical therapeutic and training methods exclusively on the verbal level and on the individual dimension. The psychosynthetic perspective underscores the need to overcome these limitations and widen the range of intervention to *work on the body* on the one hand, and the *interpersonal and transpersonal* on the other.

As Bruno Caldironi[95] emphasizes, it is clear that describing, or even just listing, all the techniques involved in Psychosynthesis is impossible. Many have been developed within Psychosynthesis, while even more that have been accepted and used in Psychosynthesis have been developed by other schools. In any case, all can be considered valid to the extent that they help to transform the personality, develop deficient aspects, scale back those that are overblown, and create, wherever possible, harmony, balance and integration.

Obviously, each therapist or educator will use only some of the techniques listed, those that conform more to their way of working.

---

95   B. Caldironi, op. cit., p. 320.

CHAPTER VI

FIELDS OF APPLICATION OF PSYCHOSYNTHESIS

Psychosynthesis is first and foremost a method and practice that addresses the individual seeking Self-realization; therefore it does not have a single scope of application. Although it first emerged as a method of curing neuropsychiatric disorders, it then extended its applications to the educational field (familial and scholastic) and also to self-training or psycho-spiritual development. It was subsequently used to help deal with the problems regarding interpersonal and social relationships (between spouses, parents and children, between various human groups, between nations and extended to the whole of humanity).[96] In this context, *five principle fields of application* are discussed[97]:

1. *personal integration and self-actualization*: aimed at individual personal growth, regardless of professional position and existential situation;
2. *educational*: in effect, the area of education in general, both scholastic and for the permanent education of the adult;
3. *therapeutic*: geared toward situations of suffering or pathologies in a broad sense, for which one of the more specific applications is psychotherapy and, in a more specific sense, psychosomatics for doctors who accept the interaction between body and mind;
4. *interpersonal*: concerning the relationship between two people, of which a typical form is psychosynthesis for the couple, but can also be used for parents and children, teachers and students, managers and employees, etc.;
5. *social*: applications for various types of groups and situations: from psychosynthesis for the family, or groups within society, to groups of planetary dimension.

Assagioli also recalled that "for each field, it is important to distinguish between the personal and transpersonal dimension"[98].

---

96   R. Assagioli, *Psicosintesi - Armonia della vita*, op. cit., p. 13.

97   M. Rosselli, *Introduzione*, in *I nuovi paradigmi della psicologia*, op. cit., p. 277.

98   R. Assagioli, *Gli orizzonti della psicosintesi*, presented at the Riunione dei Centri Italiani di Psicosintesi, 1973.

1. The implications of an integrative view of Psychosynthesis applications

Distinguishing these different fields of application does not mean that there are five models of Psychosynthesis: there is only one Psychosynthesis, and only for clarity do we talk about therapeutic, self-training, educational, interpersonal and social Psychosynthesis. They are different variations of the same central idea which consists, on the one hand, in the general approach to the bio-psycho-trans-personal model of the individual, and, on the other, in its technical specificity. Psychiatrist and psychosynthesist Massimo Rosselli[99] writes that psychosynthetic applications are a way to enrich and diversify styles and methods, as each field has developed its own techniques and specifics, while new applications are constantly emerging in relation to the most diverse contexts and cultural changes.

The importance of the different applications is to confirm the *pragmatic nature* of the psychosynthetic conception, the *systemic vision* that it has of the human phenomenon and the attention of Assagioli to the individual in their entirety. In fact, a fundamental feature is that, in every field, one takes account of the others. So the therapeutic approach, the educational and the self-training approach constantly communicate with and complement each other; and in each individual path the interpersonal and the social dimensions are also present, and vice versa.

This is because Psychosynthesis, which does not believe in a clear distinction between body and mind, between health and illness, also does not believe in the existence of a true antithesis between what is individual and what is social, between individual distress and social distress.

So one can say that "if the therapy leads to the integration and pacification of a suffering person", placing them in a position to assume responsibility for their future growth, "individual self-training favors the integration of collective consciousness, therefore it is, in a certain sense, the therapy"[100]. And a society made up of self-educated individuals would also at that point manage the education of young people, and the relationships between the various groups that make it up, in the name of creative cooperation. Psychosynthesis therefore triggers a process of spiraling regeneration, which ideally involves not just the individual who takes part consciously, but also, directly or indirectly, all those with whom he or she has a relationship and the groups to which he/she belongs.

2. Therapeutic psychosynthesis

As I have already explained, I clearly distinguish the different fields of application of Psychosynthesis for demonstrative purposes only. This is even clearer if you consider the approach it has to the concept of pathology. Pathology, health

---

99   M. Rosselli, op. cit., p. 277.

100   M. Sassi, *Formazione e terapia o è terapia?*, in "Rivista dell'Istituto di Psicosintesi", a. XV, n. 2, oct. '98.

and healing are not intended in definitive terms nor are they mutually opposing. From the psychosynthetic viewpoint, one speaks only of predominantly progressive or regressive components. Therapeutic work is not dissociated from work seen as self-realizational, and we can therefore designate the psychosynthetic process as a "therapeutic–rehabilitating–self-training" process[101].

I've already talked about phases, techniques and levels of *therapeutic psychosynthesis*, and I will talk about them again later. Here I am interested in pointing out that psychosynthesis therapy transcends its immediate medical application, presenting itself as the primary purpose. It aims not only to free the individual from the impediments and limitations of their past in order to be able to live the present well, but also to help free them from those impediments and limitations to reinvest the energy thereby freed towards further growth. In other words, it tends to elicit in the subject "a dynamic conception of psychic life with its unlimited possibilities of development and self-realization"[102].

The final goal of therapy is to render the subject independent and self-responsible as soon as possible. In this regard, Assagioli wrote that "teaching the techniques and training to use them independently as soon as possible is a fundamental principle of Psychosynthesis"[103].

3. Self-training psychosynthesis

Self-training is surely the central point of the psychosynthetic concept and, we can say, its favored destination. The criteria of self-training technology proposed by Assagioli are easily understandable when one considers that the idea of autogenic growth of the psyche and of a natural tendency toward harmony and synthesis occupies his thought. If, in fact, the psyche is conceived and experienced as an organic set of more or less evolved structures, more or less differentiated, but often in conflict with each other, it is then above all true that in all this, the primary thesis is precisely the idea of an irrepressible trend towards synthesis and harmonization.

Self-training techniques therefore represent the most specific tools of psychosynthetic practice.[104] We refer mainly to autogenic techniques based on the growth of internal parts, and in particular the use of concepts, images, symbols and evocative words used to develop a wider self-consciousness.

It should be noted, however, that many proponents of Psychosynthesis emphasize the risks associated with the self-training process, mainly identified in an illusory relationship between conscious and unconscious. In this regard Sebastiano

---

101   A. Alberti, *L'uomo che soffre l'uomo che cura*, op. cit., p 117.

102   R. Assagioli, *Principi e metodi*, op. cit., p. 140.

103   Ibid.

104   S. Tilli, op. cit., p. 83.

Tilli writes[105]:

> "Self-training posits a work which can broaden the field of viewpoints, the dimension of some ways of thinking, of being, of reacting to others, and to ourselves. It goes without saying that thought structures, like emotional structures, undergo progressive transformations as something within the psyche is set in motion. Properly because the major problems are experienced by the individual in the dimension of entering into relationships with others, and since it is in the relationship with someone or something outside oneself where most projections are stimulated, the result is that rarely, without adequate psychological work, one has the possibility to use really effectively something that has seemed useful to overcome a personal problem. That is, just because most of the unconscious themes are lived in projection, the remedy we choose is not adequate because it adapts to the 'rationalization' of the problem itself, and not the problem in question, which remains an unconscious coercion."

Therefore active techniques of Psychosynthesis should not be used within a self-training project without adequate psychological preparation. Otherwise, they might reinforce the subject in their "mistakes", producing confusion rather than development, disintegration instead of integration.

4. Educative psychosynthesis

Educative psychosynthesis is primarily addressed to educators, and among them, first and foremost, to parents. Assagioli wrote[106] that "when it comes to education too often one thinks of scholastic education; but education begins at birth, if not before."

Psychosynthesis gives significant importance to the psychological relationship between parents and children, and between teachers and students. Therefore, the educator must develop a clear awareness of how much their own shortcomings, defects and conflicts affect those who are to be educated. The educator's primary task will be to recognize the great responsibility they have and to commit to preparing theirself through adequate self-training. The parent and teacher should become living models of the future psychosynthesis of the child.

I have previously outlined Assagioli's positions on schooling (see Part 1, Chapter III, Para.1.4). It seems important to me, however, to emphasize that Psychosynthesis gives preeminence to education, in its etymological sense of "bringing out what is inside", "bringing light to what is concealed", "making actual what is only potential". Less space is given to instruction, which instead corresponds to the opposite process, that is, to "put in". The latter is considered necessary, but not so much as to fully occupy the field of educational action.

For this reason, in Psychosynthesis, educating means to support the educated's

---

105   Ibid, p. 90.

106   R. Assagioli, *Psicosintesi e psicoanalisi*, op. cit., pp. 8-9.

natural tendency toward synthesis; enabling them to develop skills such as thinking clearly, the ability to use the unconscious for their own benefit, the ability to self-assert themselves in a healthy way; to help them develop their aesthetic taste, allow them to have vital and fertile interpersonal relationships, the ability to use imagination creatively, to be able to autonomously discipline themselves, to constructively channel aggression, to be able to navigate the most intense emotions, and so on. In short, according to the psychosynthetic orientation, education must be integral and balanced, differentiated, individualized and, above all, joyful.

It also seems necessary to conclude by recalling a theme that was particularly important to Assagioli which he promoted all his life: education of highly gifted children (see Part 1, Chapter III, Para. 1.4).

5. Interpersonal psychosynthesis

In Psychosynthesis an individual life plan must be coordinated, integrated and harmonized with plans that include other people. Individual psychosynthesis is therefore not, and cannot be an end unto itself since each one of us is closely tied to other people and other groups.

The *interpersonal psychosynthesis* that is usually the first to be taken into consideration is that which involves the couple, considered a "container" with high integrative and transformative potential. In addition, a good part of the family dynamic—the relationship between parents and children, which also have an effect on other special interpersonal relationships—is based on psychosynthesis for the couple.

The individual also has interpersonal relationships in the work environment that can sometimes be difficult to manage, such as those with superiors, colleagues and other employees. Psychosynthesis offers numerous techniques to help one learn to manage these situations.

As psychotherapist and psychosynthesist Piero Ferrucci[107] explains, to understand these interpersonal dynamics, it is helpful to keep the Egg Diagram in mind. People can have relationships on the lower unconscious level. In such a case, the parties don't really know each other and project their fantasies onto their counterpart; true communication is absent and can only come about on an instinctual level, such as in the case where there is a major sexual attraction for a companion although there is no feeling of love. Instead, the relationship on the levels of the personal self and middle unconscious is a formal, practical and ordinary one. Finally, in a relationship on the superconscious level, the two individuals share an ideal, an inspiration, an aesthetic experience, or unbiased love; this would be an encounter without masks, beyond social conditioning.

---

107 P. Ferrucci, op. cit., pp. 16-17.

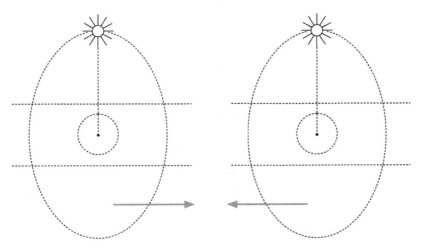

Relationship on the lower unconscious level

None of these three types of relations is complete in and of itself: the psychosynthetic ideal is a relationship that occurs on all these different levels. Obviously this cannot be actualized always and continually, but it is worthwhile to keep in mind as a possibility that guides and inspires us.

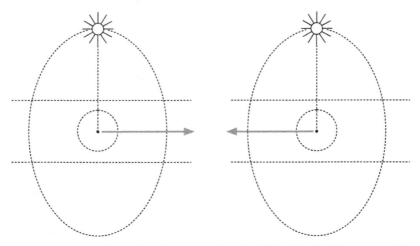

Relationship on the level of the personal self and middle unconscious

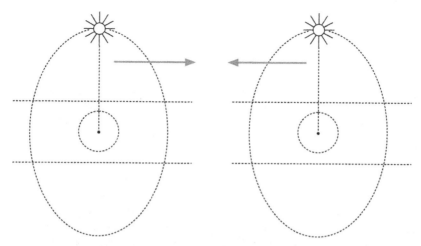

Relationship on the level of the higher unconscious

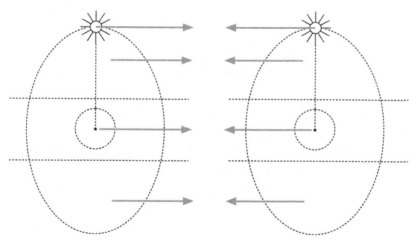

Ideal relationship: one that occurs on all the different levels of the bio-physical make-up of the individual

6. Social psychosynthesis

More than a relationship marked by irreparable contrast, Psychosynthesis considers the relationship between the individual and society as one of polarity. Assagioli wanted to consider such a relationship in the light of the principles concerning the synthesis of opposites that he developed in his essay *L'equilibramento e la sintesi degli opposti* (*The Equilibration and Synthesis of Opposites*). Of this he wrote[108]:

---

108   R. Assagioli, *L'atto di volontà*, op. cit., pp. 139-40.

"Regarding the problem of the individual and society, we have the following triangle diagram:

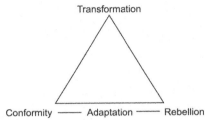

At the angles of the base of the triangle, there are two opposite poles, conformity and rebellion; the midway point of the baseline can represent a compromise situation which leaves some room for maneuvering, but it is limited and unsatisfactory as a permanent solution. But there is a synthesis point that is wider, allowing the individual to be an integrated member of society while maintaining a certain degree of independence from it. This position signifies acting in society and on society with the purpose of transforming it. (…) This is important not just for the good of society but also for the personal satisfaction of the individual who feels this internal independence."

According to Assagioli the social groups to which the individual belongs have various ways of obstructing the psychological freedom of an individual, but they can't really deny it.

Social psychosynthesis concerns an ample range of groups:

- groups in the workplace
- cultural, sport, political groups, etc.
- spiritual, religious, esoteric groups.

In these groups, psychosynthesis attempts to promote and harmonize the following types of relationships:

- between each member and the other members;
- between each member and the group as a whole, and vice versa;
- between the group and other groups.

Another aspect, less well known but not less important regarding Assagioli's contribution to group psychodynamics, is the work done over the years in different groups: training groups, cultural groups, educational groups, meditation groups, study and research groups. In this sense, Assagioli is an example of how one can belong to different groups without creating dysfunctionality, either in their own organization or in that of the groups themselves.

The goal of social psychosynthesis is to *express unity in diversity*, not just within one group, but also by connecting and harmonizing, with our activity and our presence, more groups.

7. The centrality of self-management

I conclude this chapter by agreeing with psychosynthesist Vittorio Viglienghi[109] that what distinguishes Psychosynthesis from other psychological schools is not so much a focus on one privileged field of action, but rather the presence of an active approach within each field of application. We see that with Psychosynthesis, healing is more of a self-healing process followed by the patient with the help of the therapist, rather than a passive treatment received by that patient. Education is first and foremost a process of self-education of the educator themself, who will then activate it in the student. Social and group relationships tend to be self-managed rather than being managed by someone else.

It can be said that in all psychosynthesis, the prevailing aspect is *self-management*, rather than management by others. This translates to individuals being *active and responsible subjects* at the helm of their own processs of education, training, social integration, etc. rather than passive subjects of interventions from outside. The entire structure of Psychosynthesis is constructed from and builds on this conscious and targeted intentional element.

---

109 V. Viglienghi, *Sulla natura della psicosintesi,* in "Rivista dell'Istituto di Psicosintesi", op. cit., p. 13-14. From the same author: *Orizzonti psicosintetici - Antologia di scritti sulle applicazioni e le implicazioni della Psicosintesi,* Youcanprint, 2016.

PART FOUR

THE HEART
OF PSYCHOSYNTHESIS

The Seven Fundamental Experiences

After having presented the general framework of Psychosynthesis, I will now, in this fourth part, proceed to illustrate its fundamental points.

We can derive clear indications on the subject from several notes dictated by Roberto Assagioli a few months before his death. He explained[1]:

"While Psychosynthesis is offered as a synthesis of various therapies and educational approaches, it is well to keep in mind that it possesses its own original and central essence. This is so as not to present a diluted and distorted version, or one over-coloured by the concepts and tendencies of the various contemporary schools. Certain fundamental elements exist, and their relative conceptual elaboration, deep experience and understanding are central, and constitute the sine qua non of psychosynthetic training.
These experiences are:

1. disidentification;
2. the personal self, or 'I';
3. the will: strong, skillful, good;
4. the Ideal Model;
5. Synthesis (in its various aspects);
6. the superconscious;
7. The Transpersonal Self (in most cases, it is not possible to have a complete experience, but it is a good idea to have a certain theoretical knowledge of its characteristic and the experience of a guide)."

To structure this latter part of the book, I referred to the above-mentioned notes, but made two major changes. The chapter dedicated to the topic of dis-identification will in fact be preceded by a chapter on the multiplicity of the human psyche and subpersonalities. In my view, this subject is an indispensable premise for dealing with disidentification. On the other hand, it was indeed Assagioli who indicated in his other writings how it is possible to initiate the process of disidentification and self-identification only after having sufficiently investigated the conscious and unconscious aspects of the personality.

In addition, I have decided to discuss in the same chapter the topic of 'I', or personal self, and the Transpersonal Self in order to firmly emphasize how they can be considered two different aspects of the same reality.

---

1   R. Assagioli, *Notes on Psychosynthesis Training*, dictated in the English language, May 19, 1974.

CHAPTER I

THE MULTIPLICITY OF THE HUMAN PSYCHE AND SUBPERSONALITIES

> *"At times I examine the various parts of my person-*
> *ality and remain perplexed. I realize that I am made*
> *up of diverse persons and see that the person who has*
> *the upper hand at one point will inevitably give way*
> *to another.*
> *But which one is the real one?"*[2]

Contemporary culture has moved in the direction of acknowledging the complexity of our personality, seen no longer as a solid and granitic entity, but animated by a variety of factors that often tend to impose themselves, even separately, creating internal conflicts that then have an impact on the relationships that human beings have with their fellows and the environment in general.

With perfect timing Assagioli seemed to have captured this fundamental concept that has stirred much thought over the last century. He deserves notable credit for how he interpreted the eternal struggle of humankind torn between multiplicity and a tendency towards unity, harmony and synthesis, giving rise to a new formulation of the problem of identity.

In presenting the core principles of Psychosynthesis, I cannot but start from the point where any inquiry into the human phenomenon begins: with its amazing *multiplicity*. And it is with this notion that Assagioli addresses the person who approaches for the first time the grand edifice of their psychological creation.

> "Explaining man according to only one of his components—whether it is the sexual or the spiritual, the aggressive or the altruistic, the biological, social, or cultural—means to be guilty of simplification and of not grasping precisely that varied and paradoxical treasure that characterizes each one of us."[3]

1. Multiplicity and conflict in the human psyche

In the psychosynthetic view *we are a microcosm*. In our psyche, one alongside the other, there are attitudes, emotions and thoughts quite different among themselves. However, we tend to forget about this fact for fear of the chaos that

---

2   S. Maugham, cit. in B. Carter Haar, op. cit., p. 2.

3   P. Ferrucci, *Introduzione alla psicosintesi,* op. cit., p. 11.

troubles and frightens, from time to time identifying ourselves with the state of mind of which we are aware at that moment. This tendency generates a grand illusion, that of believing that we possess a stable and integrated personality. Such a mistake, blocking every possibility of change and transformation, leads to rigidity and stagnation and to the impossibility to become other than what we are without the risk of having a serious identity crisis. In fact, Assagioli wrote[4]:

"one of the more serious types of blindness, the most harmful and dangerous illusions that prevent us from being what we could be (...), is to believe that we have a well-defined personality" while instead we are inhabited by "a variety of heterogeneous elements, contrasting tendencies from which derive the great complexity, challenge, variability and contradictions of the human psyche."

The first step towards inner research is recognizing this chaos which includes an infinity of psychic elements. Let's look at them briefly:

- first of all there is *the complexity which comes from our primitive past*, from the various evolutionary levels that coexist within us. Biologist Loren Eiseley[5] says: "There was a monkey, and its teeth are in your mouth. You are both fish and reptile as well as a warm and affectionate thing that dies if when young it has no one to cling to. You are all these things. You are a doll made of pieces from many eras and many skins";
- we then encounter the *elements of a relatively remote past: the atavistic legacy* that comes through the collective unconscious and which is revealed in dreams, fantasies and deliria; and *family inheritance* derived from parents, from distant ancestors and from relatives in general[6];
- to this set of elements determined by the past, a large group of *factors from external influences* (biological, psychological, cultural) is added. Assagioli[7] qualified them as follows:

1. various types of environmental influences;
2. prenatal and perinatal psychic influences;
3. psychic influences from infancy;
4. the spirit of the times;
5. racial influences;
6. national influences;
7. social or class influences;

---

4   R. Assagioli, *Psicosintesi - Armonia della vita*, op. cit., pp. 15 e 33.

5   L. Eiseley, cit. in P. Ferrucci, *Crescere*, op. cit., p. 37.

6   D. De Paolis, *L'io e le sue maschere*, op. cit., p. 16.

7   R. Assagioli, op. cit., p. 37.

8. psychological influences exerted by groups to which the subject belongs;

9. the generational mentality

10. personalities that are close to us, or famous and powerful taken as role models.

All of these elements contribute to creating images of ourselves, often linked to meaningful relationships, which we introject throughout our life and to which we then adapt from time to time: therein is what we believe to be, what we instead would like to be, the image of what others would like us to be, the image we think the others have of us, and so on. I will return more widely on these different images in the chapter devoted to the Ideal Model technique (see Part 4, Chapter V).

The list of influences and conditioning factors could be added to, but my intent is not to make it exhaustive. I would rather point out an idea which is a consolidated acquisition of the psychological and pedagogical sciences: the personality of the human being cannot in any way be seen *a priori* as something coherent, harmonious and unified.

It is almost superfluous to affirm that the elements generated by these influences most often do not coexist in a harmonious manner, but bring about polarity, ambivalence and conflict. In fact, there is a multiplicity of needs, desires and interests in the psychic system. This means that we find ourselves wanting various things simultaneously. That is why our impulses, our emotions and our thoughts are often in conflict with each other. But Assagioli[8] specified:

> "if there was only this, there would be an utter chaos, atomism, a psychic pulverization. But it is not so: *those elements* do not remain isolated in us, they *tend to aggregate*, to organize. For the coordinating action of the main functions, of the most important attitudes and human relationships that form the plot and the lines of our life, they tend to *form real subpersonalities*, the different 'I's we have inside."

2. Philosophical, literary and medical antecedents[9]

Psychotherapist and psychosynthesist Daniele De Paolis[10] writes that although the concept of the subpersonality assumes a peculiar connotation and scope in Psychosynthesis, it is also present under different names in various fields of human, medical, and cultural sciences: from philosophy to medicine, from psychology to sociology and literature.

Already in the mid-18th century, philosopher and Scottish historian David Hume, in his *A Treatise of Human Nature*, emphasized the lack of support for various ideas accepted by the philosophical tradition of the time, among which was

---

8   Ibid, p. 19.

9   D. De Paolis, op. cit., pp. 99-104.

10   Ibid, pp. 99.

that of personal identity. But the scholar who has dealt most with the various 'I's' inside us was American philosopher and psychologist William James. Through his phenomenological method of introspective analysis of psychic content, he contributed remarkably to the subject in question.

As far as literature is concerned, the concept of multiple identities appeared in the mid-nineteenth century in the form of the theme of the "Double". Examples of this are Fedor Dostoyevsky's novella *The Double* and the famous *The Strange Case of Dr. Jekyll and Mister Hyde* by Robert Louis Stevenson. Other authors who have dealt with the subject of the multiple facets of human personality, not only focusing on the pathological aspects, are Luigi Pirandello, James Joyce, Italo Svevo, and Marcel Proust.

2.1. The idea of multiple personalities in psychiatric and psychoanalytic literature

In classic psychiatric treatises you can usually find only a few mentions of *multiple personality* cases, presented more as exceptional examples or as historical cases. Over the last decades, however, increasing attention has been directed to the phenomenon. Accurate research and studies have been conducted and it has been found that many people are suffering from this disorder.[11] The results have led researchers and clinicians to make more precise distinctions. The following classification was composed by Swiss psychiatrist Henri Ellenberger (1905-1993)[12]:

1. *simultaneous multiple personalities*: are capable of manifesting themselves together, contemporaneously, with distinct characteristics. Each of the different personalities believes that it is living its own individuality, to the exclusion of one or all of the others;

2. *successive multiple personalities*, subdivided in:
   • mutually cognizant
   • mutually amnesic
   • amnesic in one direction only;

3. *personality grouping*. For a long time the only cases studied were those of double personality. It has since been understood that the human psyche is similar to a large container from which entire secondary groups can emerge and diversify.

On the psychodynamics front, French psychologist and philosopher Pierre Janet (1859-1947) was one of the first scientists to make important contributions to the understanding of this phenomenon: realizing that there are many psychic

---

11   P. Ferrucci, *Introduzione alla psicosintesi*, op. cit., p. 25.

12   H. Ellenberg, *La scoperta dell'inconscio*, cit. in D. De Paolis, op. cit., pp. 99-100.

processes that are not conscious, he also discovered what he called "secondary personalities" who live behind the "real personality" or alternate with it.

Even Sigmund Freud wrote that, to explain hysteria, it is necessary to hypothesize the presence of a dissociation, a split of the content of consciousness. Years later he hypothesized the existence of three structural systems: the Id, the Ego and the Super-ego. The Ego is generally under pressure to simultaneously respond not only to environmental demands, but also to the instinctive ones of the Id and the moral qualities of the Super-ego.

Many other authors have provided other formulations of subdivisions and conflicts that occur in the personality. What I want to emphasize here is that most psychological theories include a structural image of conflicts and internal division. Shapiro used the term "under-selves", Eric Berne spoke of "states of the ego", Herbert Sullivan of "personifications", Roberto Assagioli coined the term "subpersonalities".

3. The psychosynthetic viewpoint

Psychosynthesis often refers to cases of multiple personalities and phenomena of psychic dissociation because it maintains that they exasperate and highlight processes that occur physiologically in each of us. Piero Ferrucci writes[13] that in a certain sense we all have multiple personalities; we are benign cases because we maintain the continuity of conscience. Yet each of us is not a single person, but rather a crowd of individuals.

3.1. The problem of identity, the process of identification and subpersonalities

We have seen in the premise of this chapter how the original conception of dialectic multiplicity/unity had led Assagioli to formulate a new *theory of identity*. According to American psychologist and psychosynthesist Betsie Carter Haar[14], there are three classic ways of looking at the identity and the process of identification:

- the first sees the *'I' as being the equivalent of the identity*; in this view the 'I' is considered both a subject and an object of identification. This is congruent with the theory of orthodox psychoanalysis;
- instead, the second way considers the *'I' as a subject and a "false self" constructed as an object*. The 'I' is therefore the origin of the identity, but can also be identified with the "false self". Many scholars developed this theory that

---

13   P. Ferrucci, op. cit., p. 27.

14   B. Carter Haar, *L'integrazione della personalità*, Ed. Centro Studi di Psicosintesi "R. Assagioli", pp. 7-11.

can be called dual or dualistic. For example, Jung spoke of the "persona/shadow" dichotomy and warns of a lasting identification of the 'I' with the "persona" which leads to a massive removal of parts of the personality (creation of the shadow);

- the third way is that which can be defined as the viewpoint of multiplicity, which considers the *'I' as a subject and a multiplicity of selves as an object*. According to this hypothesis, the individual doesn't identify with a single false self, but instead with a group of sub-selves.

And so for the psychosynthetic viewpoint—which holds to the third way of interpreting the process of identification—we cannot consider the sense of identity as unique and coherent, but as a sense of multiple identities comprised of manifold partial identifications, the *subpersonalities*.

Identification establishes that particular atmosphere in which different subpersonalities can live and grow.[15] It consists of the process through which the 'I' coincides with the psychic content that gradually enters the field of consciousness. Identification—as a system that is typically closed and has the goal of internal coherence—urges the individual to validate only the experiences that reinforce the sense of identity of a given moment, and to refuse and discharge all the others. This phenomenon produces fragmentation in the psychic structure. In conclusion:

> "Unwitting identification with any part of the personality provokes incompatibility and produces a split in the psyche. And the more pronounced the level of identification, the deeper will be the split."[16]

This is why Psychosynthesis considers the subpersonalities *partial syntheses*, not adapted for promoting integration of the totality of the personality.

3.2. The laws of psychodynamics and the creation of the subpersonalities

The subpersonalities originate from the natural tendency, present in the human psyche, toward union and synthesis, where psychological elements tend to associate spontaneously with each other in increasingly complex structures. For Daniele De Paolis[17], among the various *laws of psychodynamics* established by Assagioli (see Part 3, Chapter III, Para. 4), three specifically *regulate the formation* and *mechanisms of subpersonalities*. They are:

> "Repeating actions strengthens the tendency to perform them. This makes them easier to do and allows them to be done unconsciously.

---

15   D. De Paolis, op. cit., p. 26.

16   B. Carter Haar, op. cit., pp. 6 e 11.

17   D. De Paolis, op. cit., p. 23.

Ideas, images, emotions and feelings, tendencies and impulses associate and group together variously in idea-forces, psychic complexes and subpersonalities.

Idea-forces, psychic complexes and subpersonalities tend to assert themselves and independently activate, beyond our consciousness and even against our will, the means for their activity and achievement."

The *first law* refers to the creation of habits and automatism, and a subpersonality features a standardized, mechanical repertoire of behaviors and attitudes.

Based on the *second law*, the elements that bring about a subpersonality do not randomly organize, but instead tend to arrange themselves around a nucleus of constellated actions. For example, a profound sense of insecurity could give rise to different subpersonalities: a dependent subpersonality seeking continued reassurance in the family environment and an arrogant, compensating, self-confident subpersonality in the workplace. A subpersonality therefore has its center (which relates to a passion, a role, a need...); a corporeal, emotional and cognitive inventory; special psychic functions; goals and motivations. It is a complete miniature personality.

According to the *third law*, subpersonalities tend to assert themselves and independently implement the means for their own affirmation often without the participation of our consciousness, or even contrary to our true existential plan. This means that in our unconscious we carry out activities we are not aware of. But these activities have their own purposes that are translated into motives, choices and actions that affect our whole being by influencing our choices, attitudes, feelings and our ways of thinking.

3.3. Roles and contexts in the origin of the more common subpersonalities

The environment, and especially the relationships we have with others, plays a key role in the genesis of subpersonalities. In fact, subpersonalities constitute all that *repertoire of roles and parts that we use to relate with others* and to stage the sometimes dramatic recitation of our life. In fact, for Psychosynthesis, subpersonalities are not just abstract constructions, but phenomenological realities, the ways of being that we experience concretely on the physical level (physical states, tensions, impediments, muscular armor), emotional level (states of mind, emotional reactions, feelings, affective experiences, needs, expectations), behavioral level (gestures, facial expressions, posture, verbal and non-language) and on the cognitive level (interpretations of reality, ideas, opinions, thoughts, convictions, beliefs).

The following table lists some of the typical subpersonalities that each of us deals with on a daily basis.[18]

Familial subpersonalities	child, father, mother, grandmother, uncle, stepmother...
Professional subpersonalities	artist, doctor, hourly employee, psychologist, banker, manager, homemaker, unemployed person...
Social subpersonalities	parishioner, boy scout, intellectual, athlete, fan, cinema enthusiast, psychosynthesist, Buddhist
Psychological subpersonalities	the aesthete, the shy, seductress, bon vivant, savior, clown, obsessive, hysterical, irrational, depressed...
Subpersonalities that follow one another in time	child, adolescent, teenager, adult, senior
Subpersonalities originating externally	various images of oneself created, induced and evoked by others

First and foremost, over the years, we experience *different family roles* from which corresponding subpersonalities emerge, those which William James called "child self", "marital self" and "parental self", each having its own different script and repertoire. "A man," Assagioli wrote[19], "has a whole set of feelings, attitudes, relationships and different behaviors as a child, husband or father; this yields a similar quantity of subpersonalities of different nature and value which are not infrequently contradictory."

There are also our *stereotyped attitudes*, typical of a given role, that give rise to our professional, class and social selves, which vary according to the people we associate with and the social, cultural and religious groups we belong to. William James, going further, maintained that "the number of social selves a man has is equal to the number of the individuals who know him and carry an image of him in their minds."[20]

And still there are subpersonalities that originate from *psychological peculiarities*, both physiological and pathological, which are organized around psychic or character traits.

Then there are those subpersonalities that *form naturally* with the passing of time: they are all very different from each other in their attributes and functions.

Finally, given the existence of the collective unconscious, we could also hypothesize the existence of *intrusive, foreign subpersonalities* belonging to other individuals who, through the interpersonal spaces, have penetrated the individual unconscious and take root there (the phenomenon of "possession").[21]

---

18   A. Alberti, *Psicosintesi e oltre*, L'Uomo Ed., Firenze, 2007, pp. 130-131.

19   R. Assagioli, op. cit., pp. 19-20.

20   W. James, cit. in R. Assagioli, op. cit., p. 20.

21   A. Alberti, op. cit., p. 131

3.4. The four primary subpersonalities[22]

From what has been described so far, we get an idea of the amazing multiplicity that characterizes the human psyche. However, in Psychosynthesis four basic subpersonalities, also called *primary subpersonalities*, are distinguished: *schizoid*, *obsessive*, *depressed*, and *hysterical*. They are a bit like the fundamental colors: from their different combinations they create the infinite nuances that characterize individuals.

But, we must bear in mind that, although one usually dominates the others, they almost never appear "pure". Therefore, in each person we find the traits of all four of these subpersonalities in variable quantities. In addition, primary subpersonalities can express themselves at different levels, covering the entire *continuum* that ranges from typology (giving rise to styles, preferences and predispositions) to pathology (manifested in a morbid, excessive and pervasive way, generating psychological disturbances of various kinds).

In the following table I have summarized the traits of the four basic subpersonalities as described by psychiatrist and psychotherapist Bruno Caldironi[23], one of Roberto Assagioli's own students.

Description	
depressed subp	committed, helpful, active, responsible, conscientious: often exploited for these characteristics; jovial, warm, affectionate, able to put others at ease; understanding, cheerful, capable of great empathy; is concerned with others, especially those who suffer; altruistic so as to gain esteem and acceptance; is willing to sacrifice greatly for affection; represses and does not heed their own desires, cannot say no, is content with little, does not assert their opinions; is pessimistic, gives up at the decisive moment; basically unable to give and receive normally, does not know how to be alone.
obsessive subp	orderly, precise, methodical, punctual, stable, persevering, with a developed sense of duty, responsible, conscientious, sober, diligent, ambitious, systematic, determined and persistent; enjoys too little of the present; well-mannered, well-dressed, acts thoughtfully; rigid and controlled in their movements, lacks spontaneity, clumsy; needs to control, watch over and thus possess; is an enemy of any Dionysian type of life, would like to force life into rules and

---

22   B. Caldironi, *Seminari di psicopatologia e psicoterapia*, op. cit.

23   Ibid.

patterns; collector, does not use things so as not to damage them; constantly monitors time, loses much time in rituals and making things lengthy; perfectionist, meticulous, doubtful, hesitation becomes a lifestyle; attacks philosophical systems or absolute thoughts, tends toward dogmatism, orthodoxy, intolerance; fears and avoids surprise and change; opposes everything, criticizes everything, has an opposing attitude typical of the "no" phase of infancy.

hysterical subp	jovial, affable, charming, brilliant, eccentric, colorful, sometimes audacious, adaptable, not very rigid; inventive, creative and has savoir-faire; great entertainer, loves to make a show; convinced that life should not be taken too seriously; their home is often hospitable, open; the way of dressing, movements, interests and career reflect the need to make an impression; is inclined to dress like a well-known character, tends to live in a fictional pseudo-reality; shrugs responsibility and is not very constant; loves stimuli and change, but thinks that what has to change is outside and not theirself; will change audiences if they become exposed, and for this reason often socializes with varied environments and companions; sometimes the creativity and acting degenerate into fiction and lies; eccentric; the facade of charm serves to cover a deep insecurity; uses seduction to impose desires and aspirations.
schizoid subp	autonomous, independent, has the courage to be theirself; rational, lucid, free of any dogma, does not make illusions and considers one the creator of their destiny; ironic, original, bizarre, an outsider; is familiar with solitude; easily evolves, is a pioneer and an initiator; ages well; always alert, has very sensitive antennas, sees the weaknesses of others and is less inclined to tolerate them; constantly experiences a great distrust linked to an exasperated conservation instinct; it is important not to need anyone, or to be beholden to anyone; has an aloof attitude, even towards groups, does not want to be part of...; is reserved and can be considered to be high-toned; in fact, fears others; relationships remain superficial, formal and proper; is not particularly attached to anyone; is like a prisoner in an ivory tower; often atheist or agnostic; reasons by a law of all or nothing, does not know the meaning of "gray areas"; hypertrophic development of the intellectual-rational side.

Family situation

depressed subp	over-protective mother excessively identified with her maternal role, replaces her child in every action; often depressed herself, tends to become dependent on the child who, unconsciously, asks to be a substitute mother; struggles to accept the crying and sadness of the child; depicts the world as a dangerous place; jealously guards her child, devaluing their friendships and inhibiting their vital drives towards independence; plays the victim (love that uses blackmail and induces feelings of guilt) and/or uses seduction (no future relationship can equal the idyllic initial relationship);
	also a mother who is openly refusing, hard, not very maternal, incapable of empathy and understanding the needs of the child, does not respect the pace of their development, unable to enjoy; next to this type of woman we often find an absent or distracted father.
obsessive subp	parents present obsessive dynamics themselves; the mother (and the father) are a constant but not gratifying point of reference; pressing expectations, persistent requests, commands, controls and punishments; many precise, meticulous and rigid rules; premature hyper-responsibility; aggressive and castrating climate that suffocates the child; repression of the natural physical, psychic, aggressive and sexual vivaciousness of the child that generates the basic doubt: can I follow my impulses and do what I want, or must I obey and adapt?; struggles between fulfillment and unfulfillment; a guilt-inducing look from the mother (or father) that paralyzes the child even before they have done something.
hysterical subp	chaotic and contradictory environment, without guidance and valid role models, the child is punished for something that will be hardly noticed tomorrow; continues to consider the child as too little or stupid to understand and for whom no sincerity is needed; also environments where appearance and social prestige are very important; often there is an exchange of sexual roles between the parents: the child does not receive any appropriate input regarding their sexual role and this makes their development difficult; in unhappy marriages, the child acts as a substitute for one of the two parents, thus being deprived of the healthy possibility of loving them as a couple: they must be an adult and a child simultaneously, generating confusion and inferiority; or the child must be the one who achieves in what the parents have failed and make their life "beautiful".

schizoid subp	possible difficulties during the mother's pregnancy (deprivation or refusal or strong ambivalence with regard to pregnancy), traumatic labor; mother too absent, often schizoid herself, incapable of showing affection, or of a spontaneous physical relationship; is a presence that engenders fear and above all sporadic; often feeds with a baby bottle; lacking in empathy, is incapable of decoding the child's needs, thus providing inadequate answers; ignores, fears or ridicules the effusions of the child, humiliating their desire for affection; or, a mother too invasive, the aggressiveness she experiences makes her feel so guilty that she tries in every way to protect her child; she becomes the child in everything, does not leave the child alone, does not allow him/her the slightest freedom; tries to satisfy any and all requests; incapable of understanding the child's crying so in order to prevent a mistake gives them everything; the father stands out in his absence.

Relationship with the world

depressed subp	relationships with others are characterized by dependence: sometimes open and direct (asks for advice, help, company, guidance) sometimes indirect (becomes indispensable); is constantly tormented by the danger of losing the other; idealizes people; strongly controls their aggressiveness, but ends up acting indirectly (lapsus, forgetfulness, mishaps, accidents, illnesses).
obsessive subp	unable to truly give, relationships with others are oriented to the assertion of their power; obstinacy enables remarkable performance (career, sports); tends toward fanaticism and can easily sacrifice for a noble cause; precision, slowness and perfectionism makes it exasperating to be with them; defends against their own aggression through theories and ideologies that value mediation, self-mastery, self-control, or idealizing the person against whom they would turn (see near-venerative relationships with sects, hierarchies, churches).
hysterical subp	aggression is placed at the service of ambition and is expressed above all in competition with others, in the need for assertion; exaggerating is part of this personality: always puts theirself in front, wants to be the prima donna; rather irresponsible, easily forgets and has no guilty feelings; attack is the best defense; due to the poor perception of their own value, even the slightest offenses can trigger intense feelings of hatred; intrigue is used as a particular form of aggression.

schizoid subp	for them everything is dangerous; panic shows itself as a fear of physical annihilation in death and/or psychic annihilation in madness; is strongly aggressive: is rigidly controlled or exhibits sudden outbursts that go as quickly as they come; aggression is the typical way they use to make contact; puts means between themselves and others: letters, phones, computers (mediated relationship); has a sharp tongue; has an attitude that is abrupt, unavailable, frustrating, cynical to the point of cruelty; can be reserved and polite with some but violent and provocative with others; aggression can be projected onto others (persecution complex); solitude is elevated to an existential value.

Sexuality and affection

depressed subp	strongly empathetic; desire to meld with the love object; needs the other; seeks a parent-like partner to lean on; tends to idealize the other; mysticism; scotomizes tensions, quarrels and conflicts for fear of loss, separation, solitude; hyper-apprehensive; loves the feeling of being in love rather than really loving the person (the object of love could be interchangeable); endures all so as not to lose the other (masochistic attitude); their dependence is expressed in two ways: directly (shows phobias, fragility, inability so that the partner will not have the courage to leave) or indirectly (being indispensable so that the other does not become self-reliant); panics if abandoned; denied aggression and aggressive equivalents; uses blackmail; absent or repressed libido; sex is much less important than affection and is used to obtain affection or similar emotional displays; sexually masochistic.
obsessive subp	the need to control and affirm their own power dominates the affective sphere; falling in love is disturbing, fearful, struggles to let theirself go since there's the risk of experiencing impotence and insecurity; indecision, doubts, endless premarital relationships, but the decision is then irrevocable; trustworthy, loyal; possible marriages of economic or affective convenience (with people who can be controlled); considers the partner as their property and this may be associated with some form of jealousy; due to their obstinacy conflicts are not readily resolved; time and money are usually issues that trigger discussions and quarrels; does not take much into account the feelings of the other and their need for affection, tends to impose their tastes and choices on the other; has difficulty in acknowledging their mistakes, but perfectly remembers the wrongs they have suffered and can become vindictive; asks that the partner be efficient, reliable, to

"function well"; sexuality is often inhibited by rigidity, sex is stable but monotonous, ritualized, predictable; fantasy is scarce if not absent; sexuality may vary with sadistic tendencies related to the subject of control and ownership of the partner; there may also be some insecurity with respect to their sexual abilities: every relationship becomes a test, or they seek endless pretexts to avoid any kind of approach; sometimes there is a clear division between sexuality and affection: sexuality considered to be dirty is not allowed to contaminate the beloved woman/man... (resorts to prostitution, taking lovers).

hysterical subp	loves love, and loves all that produces an increase in the consideration of theirself: drunkenness, ecstasy, passion; is gladly exalted, more inclined to short and passionate adolescent love rather than to mature love; little sense of responsibility; is attracted by experiences that do not consider boundaries; seeks self-affirmation above all; a master of eroticism, knows how to make the partner feel loved; would like to make the honeymoon last forever, loves love more than the partner; erotic play is more important than satisfaction; often has rapid and superficial sexual relationships; a talker or seducer whose worth depends on the number of "heads" collected; frigidity, anorgasmia, impotence, sex is actually a means to satisfy other more vital and important needs (protection, dependence); homosexuality originating in the disappointment suffered by the parent of the opposite sex and by identification with the parent of the same sex; often ends up in triangular relationships in which their position between the parents is reprised; is afraid of a liberated partner as it would require commitment, availability and responsibility; must always shock the partner by making them the audience; relationships usually do not survive crises and conflicts; only the partner's fidelity is important; uses the partner as a mirror to confirm fragile sense of self-esteem and this can lead to choosing a partner who they resemble so that they can love theirself; only when they begin to love theirself instead of the image they have of theirself can they love others also.
schizoid subp	is isolated, detached from emotions and feelings to avoid suffering; feels that love endangers their independence; empathetic and seductive abilities are foreign to them; has superficial, short, easily soluble sentimental ties, or just sexual relationships with a person-object; protects theirself from their ineptitude and inexperience in the sentimental field; rejects tenderness and displays of affection, perhaps ridiculing the partner; has remote

or sibling-type relations (for example, with older people of the opposite sex), or even refuses to legalize the relationship; puts the partner through exhausting love tests, but never reassures him/her; treats others as objects; sex, devoid of sentiment, is reduced to sexual gymnastics; there may be excessive self-esteem, the use of pornographic and erotic aids/toys, voyeurism, fetishism; in extreme cases also necrophilia and pedophilia; the sexual act is often experienced as mutual masturbation; possible impotence, frigidity or vaginismus; the partner is reduced to a sex object and is therefore interchangeable or exchangeable (exchange between couples or group sex); can exhibit sadistic behavior in which sensations are surrogates of feelings.

Body and psychosomatics

depressed subp rotund, plump appearance; poor posture, bent forward, prominent abdomen; expresses theirself poorly, speaks in low voice, without expression; poor memory; obesity, anorexia, drug addiction; recurrent diseases related to being the victim of aggression and self-aggression: various types of neuralgia, back pain, ulcers, headaches and migraines, fatigue, muscle cramps, paresthesia, tumors; insomnia in the early morning hours; children suffer from eczema, sore throat and earaches, asthma or other respiratory disturbances, dental or food-related problems.

obsessive subp stiff muscles, guard-like posture, clenched jaw; polite; measured movements, classic elegant clothing; if the rigidity is excessive, the general impression may be that of clumsiness (bumping, stumbling, getting hurt); the body is seen as something dirty, ugly, to be concealed and controlled; its functions can provoke shame; obsessed with hygiene and personal care, obsessed with the maintenance of their physical appearance; hypochondria; constipation or other difficulties related to intestinal regularity; hypertension; sleep disturbances: difficulty falling asleep, sleeps with TV, light, radio on (difficulty relaxing).

hysterical subp soft, sexually provocative movements; values the body considerably; pleasant appearance; makeup, hairstyle, well-dressed; afflicting symptoms are used to draw attention to him/herself; somatic conversion mechanisms; pretends to have the diseases of others; experiences symptoms affecting the motor system: globus pharyngis, aphonia, dysphonia, hysterical paralysis, hysterical pregnancies, opisthotonos, convulsive seizures, vomiting; even sensory systems can be easily affected: anesthesia, hypoesthesia, visual and hearing impairment; hypochondrial background

	phobias; greatly fears anything that can affect their physical or mental vitality or beauty.
schizoid subp	cold body, scarcely vital, weak, thin, rigid and tense, the joints are rigid; face has little expression that does not let emotions show, taut mouth, forced smile, superficial breathing, withholds emotions; fragmented and segmented movements; chronic tension, widespread vasoconstriction, cold feet; denial of the body as a physical place of emotions and feelings; incapable of physical contact; all mind and no body; looking in the mirror may have the feeling of not recognizing theirself; disconnected head-trunk: tension at the base of the skull, gaze is often not direct and avoids eye contact; disconnected chest-abdomen: blocking of sexual sensations, pelvic muscles chronically tensed; affected organs: skin (contact) and respiratory system (exchange), hygiene and perspiration problems.

Pathological evolution

depressed subp	depression, pathological negative mood, sadness regarding life; feelings of guilt, ruin and death; suicide (meaning the homicide of the other as an extreme act of rebellion); escape into mania, jealousy-based delirium.
obsessive subp	obsessive-compulsive, phobias, rituals, nervous tics, stuttering; tendency toward hypochondria; psychotic dissociation phenomena, deliria without total loss of consciousness, catatonia, anankastic paralysis; escape into schizophrenia (the only way to experience a bit of spontaneity); depression.
hysterical subp	maniacal states; histrionic disturbance of personality: emotional immaturity, narcissism, self-centeredness, fragility of the ego and personal identity; spectacular suicides (the need to attract attention becomes more important than life itself).
schizoid subp	ideas of persecution and paranoia; disorders of sexuality and sociality (asociality, delinquency, autism); aggression can be sexual (sadism); schizophrenia; suicide (as an extreme escape from panic).

Career-Work

depressed subp	relationship-related professions: psychotherapists, social workers, counselors, educators, teachers; association to religious institutions; activities in the field of alimentation.

obsessive subp	professions requiring precision, responsibility, patience, orderliness: judge, accountant, archivist, banker, historian, artisan, archaeologist.
hysterical subp	professions connected to the field of aesthetics, fashion, cinema, theater; artistic and creative activities.
schizoid subp	professions that require a high level of abstract thought: mathematician, physicist, astronomer, philosopher; doctor or professions that use microscopes/telescopes; interested in animals, "high-risk" professions, race car drivers, gamblers.

	Historical examples	**Literary examples**
depressed subp	Winston Churchill	Madame Bovary
obsessive subp	Adolf Hitler	Don Juan
hysterical subp	Benito Mussolini	Oedipus Rex
schizoid subp	Josef Stalin	The Stranger

Primary subpersonalities seem to derive from the early, repeated *frustration of the basic human needs*. To better understand this concept we can refer to the well-known theory of needs elaborated by Abraham Maslow, who, despite the criticisms of the last few decades, has not changed his stance regarding the validity of the subject in question. Thus, while simplifying, we can state that the development of a schizoid subpersonality is mainly related to the physiological survival needs not being met; the development of an obsessive subpersonality by the need for security and protection not being met; that of a depressed subpersonality frustrated by the need for love and belonging; and the development of a hysterical subpersonality frustrated by the need for recognition.

PHYSIOLOGICAL NEEDS	food, sleep, personal care and hygiene; essential for our physical survival in the environment; the basis of such needs is the instinct of self-preservation	schizoid subpersonality
NEED FOR SECURITY	protection from pain and danger, stability, security, dependence, order and limits	obsessive subpersonality
NEED FOR LOVE, BELONGING	acceptance, affection, belonging; regards the desire to have a satisfying sexual, emotional and relational life, to have friends and colleagues by whom he/she is accepted and with whom there is exchange and dialogue	depressed subpersonality

NEED FOR ESTEEM	appreciation, success and recognition; to be considered highly both by others and by theirself	hysterical subpersonality
NEED FOR SELF-REALIZATION	maximum development of one's own potentialities, the recognition of one's own uniqueness and individual aspiration, and to be what one really wants to be, whoever one wants to become, the search for spiritual or transpersonal qualities such as justice, goodness, beauty, harmony, truth, creativity ...	

3.5. The different levels of the subpersonalities

According to psychologist and psychotherapist Mauro Scardovelli[24], who has dedicated an interesting book to the subject, when we approach a subpersonality we must bear in mind that it is usually composed of: essence, a wound, a lower self, and a mask.

The child naturally seeks protection, security, contact, warmth, recognition and approval. When they clash with the excessive frustrations of their natural and healthy needs, they are hurt and feel pain. This *wound* transforms the original expansive energy of the *essence* into destructive energy. Part of this destructiveness is turned inward; another part goes to fuel a new psychic structure, the *lower self*, which directs the destructiveness towards the outside world against the person and the situation that caused the wound.[25]

Soon enough, however, the child realizes that freely expressing the energy of the lower self leads them further away from the outside world, making it ever more difficult to meet their vital needs. To avoid this situation, a risk to their physical and psychological survival, another structure is built, *the mask*; this is a stratagem to adapt to the environment and survive. So the child transforms destructiveness by turning it into complacency in the case of a depressed subpersonality, or turning it into seduction in a hysterical subpersonality, into surrender in the schizoid, or into control in the obsessive one.

Each subpersonality therefore contains a nucleus, a healthy need (essence) that has been frustrated or traumatized (wounded), giving rise to a reaction of sadness and/or anger (inferior self) that is controlled in different ways to guarantee survival (mask). We can summarize what has been said in this way:

---

24   M. Scardovelli, *Subpersonalità e crescita dell'io*, Ed. Borla, 2000, pp. 47-49.

25   J. Pierrakos, cit. in M. Scardovelli, op. cit., pp. 45-46.

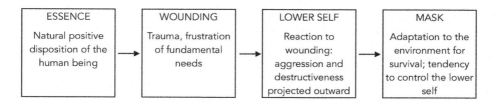

An example: the depressed subpersonality

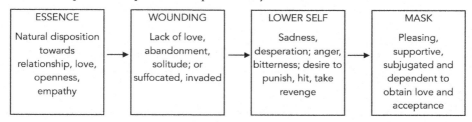

4. Life as a game and theatrical performance

It is within the metaphor of life as theater, play and drama that we can fully grasp the theoretical and practical implications of the psychosynthetic concept of the subpersonalities. The term "subpersonality" is a compound word that has its etymological roots in the Latin "person", meaning "a wooden mask worn by a character in a theatrical work".

Psychosynthesis considers daily life as a grand stage on which everyone is called upon to play their own parts, and in general we are actors who are seasoned, consummate: only that we're not aware that we're acting, precisely because we do not distinguish between the 'I' and the roles, we are identified.[26] According to this view, the individual who has not undertaken a journey of self-awareness is subject to this process. Their 'I' changes identity mechanically and constantly. Depending on the circumstances of life, at the center of their area of consciousness we can find a subpersonality now, and later find another, which, more often than not, are in conflict or even reciprocally ignored. Assagioli wrote[27]:

> "As long as the thread of memory (amongst subpersonalities) remains, it connects them very inadequately. Each one proceeds on its own, independently and often in conflict with the others. They are like characters that move on the stage of the conscience, but unlike those of Pirandello's well-known comedy, they're not in search of an author (...)."

In his book *La vita come gioco e rappresentazione* (*Life as a Game and Theatrical Performance*), the father of Psychosynthesis explained what should be the ideal situation regarding our attitudes and behaviors on the scene of life. He said that

---

26   D. De Paolis, op. cit., p. 35.

27   R. Assagioli, cit. in D. De Paolis, op. cit., p. 34.

we all play parts, so why then, he asked provocatively, don't we act them out consciously, since acting is unavoidable? He wrote[28]:

"In life, reciting a part, or rather 'parts', is a fundamentally important technique in Psychosynthesis. One might think of it as the central technique in the art of living, with which all the others are connected and on which they depend in a certain way."

4.1 Working with subpersonalities

Psychosynthesis involves active work with the various *internal characters*. Assagioli encourages the individual to become the director of the stage play. But how? The phases contemplated by the psychosynthetic process are also applicable to work with subpersonalities:

1. first, we need to know the various parts that make up our personality, and this is possible through the use of analytical techniques and the development of the inner observer's attitude. The investigation starts with the subpersonalities more accessible to the field of consciousness, eventually reaching the unconscious ones which have undesired effects or, on the contrary, are not yet sufficiently perceptible in our lives.

   It is therefore extremely important to elicit a general attitude of accepting our psychic multiplicity. Work on super-egoic applications is essential to allow real access to mastery and transformation of oneself. Using a metaphor, it is as if acceptance allows every subpersonality to be welcomed and invited to sit at the table together with all the others, regardless of their appearance and origin;

2. one then passes to the stage of *mastery*: the gradual process of disidentification leads to the creation of a psychic space that allows the emergence of a larger unifying center: the self. The subject begins to experience a greater degree of movement and inner freedom;

3. finally, we come to the transformation that comes about primarily through the development of the will and through the use of various active techniques such as visualization, dramatization, balancing, free drawing, and synthesis of opposing subpersonalities. At this point in the work, it is possible to create new subpersonalities and dissolve or transform the ones who are damaging and obsolete.

4.2. Subpersonalities and conflicts of the human psyche

The first step is thus to discover the various personalities that inhabit us. Then, once the different subpersonalities are identified, one must recognize that they are

---

28   R. Assagioli, *La vita come gioco e rappresentazione*, Ed. Istituto di Psicosintesi, p. 4.

often in conflict with each other. This is because, as we have noted, subpersonalities may have different and conflicting needs and interests, arising from their "placement" within the psychic structure. For there are those who are forgotten or segregated in the basements of the lower unconscious and who, often following this imprisonment, have taken on a repugnant or frightening aspect; there are those who live on the ground floor, in the middle unconscious, that we can relatively easily recognize and contact, as they are "ordinary" subpersonalities; finally there are those who live in the bright and airy penthouses of the super-conscious that we crave but also fear as they are unknown aspects of our being. We can represent this idea in the following sequence:

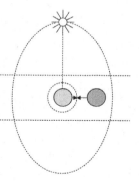

In the image here on the right there are four subpersonalities: one in the lower unconscious (angry subpersonality), one in the higher unconscious (creative subpersonality), and two in the middle unconscious (efficient subpersonality, lazy subpersonality).

Obviously, in each of us, there are many more subpersonalities than those here illustrated as examples.

Different subpersonalities interacting with each other can create conflicts of a different type depending on the level of the unconscious from which they come. Psychosynthesis distinguishes three, each with special characteristics and dynamics: *psychic conflicts*, *moral conflicts* and *spiritual conflicts or crises*.[29]

Psychic conflicts take place on a "horizontal" plane, that is amongst sub-personalities that reside on the same level of the unconscious (usually lower or middle).

This next graphic represents the psychic conflict between an efficient subpersonality and a lazy one, both of which belong to the middle unconscious. In this situation, the 'I' can identify itself in a stable manner with one against the other, or alternate between the two identities.

Moral conflicts, however, arise mostly from clashes between judgmental identifications built around prohibitions (super-ego instances) and other parts of the personality that are condemned and judged unworthy, and are characterized by guilt, remorse and shame.

---

29   D. De Paolis, op. cit., p. 46.

In this next image, moral conflict is represented where the 'I' identifies with a judging subpersonality that represses and condemns the angry subpersonality that tries to emerge from the lower unconscious.

Finally, *spiritual conflicts and crises* occur between our conscious personality (our 'I' identified with certain mental content) and the superconscious, that is, the spiritual drives that seek to enter into the consciousness and the resistance that the personality puts up in order not to accept them. In this case the clash between our various parts happens "vertically".

In this last illustration, spiritual conflict is represented where the 'I' identifies itself with an insecure subpersonality that defends itself from the creative thrust that attempts to reach the field of awareness from the higher unconscious.

It's good to keep in mind that the locations indicated in the diagrams are not permanent. Every subpersonality can, over time, become transformed and shift from the lower unconscious to the middle, to the higher, and vice versa, and more or less enter into the field of consciousness. This emphasizes that you cannot speak of "negative" or "positive" subpersonalities in the absolute sense. All of them are expressions of vital elements of our being which are open to be transformed, even if at first they seem quite the opposite, perhaps degraded and monstrous. Subpersonalities are considered to be truly damaging only when they control us, only when we experience them passively, instead of knowingly.

4.3. Preventing identity crises: partial and integral syntheses

Working on subpersonalities also has an important *preventive aspect*. Often, the role we most identify with, for example the part we recite in society, is limiting and imposes mutilations on us. "Total identification with a function, however noble it may be, tends to favor repression in the unconscious of parts of the psyche that do not fall under that function, but which are also vital and that would merit proper development and appropriate expression"[30]. This may result in lacerating conflicts and inconsistencies between the public and private individual, and, what's worse, one can become completely lost when no longer able to impersonate a given function because its task is exhausted. For many people the loss of a

---

30   R. Assagioli, op. cit., p 45.

role is akin to true death, leading to a profound identity crisis from which some never emerge. Assagioli wrote:

"How can this crisis be reversed, or better yet, prevented? The answer is: through psychosynthesis; not a partial psychosynthesis, such as that of one's own function, of one's own office, of the part rooted in the social world, but with a broader and more complete psychosynthesis; which includes all the personality."

The distinction between integral and partial psychosynthesis is very important as it brings us closer to the subject discussed in the next chapter: *disidentification*. Subpersonalities, Assagioli maintained, are centers of partial psychosynthesis since they cannot include all the elements of the bio-psycho-spiritual being.

Now, these partial syntheses can be organized in two different ways: they can generate a "segregated" system, in which each subpersonality decides for itself without taking into account the other variables in play and attempts to accomplish its objectives by creating profound contradictions and conflicts in the person; or they can give life to an "integrated" system where there is a higher center, the Transpersonal Self, which coordinates and manages the whole, makes decisions and succeeds in pursuing its goals. In the first case subpersonalities assume the function of "ends", in the second of "means"; they are rightly considered as transitional identifiers, stages of passage to broader and global synthesis.

We conclude with Assagioli's own words[31]:

Subpersonalities "are not capable of producing a complete psychosynthesis, in which all the elements that form us are coordinated and harmonized in a living unit; nor an independent and autonomous psychosynthesis, that is, not based on elements outside the true individual being. In order to implement a psychosynthesis of this kind, a unifying center is needed which has other elements. First, this center must be of a different nature from that of all the individual and particular elements that constitute our psyche. It must be different and superior to them, because only in this way can it have the power to direct them and render them an organic unity. Secondly, that center should not be something external to the personality, but intimate with it, something really central. In short, the unifying center must coincide with our 'I' or Self."

"In the process of recognizing subpersonalities, one realizes that the Self, which observes, cannot be identified with any of them, but is something or someone different. This is a very important recognition which constitutes the first step on the path to future psychosynthesis"[32].

Therefore, the most important objective of work on subpersonalities is to *intensify the sense of self* so that instead of disintegrating into an infinite number of elements in conflict, we can begin to perceive the unity of our profound essence.

---

31   R. Assagioli, *Psicosintesi - Armonia della vita*, op. cit., pp. 85-86.

32   R. Assagioli, *Principi e metodi della psicosintesi terapeutica*, op. cit., p. 76.

CHAPTER II

IDENTIFICATION, DISIDENTIFICATION, AND SELF-IDENTIFICATION

> *True disidentification increases the awareness of our presence.*

A brief premise on the etymological meaning of the terms that we will consider in this chapter, namely *identification*, *disidentification* and *self-identification*, can be extremely illuminating. Assagioli himself, in the use of words, always held to their original semantic content and advised his students to do the same.

In this sense, to identify, from the Latin term *idem fieri*, means "becoming the same, equal, identical"; disidentify, with the addition of the prefix *dis-* which means separation, departure, means the opposite process: to "distinguish or separate something (from what it had become equal to)"; finally self-identification, with the addition of the prefix *self* might be translated as "identifying oneself" in the sense of recognizing, discovering the original part of oneself, and also how to "become equal to oneself".

And it is precisely this process, which goes from identifying with objects unrelated to oneself, passing through the phase of disidentification, and on to identification of (and) with oneself, which is the central nucleus of the psychosynthetic vision of psychic dynamics.

1. The naturalness of the identification and disidentification processes

It should be pointed out that if the tendency of the 'I' to identify itself with the changing contents that gradually enter the field of consciousness on the one hand can lead the human being to a state of confusion, limitation and detachment from theirself and their true nature, on the other hand, it expresses itself with the process of disidentification, allowing it to continue to develop and evolve. The phenomenon of *identification* accompanies the entire course of all human existence. In fact, any growth path can be considered as an evolution departing from a series of partial identifications to identities with increasingly complex and inclusive elements, then moving up to self-identification or identification with the Self, essentially up until the discovery of what we really are. This means that the process of identification can in no way be regarded as pathological in itself. As

Alberto Alberti writes[33]:

"It (the process of identification) gratifies in part a person's need of identity; one feels strongly the need to know who one is, to give oneself a name and an identity, hopefully an authentic one, but in the absence of that, even fictitious. In fact, the need for identity is very strong and rooted: it is not only a cognitive need but also a structural one. It is necessary for one to maintain their supporting structure, in short, to 'remain standing'."

The process of identification only becomes pathological if it becomes arrested at a particular stage, impeding advancement towards successive disidentification and, consequently, the entire process of development which is constantly followed by the individual.

In the age of development, this passing from identification to disidentification usually progresses spontaneously, physiologically. Psychiatrist and psychosynthesist Luce Ramorino writes[34]:

"Developmental psychology teaches us that the newborn child has an undifferentiated identity (...) and responds to the natural tendency of evolution by identifying itself, i.e. recognizing itself, in the partial and extremely fragmentary experiences related to the dominant sensory-motor functions.

At three years the child begins to use the pronoun 'I', giving this 'I' the meaning of "I am a body": an identity that expresses the result of a primitive identification in the sensory and motor faculties, followed by disidentification and acquisition of a psychic space for processing and integrating this experiential information, leading to a new and more inclusive identification in the global physical instrument (...). This identity expresses the fact that the child has reached the first stage, the first point of support from which once again to detach in the integration of other elements, always the result of identifications, that is experiential moments, and of disidentifications, that is the acquisition of psychic space that allows elaboration of the experience.

In the next phase, the emotional function predominates; it is mostly about emotional identification, "I am good, I'm bad, I'm nice, etc." The resulting identity expresses the integration of the physical and the emotional-affective instrument, as a second step in development. With the emergence and prevalence of mental function, another possibility is opened up in the evolutionary process. At this stage, through the usual mechanism, the individual identifies theirself with the mental contents, which they develop and introject, and with the mind builds an identity that integrates the physical-emotional structure with the mental one, thus tending to identify theirself with the entire personality. (...) Identity is therefore more inclusive, but still confused, as such maturation has hitherto occurred without the conscious participation of the individual. There is still no clear self-awareness."

---

33   A. Alberti, *Psicosintesi e oltre*, l'Uomo Ed., Firenze, 2007, p. 129.

34   L. Ramorino, *Identificazione, disidentificazione, autoidentificazione*, in *I nuovi paradigmi della psicologia*, op. cit., pp. 223-225.

Actually, the process is not so schematic and coherent since, as we have seen, the individual arrives to adulthood with multiple identities, either fragmented and wavering, or rigid and fossilized. Often, the individual tends to glue theirself into a limited series of identities, preventing the chance for further growth and development processes, with all the consequences that result.

Psychosynthesis intervenes with the disidentification technique right at this point in the process with the purpose of promoting and motivating the conscious use of that capability of the psyche.

2. Disidentification and self-identification

2.1. What does disidentification mean?

Firstly, disidentification means starting to put a psychic space between us and the multiform elements that make up our psyche; to no longer align the sense of our identity with the more or less structured content of our consciousness. Assagioli explained that what is needed is an internal doubling. Developing the capability to disidentify means therefore acquiring a third dimension, giving depth to our psychic life:

> "For instance, think of the two or three geometrical shapes that Einstein made popular with his relativity. For the flat person, having only two dimensions, the psychic circle is everything, he is in it and stays there. But the three-dimensional person comes and goes"[35].

Disidentification allows one to be the observer and develop an ever-increasing awareness of what is happening within the mind. Consciously and voluntarily putting a psychic space between the contents of the consciousness and the subject that perceives them allows one to know more about these contents, to relativize them, to welcome them, to evaluate them, to learn how to handle them and eventually transform them. According to Psychosynthesis, this inner doubling, this ability to see oneself, is the key to all learning.

Luce Ramorino[36] writes that addressing the theme of disidentification/self-identification, also means being confronted with the fundamental process of life. In fact, what is living, if not to evolve and transform, if not to respond in an ever-wider, inclusive, profound and essential way to the fundamental question: "Who am I?" It is this question that Roberto Assagioli puts to us with the disidentification/self-identification exercise. It has us face the responsibility and the freedom to see that the answer no longer arrives without our conscious collaboration, left to the rhythm and deformation of our conditioning, but begins to be the fruit of deliberate and conscious research.

---

35   R. Assagioli, *Psicosintesi - Armonia della vita*, op. cit., p. 107.

36   L. Ramorino, op. cit., p. 223.

In his writings, Assagioli[37] pointed out how some individuals derive their identities from their bodies, others from their sentiments, others from their thoughts, and still others from their roles in society or from some subpersonality:

"Some people identify with the *body*. They perceive and speak about themselves mainly in terms of sensations, (...). Others identify themselves with their own *feelings*; they perceive and describe their state of being in affective terms, and consider their own feelings the most central and intimate part of themselves, while thoughts and sensations are perceived as more distant, perhaps something separate. Those who identify with the *mind* tend to describe themselves with intellectual constructs, even if asked how they feel. They often see feelings and sensations as peripheral, or are largely unaware of them. Many people identify with a *role*: they live, work, and experience themselves in terms of that role, such as 'mother', 'husband', 'wife', 'employee', 'teacher', etc.."

But these *partial identifications* are harmful, restrictive, limiting, and as such, they destroy personal freedom. They prevent us from realizing the experience of the self, the profound sense of self-identification, from knowing who we are. Disidentification thus means giving ourselves the opportunity to respond in a new way to the question "Who am I?", consciously asking it as Assagioli invites us to do with his disidentification exercise.

2.2. Disidentification/self-identification exercise

Psychosynthesis identifies the key to inner freedom in the *disidentification exercise*. It should lead to the discovery of one's own inner power of choosing whether to "identify with" or "disidentify from" each aspect of one's personality. This exercise is meant to be a tool to train the awareness and ability to focus attention on the main aspects of our personality. I have summarized its sequence as follows:

1. Take a comfortable position that facilitates concentration.

2. a) Be aware of having a *body* and perceiving sensations.
   b) Observe your own body and the sensations that enter into the field of consciousness.
   c) Realize that your body and the sensations perceived are changing continuously.
   d) Recognize and affirm that your 'I', your own deepest essence, is not (exclusively) identifiable with the body and its sensations.

---

37   R. Assagioli, *L'atto di volontà*, op. cit., pp. 156-157.

3. a) Be aware of feeling *emotions* and *sensations*.
   b) Observe the emotions and sensations that enter the field of consciousness.
   c) Realize that the perceived emotions and sensations are changing continuously.
   d) Recognize and affirm that your 'I', your most profound essence, is not (exclusively) identified with the emotions and sentiments.

4. a) Be aware that you have *thoughts*.
   b) Observe the thoughts that enter into the field of consciousness.
   c) Realize that the thoughts you perceive are changing continuously.
   d) Recognize and affirm that your 'I', your most profound essence, is not (exclusively) identified with the thoughts.

5. a) Ask yourself the question: Who am I?
   b) Answer, identifying yourself, in pure self-awareness and will.

Over the years the exercise has been presented with many changes by different authors. Here below is the original version developed by Assagioli[38] which he himself considered just as an idea that could be modified according to the specific needs of those who practiced it. For example, there could be the inclusion of disidentification from one's own desires, from inner images, from one's own roles, specific subpersonalities, and so on.

> "I have a body, but I am not my body.
> I have emotions but I am not my emotions.
> I have a mind, but I am not my mind.
>
> And so, who am I? What remains when I disidentify from my body, from my sensations, feelings, desires, mind, and actions?
>
> My essence: a center of pure self-awareness. The permanent factor in the changing flux of my vital person. This is what gives me the sense of being, of permanence, or inner balance. I assert my identity with this center and recognize its permanence and energy, declaring:
>
> I am a center of will and pure self-awareness.
> I am.
>
> I recognize and confirm myself as a pure center of self-awareness and creative, dynamic energy. I recognize that from this center of true identity I can learn to observe, manage and harmonize all the psychological processes and my physical body. I want to reach a permanent awareness of this fact, in the middle of my daily life, and use it to help give my life a growing significance and sense of direction."

I wish to conclude the presentation of this disidentification/self-identification exercise by making a brief but fundamental specification. As psychosynthesist

---

38   Ibid, p. 160.

Marialuisa Macchia pointed out in a timely fashion,[39] in studying this fundamental topic it is extremely important to keep in mind the distinction between:

- the disidentification/self-identification *exercise* (technique);
- the *inner attitude* that is the result of the regular and appropriate use of the exercise (but which can also be the result of other techniques and existential experiences)
- the *process*, that is the gradual and continuous elaboration of the effective disidentification/self-identification experience;
- the *state of awareness*, more or less permanent, more or less total of the experience of the 'I' aware of itself, of one's own reality, stability and independence.

2.3. A reformulation

Alberto Alberti[40] proposed a reformulation of the exercise applicable to interpersonal relationships, aimed at encouraging disidentification from others and the establishment of good human relations. This reinterpretation reads as follows:

"I am not you, and You are not me.
I am I, and You are You.
We are two distinct persons.
I have a body, my body. You have your body.
I have desires, my desires. You have your desires.
I have emotions, my emotions. You have your emotions.
I have thoughts, my thoughts. You have your thoughts.
I have a will, my will. You have your will.
I have my personality. You have your personality.
I live my life. You live your life.
I have my freedom. You have your freedom.
I have my feelings. You have your feelings.
I am my spirit. You are your spirit.

Based on this distinction and recognition of oneself and of the other, it is possible to share an authentic, adult love, free within its sentiments:

So! Now we can start to love each other.
My body meets your body.
My desires meet your desires.

---

39   M. Macchia, *Roberto Assagioli: la psicosintesi*, ed. Nomina, 2000, p. 50.

40   A. Alberti, *Il Sé ritrovato*, op. cit., p. 131 and A. Alberti, *Psicosintesi e oltre*, op. cit., pp. 81-84.

My emotions meet your emotions.
My thoughts meet your thoughts.
My will meets your will.
My life meets your life.
My freedom meets your freedom.
My feeling meets your feeling.
My poetry meets your poetry.
My spirit meets your spirit.
I meet with You, and You with Me."

The author explains that this reinterpretation allows us to recognize that the disidentification/self-identification exercise is not merely facilitating a new experience of identity, but also tends to promote the experience of that 'I' which belongs to the personality ("I have *my* body, *my* emotions, *my* thoughts, etc."). This existential affirmation is not only an act of affirmation of our specific individuality in its totality, both corporal and mental, but also a profound act of acceptance of our human condition. Alberti[41] writes: "It's like saying: I'm also human! I sink my roots in the human. My place is on this earth! It's here that I have to live with everything I have: my body, my ability to feel, my ability to think."

It is very important to underline this point because, as we will see in the next paragraph, the dangers of indiscriminate practicing of disidentification are serious.

3. Risks and difficulties in the disidentification process

Although Assagioli insists on the importance of disidentification, one might not often realize that it is not just a technique, but a long and complex process that requires great commitment and some degree of mental health in the absence of which this practice can even become iatrogenic and be used as a means of division and isolation. Laura Boggio Gilot[42] notes in an article that "even when the mental structure allows, the process of disidentification can easily become illusory". This is because of a fundamental difficulty consisting in the fact that the observer, rather than being pure consciousness differentiated from mental contents, is often a super-egoic subject that judges what he observes, even, more often than not, unconsciously.

If this discrimination between the *authentic self* and *super-egoic subpersonality* is not fully understood and experienced, disidentification risks being used as a means to distance oneself from unacceptable or overly painful psychic contents. It becomes a system to protect oneself from the intense emotional reactions caused by such content. This way of practicing disidentification, far from facilitating a process of

---

41   A. Alberti, *La volontà di sintesi*, Ed. Centro Studi "R. Assagioli", 1986, p. 15.

42   L. Boggio Gilot, *Disidentificazione e integrazione nella terapia psicosintetica: il ruolo della meditazione vedanta di autoosservazione*, in "Rivista di psicosintesi terapeutica", Anno II, n. 2, p. 31.

integration and self-transformation, merely pushes the intolerable parts of one-self toward the lower unconscious, thereby increasing the internal division. True disidentification instead:

"divides the essence of the subject from the contents of their field of consciousness; it places space between consciousness and the multiform, colorful elements of the psyche, emotional states included, in order to know, relativize and manage them; if necessary it can transform their emotive energy without denying or hiding it. Disidentification places emotion in the overall design of personality and assigns its function and place; it does not divide it, deny it or isolate it, but includes it"[43].

In the following diagram I have attempted to clarify which different reactions we can notice at an experiential level when we take the position of the observer of our inner world to distinguish between the self identified with the super-egoic subpersonality and the truly disidentified self, or 'I':

	Observer 'I' identified with a super-egoic subpersonality	Observer 'I' truly disidentified
Bodily sensations	Stiffness, closure, tension, numbness, heaviness, blockage, stagnation, pain	Looseness, openness, relaxation, sensitivity, lightness, fluidity, movement, savoring
Actions	Censors, hides, represses, oppresses, unreal expectations, distances, separates, warns, orders, divides, suffocates, contrasts, hinders	Encourages expression, accepts, listens, reveals (in the sense of shedding light onto something), liberates, develops, supports growth, encourages, waits faithfully, contains, unites
Impulses and desires	Of immediate change, of perfection, partial (only takes into account a part and not the whole of our being), selfish (doesn't take the global good into account, only their own)	Of profound change, of authenticity, global (takes into account the totality of our being), of change in harmony with internal rhythms and times; more than desires, it is rather the will-ing of good (of the greater good for the majority of our "parts").
Emotions and sentiments	Anger, fear, contempt, rejection, guilt, shame, sadness, depression, anxiety	Acceptance, equanimity, compassion, trust, caring, concern, dignity, loving, humor, joy, serenity
Images	Clash, fight, rejection, condemnation, indifference; see for example: *Jacob Wrestling With the Angel* (Doré), *The Lovers* (Magritte), *Ashes* (Munch)	Of welcoming, understanding, forgiving, participating, loving embrace; see for example: *The Return Of The Prodigal Son* (Rembrandt), *Cupid and Psyche* (Canova)

---

43   P. M. Bonacina, *L'uomo stellare*, op. cit., p. 210.

Type of thought	Focuses on defects and shortcomings, analytic, critical, cerebral, dissects reality, rigid, stereotypical, schematic, logical "if ... then ...", theorizes and resists new and different experiences, uses ways of functioning like "always/never", "everything/nothing", "everybody/nobody..", "either/or"	Focuses on the merits and the good that is already present, synthetic, good-hearted, sees globally, flexible, spontaneous, new, original, unusual, originates out of the experience of reality and transforms through the experience of reality, uses ways of functioning like "sometimes", "at this time", "some", "both/and"
Typical expressions	"I don't think of you", "You're not important", "Go away", "I don't want anything to do with you", "I don't like you", "Leave me alone", "Shame on you!", "You bother me, you disgust me...", "I don't recognize you, you don't belong to me."	"Come here", "Even if you sometimes say/do...I accept you completely", "You're fine the way you are", "I'm here for you", "You're unconditionally worthy of love", "I recognize you and you are a part of me"

One of the fundamental prerequisites for implementing disidentification is in the *true awareness* and *acceptance* of what we are disidentifying from. Declaring "I have my body, my sensations; I have my impulses, my desires, my emotions and my feelings; I have my thoughts, etc." means two things: recognizing the fact that we have a human identity and have to submit to the laws of human life where there is also suffering and death, and also recognizing the fact that we have available a very specific psycho-physical personality and none other, with the limitations that this implies.[44] If disidentification thus leads to the discovery of a point of strength and power, it does not in any way favor taking a position of omnipotence, but leads to the recognition of its limits.

Recognizing these risks, Assagioli had already warned in his writings[45] that disidentification "is not repression, condemnation, passivity, renunciation, insensitivity" but is rather "a state of full vigilance and awareness, (...) which has the double advantage of conferring domination as much on the inner world as on the outer", where domination doesn't mean suppression of the contents of consciousness. They "must not be condemned, they must not arouse fears or guilt feelings. Domination produces a right direction, regulation and transmutation of energies and emotions ... it allows their expression in harmless or, better, useful and constructive ways"[46].

Disidentification is therefore not to be seen as asceticism, nor an antithesis; it is not opposed to anything, but it is a true synthesis that provides a completely different perspective than the previous one. Ferrucci[47] writes:

---

44   A. Alberti, *Il sé ritrovato*, op. cit.

45   R. Assagioli, *Psicosintesi - Armonia della vita*, op. cit., p. 105.

46   R. Assagioli, *Principi e metodi della psicosintesi terapeutica*, op. cit., p. 106.

47   P. Ferrucci, *Crescere*, op. cit., p. 52.

"Actually, disidentification does not impede us from re-identifying ourselves, with any part of ourselves, if we so desire. What it helps us to avoid is a continuous, unconscious and random identification with any element that appears to us through the flow of consciousness."

4. The simplicity of being: self-awareness and self-identification

Disidentification is used, on the one hand, to create a psychic space between oneself and the contents of one's consciousness, on the other hand "as a technique to conquer pure awareness of self-identity"[48]. When an individual abandons all identification, what remains? Who are they then? Psychosynthesis says that the individual is not what they are aware of, but is he/she who is aware. Assagioli[49] explained:

"Self-consciousness is what distinguishes us from animals. (...) Human beings go beyond the simple perception of animals: humans know that they are perceiving. But in truth this self-consciousness is usually "implicit" rather than explicit. It is perceived in a somewhat cloudy, distorted way since it can be confused with the contents of the consciousness (sensations, emotions, thought, etc.). This continuous impact veils the clarity of consciousness and promotes a false identification of the self with transient and mutually changing contents. So if we want to make our self-consciousness clear, explicit and alive, we must first disidentify ourselves from all these contents, then identify ourselves in the self. This can be achieved with some types of meditation, but especially so with the Disidentification/Self-identification Exercise."

Even though it is good to point out that practicing disidentification/self-identification does not mean that the experience of the personal self has already been reached, for the person who practices it, the purpose of this exercise is to come as close as possible to that goal. True disidentification increases the awareness of our presence. And the individual's discovery of being a subject will allow him/her to face life's situations differently and to energetically act on them. Thus, the process of disidentification has the purpose of recouping subjectivity until one achieves true *self-identification*: "the existential experience of pure self-awareness, the direct perception of oneself, the discovery of the self"[50].

Self-identification means allowing the consciousness to perceive itself without any content and any point of support. It is "awareness of oneself" which gives us the sense of being, absolutely being, without attributes"[51]. It is a state of psychic

---

48   R. Assagioli, op. cit., p.71.

49   R. Assagioli, *L'atto di volontà*, op. cit., p. 156.

50   Ibid, p. 16.

51   R. Assagioli, *Comprendere la psicosintesi*, op. cit., p. 25.

nudity in which all our clothes have been removed: thoughts, feelings, images, physical sensations. Then what the subject faces is the *ontological experience of being*, pure self-consciousness. One is no longer overwhelmed by the never-ending flow of emotions, images, thoughts and desires, or the confusion caused by the various subpersonalities. The feelings of conflict and fragmentation vanish temporarily; the moods one used to live with, such as anxiety and guilt, disappear. This experience can last only a few seconds, but its effects last much longer.[52]

This increase of self-awareness may have several positive consequences: the discovery of a reference point, a deepening sense of identity, the emergence of a more objective, panoramic view of one's own psychic life, the beginning of personal independence and finally, the creation of a space within which the function that Psychosynthesis considers to be the most important, the will[53], may be able to act.

4.1. Fear of freedom

But the process of abandoning our old identities is not linear and can initially lead to the feeling of losing every identity. And, as Steven Kull[54] writes correctly, "the anxiety created by this situation has highlighted a *strong ambivalence towards freedom*. Although many people talk of freedom in positive terms and consciously desire it, when they find themselves face to face with the possibility of new choices and new ways of being, they retreat in fear and return to the safety of old models. It is that 'escape from freedom' which Erich Fromm also talked about."

Abandoning old identities refers symbolically to the process of dying. And death, though symbolic, generates an infinity of fears. To die, you must have courage and faith in what comes next, a subsequent rebirth. Only the strength to support the vacuum, the absence of pre-established reference points, and silence build a bridge over which the new comes to transform the old existing shapes. Of this, Piero Ferrucci[55] writes:

"Many people prefer to identify themselves with a limited and negative self-image rather than endure the anxiety of not being identified with anything. The freely fluctuating state in which there are no definitions or handholds terrorizes us, because we fear it leads to disintegration and death. Being zero: this, which although is at the epicenter of our terror, can become the beginning of our liberation. Knowing how to be simply, without the support of a role, without the reassurance of a qualification, without the support of good self-esteem. Recognizing our essence in its purest state, without qualifications and without adjectives, is the highest state of freedom: it is our Self."

---

52   B. Carter Haar, op. cit., p. 15.

53   P. Ferrucci, op. cit., p. 59.

54   S. Kull, *Evoluzione e personalità*, Centro Studi "R. Assagioli", p. 21.

55   P. Ferrucci, *Introduzione alla psicosintesi*, op. cit., pp. 62-63.

CHAPTER III

THE PERSONAL SELF AND THE TRANSPERSONAL SELF

Two nice birds
One the companion of the other
live together in the same tree,
one eats the tree's fruit,
the other, without eating
with its vision witnesses all."[56]

1. A premise

I have already pointed out, commenting on the topical model of the psyche as proposed by Assagioli (see Part 3, Chapter III), how in Psychosynthesis the contrast between the personal self (or 'I') and the Transpersonal Self is purely verbal, since they are essentially the same thing. In fact, our author[57] wrote:

"Speaking of a personal self and of a higher 'I' (the Self) must not induce us to believe that there are two separate and independent selves (...). The 'I' in reality and in essence is ONE. What we call "ordinary" self is that part of the "higher Self" that the wakeful consciousness can accept, assimilate and implement at any given moment. It is therefore something contingent and changeable, a variable quantity. It is a reflection that can become ever more clear and vivid and that one day might come to unify with its Source."

Therefore, the *personal self* has no substance of its own, but is to be seen as a *partial experience of the Self*, its reflection in the field of awareness, "its manifestation in ordinary consciousness"[58]. The Self is, therefore, at a level that can be defined as both "personal", and "transpersonal". This double experiencing of the Self can at first confuse and actually render a clear understanding of the matter more difficult, especially since the distinct contrast between the personal dimension and the transpersonal dimension has a didactic value, while in practice it has an immense amount of nuances. To achieve some clarity, however, I will maintain this distinction.

---

56   *Katha Upanishad*, cit. in L. Boggio Gilot, *Crescere oltre l'io*, op. cit., p. 67.

57   R. Assagioli, *Psicosintesi - Armonia della vita*, op. cit., p. 90.

58   Ibid, p. 87.

The two levels of experiencing the Self correspond to the two types of realization outlined by Assagioli. As I have already mentioned, according to the founder of Psychosynthesis, the path of integral development of the personality has two fundamental phases: one leading to *self-realization*, or personal psychosynthesis, and one leading to *self-transcendence*, or transpersonal psychosynthesis.

Personal psychosynthesis aims to organize the bio-psychic elements around the 'I'; the development and harmonization of functions and human potential at all levels of the lower and middle areas of the individual's constitution; the cooperation of the various "parties" to be represented, no longer in conflict with each other. At this level of synthesis all of the above elements are coordinated into a living unity, but the Self remains latent. Assagioli wrote[59] that:

"The complete, integrated, self-realized personality can in fact be quite selfish or at least self-centered. Self-realization at the personal level does not necessarily mean a higher motivation; it can be determined by the craving for success and the impulse to flaunt one's individual powers. Not only can a self-realized person at this level be satisfied with theirself, but may even end up in an antagonistic position toward any further growth."

Instead, *transpersonal psychosynthesis* corresponds to a higher type of synthesis, and aims at the manifestation of superconscious forces and the organization of the bio-psychic elements around the Self. Development "beyond the self" includes the integration of the potentialities of the higher unconscious and its translogical structures up to the realization of the Self. The transpersonal consciousness has access to the perception of the interconnection of reality which reveals the deep ties and the indivisible unity between biological, psychological, ecological, sociological and cosmic phenomena; this leads to the discovery of order tied to disorder and the connective fabric of the apparent multiplicity.[60] Realization of Self is, consequently, something very different from normal self-consciousness and realization of the personal self.

Assagioli[61] maintained that self-actualization could be achieved on different levels:

"...it's important that the subject gets to a certain level of self-identification; meaning, that they, as a conscious subject, are able to distinguish theirself from the various contents with which they usually identify. (...) In many cases one can only help initiate a good personal psychosynthesis and integrate all the elements and psychic functions around a center of awareness of oneself.

Instead, when there are subjects who already have problems of a spiritual or religious nature (...) the therapist has to adapt to the patient's interests and meet

---

59   R. Assagioli, *L'Atto di volontà*, op. cit., p. 92.

60   L. Boggio Gilot, *Lo sviluppo transpersonale verso la non dualità*, in *I nuovi paradigmi della psicologia*, op. cit., pp. 41-42.

61   R. Assagioli, *Principi e metodi della psicosintesi terapeutica*, op. cit., p. 84.

the patient in the area that constitutes their main concern: in this way, we are
assured that the best relationship can be instilled."

The distinction between the various levels of manifestation of the Self has
therefore a notable utility in the practice of Psychosynthesis.

2. The personal self or 'I'

Piero Ferrucci writes[62] that many psychologists have tried to create various
definitions of the self—and here the term "self" is understood in its classical psychological sense, not as Transpersonal Self—sometimes calling it "ego" or, like
Psychosynthesis does, 'I'. The self has been seen as the director of personality, the
behavior coordinator, the meeting point of the conscious and the unconscious, or
as the constellation of our more stable attitudes and states of mind. Other conceptions describe it as the specific style of an individual, the result of our interaction with others, the totality of the psycho-physical organism, or as an illusory
aggregate of ephemeral elements.

Psychosynthesis deals very simply with this topic, and sees the self as our
essence.[63] Beyond the psychic multiplicity, Psychosynthesis recognizes the existence
of a self, or a center of consciousness; and it considers that center, which is not
identified with any of the psychic elements, a fundamental experience in the more
profound sense, i.e. connected to the base of our existence, to its foundation.

Assagioli, after describing the countless external influxes that condition us and
the internal multiplicity that is thereby derived (see Part 4, Chapter I), reveals
how, alongside those elements there is

"a profound individual part that we feel is different from all our other more intimate
parts; its origins are mysterious, but it seems like a direct expression of our true
self"[64].

In summary we can say that, in a negative sense, the personal self is distinct
from the contents of the field of consciousness and personality; in a positive sense
it is instead defined as a center of *pure awareness*, *pure self-consciousness* and *will*,
capable of directing, dominating and using all the psychic and body functions.

Bruno Caldironi writes[65]:

"The self is assigned three fundamental categories of characteristics: self-
consciousness, awareness and volition. The first two give it the nature of a
cognitive process in which self-consciousness is a central and privileged element,
albeit not an exclusive one. (...) Alongside the cognitive processes, the volitional
ones, not detached from the first ones, are set up in a constitutive way, and are

---

62   P. Ferrucci, *Crescere*, op. cit., p. 49.

63   Ibid, p. 49.

64   R. Assagioli, *Psicosintesi - Armonia della vita*, op. cit., p. 19.

65   B. Caldironi, op. cit., p. 313.

specifically assigned to the organizing function of the personality. As we have already emphasized, the volitional function appears intimately connected with the egoic response."

2.1. The self as "center"

The image of the *self as center* is seen in all the literature devoted to Psychosynthesis. For Psychosynthesis, the center can and must be found because it alone is capable of integrating the totality of the personality; only it is the source of true harmony and balance. When we are "off-center", when we forget ourselves, we live on the margins of our being, and we fall prey to many ghosts. Then, destructive impulses, emotions difficult to deal with, anguishing thoughts and fantasies and images of us that make us suffer take possession of our self that, identifying with them, becomes those impulses, those emotions, those thoughts or fantasies. Instead, Piero Ferrucci[66] explains that the "center":

"is that part in us that is always healthy, corresponds to our true identity and always remains true to itself. (…) In the Center, we are masters of ourselves, we feel at home rather than slaves exiled in a far-off land; we are alert instead of falling prey to anguishing dreams; we are ourselves, we are not something or someone else. The Center is our 'I'."

Finding your own deep center, your true 'I' gives a strong sense of mastery: you discover how you feel when you come home, when you open yourself up to your inner intimacy and simplicity. It is a fundamental experience that is the basis of psychic health because it has the effect of synthesis on the personality. As soon as the self is free from false identifications, it acts as a unifying center for all the parts and elements of the personality that can now be accommodated according to a new, more harmonious and inclusive organization.

The self is a point with a nature higher to other psychic content because there are no elements of the personality that are foreign to it. In fact, it is not part of the personality, but transcends it. Therefore, it is no longer necessary to choose between opposing poles and conflicting elements; all elements can be integrated around it. The person who experiences the self will then have many valid functions and qualities that can be refined, developed and integrated, and can perceive themselves as a unified whole, composed of various elements related to each other.[67]

2.2. The self as a process

Yet this image of the personal self as a center easily tends to create confusion and leads the mind to construct an idea of the self as an object to possess, or a

---

66   P. Ferrucci, *Introduzione alla psicosintesi*, op. cit., p. 56.

67   B. Carter Haar, op. cit., pp. 17-18.

destination to reach. To further clarify the psychosynthetic idea of the self, it will be useful to introduce the distinction between "self as an object" and "self as a process".

The self as an object is seen as "the whole set of attitudes, beliefs and emotions that regard one's own individuality"[68]. Within this frame of reference, various authors assume the existence of a certain psychic response. This can be defined as that part of the personality qualified by a series of subjective attributes and attitudes of self-evaluation and self-perception. In Psychosynthesis, we tend to define this set of characteristics, with which the self identifies itself in a relatively stable way, as the so-called "sense of identity", distinguishing this "sense of identity" from authentic identity, i.e. from the self seen as a center of pure self-consciousness and will.

Instead, the *self-process* can be defined as a "complex of functions, or as a psychic response that assumes certain specific functions, without necessarily having relations with the object of self-perception"[69]. This means that the self is not defined as a perceived, living entity, but rather as a process that plays certain roles in the dynamic of psychic life and manages certain functions. In the wake of this we mention British psychoanalyst Edward Glover (1888-1972), who references the self as the organization of the mnemonic imprinting, Austrian psychiatrist Heinz Hartmann (1894-1979), who sees it as the mediator between endopsychic requests and external environmental needs, and American psychologist Henry Murray (1893-1988), for whom the self corresponds to the organizing function of consciousness.[70]

To understand how the concept of the personal self, as accepted by Psychosynthesis, is often misconstrued, I feel it useful to return briefly to another idea mentioned previously, that of the subpersonality.

Every subpersonality appears as the result of of the interaction, governed by the laws of psychodynamics, of the various psychic functions. So are the sensations, impulses, emotions, thoughts and images that contribute to the formation of what can be defined as a "self-object", a "subpersonality". But the self, as seen by Psychosynthesis, is distinct from the contents of consciousness and cannot be reduced to any of them. Assagioli states that between the self and the various psychic contents there is the same relationship between vessel and content, or between a cinematographic screen and the images projected on to it.

"The self is therefore not an object, but a process that presides over the organization of individual personal content. It is not identified with any of the contents, which are characterized by change, inconstancy, and relativity. The contents contribute

---

68   B. Caldironi, op. cit., p. 327.

69   Ibid, p. 328.

70   Ibid.

to forming a perceptive unit experienced as a bearer of identity, but none of them has the characteristics of identity"[71].

Therefore, the stability provided by a center considered "pure self-consciousness and will", around which rotate and organize the changing bio-psychic contents, cannot be seen as definite, absolute, given, or definitely achieved. In actual experience, self-consciousness and volitional ability constantly pass from extremely high to extremely low levels. The balance provided by the discovery of the self is not a static, constant balance, but a dynamic balance that needs to be managed moment by moment, requiring constant vigilance, attention and awareness. Using a metaphor, the balance we are talking about is much more like that of the tightrope walker performing acrobatics balanced on a rope, rather than the equilibrium of a ruler firmly seated on a throne.

These observations bring us to the point where our discussion began, that is, to the fundamental recognition that the personal self is nothing other than the function of the different levels of manifestation, implementation and awareness of the Transpersonal Self.

2.3. The self as experience

I think it is appropriate to conclude this attempt to define the personal self with the words of Assagioli that, better than anyone else, can bring us back to its original concept. I took the passage from a transcript of an unpublished interview given by the master to his pupil and collaborator Alberto Alberti in March 1973.

"AA: According to Psychosynthesis, what is the self? How can we define it?

RA: I think we *need to insist on experience*. But scientifically, in order for an experience to be valid, it is necessary to create the appropriate and necessary conditions for it to occur. For a physical experience, the conditions suited to that experience must be created. So, those who want to know what the self is must do the disidentification exercise and then silence—arriving at pure self-consciousness. If one really wants to go see if the self is there, you have to go find it at its home!

It is therefore useless to continue to intellectually discuss what the self is, as if it were an object. It is a direct subjective experience, one of those "immediate facts of consciousness," as Bergson calls them. The disidentification exercise is nothing other than the negative and preparatory part for self-identification, and I would say we should speak more and more of this self-identification exercise, the first stage of which is disidentification.

Knowing that we exist is, in the end, the most important thing. And whoever wants to discover this, with all its relative consequences, like the unleashing of energies, must undergo specific training.

---

71   Ibid, p. 332.

AA: Isn't it necessary to explain what the self is, if it's energy, or spirit, or…?

RA: No. It's an experience, an immediate fact. It's better not to add further clarifications. One thing is an experience, another thing is a doctrine.

The example of aesthetics is significant. Benedetto Croce wrote a very interesting book about aesthetics (...) But Croce did not have a true aesthetic sense. He did not understand Dante's poetry, and said very questionable things, for example the Divine Comedy has value only for some lyrical passages, but doesn't have a value in and of itself (...) so we can develop theories about aesthetics without having an aesthetic sense. You can be uncultured, but still have aesthetic sense and enjoy aesthetic experiences (…)"[72].

It seems to me that, in the final analysis, in Psychosynthesis the self is essentially not an object or structure, but an experience that has certain structural features, certain functional prerogatives, and precise fundamental aspects. With this, asserts Sebastiano Tilli[73], Assagioli launched a message of further development, which dynamically explains and understands the recognition of the complex and fragmentary nature of the human personality, as well as its need for synthesis, identity and constant renewal. Below is the excellent summary from Alberto Alberti[74]:

Characteristic structure of the experience of the self

Centrality	In every existing structure, from an atom to a constellation, there is a Center that supports, organizes and vitalizes
Identity	The center is "one," makes us feel "unique" and "united", individual, unrepeatable, equal to ourselves, different from what is non-self, distinct from external objects and with the feeling of some delimitation in space (the boundaries of the self); the center gives us a sense of identity as it is "identical to itself" (sameness).
Continuity	In fact, centrality is maintained equal and identical to itself in the various stages of development. Centrality as the guiding principle of life, which has the characteristics of stability and permanence. Stability in time, permanence (immobility: self, reflection of Self, resides in the dimension of Being, and not of becoming).

Functional characteristics of the experience of the self

Synthesis	The center has the function of cohesion and synthesis of the multiplicity of energy aspects in a unit (unifying center)

72   R. Assagioli, intervista inedita, 1973.

73   S. Tilli, *Spunti per una lettura prospettica della "psicologia" di Roberto Assagioli*, in *I nuovi paradigmi della psicologia*, op. cit., p. 207.

74   A. Alberti, *Psicosintesi e oltre*, op. cit., pp. 48-50.

Evolution	The self has the function of evolving and maturing the human personality by refining its functions (affective, cognitive, and active), and making it an adequate instrument of expression of the Self.

Fundamental aspects of the experience of the self

Freedom	Assagioli comes to the experience of the self through the disidentification exercise, which is basically a work of liberation, of acquiring a margin of inner freedom. The self is located in a specific dimension of freedom: the experience of the self occurs in a specific interior setting, consisting of a space-atmosphere of freedom.
Consciousness	The self is a center of self-consciousness that has the fundamental function of observation.
Will	The self is also a center of will, meaning it possesses a vital energetic aspect which means that, besides observing, it can also act on what it observes of itself, of others, of the surroundings
Relation	The self is not isolated; but is in relation with you, with others, with objective reality and with the world; the self is a Center of love, i.e. a Center of a relational, osmotic, empathic, resonant field, giving and receiving love
Presence	All of the above aspects give the sense of "presence" (consider that illness may be, in some ways, considered as a form of "absence"). Presence, as a feeling of the true and authentic self, is not a cold and abstract awareness, but rather a warm and living state of consciousness. We could mention a: • living presence: the presence is what "animates" and "vitalizes" the personality. It is the "breath of life". The essence of the self is life, which is experienced in the form of a feeling of existence; • gentle presence: presence is gentle and manifests itself as feeling, which is the musical key of the spirit (sound, vibration of individual subjectivity, word, song, dance of the spirit).

3. The I-Self connection

> "... the thread of contact with the Self, that
> 'Thread of Ariadne',
> that enables the 'I' to not become lost
> in the multiplicity of human experiences,
> both internal and external."[75]

Given that the personal self or 'I' is not that part of the Transpersonal Self which, projected in existence, experiences and identifies with the multiplicity of

---

75   A. Alberti, op. cit., p. 95.

human experiences, the relationship between the two takes on a fundamental importance in the psychosynthetic process.

In effect, the personal self is in a specific and precarious intermediate existential position between Self and non-Self, between past and future, between multiplicity and unity, between disintegration and synthesis. Its purpose, after affirming itself and having distinguished itself from the contents of the field of consciousness, is to join its root and origins. This is what Maslow also found when he wrote[76]:

> "I want to emphasize a fundamental paradox that we must face even if we do not understand it. The goal of identity (self-realization, autonomy, individualization, Horney's "real self", authenticity, etc.) seems simultaneously to be a final goal in itself, and also a transient goal, a kind of rite of passage, a step along the path leading to transcendence of identity. This almost means that its function is to cancel itself."

In short, it seems that achieving self-realization on a personal level often coincides with the beginning of the transpersonal journey; it seems that the maximum attainment of the self and of self-consciousness corresponds to a transcendence of oneself, going beyond the individual dimension. Assagioli[77] agreed, affirming:

> "When certain exercises help to eliminate the psychic contents of the 'I' the conscious self tends to climb back naturally to its origins."

In Assagioli's Egg Diagram the I-Self connection indicates that the *realization of Self is a function of the level of self-identification reached*. For Pier Maria Bonacina[78] the fact that the 'I' may recognize itself in the Self, and that the recognition of the connection between 'I' and Self consists in coming to the real awareness of one's own deep identity, constitutes the essential crossroads of the individual's evolutionary process. Thus, the unification of the 'I' with the Self becomes possible only when the sense of self has attained sufficient intensity, such that it can freely and deliberately disidentify from the functions and contents of the personality. In fact, the self can move consciously and voluntarily toward its essence, towards the Self, but it is also possible that, being free, it can decide to take another path, that towards the non-Self (see Part 2, Chapter III, Para. 5.3). In this case, the individual follows a path that leads to losing their way, to becoming overwhelmed by the chaos of psychic multiplicity, to a distancing from essence, and ultimately to the loss of theirself.

---

76   A. Maslow, op. cit., p. 119.

77   R. Assagioli, *Lo sviluppo transpersonale*, op. cit., p. 37.

78   P. M. Bonacina, op. cit., p. 23.

But we must bear in mind that there isn't just *movement of the 'I' toward the Self*, the journey which consists in the laborious recomposition of their divisions and conflicts and in the creation of "synthesis" through consciousness, will and love; there is also another movement that originates and starts directly from the Self that manifests and reveals itself, unfolds and expands with ease and lightness.[79] This *movement of the development of the Self* happens when the circumstances of existence create a climate that favors its manifestation: whenever we perform an act of synthesis, whenever we open ourselves to the beauty of life, every time we observe and treat another being with respect, every time we unveil our will, whenever we give voice to our humanity and our feelings.[80]

The Self is the authentic and profound essence, it is what the human being intimately already is and, at the same time, what they want to become. Its fundamental instinct is to manifest itself, to show itself, to exist fully and totally. So:

> "Striving to show itself, the Self exerts a kind of attraction from above on the human personality, and a pressure from inside the personality from which it derives a transpersonal thrust of the self, which feels moved and oriented towards overcoming self-centeredness, to de-center itself in relation to others and to over-center themselves in relation to universal life"[81].

In the Egg Diagram, this process of dialogue and approach between the self and its source can be visualized by imagining the conscious 'I' gradually moving along the line that connects it to the Transpersonal Self. However, this way of presenting the I-Self relationship must not be misleading: the position of the Self at the top of the ovoid does not imply that its realization by the self can only occur in the higher unconscious. If we are sufficiently disidentified, the Self can be encountered at any level of the psyche. Indeed, as I have already pointed out, sometimes super-conscious experiences can divert from the realization of the Self, because it is more difficult not to identify itself in transpersonal states that are so joyful, ecstatic and attractive.

The more the self empties itself of its own identifications, of all identifications, the more one approaches the experience of the Self, or perhaps it is better to say, the more one comes back to being what one really is, the Self. The self can become master of its own personality, can be the unifying center, can acquire the tools to best manage the complexity of psychic life, but cannot do other than recognize itself as a channel and instrument of the Self. To be able to receive without being overwhelmed, it must be emptied, gradually renouncing its comfortable and reassuring identities and abandoning itself with confidence. In fact "it is only in an empty, and therefore truly humble consciousness, that a genuine transpersonal experience (of the Self) can be received: a moment of fear, a moment of presumption is enough for it to be distorted and contaminated,

---

79   A. Alberti, op. cit., p. 253.

80   A. Alberti, *Psicosintesi - una cura per l'anima*, L'Uomo ed., 2008, p. 48.

81   Ibid, p. 43.

transforming it into an experience of annihilation or exaltation, creating psychic imbalance"[82]. Assagioli[83] also warned:

> "This fact (the reuniting of the 'I' with the Self) that can be expressed so simply (...) is a long and difficult task that is not for everyone. Between the starting point on the plains of consciousness and the lofty peak of full spiritual self-realization there are various intermediate steps, (...). These intermediate stages mean new identifications. The 'I' that does not know how to consist fully in its highest Self, must look for other vital support and connections (...)"

So before attaining reunification between the 'I' and the Self, only possible in rare cases and usually temporary, there is the period of the dramatic internal dialogue between the two aspects. Though identical in essence, in experience, the personal self, uniquely identified with certain psychic content, may even feel its relationship with the transpersonal Self as threatening. But then, writes Caldironi[84], if the identity between 'I' and Self is verbally impossible, what is it that makes them the same thing? Where do they join? The answer is: at the moment of the experience.

4. The Transpersonal Self

The description befits things,
to being the experience.

4.1. The Self as experience and the inadequacy of language

Though Assagioli declared on several occasions that he does not want to confuse psychology with religion and philosophy in any way, it is undeniable that his proposed conception of the Transpersonal Self—as well as that of Jung—naturally lends itself to being linked to spiritual traditions. In the history of humanity, all mystical and metaphysical traditions have dealt with this mysterious concept by calling it in dozens of different ways. It was known by the name of the Divine Son, Adam-Kadmon, Ruach Adonai, Nous, Pneuma, Purusha, Brahman-Atman, The I am, Dharmadhatu, the Void, Talezza, the Divinity, etc.

According to Assagioli these terms are nothing more than different symbols of a single concept experienced in every corner of the world and in every culture. And it is the *experience* that Psychosynthesis is interested in, especially the *effects it produces* on the psychic life of the human being. Leave the intellectual dissertations on what the Self ultimately is or how it can be satisfactorily defined in the background. What matters in the psychosynthetic approach is that the Self "is a true

---

82   A. Alberti, *La volontà di sintesi*, op. cit., p. 14.

83   R. Assagioli, *Principi e metodi della psicosintesi terapeutica*, op. cit., p. 30-31.

84   B. Caldironi, op. cit., p. 333.

phenomenal experience, an internal reality that can be empirically verified and deliberately produced with the appropriate techniques"[85].

This approach comes out of the recognition of the natural inability of language to fully describe such an experience. Indeed Psychosynthesis considers fully definable only the psychic contents, the "objects" that appear in the field of consciousness. On the contrary, the living essence of a human being does not lend itself to being described as a thing. Erich Fromm[86] says:

> "Words describe an experience, but they are not the experience. As soon as I try to describe what I experienced, that experience goes up in smoke: it dries up and dies, and becomes a mere idea."

Thus we have to remember that any idea or image we may have of ourselves before having a real experience can be an obstacle to it, and, if taken literally, even takes us in the wrong direction. According to Assagioli, the Self is indescribable with words. It is direct, immediate, non-verbal awareness. For this reason he always underlined that this reality lies beyond names, shapes, words, thoughts; above and beyond rationality:

> "Essential Reality is so far above any mental concept. It is inexpressible. It must be lived (...) The joy inherent in life itself (...) The realization of one's own Self, which is based on oneSelf and resides in oneSelf (...) The 'I' without 'I' (...) The three aspects of the supreme paradox: absence of the 'I' (Buddhist aspect), Unity with God (mystic aspect), Realization of the True Self (Vedic aspect)"[87].

What emerges from this passage is that the experience of Self-realization possesses profoundly paradoxical features that make it unattainable to a mind that operates according to logical-rational criteria: it is both transcendent and immanent, it is the absence of any specific quality and also the synthesis of all the qualities, an experience of emptiness and at the same time expression of the utmost fullness, it is ecstatic and terrifying. For this reason, it can be captured *only intuitively*.

In addition to its inadequacy to describe the experience of the Self, language poses an additional problem. Those who have testified over the centuries have described their experiences in terms of their individuality, the methods used or their own particular religious or philosophical beliefs.

From these findings Assagioli derived the conclusion that the experience of the Self, being a "true phenomenal experience" empirically verifiable by the individual, should in no way be limited to a type of experience that we could call religious or mystical, or delegated to theology, ceremonies and various churches.

---

85   R. Assagioli, op. cit., p. 15.

86   E. Fromm, *Avere o essere?*, Ed. Mondadori, 1977, p. 120.

87   R. Assagioli, *Libertà in prigione*, notes from unedited manuscript.

According to our author, the time has come for the human being to discover the essential truths of life by having a direct experience.

4.2. Characteristics of the experience of Self

If defining the Transpersonal Self is an arduous endeavor, it may be less difficult, and certainly more useful, to list some characteristics of the mental states that are produced when it manifests itself in the field of consciousness. These can be indicated by symbolism and analogies from testimonies of direct experiences. It is interesting to note that these symbolisms and analogies have characteristics that are exactly opposite to those that distinguish the psychic and psychosomatic disturbances,[88] allowing us to emphasize the *therapeutic value of the experience of Self*. For Assagioli[89] this experience is connected to the following features:

Characteristics of the experience of Self	Positive assertion	Opposite assertion
Sense of clarification	I arrive at the roots of my being, leave the surface and reach my "depths"	I have no roots, I belong nowhere, I have no safe place
Sense of internalization	I go from the periphery to the center of my being, I am centered, balanced	I feel shallow, inconsistent, I feel empty inside
Sense of elevation	I go to a higher level, I'm elevated, raised	I'm at the bottom of a pit, I'm sinking
Sense of expansion	I expand, my consciousness expands, I participate in a more ample reality	I feel small, miserable, selfish, closed in myself
Sense of development	I blossom, emerge, remove veils and thickets that close and impede, I express myself and show my face	I am turned inward, wrapped in a cocoon, I hide
Sense of following a path	I walk a path, I'm on the right way, my way	I feel lost, disoriented, I don't know where to go
Sense of empowerment	My existence is full, I am, I feel strong, energetic and dynamic	I feel weak, tired, impotent

---

88   A. Alberti, *Il Sé ritrovato*, op. cit., p. 27.

89   R. Assagioli, *Lo sviluppo transpersonale*, op. cit., pp. 72-83.

Sense of awakening	I am alert to a new reality, I feel inspired, attentive	I feel sleepy, numb, unsteady
Sense of illumination	I see reality in a new light, I clearly understand, I am confident in my perceptions	I feel uncertain, doubtful, confused, as if I were in a fog or, even worse, in the dark
Sense of joy	I am at peace, feel rewarded, in ecstasy	I am anguished, suffering, tormented
Sense of renewal	I am regenerated, renewed, reborn	I feel degenerated, old, dying
Sense of resurrection	I've come home, back to a previous and forgotten state	I am getting away from myself, forgetting myself
Sense of liberation	I am free and I feel free	I feel imprisoned, oppressed, closed
Sense of purity	I feel innocent, clear, genuine, uncontaminated	I feel impure, guilty, dirty

It seems important to conclude this paragraph with a specification. The full and harmonious experience of the Self, as described here, is usually only possible when one has reached a sufficient level of personal psychosynthesis, that is, when the individual has "realized and passed through all the earlier phases of identity development"[90]: renouncing their own desires of omnipotence, developing an attitude of essential trust in existence, recognizing themselves as being autonomous and free, discovering themselves intrinsically connected with other human beings and with the universe, humbly accepting life in its entirety and beauty (see Part 3, Chapter II, Para. 5).

When, on the other hand, this experience arises in a personality that is not sufficiently integrated, in an individual seeking realization of the Self out of presumption, greed, desire for power, or need for recognition, it may lead not only to erroneous interpretations in the egoistic and separative sense, but also to imbalances and severe psychological disturbances.

For this reason, instead of taking the path of realization of the Transpersonal Self through the use of specific techniques, it would be preferable to take an indirect path which aims to embody on a daily basis an essential quality: Synthesis. This path, Alberti[91] writes, even if not necessary, makes it easier to avoid the risk of exaltation and inflating the ego. Indeed, we may paradoxically state that the indirect path is the most secure and "direct" one for the gradual realization of our Self.

---

90 A. Alberti, *Psicosintesi e oltre*, op. cit., p. 109.

91 A. Alberti, *Psicosintesi - Una cura per l'anima*, op. cit., pp. 47-49.

4.3. Meaning of the graphic representation of the Self

Even though language is an inadequate instrument to express the real consistency of the experience of the Self, it is useful in the comprehension of meanings that the graphic representation wishes to convey.

First of all, it is important to emphasize that the Transpersonal Self is depicted in the Egg Diagram as *unconscious*. This means that it is normally not perceived and that the identification of the personal self with its source rarely occurs; it is usually temporary and is often the highest peak that one reaches after years of discipline. But it is good to point out that the Self, placed at the top of the ovoid, does not indicate a static and definitive point of arrival, "something to evolve toward and change into. If it were this way, it would only be an object frozen in time and space, something static and destined to death"[92]. Rather, it represents the synthesizing center of our whole being. "It is the transforming process itself"[93], the flowing of the joy of life.

The Transpersonal Self at the top of the ovoid is an effective symbol of the initiatory journey that everyone makes toward light, fullness, and joy. It is a reference point, the guiding star showing Ulysses the way home. As Alberto Alberti writes[94], it is simultaneously "a purpose and an evolutionary goal in time, a center of synthesis and cohesion in space".

But I have already had the occasion to point out that placing the Self at the apex of the higher unconscious does not mean that it is associated only with the sublime energies of the superconscious. The Egg Diagram represents the Self, both in its *transcendent dimension* (Self), distinct from all the contents contained in the various levels of the unconscious, as well as in its *immanent dimension* (personal self or 'I'). The Self is therefore potentially present on all psychic levels, able to emerge in every experience, regardless of the level from which it comes. In Psychosynthesis, transcending "does not mean going further, in the sense of rising up, leaving behind the transcended like a useless burden; transcending means extending the consciousness to that part, to that previously unknown dimension which is now conquered by the 'I'"[95]. "In fact, human nature is not only 'aerial' and 'volatile': it is also concrete, material, similar to a tree, which extends its roots into the earth even as its branches reach to the sky. Transcendence by itself risks losing immanence: and the Self, the true Self, is at the same time immanent and transcendent"[96].

In summary, we can say that in psychosynthetic thought such a graphic representation of the Self indicates a convergence of transcendence and

---

92   A. Alberti, *Psicosintesi e oltre*, op. cit., p. 69.

93   A. Alberti, *L'uomo che cura, l'uomo che soffre*, op. cit., p. 212.

94   A. Alberti, *Il Sé ritrovato*, op. cit., p. 31.

95   A. Galoppini, *Il Sé transpersonale*, in *I nuovi paradigmi della psicologia*, op. cit., p. 270.

96   A. Alberti, *Psicosintesi e oltre*, op. cit., p. 64.

immanence, a convergence that is verified in an experience that is always an experience of integration, synthesis and totality.

The absence of a real controposition between immanence and transcendence assumes a further nuance in the absence of a clear opposition between the *universal dimension* and the *individual dimension* of the human being. The Self is precisely represented half within and half outside the Egg Diagram, indicating the possibility of "encounter and synthesis between the 'I', the others, and the universal Self, between the individual, humanity and the universe, between the human dimension and that of the divine"[97]. Alberti writes:

> "The full experience of the Self in its completeness is simultaneously individual and universal. It is an experience of harmony and synthesis in which the subject feels unique and united with theirself and at the same time in communion with others and the universal reality. The subject that lives this experience doesn't stop at individual consciousness, but enters into a state of wider consciousness where, in a breath of love and freedom, they perceive the sense of unity of all life"[98].

In this sense, "it is possible to perceive the meaning of the Self, as the pontiff (Ed. "bridge builder") of human existence, as a bridge between the personal and universal aspects of the human being, and the synthesis of individuality and universality"[99]. One might even say, using an existentialist expression, that the Self is "the connection between Being and Existence, between 'Sein' and 'Dasein'"[100]. How can there be the experience of universality without individual self-consciousness?[101]

4.4. The Jungian Self and the Psychosynthetic Self: differences and clarifications

Although in many ways the Transpersonal Self of Psychosynthesis is similar to that of Jung, it is important to highlight a point where the two orientations differ radically. The psychosynthetic definition of Self as transcendent-immanent provides us with the opportunity to reiterate that it "is not simply the totality of the personality (Jungian conception), nor an aggregate of the content and processes of the psychosomatic entity; the Self is distinct, but not separate from all levels of the person"[102].

Jung said that "from the intellectual point of view, the Self is nothing more

---

97   Ibid, p. 117.

98   Ibid, p. 36.

99   P. M. Bonacina, op. cit., p. 23.

100   B. Caldironi, op. cit., p. 315.

101   B. Caldironi, op. cit., p. 316.

102   J. Firman, *Suggerimenti per un cambiamento dell'ovoide*, in "Rivista dell'Istituto di psicosintesi", Anno XII, n.2, ott. '95, p. 39.

than a psychological concept, a construction that tends to express an essence, be it imperceptible and inconceivable, because it goes beyond our understanding"[103]. In summary, for Jung the Self is just a symbol and an archetypal structure of consciousness, a transcendent postulate that can only be justified psychologically without scientific proof, and therefore should not be considered a reality. According to this orientation, only the symbols of the Self, for example the mandala, can be part of the conscious experience of the individual.

Precisely because of this position, Assagioli asserted in his conferences on *Jung e la psicosintesi* (*Jung and Psychosynthesis*) that the most obvious difference between him and the great Swiss psychiatrist was that the latter regarded the Self as a non-verifiable theoretical concept and not as a living experience. The father of Psychosynthesis, on the other hand, always spoke of the Self as a directly experienced reality, a real existential experience, an immediate, self-evident experience, an "immediate fact of consciousness." Assagioli wrote[104]:

"In Psychosynthesis the Self is considered a reality, a living Subject, of which one can have direct and certain awareness."

4.5. The Self as center and will of Synthesis

Though it has been said that an exhaustive definition of the Self is impossible, there is a way of considering it on which all the authors of psychosynthetic orientation who have written about this subject agree, that is, the definition of the Self as "center and will to synthesize". Alberto Alberti writes[105]:

"The Self can be considered as a center of synthesis that integrates and unifies the totality of humankind."

The Transpersonal Self is thus an essential point of reference, a destination that prevents individuals from losing themselves in the multiplicity of their experiences. The Self, understood as the *will of synthesis* that actuates itself, determines a process that appears as a harmonious evolution towards increasingly broad, elevated and complete integration. In this perspective, the Self seems to essentially exert a threefold function[106]:

1st function	Maintain a sense of personal identity	Individual synthesis
2nd function	Actuate synthesis between the individual and others	Inter-individual synthesis
3rd function	Connect individual and universal dimensions	Trans-individual synthesis

103   C. G. Jung, cit. in J. R. Staude, *Dalla psicoanalisi alla psicosintesi: Freud, Jung e Assagioli*, in *I nuovi paradigmi della psicologia*, op. cit., p. 101.

104   R. Assagioli, *Carl Gustav Jung e la psicosintesi*, manuscript, 1966, p. 7.

105   A. Alberti, *Il Sé ritrovato*, p. 20.

106   A. Alberti, *La volontà di sintesi*, op. cit., pp. 12-19.

The *first function* of the Self is to *maintain the sense of personal identity* through the thread that connects it to the 'I' or personal self (individual synthesis) thus preventing the subject from dissociating and fragmenting under the pressure of the disruptive tendencies of psychic multiplicity.

The *second function* is the *actualization of synthesis between the individual and others* (inter-individual synthesis). Indeed, to the extent that the 'I' maintains its contact with the Self, it experiences an inner drive to overcome its self-centeredness and become authentic.

Lastly, the individual feels inside theirself a deep longing, which is aspiration and hope, *an irrepressible need for union with a wider reality that includes him/her* and to which they feel a part of (trans-individual synthesis). The Transpersonal Self is then the point of encounter and synthesis between the individual and the universal dimensions.

The experience of the Self is therefore an experience that includes the personal identity (the 'I'), the identity of others (You and Us) and the identity of the universe.

CHAPTER IV

THE WILL

"When all is well internally,
the external part takes care of itself,
automatically."
Goethe

1. Between determinism and mechanism: the will as "Cinderella" of psychology

Assagioli defined the *will* as "the Cinderella of psychology"[107]. And rightly so, since experimental psychology has always ignored the study of voluntary processes, focusing instead on psychic functions and activities such as cognition, affectivity, perception, and memory.

On the other hand, *behaviorism* and *psychoanalysis* have considered the will, intended as "motivation" or "behavior", only to substantially deny it. The behaviorists in fact see the individual as a "machine" operated by the mechanism of "stimulation-response"; psychoanalysts regard human behavior as determined by unconscious motivations and the 'I' responding to the impulses of the Id, to the rigid impositions of the Super-ego, and to the pressures of the outside world.

For Psychosynthesis, these two visions of the human being had the merit of highlighting some of the mechanisms that regulate psychic functioning but, obscured by reductionism and mechanical philosophy, were unable to take into account the "incontrovertible phenomenological reality of the voluntary experience"[108]; they did not know how to validate the idea and the experience of a free and responsible will directed towards an intentionally chosen goal.

Renewed interest will be gained by the topic of will with the emergence of *humanistic psychology*. For this approach, the dimensions of freedom, responsibility and intentionality are what intimately characterize the human being. After determinism and mechanical philosophy as mentioned above, one comes to a "finalistic" point of view.

Many scholars adhering to this school of thought have formulated theories about the will that are close to those of Assagioli. For psychoanalyst Otto Rank (1884-1939) for example, the purpose of a therapeutic work is to unlock the will

---

107   R. Assagioli, *La volontà: Cenerentola nella psicologia e nella vita*, Istituto di psicosintesi, 1970.

108   B. Caldironi, op. cit., p. 317.

and to put the individual in a position to choose and act so that they can, through the consciousness of their deep desires, design their future. German theologian Paul Tillich (1886-1965) states that a person becomes completely human only when they decide. Viktor Frankl maintains that therapy consists of leading a person towards the ability to decide, and speaks of the "will of meaning", intending that which is a fundamental impulse and need in humans. Rollo May affirms that we are who we choose and how we choose because it is with intentionality that the human being discovers who they really are, their identity: the 'I' is therefore the 'I' of "I can".

Assagioli, too, in keeping with the humanistic orientation of Psychosynthesis, entrusts the human being with the responsibility of their identity, their actions and the use of their psychic faculties. This means that every person can first decide how to deal with, how to react and how to use feelings and thoughts in the face of events that life presents: each behavior can turn into a free choice. Assagioli puts human existence in the hands of the individual, and makes him/her choose whether to live or let live, whether to adapt passively to the environment or to create their own way.[109]

In Psychosynthesis the will is seen as fundamentally linked to the processes of *change*, because it allows the person to retake control of their own individual plan. Concerning oneself with the will means thus making a fundamental passage: leaving the world of symptoms and opening up to the dimension of symbols; freeing oneself from the sense of impotence to open up to a vision of oneself as a free, responsible, and capable being; going from limitation and conditioning to creativity and the infinite possibilities of growth; being emancipated from the past to build the future.

2. Voluntarism, will and freedom

This premise makes it clear how the will, in a psychosynthetic sense, has nothing to do with the legacy of the so-called "Victorian will". Piero Ferrucci[110] writes:

"The will as an anxiety-ridden sense of duty, as condemnation, as repression of a part of ourselves, as a refusal of what we are, is always a kind of will that is a detriment to something and thus represses. Instead, the will that originates from the center of our being does nothing at the expense of something else; does not impose but coordinates, does not push, does not force, does not condemn or repress, but simply directs."

---

109   P. M. Bonacina, op. cit., p. 11.

110   P. Ferrucci, op. cit., p. 141.

Assagioli himself explained in an interview granted to Stuart Miller[111]:

"To repeat, the will is not something hard, rigid, imperative and excluding. Rather, it has basically a *regulating* function. It is the psychological function that directs and regulates the play of all the others. An analogy is the conductor of an orchestra, who does not play himself but directs the players of various instruments.
This helps distinguish the will from what the Victorians called "will power." Another analogy may help: the automobile. The Victorian will, which gave such a bad press, so to speak, to the concept, was like a man who wanted to go somewhere placing himself behind his car and trying to push it toward a destination."

Just to emphasize this conception of the will, it's considered inextricably tied to another fundamental experience: the *feeling of freedom*. Alberto Alberti writes[112] that "the feeling of freedom of the 'I' seems to be what enables the correct and authentic experience of the will, as it avoids the degeneration of this last into voluntarism." Recognizing the fundamental value of freedom and its connection with the experience of will removes the risk of a distorted understanding and misuse of the voluntary function. Often, what we believe to be will is really stubbornness or rigidity, traits that seem to belong instead to a subpersonality and not the personal self. "Only a free will is an authentic will"[113].

Another characteristic feature of the experience of will is the *lack of effort*. Effort is usually linked with a distancing from ourselves because it originates from the dissatisfaction with what one is. That is why the use of genuine will is possible only if a sufficient degree of self-consciousness and self-identification is achieved and, with it, the ability to take in and accept the reality of what we are. Otherwise, its use will be dangerously distorted by unconscious motives.

3. Anatomy and physiology of the act of will

As I have already pointed out, for Psychosynthesis, *self-consciousness* and *will* are two sides of the same coin. It could be said that ideally self-consciousness is the *static moment* of being, while will is its *dynamic aspect*: the self is simultaneously an observer of the psychic multiplicity in which it is immersed and a participant able to act on it.

Obviously, in the reality of experience these two situations are not disconnected from one another. The experience of the self and that of the will go hand in hand. When the self, finally free of unconscious identities, expresses itself in the world, it does so through the will. Daniele De Paolis[114] writes that: "the central

---

111   S. Miller, *La volontà di R. Assagioli*, in "Intellectual Digest", 1972.

112   A. Alberti, *L'Uomo che soffre, l'uomo che cura*, op. cit., p. 35.

113   A. Alberti, *Psicosintesi e oltre*, op. cit., p. 137.

114   D. De Paolis, *La scoperta della volontà*, in *I nuovi paradigmi della psicologia*, op. cit., p. 234

experience of the will is to feel inside oneself that unity between self and desire, to feel that there is an "I-that-wills", a "Willer".

Assagioli[115], too, maintained that the will is above all an experience, a subjective event that is lived through, *articulated in three different moments*:

> "*The first* (don't be surprised) is to *recognize that the will exists*; In fact many people— and among them also many modern psychologists—do not accept it; some even deny its existence. It is therefore necessary to recognize the reality and the nature of the will, (...).
>
> *The second* stage is the *discovery of having a will*. One can arrive directly through internal experience as an immediate fact of the consciousness; many who do not have a philosophical mind succeed in this way, even more easily than others, and for everybody it is the most convincing way. Such direct discovery can be spontaneous, or facilitated, or even provoked by a special exercise; (...).
>
> *The third* stage of discovery, which makes it more complete and effective, is to *be a will*, which is different than "having" a will. This discovery can also be made in the same two ways: the direct way, which consists in the continuation and deepening of the preceding one, and the indirect, rational one based on the tenets of the "voluntaristic" conception. This involves the discovery of oneself as a conscious subject, distinct from any content or determination; it is the revelation of true self-consciousness, of the "I am."

The father of Psychosynthesis dedicated an entire book on the study of the will, analyzing its aspects, qualities and phases. Here below I will take into consideration just these topics.

3.1 The aspects of the will

> "The aspects of the will in its full development are the strong will, the skillful will, the good will and the transpersonal will."[116]

According to Assagioli, each one of these aspects (strength, skill, love and transpersonality) can be trained in a specific and appropriate manner.

The strength aspect is what is most immediately associated with the will, perhaps due to that Victorian imprint which I referred to previously. In Psychosynthesis, however, the strength of will does not indicate a repressive attitude of condemnation which leads to an intensification of removal and internal disintegration; it refers instead to the energy, to the momentum which provides the voluntary act with sufficient intensity to achieve its purpose. The strength aspect of the will has two ways of manifestation: it can stimulate or contain, just like driving a car when we can accelerate or brake. This aspect, for those who have little or no will, is the first to develop.

---

115 R. Assagioli, *La volontà dal proposito all'attuazione*, Lesson manuscript, Istituto di psicosintesi, 1967, p. 4.

116 R. Assagioli, *L'atto di volontà*, op.cit., p. 19.

The will must then be skillful or knowledgeable. This aspect consists in the ability to achieve the desired results with the least amount of energy and implies the knowledge and correct use of the laws of psychodynamics (see Part 3, Chapter III, Para. 4). About the knowledgeable will, Assagioli says[117]:

> "In order to go somewhere, one does not proceed by walking in a straight line across open country or by climbing over buildings. One rather studies a road map, and uses existing roads, which, although not in a straight line, can lead one to one's destination with the least amount of effort. (...)

> Similarly, in order to use our will most skillfully, we need to understand our inner constitution, become acquainted with our many different functions, drives, desires, habit patterns, and the relationships between them, so that at any one time we can activate and use those aspects of ourselves that already have the tendency to produce the specific action or condition we are aiming for."

But even when the will is strong and wise, it is not complete. It can become an extremely dangerous weapon if used for selfish or sinister purposes. It is for this reason that the will must also have an element of *goodness* that particularly impacts inter-individual psychosynthesis. "Practically dealing with the good aspect of the will is to ask: how do I harmonize my will with the will of others and with nature?"[118] For this reason Assagioli stated that learning to choose the right goals is a fundamental aspect of psychosynthetic training. And the goals of a good will are: love, trust, cooperation, harmony, synthesis, understanding. It is important to emphasize that a good will is not to be confused with idealistic desires and aspirations: "True goodness is not weakness but strength. The weak man is good only in appearance"[119].

The three above-mentioned aspects constitute the whole of the characteristics of the will at the personal level. But when there is an opening towards the transpersonal dimension, the will of the 'I' or personal self connects to that of the Self. If this happens, the 'I' becomes a channel that allows the *transpersonal* will of the Self to manifest itself and result in effortless action, the *Wu wei* of the Taoists.

We can conclude by saying that in the different aspects of the will, its complete development is represented schematically. In fact, when Psychosynthesis speaks of the will, it always refers to a fully developed will in its elements of *energy* (strong will), *consciousness* (skillful will) and *love* (good will). Daniele De Paolis[120] specifies:

> "At the beginning there is a necessarily self-centered period aimed at the discovery and growth of the 'I'. Such 'centricity' is characteristic of the strong and skillful

---

117   Ibid, p. 20.

118   D. De Paolis, op. cit., p. 237.

119   R. Assagioli cit. in D. De Paolis, op. cit., p. 234.

120   D. De Paolis, op. cit., p. 242.

will, of the individual will, and regards personal psychosynthesis above all. This is followed by a horizontal enlargement, which is the typical movement of good will and is connected to inter-individual psychosynthesis. Finally, we have the alignment between 'I' and Self and the activation of the transpersonal will."

We can summarize what is said in the following table:

Aspect of the will	Type of movement	Type of psychosynthesis	Dimension
Strong	self-centered	personal	I
Skillful			
Good	horizontal enlargement	inter-individual	I-You
Transpersonal	vertical alignment	transpersonal	I-Self

3.2. The qualities of the will

Assagioli maintained that in studying the phenomenology of the will in action, meaning the characteristics of individuals involved in willful acts, we find a number of qualities that each of us possesses to a certain degree. These qualities, if necessary, can be revived from their dormant state. They represent the ways in which the will is detailed[121]:

1. Energy, Dynamic Power, Intensity

2. Mastery, Control, Discipline

3. Concentration, Convergence, Attention, Focus

4. Determination, Decisiveness, Resoluteness, Promptness

5. Perseverance, Endurance, Patience

6. Initiative, Courage, Daring

7. Organization, Integration, Synthesis

It is clear that some of these qualities are closely related, while others have different characteristics. From a psychosynthetic perspective, the individual with a harmoniously developed will is able to use and balance the different qualities according to the needs of the moment.

Energy is the essential characteristic of the strong will. It is the quality *par excellence* with which the will is usually identified. But is not the only one, and if it is not associated with other qualities and balanced by the action of other psychological functions, it may become self-defeating.

---

121   R. Assagioli, op. cit., p. 22.

Mastery is the property most closely linked to the previous quality, being that *mastery* and *control* require energy, and also because one of the main uses of the will is to regulate the expression of other psychic functions.

Concentration is a particularly important quality. Its absence can in fact also neutralize a strong will, while its use can effectively compensate for relative weakness. It is obtained with the *attention* that is comparable to a lens that focuses the rays of the sun, concentrating and intensifying the heat.

Determination is necessary during willful action, but is not to be confused with impulsiveness. It is closely tied to initiative, courage and boldness.

For certain enterprises that require a lot of time, *Persistence* and *Endurance* are even more important than, and can substitute, energy.

The qualities of *Initiative*, *Courage*, and *Daring* are rooted in the recognition that there is no absolute security in life. There is another incentive to courage: stimulus and excitement, which are part of the risk. Of course this does not mean that the risk must be misguided: bravely facing a risk is justified and appropriate when it has value and purpose, but not if the risk is an end unto itself.

Finally, the prerogatives of *Organization*, *Integration*, *Synthesis*, are considered the most important, those which render the will capable of fulfilling its unique and specific function. They act in various ways. Firstly, as an inner synergy that coordinates the various psychological functions: the unifying quality that enables personal psychosynthesis and places us in a position to achieve it. Then, they are also active at the transpersonal level and work by facilitating the unification of the 'I' with the Self, and the corresponding harmonious cooperation of the personal will with the transpersonal will.[122]

3.3. The stages of the willful act

Now we will analyze the *stages* of the will. If we examine the willful process we can divide it into two fundamental moments:

- *a first sizable, introspective phase* that concerns the choice of the internal purpose and action (stages 1 – 5)

- *a second, dynamic phase* which represents the direction of the action, i.e. the coordinating of the various psychic functions aimed at the true, exact action (stage 6)

The first phase includes:

1. *Formulation of the purpose (or purposes)*: the distinctive element of the willful act is the existence of a purpose to be achieved, the clear vision of a goal to be reached. The choice of purpose is based on its evaluation, which implies a scale of values that in turn is based on a conception of life and the world.

---

122   Ibid, pp. 22-32.

Usually this conception is not formulated consciously and is often inconsistent or contradictory. Clarifying one's own position and attitudes towards oneself, others and the world is therefore a particularly important moment of this stage of the willful act. In turn, the assessment of purpose triggers the intention to achieve it and the motives to do so.

One of the most important points at this stage is the uncovering of unconscious motives and the ways in which they seek to be accepted by the conscious self. Assagioli warns that one must not fall into the error of condemning or suppressing them: the will is able to use them to its advantage.

2. *Deliberation*: evaluation is followed by deliberation, consideration and weighing the various possibilities. Deliberation takes into consideration the various objectives and the concrete possibilities we have to reach them, their correspondence with our life plan, their priority over the needs of the moment and the effects of their achievement. Many times the goals that motivate us are many, or we can reach the same goal in different ways. It is therefore necessary to thoroughly examine the various purposes in order to decide which of them get priority or to decide which tactic is best to use.

3. *Decision*: you have to set a goal by renouncing, at least temporarily, the others. This is a very important step, since choosing goes against the strong tendency of the human being to have contradictory needs. However, Psychosynthesis replaces the negative term "renunciation" with the positive term "preference". Another difficulty in making a voluntary decision is that the individual realizes that it is an act of freedom and therefore necessarily implies assumption of responsibility.

4. *Affirmation*: during this phase we have to be conscious of the purpose we've chosen to pursue, feeding it with the energy of emotions and desire and managing well any moments of discouragement and frustration. The purpose becomes the magnet that arouses and directs the dynamic and creative energies needed to attain the objective: it evokes confidence in our capabilities, the courage to attempt, the daring to risk, and so on. Assagioli said that it is advisable to be aware that the affirmation stage sometimes provokes a reaction of opposing subpersonalities that put up resistance.

5. *Planning*: this is the stage that concludes the introspective phase of the willful act. At this point we have identified our purpose, we've thoroughly evaluated it and we've decided to pursue it, and now we have to choose the best methods for effectively achieving it.

To this end, the so-called "trifocal vision" can help. This technique involves simultaneously keeping in mind the chosen goal, the intermediate path to achieve it and the concrete method to achieve it in the here and now. Two errors are typical of this phase. One is to keep the focus and direction of the will firmly fixed on the final goal while not taking sufficient account of the intermediate tasks to be carried out; the other is to overestimate and get so occupied with the means to be used that sight of the ultimate goal is lost.

The organizational phase also takes into account the execution times and the possible external collaborations or assistance that may be required as well as the existing conditions and possibilities: it is therefore a stage that can require much attention.

Thus we have arrived at the second phase of the willful act, the dynamic phase. That, surprisingly, this is the only active phase, actually helps us to understand what the authentic task of the will is.

6. *Directing the execution*: is the most specific task of the willful act, whose real function is not to perform the actions directly but to direct them. The will can and must make use of other psychological and physical functions together with the physical energies existing in personality: thought, imagination, sensations, intuitions, feelings, desires, as well as the physical organs nominated in the action. This direction must also include the constant supervision of the execution.[123]

Assagioli explained[124] that these six stages are like links in a chain; the chain is only as strong as its weakest link. And so a single willful act will only be as effective as any one of the individual phases.

Here we have taken into consideration the willful act in its entirety and in its ideal state, as a guide to a complete, intentional action. Obviously certain acts of will require great care in the execution of each stage. In other cases, some stages may be of particular importance, while others may require only a minimum of attention. But even if in everyday practice not all stages of the will can be equally important, in order to be able to act effectively in every circumstance, we must be able to be efficient in each of them. In fact, Assagioli wrote[125]:

"I have observed, and it can be easily verified, that the main cause of failure in completing an act of will is that it is often difficult to accomplish this or that other specific stage: in other words, it remains locked in a particular point in the sequence. Understanding the various stages and their functions is therefore crucial to discovering the specific weak point or points where we must become more skilled in order to discover the best suited approaches and techniques."

4. Techniques for training and developing the will

First of all, the will is necessary to decide which technique to use and then to persist in using it.[126] And so a first and immediate use of the techniques to train

---

123   D. De Paolis, op. cit., pp. 238-240 e R. Assagioli, op. cit., pp. 103-145.

124   R. Assagioli, op. cit., pp. 103-104.

125   Ibid, p. 104.

126   R. Assagioli, *Principi e metodi della psicosintesi terapeutica*, op. cit., p. 111.

the will is just that of arousing and consolidating the will to do so.

Psychosynthesis holds that everyone has at least a small amount of will, even if dormant. So the first task in training the will is to increase the existing capital, i.e. to train the will to will more effectively. For this purpose Assagioli has provided a number of exercises[127] to mobilize the necessary energies and to arouse the desire to have an effective will. The program includes the following steps:

1. *Mobilizing the energies*

   This is possible through:
   - specific imaginative exercises: preparatory exercises for training the will[128]; imaginative evocation on the topic of will
   - reading appropriate books or watching films (for example biographies of people who are/were particularly gifted with a undisputed will)
   - deciding to want to develop the will

2. *Performing "useless" exercises*

   Performing acts and exercises whose only use is that of training the will (for example slowly emptying a box of matches and then putting them all back in again).

3. *Exercising the will in daily life*

   For example getting up 10 minutes earlier every morning; fully tasting every bite of food; saying no to certain people and certain situations.

4. *Do physical exercises or sports* in order to specifically train the will.

   Assagioli believed that every physical movement is a willful act, and that repeating these acts with attention, effort and resistance serves to reinforce the will.

---

127 Ibid, pp. 112-120.

128 This exercise as described by R. Assagioli is cited in D. De Paolis, op. cit., pp. 243-244.

CHAPTER V

THE IDEAL MODEL: THAT WHICH WE CAN AND WANT TO BECOME

I want to make it immediately clear that talking about the Ideal Model does not merely refer to one of the fundamental active techniques used by Psychosynthesis to facilitate transformative processes. Speaking of the Ideal Model means, above all, presenting a tool that promotes the building of an *inner attitude* to undergo the inevitable transformations that face us daily with ever greater awareness and fluidity. Psychotherapist and psychosynthesist Alba Piccitto writes in this regard[129]:

"Changing our personality can happen accidentally and unconsciously, due to unconscious pressures or stress of an environmental, familial or social nature. In this case, we are passively subject to it. Or it can become a mode of active and positive action, based on the knowledge of ourselves, on the clarity of what we want to achieve and why we want to do it, and on the conscious use of the laws of psychodynamics."

1. The preparatory phase: the images of oneself

The purpose of the Ideal Model technique is to use the creative and dynamic power of images, especially visual images. "More precisely," Assagioli explained[130], "this method aims at substituting a superior, but viable 'human model' for the existing one that does not have these qualities." And he goes on to say that to do this, we must first realize that we all have different images of ourselves, or more precisely, of our personality, and that these images are not only profoundly different in both their quality and origin, but may also be in conflict with each other.

"Acquiring a clear awareness of those images is a necessary preparation in Psychosynthesis."[131]

---

129 A. Piccitto, *La crescita psicologica attraverso il modello ideale*, in *I nuovi paradigmi della psicologia*, op. cit., pp. 247-248.

130 R. Assagioli, *Principi e metodi della psicosintesi terapeutica*, op. cit., p. 141.

131 Ibid.

This process of awareness is the most important part of the analytic phase that, in Psychosynthesis, consists not only in the search for past traumas or experiences, but also in the analysis of the present situation. It is in fact in the present existential situation that these different images and models of oneself carry out their activity and influence.

So before we can use the Ideal Model technique, we must be aware of the different images we have of ourselves, the ones that others have and project upon us, and their consequences on our inner and outer life. Assagioli[132] proposed to use the following guidelines:

1. *what we believe to be.* These images can be divided into two categories: those in which we over-rate our value (sense of superiority) and those in which we underestimate it (sense of inferiority) or their exchanging over time.
2. *what we would like to be.* In this case, we are not referring to the Ideal Model that is viable, but to the idealized self-image that is unattainable and as such a source of continuous frustration.
3. *the images that others have of us,* what they believe we are. Each of these images is different from the others and are often contradictory.
4. *what others would like us to be,* the 'models' created by others according to their expectations, their desires, or their preconceptions. These images often constitute real psychic impositions.
5. *what others are able to make us be,* the images that others evoke and produce in us. Here it is good to highlight an important fact: often we refuse and reject the images that others have of us (points 3 and 4), because we recognize their extraneous origin which does not correspond to personal reality; instead, the images in this category refer to the 'models' that others are able to impose on us, and therefore may be the most damaging.
6. *what we would like to seem to others,* what we are supposed to be. These are the masks that we put on for pride, convenience, and sometimes even for necessary self-defense. They are different masks for each of our interpersonal and social relationships.
7. *finally, what we can become.* This constitutes the Ideal Model, the goal of Psychosynthesis.

This path toward the discovery of the different images of oneself must be accompanied by their progressive elaboration and the practice of disidentification. This process leads us gradually and naturally to the discovery of our Ideal Model,

---

132 R. Assagioli, *Tecnica del modello ideale,* in *Corso di lezioni sulla psicosintesi,* Istituto di psicosintesi, 1967, pp. 1-2, and *Principi e metodi della psicosintesi terapeutica,* op. cit., pp. 141-142.

of *that which we can and want to become*, and of the evocation of the function that allows us to implement it: the will in its various aspects.

2. The use of the creative power of imagination

As I have already mentioned, the Ideal Model method is the proper and appropriate use of the imaginative function in its two aspects, reproductive and creative, especially of visual images, and of the suggestive power, through activation of these images, on both the plastic unconscious of the individual as well as the conscious.[133]

Imagination has the incredible power to profoundly shape our lives, both in a positive and a negative sense. We know that the forces of the lower unconscious, with its ghosts, can profoundly influence and deform our existential project at the price of great suffering. Other images, especially when used systematically and explicitly as in the Ideal Model technique, have the power to actually stimulate what is good in us, to evoke new abilities and qualities, to foster the expression of who we really are, to accomplish our true existential project.

The *psychological law* on which this technique is based has been formulated by Assagioli as follows (see Part 3, Chapter III, Para. 4):

"Images or mental pictures and ideas tend to produce the physical conditions and the external acts that correspond to them"

This law means that each image is an action in a latent state, and that action contains a motor element. So the more the image of what we want to achieve is clear in our mind, the more we think and imagine it materializing and manifesting itself in reality. Moreover, every realization, every unconscious act, is preceded by an idea, a motivating pattern, a project.

The technical assumptions on the use of the Ideal Model are:

* *the capability to use thought*
* *the capability to imagine*
* *the capability to predict (in the sense of seeing before).*[134]

Being able to use good thinking means being trained to keep focused and concentrated attention on certain thoughts and ideas. Instead, using the imagination better means having the ability to embellish these thoughts and

---

133   A. Piccitto, op. cit., p. 249.
134   A. Piccitto, op. cit., p. 248.

ideas with an image, above all visual. Finally, being able to predict implies having achieved a good level of self-awareness and a clear vision of the direction in which you want to move; it involves the ability to distinguish what is part of us and what is not.

And if we sometimes fail to achieve a certain purpose, it is because in our unconscious there are different and conflicting images that neutralize each other, or because we are unable to go through all the stages that comprise the will in action.

2.1. The phases of the creative process

According to Psychosynthesis, the phases of the creative process, both that which lead to the creation of an object (a work of art, a tool, an apparatus), as well as that which leads to the creation of new qualities, capabilities and attitudes, are the same and can be summarized here[135]:

1. *the first phase is that of the image-idea.* In reality, the idea and the image are different from each other, but in practice, an idea immediately arouses an image or even emerges into consciousness in the form of an image. This stage can be compared to that of drawings and 'pre-production models' of objects that will then be manufactured.

2. *the second is the action of the motorial element in the image.* Imagination, as we have seen, tends to materialize, to generate external acts or corresponding physiological modifications. According to Assagioli, there is a clear confirmation of this fact in hypnosis.

3. *the third phase sees the contribution of the energy of desire.* The idea-image becomes an admirable and desirable ideal that sets in motion all the means necessary for its gradual creation or implementation.

The sequence is thus the following:

idea → image → model → desire → creative activity → manifestation

The Ideal Model technique is therefore based on the directed and focused use of an idea-image, along with its motor impulse; on the ability to stimulate and channel the energy of desire; on the qualities required during the design phase and finally on the ability to achieve its realization.

---

135   R. Assagioli, op. cit., p. 143.

3. Practical application of the Ideal Model

We must say that there are various degrees, different levels in the implementation of the Ideal Model. Firstly, the technique can be used in a very targeted manner, limited to a *single function or quality*, or directed to a subpersonality that one wants to transform. Subsequently, the project can be expanded to include the entire personality. In fact, *personal psychosynthesis* is the creation of one's own Ideal Model. Finally, the technique can be employed to accomplish one's own *transpersonal psychosynthesis*. I have already said that the task of bringing the personal 'I' to its source, the Self, is difficult and very long. Regarding this, Assagioli wrote[136]:

"Intermediate stages imply new identifications. The 'I' that does not know that it is fully contained in its highest Self (...), must look for other support structures and vital connections; it must create or choose an image, an 'Ideal Model' of itself appropriate for its strength and its psychic constitution so that it can then be implemented."

As regards putting the Ideal Model into practice, meaning the psychological techniques used to accomplish this, Assagioli stated[137]:

"The various phases are:

1. Above all, choose the model

2. Declare the will to implement it

3. Visualize it vividly, accurately; imagine yourself in possession of the desired qualities and assume a physical attitude, including facial expression, which reflects it.

Repeat the exercise, visualize the image over and over again until it becomes more effective. (...) But the use of this technique will differ depending on the case and the situation."

Reading these words it seems obvious how the Ideal Model technique refers to an advanced stage of the individual path, the *transformative phase*. It assumes that the often-undesired images of oneself lurking in our unconscious have been cleaned out, thereby making it possible to choose an Ideal Model corresponding to one's true existential plan. It also assumes that the stages of the creative process are known and that the volitional function has sufficiently developed. Last, it assumes that the necessary tools have been acquired for the proper use of imaginative techniques.

3.1. The importance of choosing the model

The choice of the model must be carefully evaluated on the basis of differential psychology and, above all, on the typology (see Part 4, Chapter VII, Para. 5).

---

136 Ibid, p. 31

137 R. Assagioli, *Tecnica del modello ideale*, op. cit., p. 7..

For example, from the outset some people clearly see the goal to achieve and are able to delineate a very precise and detailed image of what they want and propose to become. Others, of a more pliant, spontaneous and less structured nature, cannot clearly imagine such a model, and instead they run from it. They feel that their task is rather to work on the obstacles and resistance of their personality, and then let the creative power of the transformation work of its own accord.

One must have both approaches in mind, with their advantages and disadvantages, as both are valid and appropriate to the corresponding psychological type. It is also appropriate for those who immediately have a very clear picture of the goal to cultivate a flexible and open attitude, remaining ready to change the chosen model if the introduction of new circumstances makes it necessary. Instead, those who follow the second method must shield themselves from excessive passivity, developing the discrimination necessary to avoid the interpretation of desires and images originating from unconscious complexes as impulses originating in the higher unconscious.

In addition, the model that we choose as a reference may be the result of internal processing or inspired by external models, for example individuals who have already achieved the desired qualities that embody the ideal we aspire to.

The most common case seems to be the often-unconscious choice of an external human model, a person who has our esteem and appreciation, and thus represents an example. It can be a well-known individual, perhaps mythical, a historical character or a person in the family: father, mother, other relative; or even a teacher or mentor. In the therapeutic relationship, the "model" can even be the therapist theirself.

However, Assagioli warns that "these external models may sometimes have serious disadvantages"[138]. First of all, they may not be suitable for the character and the natural inclinations of the subject. And even when the model is appropriate, one must be careful not to fall into automatic imitation. Each of us is unique and original, and trying to become identical to someone else would only divert one from theirself and from their existential project.

Another risk is the excessive idealization of the person chosen as a model who is initially considered to be truly infallible and perfect. But afterward, the inevitable discovery of defects and faults can cause disappointment, resentment and an attitude of criticism; it can even lead to a loss of confidence in both one's ability to properly judge people and in people in general.

Where, however, this disappointment does not occur, there may still be an excessive personal attachment to the chosen personality, an affective dependence that hinders or slows the process of developing one's own individuality and thus the attainment of one's existential project.

---

138 R. Assagioli, *Principi e metodi della psicosintesi terapeutica*, op. cit., p. 144.

In reality, the Ideal Model should represent the link between the 'I' and the Self, seen as the custodian of the existential project of the individual, which mirrors, reflects and symbolizes the person chosen. The ideal action of the technique used with an external model can therefore be schematized as shown in the diagram here on the right.

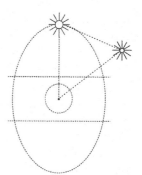

Considering all the dangers associated with the use of an external model, the *ideal internal models* are considered the most important for the purpose of Psychosynthesis. They are a stimulus, indicating a direction, and represent a destination towards which the development process should be directed.

First of all there is the *Ideal General Human Model*, based on the knowledge of the bio-psycho-transpersonal make-up of the human being and of the great latent possibilities in the superconscious and in the Self. However, this model must not remain too vague, or be a remote, undefined vision. It must be constructed and clearly divided into each of the steps that must be taken and experienced to really embody it. Assagioli wrote that "every stage of psychological development must be known and envisioned so that it can be approached, experienced and, at the right time, surpassed."[139]

From the general model of development we then go to the *special models*, adapted to the individual's specific make-up and possibilities. As I have already mentioned, to properly identify the appropriate model a good knowledge of differential psychology and typology is necessary. We can simply recall the great categories of extroverts and introverts and the various types of qualifications covered by Psychosynthesis that correspond to the self-realization paths illustrated in chapter VII (see Para. 5).

3.2. Risks and counter-indications

As I've mentioned previously, various complications can arise from use of the Ideal Model technique. Piero Ferrucci illustrated them in the following way.[140]

First of all, it is not advisable to use the technique in a compensatory manner to directly counteract some personality issues; doing so will only result in repression or an intensification of the conflict in question. In these cases, Assagioli recommends a preventive application of the desensitization and disidentification techniques.

But the biggest risk is haste, both in the conceptualization of the ideal and also in its implementation. In this way, it is likely to lead to delusions of various

---

139   R. Assagioli, *Tecnica del modello ideale*, op. cit., p. 5.
140   P. Ferrucci, *Crescere*, op. cit., pp. 151-159.

kinds, or to becoming trapped in a categorical and perfectionist attitude. We must remember that in the human psyche the number of ways in which growth is achieved is, perhaps, infinite. It is therefore important to proceed cautiously in formulating the model to which we aspire and take the time to experiment and review the initial idea as we walk the path of inner evolution.

Another common mistake is to confuse the Ideal Model with a daydream. Many people struggle to live their daily lives, and dream of an extraordinary life made up of amazing exploits, memorable moments and fantastic people. These fantasies have the obvious purpose of meeting unsatisfied needs, of compensating for one's frustrations. In these cases we are faced with the exact opposite of the Ideal Model: the latter is oriented towards reality, it manifests itself slowly and gradually and is the expression of the true self, while daydreams are compensatory, reflect the frustrated desires of an individual and provide only a fleeting and illusory fulfillment.

Another possible risk in working with the Ideal Model is the "reverse effect". It can arouse our deeper resistance to change, instill fear of becoming something other than what we believe ourselves to be and unleash the conservative tendencies of our personality. This in itself is not a bad thing, and in fact it allows us to further deepen the knowledge of ourselves and to work on the defenses we put up against the transformative process.

Lastly, I'll mention a deceptive danger: some fear that this technique inhibits spontaneity. This fear originates from a misunderstanding about the function of images. An image that aims to shine light on our deep potentials, which makes us move towards the realization of our personal self/our Transpersonal Self, can in no way be a ploy or a means of self-deceit. The Ideal Model is a seed present in us from the beginning of our lives and its rediscovery and activation leads us in the direction of authenticity, of true spontaneity.

Ideally, all these dangers can be avoided and prevented by the preparatory work on the image of oneself, which should culminate with the discovery of the 'I', of self-identification, that is, with the discovery of what we can and want to become. The discovery of the 'I' is then tied to the activation of the volitional function, essential to succeed in the implementation of our Ideal Model.

We can summarize the entire process that has been outlined up to now in the following steps:

1. *development of awareness* of the various images that we have of ourselves and images that others have and project onto us
2. *processing, integration, and disidentification* from these various images
3. *self-identification*
   • discovery of one's Ideal Model, of what we want to become
   • evocation of the instrument that allows us to implement it: the will
4. *use of active techniques* for concretely manifesting the chosen model.

CHAPTER VI

THE PRINCIPLE OF SYNTHESIS: UNITY IN DIVERSITY, DIVERSITY IN UNITY

> *"Whoever wants to know the great secrets*
> *of nature regards and contemplates on the*
> *minimums and maximums of opposites and*
> *contraries.*
> *Deep magic is the ability to find the opposite,*
> *after having found the point of union."*[141]

Speaking of *Synthesis* means approaching the *guiding principle* of Assagiolian psychology, both the means and the goal of the entire psychosynthetic pathway. The etymological meaning of the word "synthesis", derived from the Greek "syn" + "thésis", is "putting together, composing". Obviously, this concept assumes a variety of elements that need to be "compounded", a multiplicity of parts to be "put together".

Synthesis is a process that involves the creation of a relationship between two or more elements through a third entity, in order to create a new reality. Psychotherapist and psychosynthesist Anna Maria Finotti[142] defines synthesis as "a creative process which establishes a dynamic relationship between two or more different entities that, while maintaining their distinctiveness and individuality, open themselves to cooperating toward a new function and new possibilities".

1. Synthesis as a universal trend

For Assagioli[143], Synthesis is "a trend that is the expression of a universal principle" whose manifestations can be found in all aspects of reality: from the world of inorganic matter to the organic vegetable and animal world, from the psychic world of emotions and ideas to the world of interpersonal and social relationships, to the spiritual worlds. Speaking of Synthesis therefore means dealing with a very wide subject: in fact, creation, growth and the evolution of all that exists depend on the principle of synthesis.

---

141 G. Bruno, cit. in R. Assagioli, *Psicosintesi - Armonia della vita*, op. cit., p. 38.

142 A. M. Finotti, *Sintesi: principio e tecnica*, in *I nuovi paradigmi della psicologia*, op. cit., p. 121.

143 R. Assagioli, op. cit., p. 34.

And so Assagioli wrote:

"The basic principle of synthesis is clearly found, in its simplest form, in inorganic matter, and is apparent in the difference between the mixture and the chemical combination. (...) The atom itself is actually a dynamic synthesis of electrical charges (...). Let's go to the organic world. Biological life immediately appears to us as a synthesis. We see that the individual organs of an animal or human organism are coordinated in their action by a superior unit. There is a unifying, vital principle, which from many manifestations appears intelligent, thereby rendering life possible for the organism (...)"[144].

In nature there is therefore an innate tendency toward unity and harmony. This tendency, also called *syntropy*, is an aspect with which scientific research has not been occupied for a long time, preferring to study its opposite, *entropy*. But, although it is undeniable that at the molecular level there is a propensity towards disorder and disorganization, Assagioli has never shared the unilateral and excessive philosophical claims that have been deduced from this statement. Indeed, many of the studies carried out in recent decades about spontaneous tendencies in the natural world toward order and self-organization seem to support his position. For example, I refer to the general theory of systems formulated by Austrian biologist Ludwig Von Bertalanffy (1901-1972), ideas on the science of complexity from Russian scientist Ilya Prigogine (1917- 2003), and those on synergetics by the German physicist Hermann Haken.

Mentioning these scholars means naturally tying the principle of synthesis to a *systemic perspective*. In fact, synthesis can also be defined as a process of integration of individual subsystems, which have completed their development process, into a new super-system that "preserves distinction and individuality by transcending them and giving them another role and another meaning"[145].

In this process, the parts that contribute to the creation of the new entity are not deleted, but incorporated and modified. In fact, the synthesis is more than the sum of the individual parts. It creates a new reality transforming the elements that make it up into a unit that has original features and qualities. Transformation therefore does not involve individual elements taken separately. What are transformed are the relationships that exist between them. To clarify, we can say that creating a new synthesis does not mean eliminating our fragile and vulnerable parts, but it makes it possible for them to benefit from a different kind of relationship with other components of our personality and, in particular, with the 'I' and with the Self.

---

144   Ibid, pp. 35-37.
145   P. M. Bonacina, op. cit., pp. 86-87.

2. The various syntheses contemplated by Psychosynthesis

The tendency towards order in the physical world was used by Assagioli as an analogy to explain some psychic phenomena. And, as I have already pointed out, all the psychosynthetically oriented self-training, educational and therapeutic work is aimed at encouraging this natural tendency of the psyche toward harmony and union.

> "This is especially of interest to us as an analogy for the study of psychic life. In this, the tendency toward synthesis is no less strong and fundamental (than inorganic matter and biological life); on the contrary, it even rises to higher complexity and refinements"[146].

The principle of Synthesis acts throughout the biopsychism (mind-body unity) of the individual, generating different configurations and structures over time. But it finds its main manifestation in the organization of the various parts that make up the personality around a unifying center. Depending on the case, this center may consist of a subpersonality, a role, a passion, an idea or the personal self or even the Transpersonal Self. This process ensures the maintenance of a relatively constant sense of identity.

As psychotherapist and psychosynthesist Vincenzo Liguori explains,

> "In the healthy development of the individual, the unifying center tends to become from implicit and unconscious, at least in part explicit and conscious; it tends to move away from being identified with aspects of personality that give rise to partial synthesis, to identification with the true center, the 'I' which is innately different from the components of the personality" [147].

2.1. Automatic and partial Syntheses

Before the 'I' begins to emerge thanks to the work of self-realization, some *partial syntheses* form in the psyche, syntheses that concern only some elements of the personality while excluding others. Usually the 'I' is not fully aware of these syntheses: it automatically identifies with certain elements and, just as automatically, rejects others.

Partial syntheses are generated by what sparks our interest, by what fascinates us, and consist in the organization of some psychic content around a dominant element of our life (for example a role, a subpersonality, a complex, a passion, an idea) that acts as a unifying center. In this type of Synthesis, sensations, desires, emotions, thoughts and images are aggregated according to the purpose of the

---

146   R. Assagioli, op. cit., p. 37.

147   V. Liguori, *La sintesi in psicosintesi*, in *I nuovi paradigmi della psicologia*, op. cit., p. 153.

unifying center of the moment; those that are inconsistent with this purpose are excluded and relegated to the unconscious in various ways (through mechanisms of division, negation, removal...).

Automatic and partial syntheses are not in themselves negative. They have the function of organizing the psychic chaos, giving it some order and stability, and although they have a transitory importance in development, "for some, perhaps many, they are the maximum they can aspire to, or, in any event, reach"[148]. When partial syntheses are possible, especially those that are obsolete or damaging, they are made conscious and dissolved through the process of analysis, and the energy thus liberated is engaged in a voluntary and conscious synthesis: in personal and/ or transpersonal psychosynthesis.

2.2. Conscious and voluntary syntheses (Personal and Transpersonal Psychosynthesis)

Personal Psychosynthesis is the first important *conscious and voluntary synthesis* in the maturation process of the individual. It is made possible by the awakening of the self, in its dual aspect of self-consciousness and will. The personal self becomes the unifying center around which all the elements of biopsychism are organized. Facilitating this accomplishment are the investigation, elaboration and integration of the conscious and unconscious aspects of personality and the patient process of disidentification. Self-consciousness and will are thus those forces that guide towards Synthesis, and the Ideal Model technique that I have described extensively in the previous chapter is an essential tool for achieving personal psychosynthesis.

The second major synthesis is termed Transpersonal Psychosynthesis. It aims at awakening and implementing the dormant potential and qualities in the human psyche. Transpersonal Psychosynthesis is a process that tends to integrate, in addition to the aspects present in the middle and lower unconscious, also those of the superconscious into the personality, "elevating the center of consciousness in order to achieve union between the 'I' and the Self, thus fulfilling the process of growth that leads from multiplicity to unity, from mass consciousness to self-consciousness and thus to consciousness of the Self: a Synthesis of the universal and individual"[149].

We can summarize these concepts as follows, keeping in mind that a table only has educational value and that reality is much more complex:

---

148 Ibid, p. 154.
149 Ibid.

Type of (psycho) Synthesis	Unifying Center	Content that is Integrated	Content that is Rejected	Effect on the Psychism
Partial	a role, a task, a subpersonality, a passion, an idea, a model...	those in harmony with the goals of the partial unifying center	all the rest	stagnation, oscillation, conflictuality
Personal	personal self	those of the middle and lower unconscious	those of the upper unconscious	balance, mastery, rhythm
Transpersonal	Transpersonal Self	those of the upper, middle and lower unconscious	none	evolution, transformation, harmony
Automatic	mechanical aggregation of psychic elements that occurs without the contribution of consciousness and will			
Voluntary	targeted aggregation of psychic elements that occurs with the contribution of consciousness and will (personal self/Transpersonal Self)			

2.3. Interpersonal syntheses

So far I have illustrated the syntheses that take place at the intrapsychic level, but humankind are relational beings, so the principle of Synthesis involves and governs the relationships that one has with others and with the world. The degree of integration and synthesis that an individual has reached internally will tend to reflect on the type of relationships that they will build with the outside: within the couple, within the family, with the associations and groups to which they belong, with the community, the nation, the planet and the whole cosmos.

Similarly to what is stated in the previous paragraph, a person who has not yet reached a sufficient level of personal psychosynthesis will tend to build *inter-individual automatic and partial syntheses*. He/she can consciously bring only some of the aspects of theirself into the relationship with the other, while those aspects relegated to the unconscious will tend to act unconsciously through various defense mechanisms consisting mainly of projection, generating conflicts of various kinds.

On the other hand, a person who has achieved a sufficient degree of personal psychosynthesis will tend to establish relationships with other individuals at the level of the 'I' or Self by implementing *conscious and voluntary inter-individual syntheses* of positive evolution and harmony for all the elements in play. These syntheses, thus, by activating good relations with others, will tend to create larger units of which each one is part: from interpersonal syntheses, to syntheses between groups and to the syntheses of humanity and the planet, conceived as a single being where each one finds his place and his function[150].

3. The synthesis of opposites

Regarding the principle of the *synthesis of opposites*, I'm treating it separately since it is a more general type of synthesis compared to the others. This means we find the principle of polarity in all the fields considered in the previous paragraphs: the personal, the transpersonal, the interpersonal and the social fields.

3.1. Philosophical and spiritual antecedents

Anna Maria Finotti[151] states that addressing the argument of the synthesis of opposites means reinforcing the intuition that, from Heraclitus to Plato to Hegel, through Nicola Cusano and Giordano Bruno, has been transmitted to us by Western philosophy. This asserts that the *principle of polarity* is subject to the whole of manifestation, therefore everything that exists has its opposite: everything is duplicate, everything is bipolar, as if the One during manifestation was split into two.

This condition, Ferrucci notes[152], has been illustrated in many ways by many traditions: the Bible says "the wolf will dwell with the lamb, the leopard will lie near the goat, the calf and lion cub will graze together, and a little child will guide them"; in the alchemical tradition, with the *coincidentia oppositorum*; in the Chinese symbolism of Yin and Yang; in Indian tradition, from the dance of Shiva that symbolizes the divinity including and expressing all the good and evil of our lives.

3.2. Polarity as a universal principle[153]

Like the tendency toward synthesis, *polarity* also is considered a universal principle detectable at every level of the manifestation.

According to Assagioli, the most general polarity in the physical world is that between positive and negative electricity. In the three realms of organic life (plant, animal, human) the most important and widespread polarity is that of the sexual. This, however, is not exclusively relegated to the physical dimension because it extends to innumerable manifestations of life. In the sphere of sentimental life

---

150 Ibid.

151 Finotti, op. cit., p. 124.

152 P. Ferrucci, op. cit., p. 189.

153 R. Assagioli, *L'equilibramento e la sintesi degli opposti*, Ed. Istituto di Psicosintesi.

we find well-known dualities such as pleasure and pain, excitement and depression, attraction and repulsion, love and hatred. Within the mind we find a clear antithesis between analytic and synthetic activity, between the inductive and deductive processes. Finally, if we consider human personality in its entirety, we find various polarities that have been extensively studied by modern psychology: body and psyche, unconscious and conscious, lower unconscious and superconscious, extroversion and introversion, passivity and activity, eros and logos.

In addition, Psychosynthesis also considers *inter-individual polarities*. The first and most fundamental is that between man and woman, which is complementary at all levels (bodily, emotional, cognitive, intuitive, etc.). There is also the polarity between adults and children, especially in the form of the relationship between mother and offspring; the one between the individual and the various groups to which they belong (family, social class, professional class, cultural groups, homeland, church, race); and that between different social groups. Of this last type, the polarity between the northern and southern regions (both within the continent and within each individual nation) and between the western and the eastern ones is of particular importance.

In his article devoted specifically to this issue, *L'equilibramento e la sintesi degli opposti* (*The Equilibrium and Synthesis of Opposites*), Assagioli specified that:

> "It is opportune to clarify that each polarity is a relationship between two elements and that, as such, is never absolute, but relative to that given pair of terms. Therefore, the same element can be positive compared to a given "pole" and negative compared to another." [154]

Following the above comments, the dialogue on existence appears to be based on the synthesis of opposites, and the creative moment is characterized by the encounter of two forces, which combine at a higher level. Thus, the process of growth and evolution of our personality depends for its dynamics on the tension of multiple polarities, for which it is necessary to find ever more differentiated levels of synthesis. [155]

3.3. Possible relations between opposites[156]

Stagnation

Though Psychosynthesis stems from the assumption that polarities exist in each of us, in some people it is very difficult to recognize them. In these individuals, the self is totally and consistently identified with one of the two poles, while

---

154   Ibid.

155   A. M. Finotti, op. cit., p. 124.

156   P. Ferrucci, op. cit., pp.192-195 and M. Macchia, op. cit., pp. 110-111.

the other remains unconscious. We are talking about people who, for example, are driven by sense of duty and do not give any space to the principle of pleasure, or they always listen to their hearts but never to reason; they may cultivate an austere attitude towards existence, even coming to condemn the sensual side.

In these situations one of the two poles is intensified while the other is rejected by defensive mechanisms that may vary depending on the intensity of the underlying conflict. There is even a lack of awareness of a possible relationship between the two polar elements. Evidently there is neither struggle nor contrast and the result is stagnation, stalling. The evolutionary process of the individual is blocked, there is no creative current.

The first step for those who find themselves in such a situation is making the stagnant pole conscious.

STAGNANT STATE

EXCITEMENT
active pole, conscious

DEPRESSION
negated pole, unconscious

"I am (always and only) excited"

Oscillation

In other cases, however, the self tends to identify alternately first with one pole, and then with the other, losing contact each time with the opposite. The two elements of polarity, while both reaching the field of consciousness, continue to be mutually exclusive through the use of defense mechanisms. These oscillations can be brief or prolonged over the years.

The misunderstanding that underlies these continuous oscillations consists in trying to suppress one of the two poles, assuming that it can only exist in a certain way, that is to say, according to the *either-or* logic: either I am a serious and conscientious person or I am an insignificant hedonist; I either follow my emotions and feelings, or I am cold and detached; I either dedicate myself to harsh austere practices or I let myself be taken by sensual pleasures. But these attempts to suppress one of the two poles do not work, and sooner or later the denied part will reappear in the field of conscience with all its strength. And the more the identification with one of the two poles has been intense, the more forceful will be the oscillation at its extreme.

OSCILLATING STATE

EXCITEMENT	DEPRESSION
active pole, conscious	negated pole, unconscious

Before: *"I am excited."*

EXCITEMENT	DEPRESSION
active pole, conscious	negated pole, unconscious

After: *"I am depressed." (and so on..)*

Balance

The solution proposed by Psychosynthesis consists in accepting and simultaneously rendering the two aspects of the polarities living in our psychic structure aware, giving up the illusion of being defined by one single characteristic. The process that makes this development possible is disidentification from both poles and the subsequent self-identification, or identification with the 'I' (personal self) or the Transpersonal Self, according to the level we set for ourselves.

This leads to a situation of dialogue and inner freedom that allows us to evaluate and appreciate the gifts of every aspect of our being, and to regulate their mutual relationship. One comes to a rhythmic and creative movement that leads to the cyclical expression of the two aspects: I can be serious and conscientious when the situation requires it, and I can let myself be light and frivolous in the appropriate moments; I am capable of listening to my emotions and feelings and I can properly take into account the suggestions of my rationality; I travel a path of spiritual research and rejoice in the beauty and sensuality of life. The ideal of maturity proposed by Psychosynthesis sees, as Piero Ferrucci maintains, "the ability to move gracefully, rhythmically, almost musically, from one to the other" [157].

BALANCED STATE

| EXCITEMENT | ⟵ | I / SELF | ⟶ | DEPRESSION |

Both poles are active and conscious

"I have an excited part, but I am not excited.
I have a depressed part, but I am not depressed.
I am in dynamic equilibrium"

---

157   Ibid, p.194.

Synthesis

Following this, the activation of the personal self, or the Transpersonal Self, can bring the different aspects of polarities closer to one another until they merge bringing about a synthesis, a mode having new qualities. Assagioli said:

> "Opposites are 'opposite' to themselves, but are not opposed to unity, since real and concrete unity is but unity and synthesis of opposites."[158]

Identified with the 'I' or the Self, we no longer need to refuse and defend ourselves from the element of polarity we considered negative. Through synthesis a new reality is generated with new and original features. In it we can be both responsible and frivolous at the same time, we have the ability to integrate head and heart, we know how to combine spirituality and sensuality in a new way. Indeed, the synthesis is greater than the sum of its parts and, by virtue of this fact, there are no words that can fully describe it.

To illustrate this process and highlight the radical difference between what can be called an intermediate solution, or a compromise, and a true Synthesis, Assagioli proposed the following graphic representation.[159]

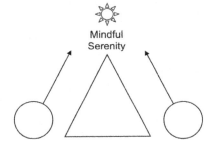

STATE OF SYNTHESIS

Mindful
Serenity

Excitement   Apathetic Calm   Depression
Both poles are active and conscious

"I know and accept both aspects of polarity and go beyond.
I attain a new dimension.
Notwithstanding moments of excitement and depression,
I am mindfully aware."

As is seen in the graphic, the two opposite poles and the resulting compromise are all on the same plane, while the result of the synthesis is the vertex of the triangle, symbolizing a change of level, thus, a moment of growth, a new dimension in which the two elements are absorbed into a unit having superior quality that transcends both.

---

158 R. Assagioli, *Psicosintesi - Armonia della vita*, op. cit., p. 39.

159 R. Assagioli, *L'equilibramento e la sintesi degli opposti*, op. cit., pp. 11-13.

4. How is the Synthesis process activated?

Vincenzo Liguori[160] answers the question: "How is the Synthesis process activated?", asserting that the practice and methodology of Psychosynthesis provides a specific development plan for each person, as part of the path of uniqueness of each. And many active methods and techniques are used that will be different at different times during the process, with therapeutic, training or educational overtones.

However, we can identify the fundamental method in the process of *disidentification* that leads to self-identification, that is, the discovery of I/Self in its aspects of self-consciousness and will. This position massively favors a genuine process of integration and synthesis. The techniques for the development of the *will* and that of the *Ideal Model* already set out in the previous chapters are fundamental. Another method that can be employed is the *transformation and sublimation of energies*, especially the sexual and aggressive.

More specifically, to promote transpersonal synthesis, Psychosynthesis indicates *methods to awaken the energies of the higher unconscious* or to facilitate contact with its contents: the use of anagogic symbols, meditative techniques, guided visualization, evocation of superior qualities and techniques for the development and use of intuition.

Finally, there are *methods to facilitate interpersonal and group synthesis*: group analysis, role playing, techniques to eliminate prejudice, techniques for developing cooperation, sharing and empathy, coordinated group activities, techniques to promote "right" human relationships.

I would like to conclude this chapter with a splendid quote from Alberto Alberti[161]:

"We could say that every synthesis experience is a movement in the direction of the Self: every expansion of consciousness, every sentiment expressed and shared, every act of will, every moment of encounter, in short every gesture of union and Synthesis in us, between us and others and between us and the world, are steps forward in moving towards the human Self."

---

160   V. Liguori, op. cit., pp. 154-155.

161   A. Alberti, *Psicosintesi e oltre*, op. cit., pp. 90 e139.

CHAPTER VII

THE SUPERCONSCIOUS OR HIGHER UNCONSCIOUS

1. Premise: the phenomenological reality of the spiritual experience

"The superconscious, or higher unconscious, is one of the most exquisitely psychosynthetic notions (...). It is definable in terms of the noetic, transpersonal dimension of personality, and refers to the contributions of the humanistic, anthropoanalytic and existential psychologies of contemporary psychology. The superconscious is the seat of the instincts that Maslow has called "instinctive" and that bring man to positive, creative and joyful experiences such as expansion of consciousness, creative inspiration, peer experience, archetypal intuition, ecstasy, and states of illumination. In the higher unconscious, there are ethical, aesthetic, and artistic rules together with, in general terms, all those potentials that are a peculiar trait of human nature."[162]

It is very important to emphasize from the very beginning that Psychosynthesis clearly distinguishes the religious dimension from religion and religious beliefs. When referring to instances of a transpersonal nature, it means referring to the former, not the latter. There are also superconscious experiences that have nothing to do with commonly understood religiosity, such as certain great scientific intuitions, certain artistic inspirations, or certain impulses toward heroic or ethical actions.

As I have already mentioned elsewhere, Psychosynthesis, with the introduction of the hypothesis of the existence of a superconscious dimension in the individual, refers to and affirms the phenomenological reality of spiritual experience. In Assagioli's investigations on this subject, he always tried to stick to the facts, meaning "to verifiable psychological experiences and experiments, and to established results of the application of psycho-spiritual techniques"[163]. The psychosynthetic vision of the transpersonal is therefore not moral, philosophical or religious, but has scientific pretenses.

The father of Psychosynthesis believed that it was not the subject that made a study scientific, but the way this subject was studied. He was therefore persuaded that the first step in scientific study of transpersonal phenomena was to point out that the contents and functions of the superconscious are psychic 'facts', are

---

162 B. Caldironi, op. cit., pp. 313-314.

163 R. Assagioli, *Principi e metodi della psicosintesi terapeutica*, op. cit., p. 166.

'reality' in a pragmatic sense, because they are 'effective', that is, they produce changes, both within the human being, and also by influencing their external activities"[164]. Therefore, the interest of Psychosynthesis in transpersonal experiences must be read in the light of the real and important transformations that these experiences produce on the sense of identity, on the way of thinking, feeling and behaving, and sometimes even on the whole relationship that the individual has with their fellows and with life.

In his book titled *Lo sviluppo transpersonale* (*Transpersonal Development*), Assagioli himself clearly outlined the aspects and stages that need to be considered for a scientific study of the subject[165]:

- "Firstly, the *phenomenology*, that is, the collection of the spontaneous experiences; of the observed facts as described by many people from all times and places
- the methods of the *process for passing* between the superconscious and conscious
- the *techniques* used to produce or facilitate that passage; these include the various practices, external and internal, of various religions, and the various exercises that have different names but which are known by the generic term of yoga
- the immediate *results* and the subsequent effects that result from them
- the *methods* to prevent risk and repair damage that can be produced by the "descent" or the invasion of transpersonal energy
- the *ways* for the best and most useful uses of those achievements and energies."

Studies performed in the last decades of the previous century, especially in the United States, have in effect demonstrated that individuals of various ages and civilizations have adopted very similar techniques and attitudes to achieve particular spiritual accomplishments. These techniques and attitudes therefore transcend to some degree the history of events and cultural diversity. These findings prompted researchers to formulate two hypotheses:

- that such experiences are natural to the human being and must be the expression of the unexplored powers of the unconscious and cognitive functions that go far beyond the limits of rational intelligence, still unknown to psychology
- that every individual, at least in an embryonic way, possesses these potentials, which can then be suitably developed, at least to a certain degree, by specific techniques.

---

164   R. Assagioli, *Psicosintesi - Armonia della vita*, op. cit., p. 171.

165   R. Assagioli, *Lo sviluppo transpersonale*, op. cit., p. 56.

And this is an idea in which Assagioli believed deeply, devoting his whole existence, writing books and articles, holding lectures and lessons all over the world. But above all, he worked personally with individuals and groups to promote the experience of what he metaphorically considered "an unknown territory, rich in oil and precious metals, a source of immense wealth and unlimited possibilities for the whole of humanity": the superconscious.

2. The higher unconscious and the states of transpersonal consciousness

I have already said how important it is not to confuse the Self with the superconscious. Now, before proceeding on this subject, it is also worth mentioning the difference between the *superconscious dimension and the higher states of consciousness*, or transpersonal consciousness. For Psychosynthesis, the higher states of consciousness are characterized by the personal self remaining, for a certain time, in a transpersonal dimension, and emanate from the activation of a specific structure, the superconscious. It is therefore considered to be a structure which, having become operative, generates states of consciousness other than those generated at other levels by other structures, those which can be called lower and middle.[166] Assagioli explained[167]:

> "In this regard, a possible misunderstanding should be avoided and a doubt clarified. How can we talk about experience, about awareness, about what is outside or above consciousness? The answer is easy, and it is the same that can be given to any other aspect or level of the unconscious. We can have the conscious experience of elements that are usually outside our awareness when, at certain times or under certain conditions, they enter the field of consciousness."

Let's remember that all the lines in the Egg Diagram are dotted to indicate that there is a continuous exchange between the unconscious and the conscious. That which is superconscious can then become conscious at any given moment, entering into the field of consciousness of the 'I', remaining there for a somewhat extensive period of time, and then returning to the superconscious. It is useful to repeat that "unconscious", "conscious" and "superconscious" are adjectives, that is temporary conditions of a psychic fact.

3. Modes and stages of the passage of superconscious content in the field of consciousness

One of the key themes of Transpersonal Psychosynthesis is the relationship between higher unconscious activities and conscious life. Assagioli has indicated

---

166 A. Galoppini, *Il Sé transpersonale*, in *I nuovi paradigmi della psicologia*, op. cit., pp. 267-268.

167 R. Assagioli, *Lo sviluppo transpersonale*, op. cit., p. 21.

two modalities by which contact can be made between the superconscious and the conscious.

The most common way is what can be called *descendant* and consists of the influx of elements from the higher unconscious into the field of awareness. These contents can take the form of intuitions, inspirations, artistic creations, impulses to humanitarian and heroic action, and so on. Assagioli also included some parapsychological phenomena among these experiences, "some of which would lead one to admit that through the unconscious, on all of its three levels, influx of extra-individual origin arrives to consciousness"[168].

The other type of contact that can be established with the superconscious is that called *ascendant*. It consists in elevating the 'I' and its field of consciousness to the threshold of an area we normally ignore, since it is above the ordinary level of our consciousness.

3.1. The descendant mode

According to Assagioli, the descent of the contents of the superconscious can occur spontaneously or can be stimulated with the utilization of special techniques.

The most notable mode of spontaneous descent is *inspiration*. Superconscious content can, however, become conscious in very different degrees of processing: simply sketched, or partly elaborated, or in other cases well-structured. A typical example of this latter mode is the musical inspiration that sometimes appears in the consciousness of the composer in an almost complete form.

In contrast, the simplest way is *intuition*. Intuition can be compared to flashes of light that illuminate the field of consciousness, or to the opening of an "inner eye" that allows one to see objects in their entirety, to perceive reality that the normal mental vision, based on logical-rational criteria, is not able to grasp. In this sense, Assagioli has always considered intuition a valid means of knowledge, especially useful for investigating the superconscious dimension. However, it should be noted that in Psychosynthesis, intuition, as a psychic function, is clearly distinguished from intuitions, that is, the results of its activity.

Often intuitions do not appear to the consciousness in an abstract, "pure" way, but rather through the assistance of the *imagination*, which is another way of descent of the superconscious contents. It is therefore very important to be able to distinguish the content that constitutes an intuition from the form that covers it. The father of Psychosynthesis wrote[169]:

"This form has a symbolic character, and this raises the important and complex issue of symbolism. (...) Now I will only recall the twofold, and somewhat

---

168 Ibid, p. 28.
169 Ibid, p. 59.

contrasting, nature and function of the symbol. It can cover or reveal. When it is mistaken for the reality that it expresses, it covers, and it is therefore a source of illusion. Instead, when it is recognized as a means of expression, it is a useful, and sometimes necessary, way to capture and then recognize a transpersonal reality."

An example of this is how St. Francis understood the command he had received: "Go and repair my church." At first, taking the message literally, he began to rebuild a small church in the area. Only afterward did he understand the wider, symbolic meaning of the invitation, which then prompted him to reform the institution of the church, which had become corrupt and degenerate.

Another of the most common modes of manifestation of superconscious content in the field of consciousness is that of *illumination*. Illumination and intuition resemble each other in some ways but in others they are very different. I mentioned how intuition is like a flash of light illuminating a specific aspect of reality. Illumination, on the other hand, is a wider and more lasting experience; "It is a vision that usually shows the essential nature and the unity of all reality, or great aspects of it"[170].

There is then an ultimate type of illuminating experience that Psychosynthesis considers: it is the intimate and often sudden *revelation*, the awareness that a human being has regarding theirself, of what they profoundly are. The effects of this discovery can be different and contrasting. For some individuals it translates into a positive and joyful understanding of the potentialities and qualities that lie in the higher unconscious that leads to a true understanding of themselves and others. For others, especially when this revelation is too unexpected or intense, it translates into a sense of exaltation and megalomania. For some, it may be the revelation of the shadow, the dark sides of the personality, and this revelation can even produce very intense depressive states, fear, and despair.

As previously mentioned, Psychosynthesis considers various methods and techniques that can facilitate the descent of the transpersonal elements into the field of consciousness.

One of the simplest, which Assagioli thought was very effective, is *free drawing*, another is *writing*. There is also the technique to encourage the *reawakening of intuition*, which consists in the emptying of the field of consciousness of the psychological contents of the normal waking state followed by the tranquil wait for contact with the examined reality. The most important method for this is that of *inner silence* followed by the use of various types of *meditation* (reflective, receptive, creative).

All these methods should be used bearing in mind that expansions of consciousness can take place in three different directions: upward, downward and horizontally. Therefore, consideration should be given to the possibility that the contents that emerge could come from not only the higher unconscious, but also the

---

170   Ibid, p. 60.

middle or lower unconscious. For this reason, before exploring the superconscious territory, it is important to have explored and sufficiently integrated the contents of the middle and lower unconscious.

3.2. The ascendant mode

Assagioli would metaphorically define this mode of contact with the higher unconscious as "psychological mountain-climbing"[171].

A first analogy between the inner ascent and the actual climbing of peaks regards the *motives*. In the climb we can be guided by countless reasons, more or less conscious, more or less elevated. We could be driven by a certain willfulness for power, that is, a desire to dominate others through the acquisition of extraordinary, "magical" powers; or by the desire to escape from the difficulties and monotony of daily life; or the need to stand out from others, to feel special, superior, "chosen"; or even by the desire to explore the unknown, to embark on an adventure. But there may also be a genuine desire to contact what is superior and wonderful in the human being, to go beyond known limits. In the end, you may want to climb towards the higher states of being for the sake of humanity, to help create a different and better world. Often, these different levels of motivation coexist with each other in degrees and intensity that vary from person to person.

A further, very important analogy is the *practical preparation*, the training required to create the conditions for success in the enterprise. Psychosynthesis insists on the need for adequate preparation, which consists in achieving a sufficient degree of personal psychosynthesis through the exploration and the integration of the elements of the middle and lower unconscious. When this fails to be done, serious psychological disorders may be generated.

But practical training itself is not sufficient. According to Assagioli, a *theoretical knowledge* of the mountain that one is going to climb is also needed. This can be acquired by reading those authors who have had direct experiences, or by personally getting in touch with those who have been exploring them, or with valid and expert spiritual guides.

There are various methods available for the active exploration of superconscious levels: *prayer*, *meditation* and various special exercises, including the use of *anagogic symbols* and *guided visualizations*. It is also important to mention the fact that there are also different ways, different paths that lead to the experience of the superconscious dimension: the heroic path, the path of illumination, the ethical-regenerative, the aesthetic, the mystical, the scientific, and the ritual. I will dedicate an entire paragraph of this chapter to this theme (see Para. 5).

Assagioli[172] loved to emphasize that in this process of elevation of the

---

171   Ibid, pp. 28-31.

172   Ibid, p. 40.

consciousness a good command of the volitional function is needed. It is useful as an incentive to start the exploration and to persevere in moments of difficulty; to eliminate the many obstacles blocking the way; to maintain a calm, receptive and confident state; as propellant for an ever-higher elevation, and to stabilize the consciousness at higher levels; to channel and effectively utilize the energies emitted from the contacts that have been established.

4. Shadows and light in transpersonal development

4.1. The obstacles and their overcoming

It is often clear that some transpersonal achievements can prove to be very demanding because they have one face issues and responsibilities from which the 'I', or personal self, not yet aligned with the Transpersonal Self, wants to escape. So sometimes it happens that the influx of energies from the higher unconscious triggers a true inner struggle between the 'I', still identified in its emotions, thoughts, and subpersonalities, and the Transpersonal Self that spurs the whole personality to change.

Assagioli identified three sets of challenges that must be overcome by those who are about to undertake, or who have already embarked on the path of transpersonal development: mental, emotional and volitional obstacles.

He considered those involving emotion very important, both because they are the most frequent, and because mental obstacles, such as doubts and skepticism, are often produced or accentuated by emotional or volitional obstacles. Among the emotional obstacles the primary consideration is *fear*, identified in five main types: fear of death, fear of solitude, fear of insecurity and weakness, fear of failure, of being disliked and ridiculed, and fear of the unknown.

Another fear that can be an obstacle to transpersonal development is the *fear of suffering*, the inability to accept pain that can be inevitable in further growth, development and transformation.

Another obstacle is the *human tendency of attachment*. Attachments can be of two types: active, such as instinct, passions, ties to people and things; or passive, such as inactivity, laziness, habits.

There is also *aggressiveness* in its various manifestations. Anger, resentment, condemnation, blame and criticism can all hinder the individual from exploring the worlds of the superconscious.

For all these obstacles, Assagioli proposes methods, techniques and exercises aimed at their transformation.

It is, for example, possible to overcome fear using both psychological and spiritual methods. Psychological methods involve the use of the mind, reflection, and persuasion; the exploration of the unconscious to find and dissipate the causes of fear; diversion and substitution through physical activity, the use of imagination, humor and the evocation of positive emotions; psychagogic exercises such as positive affirmations and imaginative training. Spiritual methods encompass various transpersonal accomplishments induced by meditation on certain key issues such as death, spiritual love, awareness of one's own powers, communion with life, trust, and so on.

The fear of suffering is overcome by accepting the pain, and through the search, and deep understanding, of the meaning of the experience the person is undergoing.

The methods for dealing with attachment are varied: there is that of "tearing away", radical and rapid but usually very painful; there is that of transmutation by replacing the objects to which one is attached; there is that of minimizing and humor; and finally that of inner independence, of spiritual autonomy.

We can be liberated from the tendency to be aggressive and to criticize by transformation and sublimation, that is by altering our attitude towards the defects of others (and ours!) and developing the opposite qualities like goodness, sweetness, acceptance, empathy, generosity, understanding, appreciation and gratitude.

4.2. Crises and dangers

> "Man's spiritual development is a long and difficult adventure, a journey through strange countries, full of wonders, but also of difficulties and dangers. It involves a radical purification and transmutation, the awakening of a series of previously inactive faculties, the raising of consciousness to levels previously unreached, its expansion along a new inner dimension. We must not be surprised that such a big change takes place through several critical stages, often accompanied by neuropsychic and even physical (psychosomatic) disorders"[173].

For this reason, Psychosynthesis considers it desirable to carefully consider these disorders, providing a general outline of the crises that may arise in the various phases of spiritual realization. It distinguishes for clarity *5 critical stages*[174]:

Crises that precede spiritual awakening

Crises resulting from spiritual awakening

Reactions that follow the spiritual awakening

The phases of the transmutation process

The "dark night of the soul"

---

173 Ibid, p. 97.

174 Ibid, pp. 97-111 and R. Assagioli, *Principi e metodi della psicosintesi terapeutica*, op. cit., pp. 40-60.

Crises that precede awakening

Sometimes a sudden change occurs in the inner life of a person. This change may arise following a series of disappointments and failures, or after a significant emotional trauma, such as the death of a loved one. Other times, however, this change occurs without a clear and identifiable reason, perhaps at a particularly happy and satisfying moment in life.

Usually the process begins with a generic sense of dissatisfaction. The individual feels dissatisfied with the life they lead, perceives a sense of "lack" but struggles to define it as he/she does not have concrete and material desires. The search is for something that seems elusive. Over time, these feelings intensify and the person may experience an increasing sense of unreality. An investigation on the origin and purpose of life may begin, a search for meaning, and in particular, what is the meaning of the suffering that so often accompanies it.

A strong moral crisis may subsequently add to this state of emptiness and lacking, characterized by severe self-criticism and very intense guilt feelings. In extreme cases, the situation can lead to such deep discouragement as to give rise to suicidal thoughts. Obviously this description is a general picture. Many in fact never reach such an acute stage, while others may arrive there suddenly and without warning.

According to Assagioli, when a person has arrived at this point they often do not understand and cannot comprehend their condition. The various manifestations of the crisis preceding the transpersonal awakening are in fact similar to some of the symptoms of common psychological disorders and certain states at the borders of psychiatric pathology. Since the two kinds of difficulties require different therapeutic approaches, it is important that the psychosynthesist is able to distinguish them.

Crises resulting from awakening

Generally, the awakening to the superconscious dimension is accompanied by sensations of intense joy and a full flow of energy. Internal conflicts and suffering seem to disappear, often with astonishing speed, and life takes on a new and clear meaning. We can well say that in these cases, the contact with the transpersonal dimension seems to be the proper cure for the state of exhaustion described above.

But this does not always occur in such a linear manner and, in certain circumstances, the same awakening can create imbalances and disturbances. According to Assagioli, this can happen when contact with the superconscious dimension is too sudden and impetuous. Or it occurs in those who do not yet have a sufficiently integrated personality and therefore have a very fragile nervous system, emotional hypersensitivity, an unstable mind or a confused and overactive imagination. In these subjects, states of emotional excitation can occur accompanied by vociferations, crying, and psychomotor agitation, or significant inflation of the ego which entails committing the mistake of attributing the qualities and powers of the superconscious and Transpersonal Self to the personal self which is not yet sufficiently disidentified.

Others, particularly those who tend to be enterprising and combative, are likely to interpret the influx of energy as a signal to assume the role of the prophet or savior, leading to associations with sects characterized by excessive fanaticism.

Finally, in certain overly strict and categorical people, transpersonal awakening can painfully accentuate the perfectionist tendencies of some super-egoic subpersonality, and lead them to believe that they must immediately conform to what they perceive as potentialities. In reality, this accomplishment "can only be the goal of a long and gradual transformation of the personality; and therefore such a requirement can only be in vain and provoke reactions of depression and self-destructive desperation."[175]

Reactions that follow the awakening

The reactions that accompany this phase are many and often occur some time after the awakening. Indeed, even where this has happened in a harmonious manner, generating a sense of joy and enlightenment, the initial state of contentment and well-being is bound to cease. The contact of the ordinary personality with the superconscious dimension was only momentary and did not lead to a real and definitive transformation.

Returning to the initial state can therefore be very painful, discouraging and cause disturbances of various kinds. Some individuals even come to deny the value of the experiences they had, and regard them as fantasies and illusions; they may refuse the values, aspirations and ideals that had guided them. But in spite of all the effort and resistance that one puts into practice, the individual cannot restore their ordinary life by erasing the memory of the beauty of what was experienced. They are tormented by "divine nostalgia", by the desire to go back home.

It is very important to recognize that this regression, or "fall", is a physiological and inevitable event. Realizing this usually generates great relief and encourages the person to consciously and responsibly walk along the path of self-realization, to begin the climb up the steep slope that will lead to a more stable transformation.

The phases of the transmutation process

Personality transmutation is a long and complex process, during which light and darkness, joy and sorrow continuously alternate. This period includes different phases: in some it is necessary to work consciously on the obstacles that prevent the influx and action of superconscious energies; others, however, are dedicated to the development of qualities and abilities which have remained latent up

---

175 R. Assagioli, *Lo sviluppo transpersonale*, op. cit., p. 102.

to that moment, in yet others the personal self must only be silent and receptive to allow the Transpersonal Self to implement its plan.

Assagioli compared this stage to that of the caterpillar that is about to turn into a butterfly: the old condition is now behind, but a new one has not yet been reached. Unfortunately, in real life, the individual can hardly stand by and close theirself in a cocoon to implement this process in solitude. Their family, professional and social life imposes tasks and roles they cannot escape. It is not surprising, therefore, that this "double life" can produce psychic disorders of various kinds, such as fatigue, insomnia, depression, anxiety, indifference and all sorts of physical symptoms.

Occasionally, the disturbances are caused by premature and erroneous attempts, usually related to overly rigid and archaic moral and religious concepts, to inhibit and suppress sexual and aggressive impulses. For Psychosynthesis the solution is always sought in a harmonious integration of all the impulses and aspects of personality.

Different issues face the individual in times when contact with the superconscious is easy and the flow of energy is intense. In these cases, one needs to be able to manage the available energy in a balanced way, without suffocating it and dispersing it into useless and hectic activities.

The "dark night of the soul"

"When the process of psycho-spiritual transformation reaches its final and decisive stage, it sometimes produces intense suffering and an inner darkness which was called by the Christian mystics 'the dark night of the soul' "[176]. This difficult state is usually characterized by deep depression, an intense sense of apathy, an anguished feeling of mental impotence, a weakening of the will, and a general aversion to life. Assagioli maintained that "this strange and terrible experience is not, despite appearances, a pathological condition; it has spiritual causes and a great spiritual value"[177].

This very dismal condition, which has also been called "mystical death", is followed by a total rebirth that definitively eliminates all suffering and discomfort. This new beginning, according to the accounts of all those who have witnessed it in time, greatly compensates for the suffering experienced and constitutes the fullness of psycho-spiritual health, that is, the realization of the Self.

Regressive disturbances, progressive disturbances

I wish to conclude by pointing out that Assagioli, while deeply engaged in psychological disorders that could accompany transpersonal development, surely did not mean to "give the impression that those who follow the path of spiritual improvement are more easily afflicted by nervous disorders than ordinary men".

---

176   Ibid, p. 106.

177   Ibid.

He specified[178] that:

- in many cases the growth of human beings to higher levels of integration takes place in a harmonious and gradual manner
- the psychic disturbances of the "common man" are often more serious and difficult to support and treat
- the disturbances that afflict those who travel along an evolutionary path are actually temporary reactions to the inner growth and regeneration process
- the sufferings caused by the evolutionary journey find their significance and compensation in the experiences of elevation, and in the intuitions and insights that they bring.

It is therefore extremely important for the psychosynthesist to be able to distinguish the psychic disturbances affecting the ordinary individual from the sufferings that torment those who travel an evolutionary path. In fact, the treatment best suited to the first group of people may be not only ineffective, but even detrimental to those belonging to the second group. I have summarized in the following table the indications provided by Assagioli on the subject[179].

Disturbance	Origin of the disturbance	Type of conflict	Therapeutic task
Involutive Regressive	Inability to undertake the necessary internal and external adjustments that are part of normal development of the personality	Between the various conscious and/or unconscious aspects of personality, or between the personality and its environment	Help the person achieve an adequate level of personal functioning. Personal psychosynthesis.
Evolutive Progressive	Difficulties related to the tensions and struggles in the various stages of self-realization, and related to the effort to grow, to elevate	Between the conscious personality and the energies that erupt from the higher unconscious	Help the person to harmoniously assimilate and integrate transpersonal energies with preexisting elements. Personal and transpersonal psychosynthesis

Obviously such a clear distinction has purely educational value. In reality, it isn't so easy to distinguish between the two types of disturbances because in the same person there are often present, to differing degrees, difficulties and suffering arising from both causes.

---

178   Ibid, pp. 106-107.

179   Ibid, p. 108 and *Principi e Metodi della Psicosintesi Terapeutica*, op. cit., pp. 56-57.

4.3. Defense against and resistance to the Sublime

But why does this process of growth and inner evolution have moments of such discomfort and suffering? What are the causes of all these difficulties? Why do we defend ourselves against happiness, from fullness and well-being?

We must look for the roots of this situation in the *instinct of self-preservation*, that is, in the natural tendency of every living thing to preserve its existence. In order to experience the transpersonal reality we must change, assume responsibility, seek and create new internal and external balances, and this process can generate substantial resistance: because we need structure and security; because we are strongly attached to our own sense of identity; because we fear being deeply wounded; because we fear disintegration and madness; because we think we have to give up what we possess; because we are terrified by solitude and death; because we do not want to risk seeming ridiculous or challenging the status quo.

The ordinary personality, therefore, perceiving and interpreting the influx of superconscious elements as a danger and a threat, tends to protect itself from this eventuality by implementing defensive strategies. Piero Ferrucci[180] has identified them as follows:

- *repressing*: attempting to deny one's own greatest potentialities and experiences, thus opening the door to even serious cases of withdrawal, anger, cynicism and depression

- *projecting*: attributing the qualities of one's own higher unconscious to someone else (guru, master, therapist, friend), idealizing them and avoiding in this way the assumption of one's own responsibility

- *compensating*: assuming attitudes contrary to the superconscious qualities that push for manifestation, for example by trying to neutralize a compassionate urge with harsh, insensitive attitudes

- *desecrating*: ridiculing everything that directly or indirectly recalls the transpersonal dimension

- *defending oneself with pessimism*: belittling and depriving oneself because "one is too tired, stupid, impeded" or "because one doesn't have time, money, connections ..."

- *making it routine*: strangling the genuine and spontaneous contact with the superconscious with a series of repetitive and empty rituals

- *dogmatizing*: making a fundamentally vital experience a responsibility, establishing rigid duties "I must evolve, grow, I must realize the Self ..."

- *degrading*: devaluing the contents flowing from the higher unconscious, canceling their power, beauty, and strength.

---

180 Piero Ferrucci, *Crescere*, op. cit, pp. 133-139.

5. The science of human typology and the various paths to transpersonal realization

The ways individuals choose to travel their own path to self-realization vary in relation to different individual make-ups. Psychosynthesis identifies *seven main paths*, but does not consider them to be separate from each other. Often, in reality, they overlap, so a person can follow more than one simultaneously. But it is useful to describe and to know their specific elements.

5.1. Classifications and irreducible uniqueness of human beings

Humankind has always been trying to sort and divide the differences and similarities between human beings into categories and groups. From antiquity to the present day the existence of various temperaments has been recognized, and many classifications have been proposed. Hippocrates, a physician of ancient Greece, divided humankind into 4 groups according to the physical humors prevailing in the body: sanguine, phlegmatic, melancholic, and choleric. Physiognomy tries to divide them according to facial features. Astrological sciences do so by date, time and place of birth. Jung classified humans into the two large groups of extroverts and introverts, further differentiating them according to the four fundamental psychological functions: thought, feeling, intuition, and sensation. Alexander Lowen, a principal student of Wilhelm Reich, identified a typology comprised of five characters - schizoid, oral, psychopathic, masochistic and rigid - each resulting from the negation of a child's fundamental right. The Enneagram system, introduced to the West by Gurdjieff, is based on the classification of individuals into nine different types: the idealist, the altruist, the organizer, the artist, the thinker, the trusted collaborator, the optimist, the boss, the mediator. And the list could continue.

Roberto Assagioli proposed a subdivision of human beings based on *7 different types* considering the first three introverts, the fourth ambiverts, and the last three extroverts. We therefore have:

- the *willful type*
- the *loving type*
- the *active-practical type*
- the *creative-artistic type*
- the *scientific type*
- the *devotional-idealistic type*
- the *organizing type.*

Before going further in the discussion of the subject, it seems essential to me to clarify that Psychosynthesis maintains a cautious attitude towards attempts to classify individuals. Experience has in fact demonstrated how difficult it is to try to organize the complexity and multiplicity of human beings into categories without committing the error of forgetting their indispensable uniqueness. And so for Assagioli it was essential to emphasize the importance of resisting the temptation to attribute too much relevance to typological classification, and even more so to the tendency to label individuals. So he wrote:

> "As helpful as typology can be to understand and treat different human beings, it fails to give us a complete, comprehensive account of an individual. Each individual is a unique combination of infinite discordant factors." [181]

On the other hand, it is true that, being cautious, the classifications allow us to highlight groups of characteristics that qualify people, thus contributing to a more complete understanding of the human being. Typologies, in the psycho-synthetic sense, arrange the individual by certain strengths and fragilities, giving them specific characteristics that will lead them to achieve more in certain fields of human activity and less in others.

5.2. The aim of typological classification

However, for various reasons, finding out what type we belong to is not easy at all. There are individuals who are difficult to classify because they are less differentiated or because they are very eclectic and multi-faceted. There are times of life in which events of various kinds (mourning, falling in love, personal and/or professional situations) can eclipse our truest and deep nature. There are also people who hide certain features by masking them with opposites, for example by compensating for an acute sensitivity with a glaring cynicism.

Moreover, pure types are unlikely to exist. Each of us tends to belong to several types simultaneously. This is because our body, our emotional and mental sphere, our personality and the Self can be of different typologies.

The purpose of psychosynthetic work on typologies lies in the usefulness of the indications that are derived in order to widen the knowledge of ourselves and to guide our bio-psychospiritual development by directing it towards the realization of our true vocation. But not only; typology can also provide us with clear explanations, to accept and understand others better, and to communicate with them more harmoniously. Assagioli summarized the fundamental points of this elaboration in the following terms[182]:

---

181   R. Assagioli, *L'atto di volontà,* op. cit., p. 193.

182   R. Assagioli, *I tipi umani,* Ed. Istituto di Psicosintesi, 1978, pp. 9-11.

1. expression of one's specific type

2. control

3. harmonizing

Discovery of your own type opens a path that leads to the full *acceptance* of that type. As always, in the psychosynthetic sense, the term "acceptance" is not meant as passive resignation, but rather "a conscious and voluntary recognition of the possibilities inherent in our type; of what it can teach us, of its opportunities and of its dangers; and finally the kind of service it can offer"[183]. *Expressing* your typology means recognizing and developing its potentialities, taking on the responsibility for the tools that life has provided us and employing them in the most complete and evolved way possible.

Subsequently, we must learn to *control* and manage the characteristics of our type, and this means developing the ability to discipline the prevailing faculties in order to prevent them from taking over, which could lead to unilateral and hypertrophic developments. Think of the "super-brainy" person that does not have the slightest relational ability, or the creative person who is unable to practically organize their own life, or even to the scientist who has no contact with his/her emotional side. These disharmonies are an obstacle to the ultimate goal of our evolution, "that is, to produce complete individuals with all their faculties developed at all levels"[184]. Knowing your own type means recognizing one's excesses and defects, and then managing and transforming them.

Finally, it is necessary to *harmonize* one's own type. This task, which is closely linked to the previous one, consists of giving space to dormant functions by cultivating those faculties that are not yet part of our current psychological make-up. In addition, this task involves resolving internal conflicts characteristic of the typology, leading to greater personal completeness. Thus, for example, a person with distinct practical tendencies can work on developing their creative and intuitive skills, while a sentimental and affectionate person can concentrate on their will, and a very impulsive person can work on their reasoning.

5.3. Psychological types and the different ways of transpersonal realization

Life inevitably presents us with questions, problems and mysteries. And it is our task to try to solve them. According to psychotherapist and psychosynthesist Piero Ferrucci[185], the pupil of Assagioli who devoted himself more than anyone else to the systematic and scientific study of the "peak experiences", the pathways of transpersonal realization are traced by the attempts people make in seeking

---

183   Ibid, p. 9.

184   Ibid, p. 10.

185   P. Ferrucci, *Esperienze delle vette*, Ed. Astrolabio, 1989.

the answers to these questions. To this end, they use familiar and ordinary aspects of everyday life, methods that are spontaneous and common to all men: choosing and taking responsibility, or being conscious, performing actions, appreciating what is good, or knowing the reality around us. We can therefore say that every path is defined by the dilemmas it poses. So, in the psychosynthetic approach, the problems that afflict the human being are not at all a misfortune. They instead give us a clear indication of what is most important, show us what is closest to our hearts.

> "In the problem he is facing, man finds the most advanced point on his path to be that where, for the time being, he was obliged to stop, but is also that which indicates the next step forward"[186]

In his book, appropriately entitled *Esperienze delle vette* (*Peak Experiences*), Ferrucci described the results of research conducted on more than five hundred autobiographies, biographies, diaries, and articles on individuals who have demonstrated exceptional abilities during human history: some of the greatest artists, scholars, wise men, philosophers, educators, mystics, men and women of action, pioneers, political leaders, actors and athletes. He wrote in the introduction to the book[187]:

> "I wanted to find the answer to these questions:
>
> What are the happiest expressions of human nature?
>
> In which way did these individuals reach them?
>
> What can we learn from them and apply to our lives? (...)
>
> We will see individuals in motion and their goal is the world of the Self. Everyone uses a different manner to move forward: each has their own way. The metaphor of the path is correct as it reminds us that every human being is in the becoming. (...)
>
> A path is not a way predetermined and equal for all. (...) Following a path towards the Self does not mean choosing a technique and then applying it mechanically until one reaches liberation. (...) Everyone has to invent their own path: one must challenge one's own dearest habits and convictions, use all available resources, expose theirself to the most unpredictable reversals. Without any guarantee of success."

Willful type: the way of the will

Summary table WILLFUL TYPE	The way of the will is the path of all those who dare: explorers who venture into the unknown, political leaders confronting hostile social forces, athletes who challenge the limits of human abilities.
Archetype	the hero, the revolutionary, the warrior, the explorer, the pioneer

---

186   Ibid, p. 134.

187   Ibid, pp. 9-17.

Psychological function	will
Path of realization	accomplished through the ability to be responsible and the freedom to make decisions
Functions	dominate, lead, govern, judge, punish, fight, destroy, conquer
Basic motivation	power, ambition
Psychosynthesis tasks	to develop love, to cultivate the ability to cooperate, to transform personal will into transpersonal will
General description	the most important trait of this human type is the strong will; its highest expression, the total succumbing of the individual will to the cosmic will
Positive features	courage, strength, resistance, sincerity due to lack of fear, ability to govern, firmness, decisiveness, sense of justice, ability to grasp wide-ranging problems with broad vision
Negative features	ambition, arrogance, pride, cruelty, hardness, anger, obstinacy, desire to dominate others, selfish isolation, destructiveness, violence, abrasiveness
Characteristics to be developed	tenderness, humility, compassion, tolerance, tact, patience, sweetness, love
Psychological disturbances	those linked to schizoid subpersonality
Notable people	Amundsen (the first person to reach the North Pole), Lindbergh (the first aviator to accomplish a solo transoceanic flight), Enzo Majorca (record-holding freediver); Gandhi; Martin Luther King

In living organisms, attachment to life is, among the various instincts, the most archaic and tenacious. Yet some individuals experience the need to explore the dangerous area between life and death. By doing so, they "discover that challenging their attachment to life they are transformed and regenerated. There is a violent jolt to their entire being, and thanks to this, a profound renewal takes place. This is the way of the will"[188].

This difficult journey is undertaken by very different individuals who share a fundamental characteristic: they all go beyond collective limits, confronting fear and staring in the face of the unknown and death. They are the explorers and pioneers who dare to venture beyond the boundaries of the known world; they are the political leaders who have the courage and strength to rebel against the dominant model of society, sometimes jeopardizing their own lives; they are the athletes who, through extraordinary discipline, succeed in overcoming the limits of the imaginable.

---

188 Ibid, p. 231.

The way of the will is the quickest, the hardest, and even the most solitary. In this, unlike other ways that are more codified, there are no fixed reference points, rules to follow, models to imitate, communities to belong to, or guides to indicate a path that has already been established. Whoever travels this fearful route incarnates the warrior archetype. The transpersonal world not only includes peaceful qualities such as serenity, joy, love and trust, but also intense and burning qualities such as strength, courage, power, and boldness.

Obviously, the main danger we encounter along this path is the illicit use of these characteristics leading to the mutation of force into violence, the will into inflexibility and power into arrogance.

Loving type: the way of enlightenment

Summary table LOVING TYPE	The way of enlightenment is based on the practice of meditation and it is the way of the great thinkers, wise men and philosophers of all ages.
Archetype	the enlightened wise one, the passionate educator
Psychological function	emotion-feeling
Path of realization	through relationships and the ability to love
Functions	unite, protect, understand, teach
Basic motivation	love (for loved ones, a cause, a homeland)
Psychosynthesis tasks	achieve non-attachment and develop a strong will
General description	the emotional sphere is the center of their attention and their vital force; in some higher representatives the quality of love prevails, in others the aspect of wisdom; it needs, in order to express itself, the stimulus of interaction with others
Positive features	serenity, strength, calmness, patience, acceptance, understanding, tolerance, tact, spirit of cooperation, love for study, trust, clear intelligence, intuition, sensitivity, communicativeness, generosity, foresight, sympathy, compassion
Negative features	insensitivity, indifference to others, selfishness, indecision, procrastination, laziness, love of comforts, lack of will, impossibility of being alone, hypersensitivity, fear, attachment
Characteristics to be developed	will, firmness, activity, energy, decisiveness, enthusiasm, sense of justice
Psychological disturbances	those associated with a depressed subpersonality
Notable people	Buddha, Patanjali, Meister Eckhart, Hildegard von Bingen, Krishnamurti, Sri Aurobindo, Rousseau, Pestalozzi, Montessori

Being aware. This path is based on the recognition of this evident, truly exceptional characteristic of the human being. The mystery of the consciousness impassions certain individuals to such an extent that it brings them to consider their inner world as a sort of laboratory for conducting experiments of all sorts. As time passes, they come to discover that consciousness can take on different forms and that, among these, some seem more sensible and convincing, more real than others.

Exploring the different dimensions of consciousness then becomes a path of self-realization, a path that leads to the experience of the Self. In truth, every path is a journey that leads to the Self, but this, unlike the others that are based on an "external" element, such as action, beauty, scientific research, or ritual, is based on internal, indefinable elements. Usually, the exploration of one's own inner world starts with a preliminary work of purification that serves to make the subject's personality as transparent as possible. This work involves the corporeal dimension, the sphere of emotions and desires, and the sphere of thought. Once a sufficient amount of preparation is achieved, the actual work begins. Over the centuries, entire reference systems have been codified with different types of techniques designed to guide and facilitate those who follow the path of illumination. There are three main operations that Ferrucci identifies:

> "I, a living subject, can open my conscience panoramically to all that exists within me and without me; in this way I am awake and present, and I am aware of everything without filters and preferences.
> I can, on the contrary, concentrate the consciousness on a single subject, to the exclusion of all others, bringing it to maximum intensity.
> I can withdraw the consciousness to its origins and gather it in itself, so that it can be perceived as pure awareness, without content and not subject to time and space."[189]

As with any other path, there are also dangers and deviations. We have already spoken of the need for an adequate and preliminary purification of the personality. The inner world is vast and boundless, and can swallow those who have not been sufficiently prepared. Exploration of the peaks and abysses of consciousness can render the individual no longer capable of discerning dream from reality. The individual may believe theirself to be chosen and in possession of the supreme truth, invested with a special prophetic task, only to wander in the grip of the illusions of a fragmented consciousness.

Active-practical type: the way of action

Summary table ACTIVE-PRACTICAL TYPE	The way of action leads to the Self through active engagement in society and unselfish service.

---

189 Ibid, p. 93.

Archetype	the servant of the "last", the paladin of the outcast
Psychological function	imagination
Path of realization	achieved through doing and transforming intelligence into concrete action
Functions	manifest, concretize, produce, adapt, invent
Basic motivation	money, profit or, if more evolved, philosophical and abstract knowledge
Psychosynthesis tasks	cultivate the recognition of the intangible world, control activism, unify the practical aspects and transpersonal aspects through elevation of the activity
General description	intelligent activity is a fundamental quality, the ability to manipulate something and take advantage of its many uses
Positive features	broad vision, ability to synthesize and reason, clarity and mental elasticity, detachment from smaller daily worries, ability to recognize the essentials, to feel the truth as a goal, adaptability, discrimination, to know how to seize the right moment, tact, to know the various sides of a question, able to reconcile, balance, objectivity
Negative features	imprecision, disorder, superficiality, physical laziness, distraction, tendency toward insincerity and scheming, curiosity, cunning, oppression, tendency to exploit intelligence for selfish purposes, hypocrisy, two-faced, wasting time to talk about meaningless things, overparticular
Characteristics to be developed	accuracy, strength, will, love, devotion, concentration, ability to accomplish, order
Psychological disturbances	those linked to schizoid subpersonality; intellectual defensiveness
Notable people	Albert Schweitzer, Mother Teresa of Calcutta, Florence Nightingale, Abbé Pierre

Individuals who travel along this path have made action, elevating it to its highest levels, a means of growth and inner achievement. We think of individuals of the caliber of Albert Schweitzer, Florence Nightingale, or Mother Teresa of Calcutta.

Action is certainly not always the harbinger of an expansion of consciousness. Sometimes it seems to take us in the opposite direction, weighing on us, dragging us down to the reality of the thousand small things we do, making us slaves of our success or of our fear of failure, making us lose contact with the dimension of our being.

It is, however, an undeniable fact that action is also an instrument capable of transmitting knowledge, strength and freedom; a means to overcome that part of us that tends toward inertia, stagnation, immobility; a way of expressing our will in the world, of voicing what we are, of manifesting our profound project.

At this point we can ask ourselves: how can action, in certain circumstances, become a true way of self-realization, a path to the Self? This occurs because through doing, it is possible to reach a higher level of knowledge. Those who follow this path have two main traits. First of all, they gradually change their attitude towards their own activity. Usually, the individual tends to identify with what they are doing and with the results that are achieved. Those who take this path gradually separate their acts from their expectations, acknowledgements and achievements so that they are internally free. Secondly, they transform the motive at the root of their actions from something selfish and self-referential to something that becomes a channel through which unconditional love can come about.

Ferrucci notes that the data on the people who have followed this route of self-realization is clear but scarce. These people have often led modest lives out of the spotlight. "By its characteristics, this path leads to finding the highest values in what, in the eyes of most, is unimportant, without dreaming of great enterprises, without looking for the immortal masterpiece"[190].

Creative-artistic type: the way of beauty

Summary table CREATIVE-ARTISTIC TYPE	The way of beauty is based on aesthetic appreciation, inspiration and creativity, where we find the masters of various arts.
Archetype	the artist
Psychological function	intuition
Path of realization	through the search for beauty and harmony (and is perpetually in conflict)
Functions	discover the profound significance of every appearance and symbol and every fragment of the cosmic manifestation
Basic motivation	the pursuit of harmony
Psychosynthesis tasks	acquire greater ability to live with rhythm, work on the synthesis of opposites
General description	has a tendency to reach harmony through intense efforts to combine contrasting elements; the problem of opposites is central, such as oscillation, even intense, between inaction and activity, between spirituality and sensuality, between anger and calm

---

190 Ibid, pp. 65-68.

Positive features	love of beauty and harmony, love for nature and animals, generosity, courage, devotion, sympathy, strong affections, rapidity of perception, intuition, vivacious intelligence, sense of humor, objectivity, impartiality
Negative features	selfishness, volubility, instability, negligence, laziness, extravagance, stubbornness, disorderly, extreme sensuality, inability to make efforts and make sacrifices, apprehension, lack of moral courage, indolence, capriciousness
Characteristics to be developed	serenity, trust, purity, self-domination, orderliness, accuracy, moral and mental balance, superior creativity
Psychological disturbances	those related to a hysteric and over-dramatic subpersonality, bipolar syndromes, manic depression
Notable people	Tagore, Leopardi, Monet, Chopin, Goethe, Keats, Balzac, Neruda, Michelangelo, Beethoven, Mozart, Dante

In Western culture, the first person to refer to beauty as a way of self-realization was the Greek philosopher Plato. Today we know that, in practice, this path is far less structured than he believed, but its essential assertion remains equally valid: beauty has a formidable power of liberation on the human mind.

This principle is regularly used in various therapeutic forms: beauty soothes the soul and, in one of its most accessible languages, music can speak to our feelings in very suitable and fertile ways. Even more positive is creating. Being creative, even at a very simple level, promotes the integration and general harmonization of the psyche.

Every true aesthetic experience is based on trust in one's own judgment and intimate contact with one's own sensitivity. In this way, identification with the wonders of the natural world is a primary source of contentment and knowledge. Many aesthetic experiences demonstrate how it is possible to recognize the Self in the flow of life, above all in nature, rather than imagining it an intangible and unchangeable entity.

Of course, along the path of beauty, we find dangers and temptations, first of all aestheticism, that is, the pursuit of beauty as an end unto itself, unconnected with other fundamental ethical values such as knowledge, solidarity, or truth. Indeed, in every expansion of consciousness, there is the danger of psychic disintegration. If the perceptual capacity expands without the expansion of the center that integrates this expansion, there is a risk of falling into mental alienation. There is also the suffering linked to the perception of the contrast between the beauty of that which is intuited and the world in which one feels obliged to live (crisis of duality). Finally, in some cases, the perceived beauty is so intense that it becomes unsustainable (crisis of excessive beauty).

Summary table SCIENTIFIC TYPE	With the way of science, the sublime is achieved through systematic research, observation, and thought.
Archetype	the scientist, the inventor
Psychological function	thought
Path of realization	realized through the investigation of how life manifests itself, the laws underlying phenomena; interest in knowledge in the pure sense
Functions	objectively describe the phenomena registered by the senses or through instruments; discover transformations and laws through observation and experience; identify the means by which individuals can use this knowledge
Basic motivation	the thirst for knowledge and investigating
Psychosynthesis tasks	sublimation of the desire for knowledge and integration of Eros and Logos
General description	its ideal and its main task is concrete, objective, impartial research
Positive features	strong principles, honesty even in minor issues, punctuality, consistency, courage of actions and opinions, persistence in research, strong observational and analytic skills, capable of prolonged attention, exacting imagination, acute and penetrating intelligence, sense of extreme justice, independence
Negative features	overly meticulous, insensitivity to the suffering of others, mentally static, materialistic, exploits others, denies what is not objectively perceived, skepticism, contempt for poetry, the arts and spiritual experiences, incomprehension and repression of feelings, lack of compassion, mentally prejudiced, critical, arrogant
Characteristics to be developed	cognitive intuition, love, understanding, sympathy, compassion, reverence, tenderness, width of vision, synthesis skills
Psychological disturbances	those related to obsessive subpersonality
Notable people	Flammarion, Einstein, Poincaré, Heisenberg, Bateson, Hawking ...

The way of science is not a declared way, in the sense that very few scientists, if asked, would support its existence or would say that they are consciously on that path. Yet, as we can see, scientific work arises from a profoundly existential question, from humankind's need to know how our universe is formed, how the cosmos works. Endeavoring to answer this question frees the mind, leading to important intuitive experiences, and therefore it has many affinities with the transpersonal path.

Indeed, it is improbable that those who follow the path of science will not be profoundly transformed. More than one scientist claimed to have experienced that "cosmic religious feeling" which, according to Einstein, is "the strongest and most noble motivation of scientific research"[191]. Sometimes it is the pure concept of the infinite that opens the mind; at other times one can perceive the presence of an intelligence greater than that of the human in what is being studied; or one can be filled with astonishment by observing the human being. Sometimes scientific understanding coincides with aesthetic experience; other times it is the study of nature that touches the heart of the researcher. Finally one of the most representative forms of transpersonal experience on the path of science is the moment of discovery or invention, the *eureka* experience.

In conclusion we can ask what the way of science offers to those who might be distrustful and are horrified at some of its more awful applications. According to Ferrucci, "it offers the possibility of new, fertile attitudes and thinking habits that are not limited to scientific practice, but are the legacy of every intelligent mind:

- honesty in the face of the facts
- the discipline of precision and concentration
- the determination not to take anything for granted
- the ability to see hidden similarities
- the art of thinking coherently
- sensitivity to conceptual elegance
- the wonder in the face of the mystery."[192]

Devotional type: the way of devotion

Summary table DEVOTIONAL TYPE	On the path of devotion we find mystics and saints of all religions; prayer is its most important vehicle, the relationship with the divine is its central theme.
Archetype	the mystic
Psychological function	impulse-desire
Path of realization	giving oneself to a superior ideal
Functions	dynamically contribute to the development and spiritual progress of humanity
Basic motivation	devotion to some person or ideal
Psychosynthesis tasks	as sustainer of what he/she believes is their truth, must develop inclusive love, tolerance and intellectual humility.
General description	the source from which all his/her traits come is devotion to an ideal: a tending towards the ideal and the impulse to materialize it

---

191 Ibid, p. 169.

192 Ibid, p. 173.

Positive features	devotion, idealism, mysticism, spirit of sacrifice, loyalty, fidelity, enthusiasm, tenderness, love, unity of purpose, fervor, sublimation, asceticism, abnegation, compassion, sincerity, helpfulness, reverence, constancy
Negative features	fanaticism, partiality, short and restricted vision, selfish and jealous emotional attachments, impulsiveness, obstinacy, prejudice, furious rage, superstition, excessive need to depend on others, self-illusion, suspicion, personalism, combative, passionate, one-sidedness
Characteristics to be developed	strength, purity, self-sincerity, tolerance, balance, common sense, disinterested and altruistic love, breadth of ideas, detachment, impersonality
Psychological disturbances	those associated with a depressed subpersonality
Notable people	Kabir, Giuliana of Norwich, St. Teresa of Ávila, St. John of the Cross, Rumi and Hafiz (Sufi Mystics), St. Francis

"Every transpersonal path starts from a situation of incompleteness and has as its goal the attainment of unity. In this task, the way of devotion is based on the feeling that, more than any other, embodies the desire to regain unity: love. In this sense the way of devotion is the closest to the human essence because it begins with the most fundamental emotion of all; basically, we all love someone or something (...)"[193]. This means that our desires, our impulses, our emotions and our feelings have a much wider meaning and greater implications than we usually imagine.

The work that we undertake along the path of devotion is to direct our love to the ideals and the highest values that we can conceive, and gradually cleanse this love of selfish residues. The relationship with the divine is here more intimate and personal than we find in other ways, for example, the cosmic and impersonal intelligence of the path of science.

Often the divine is personified and approached by the grace of humility. This is the only way that, instead of quality and talent, is based on weakness. And the admission of this weakness is the paradoxical key that allows progression.

The phenomena that characterize the way of devotion surpass in richness and variety any other path to self-realization. First of all there are manifestations that massively involve the emotional sphere: sublimated affection, total emotional submission, passionate ardor, rapture, exaltation, ecstasy. Sometimes sounds, visions or altered perceptions of the body are experienced.

And like all the ways we've considered until now, this one also has its dark and particularly dramatic moments during which a real "hell" can be encountered. And it seems quite obvious that the channeling of all sentimental life in a single direction can bring those who travel this path to face the risk of becoming fanatical and sectarian.

---

193 Ibid, pp. 203-204.

Organizing type: the way of ritual and dance

Summary table ORGANIZING TYPE	The way of ritual and dance includes the externalized and community-oriented methods for the expansion of conscience; in it we find all those who celebrate rites and also dancers, actors, yogis.
Archetype	the magician, the priest, the sacred dancer, the actor
Psychological function	sensation
Path of realization	organizing group (coordinated) activities
Functions	establishing good relations between things or persons that have no relationship to each other, or have a wrong and non-harmonious relationship
Basic motivation	create order and organize
Psychosynthesis tasks	avoid the danger of becoming too associated with the formal aspect
General description	his/her dominant note can be expressed as "ordered group activity" or "objective manifestation through organized activities"; another prevailing quality is discipline
Positive features	ability to actualize, to manipulate things, sense of order, spirit of organization, attention to detail, economic and financial capability, productivity, strength, perseverance, courtesy, self-confidence, capability in mechanical constructions, ability to interpret symbols
Negative features	formalism, bigotry, pride, narrow-mindedness, materialistic, superstitious, excessive interest in psychism and phenomenal occultism
Characteristics to be developed	achievement of unity, breadth of ideas, tolerance, love, adaptability
Psychological disturbances	those related to an obsessive subpersonality
Notable people	Isadora Duncan, Rudolf Nureyev, Ram Gopal (Indian dancer), Nijinsky, Anna Pavlova, Eleonora Duse, Kostantin Stanislaus, Sarah Bernardt ...

Dance and ritual have always been and are still common in all cultures. They seek to answer fundamental questions such as "what relationship do we establish with our body?", "how can we express in a concrete and public way what is intangible and private?" and hence "how to share with others, with a community, a similar state of consciousness?"[194]. Those who try to answer these questions through dance, movement, and ritual often discover new ways of being and, sometimes, of getting closer to the transpersonal reality.

---

194   Ibid, p. 131.

At this point, however, there is a question: why do these two seemingly different practices come together? Ferrucci answers the question by highlighting how, despite the great diversity they present on the surface, ritual and dance share many essential aspects:

> "They use space-time means, first the body and its movements, and then its extensions like clothing, settings, and supports of various kinds to pertain to a reality that exists outside time and space.
>
> They are ways of affirming and manifesting those realities on the material plane, and feeling them living in their own bodies.
>
> They are based on the rhythm and the repetition of movements. (...).
>
> They are mostly public events. (...).
>
> They are intensified by psycho-physical alterations (...).
>
> They build a subtle reality using gestures and movements (...).
>
> They clearly distinguish ordinary reality from sacred reality (...).
>
> They are based on the principle that gestures and movements, rather than leaving us unchanged, evoke the corresponding images, thoughts and emotions in our being: (...).
>
> They establish a new relationship with the body that, from a symbol of our individuality, becomes the place where the finite and infinite coincide."[195]

The greatest risk involved with this path is that of becoming trapped in outward appearance, in a devitalized ritual or in a contrived dance.

6. The characteristics of the transpersonal experience

After illustrating the various peculiarities of the transpersonal pathways, we will now look in conclusion to this chapter devoted to the superconscious at the *characteristics* that all peak experiences have in common, namely: awe, righteousness, knowledge, unity, universality and social relevance.[196]

Awe - Contact with the superconscious dimension often leads to a shock, to a true "destructuring" of the whole personality. The usual ways of thinking, feeling and perceiving reality are put to the test. New elements appear in our lives, bringing us moments of surprise and wonder. The transpersonal experience therefore tends to create a break with the psychological situation that preceded it, causing changes and transformations. "The result is *awe*, the astonishing surprise of being faced with a structurally different reality that strikes us with all its power and majesty"[197].

---

195   Ibid, pp. 131-132
196   Ibid, pp. 271-288.
197   Ibid, p. 275.

Righteousness - Those who undergo a transpersonal experience need no proofs, checks, or comparisons. It is of itself evidence that needs no further explanation, nor does it need to be dissected to determine its value. It is legitimate in itself, it is right. This feeling of righteousness concerns not only the individual, but invests the totality of existence: it is right and good that I exist, it is right and good that others exist, that there is the world and that there is the entire cosmos. In this vision, the evils of the world are recognized and accepted as part of the whole that is inexplicably perceived as right, beyond good and evil, just as it is. But this is not a way to justify and defend the sufferings that afflict humankind, nor is it an alibi for fatalism and despair.

Knowledge - Whoever has a transpersonal experience sees unknown and amazing panoramas, in comparison to which the ordinary cognitive mode seems almost futile and trivial. Knowledge given via contact with the superconscious is completely different from that coming from a rational mind: it is global, immediate, relevant, surprising and profound.

Universality - I have already said how in the superconscious experience the boundaries of one's personality are widened and mental patterns are changed. In fact, it leads to the transcendence of one's own individual dimension, one's misfortunes, and one's own needs to the point of reaching a sense of universality that illuminates one's outlook, giving meaning and a sense of relief to human life, because it goes beyond the contradictions of the individual world. There is therefore a polarity between the universal and the particular, but this polarity is resolved in the transpersonal experience. And so an immeasurable element appears also in the most banal events of everyday life.

Unity - Our mind works according to a dualistic vision of life. Compare, contrast, judge, categorize. Much pain, conflict, anxiety, sorrow, desire and frustration arise from this way of working. In the superconscious experience, the mind quiets and another way of perceiving reality takes over, a way in which desire is absent, as are comparisons and preferences: one experiences unity. Distinctions and choices are no longer necessary, we are no longer looking for other places or other moments that will eventually satisfy us: we have come home, we feel that we belong to a larger whole, we ourselves are whole.

Social relevance - Finally, a common characteristic of all transpersonal experiences is their social relevance. The influence generated by such an experience extends beyond the person and the specific moment, and continues to live through a work of art, a social or religious movement, a scientific discovery, a new possibility for the development of all of humanity. "In short, no experience comes about in a vacuum, and no experience is purely individual: what one experiences is transmitted to others ... and not only with words and deeds, but with their being"[198].

---

198   Ibid, p. 288.

I've mentioned several times the importance of distinguishing contents of a super-conscious nature from the realization of the Transpersonal Self, explaining how at times the former, poorly interpreted, can even distance us from a deeper contact with our authentic being. On the other hand, underlining what is common to all of the genuine transpersonal experiences, and with this also that which is common to the different paths of self-realization illustrated in the preceding paragraphs, enables us to indicate in a precise manner a direction, a route to follow. And to understand if the road we're all following to return home brings us closer or farther away from our common destination.

In the end, it really doesn't matter in what manner and by what way we arrive home. This belongs to the realm of the irreducible originality of each individual or human group, which must be respected and sustained. What is truly important is the commitment we maintain in the cultivation of those internal attitudes which enable us to return home ever more frequently, again and again: to open ourselves to the marvels of new visions and to the possibility of being transformed, of renewing the profound acceptance of reality as it is in any moment, to access that profound knowledge which guides us "beyond" our limits, towards the essence and the essential, towards who we truly are, our Self, towards that awareness of Unity which is then realized, necessarily, through sharing with others.

Among the characteristics described by Piero Ferrucci, this last- the social relevance of the experience offered by the practice of Psychosynthesis- calls me particularly: an impulse which tends to transcend, to go "beyond" the individual and time. Arriving at the conclusion of this book, I leave the reader with the hope that these pages can be truly relevant. Above all, I hope that they succeed in transmitting the essence and the profound inspiration that have animated the person, the life, and the teachings of Roberto Assagioli. I hope also that they may be meaningful for all those who feel a correspondence with the message of Psychosynthesis in its broadest sense, permitting each one to recognize- independently of any group or institutional affiliation, and beyond the numerous and inevitable differences- that which unites us, that which causes us to move, at times in different ways, in the direction of the same common destination. This challenge has never been more urgent or vital. Succeeding in meeting it means to develop and improve the extraordinary potential of the monumental vision that has been given to us. Roberto Assagioli's legacy gives us all the tools to realize this, as well as the methods for activating our Good Will.

BIBLIOGRAPHY

1. Works by Roberto Assagioli

Assagioli R., *Psicosintesi - Armonia della vita*, Ed. Mediterranee, Roma, 1971.

Assagioli R., *Principi e metodi della psicosintesi terapeutica*, Astrolabio Ubaldini, Roma, 1973.

Assagioli R., *L'atto di volontà*, Astrolabio Ubaldini, Roma, 1977.

Assagioli R., *Lo sviluppo transpersonale*, Astrolabio Ubaldini, Roma, 1988.

Assagioli R., *Comprendere la psicosintesi*, Astrolabio Ubaldini, Roma, 1991.

Assagioli R., *Per vivere meglio*, Ed. Istituto di Psicosintesi, Firenze, 1993.

Assagioli R., *L'equilibramento e la sintesi degli opposti*, Ed. Istituto di Psicosintesi, Firenze.

Assagioli R., *I tipi umani*, Ed. Istituto di Psicosintesi, Firenze.

Assagioli R., *Come si imparano le lingue con l'inconscio*, Ed. Istituto di Psicosintesi, Firenze.

Assagioli R., *La vita come gioco e rappresentazione*, Ed. Istituto di Psicosintesi, Firenze.

Assagioli R., *Intervista con Sam Keen*, Centro Studi di Psicosintesi "R. Assagioli", Firenze.

Assagioli R., *Interviste 1972-1974*, Centro Studi di Psicosintesi "R. Assagioli", Firenze.

Assagioli R., *Libertà in prigione*, unedited manuscript.

Assagioli R., *Gli effetti del riso e le loro applicazioni pedagogiche*, "Rivista di psicologia applicata alla Pedagogia e alla Psicopatologia", 1906.

Assagioli R., *Johann Georg Hamman e Ralph Waldo Emerson - Alcune curiose coincidenze fra le loro idee*, Verhandlungen des III Internationalen Kongresses Für Philosophie Heidelberg, 1908.

Assagioli R., *Per una nuova psicagogia*, La Voce, I, n. 2, 1909.

Assagioli R., *La psicologia della religione al Congresso di Ginevra*, Coenobium, n. 4, 1909.

Assagioli R., *Seconda riunione psicoanalitica*, "Rivista di Psicologia Applicata", a. VI, n. 3, 1910.

Assagioli R., *Le idee di Sigmund Freud sulla sessualità*, La Voce, 1910.

Assagioli R., *Die Freudschen Lehren in Italien*, Jahrbuch der Psychoanalytische und Psychopatologische Forschungen, a. 1910.

Assagioli R., *Il subcosciente*, Biblioteca Filosofica, Firenze, 1911.

Assagioli R., *Rabindranath Tagore – Poeta, Mistico, Educatore*, Ed. della Rassegna Italiana, Firenze, 1926.

Assagioli R., *Le idee di Sigmund Freud sulla sessualità*, manuscript, 1933.

Assagioli R., *L'animo molteplice*, manuscript, 1933.

Assagioli R., *L'ebraismo progressivo e la psicologia*, La Voce dell'Unione Italiana, 3 marzo 1955.

Assagioli R., *Psicoanalisi e psicosintesi*, manuscript, 1963.

Assagioli R., *La costituzione biopsichica dell'uomo*, manuscript, 1963.

Assagioli R., *La medicina psicosomatica – Interazioni psicofisiche*, manuscript, 1963.

Assagioli R., *Sintesi della psicoterapia*, presentation to the VI International Congress on Psychotherapy, London, 1964.

Assagioli R., *La medicina psicosomatica*, manuscript, 1964.

Assagioli R., *Tecniche della psicosintesi interindividuale*, manuscript, 1965.

Assagioli R., *Carl Gustav Jung e la psicosintesi*, manuscript, 1966.

Assagioli R., *Carl Jung e la psicosintesi – La terapia*, manuscript, 1966.

Assagioli R., *Carl Jung e la psicosintesi – Terapia e educazione*, manuscript, 1966.

Assagioli R., *Medicina psicosomatica e biopsicosintesi*, Acta Medica Psychosomatica, 1967.

Assagioli R., *La volontà dal proposito all'attuazione*, manuscript, 1967.

Assagioli R., *Tecnica del modello ideale*, manuscript, 1967.

Assagioli R., *La vita come gioco e rappresentazione*, manuscript, 1967.

Assagioli R., *La psicologia dell'avvenire*, manuscript, 1968.

Assagioli R., *L'educazione dei giovani particolarmente dotati*, Istituto di Psicosintesi, 1969.

Assagioli R., *La Volontà: cenerentola nella psicologia e nella vita*, manuscript, 1970.

Assagioli R., *Una tecnica della psicosintesi: il buonumore*, manuscript, 1970.

Assagioli R., *La psicologia e l'esistenza umana*, manuscript, 1971.

Assagioli R., *La terza e la quarta forza nella psicologia – La direzione transpersonale*, manuscript, 1971.

Assagioli R., *Le nuove dimensioni della psicologia*, Corso di lezioni sulla psicosintesi, 1973.

Assagioli R., *La conoscenza di sé*, manuscript, 1973.

Assagioli R., *Gli orizzonti della psicosintesi*, Presentation, Riunione dei Centri Italiani di Psicosintesi, 1973.

Assagioli R., (c/o C.A. Lombard) *Freedom in Jail*, Istituto di Psicosintesi (ed.), Quaderni dell'Archivio Assagioli, 2016.

Assagioli R., *Appunti sull'allenamento in psicosintesi*, dictated in the English language, 19 May, 1974.

2. Works by other authors

AA.VV., *Enciclopedia di Filosofia*, Garzanti, Torino, 2005.

Alberti A., *La volontà di sintesi*, Centro Studi di Psicosintesi "R. Assagioli", Firenze.

Alberti A., *Il Sé ritrovato*, Giampiero Pagnini, Firenze, 1994.

Alberti A., *L'uomo che soffre, l'uomo che cura*, Giampiero Pagnini, Firenze, 1997.

Alberti A., *Roberto Assagioli: Note e Ricordi*, in "Rivista dell'Istituto di Psicosintesi", anno XVI, n. 2, 1999.

Alberti A., *Il bimbo interiore*, Pagnini e Martinelli, Firenze, 2000.

Alberti A., *Psicosintesi e oltre*, L'uomo Edizioni, Firenze, 2007.

Alberti A., *Psicosintesi. Una cura per l'anima*, L'uomo Edizioni, Firenze, 2008.

Assagioli I., *Poesie e Diario spirituale*, Nuova Era, 1972.

Aleardi J. A., *La psicosintesi e le altre scienze umane*, manuscript, 1973.

Amariu C., *I simboli – l'uovo*, Meditarranee, Roma, 1988.

Arnold W. (edited by), *Dizionario di psicologia*, Paoline, Milano, 1986.

Bailey A. A., *Autobiografia incompiuta*, Nuova Era, Roma, 1989.

Bartoli S., *Psicosintesi formativa e autoformativa*, manuscript, 1975.

Bartoli S., *La volontà come esperienza dell'autocoscienza*, manuscript, 1977.

Bartoli S., *Metodo scientifico o letto di Procuste?*, manuscript, 1979.

Benesch H., *Atlante di psicologia*, Sperling & Kupfer, Milano, 1995.

Berti A., *Roberto Assagioli. Profilo biografico degli anni di formazione*, Istituto di Psicosintesi, Firenze, 1987.

Berti A. (edited by), *Roberto Assagioli 1888-1988*, Centro Studi di Psicosintesi "R. Assagioli", Firenze.

Biancoli R., *Aspetti umanistici della psicosintesi*, manuscript 1976.

Binswanger L., *Essere nel mondo*, Astrolabio Ubaldini, Roma, 1973.

Bocconi A., *Gli sviluppi della psicosintesi educativa*, in Rosselli M. (edited by), *I nuovi paradigmi della psicologia*, Cittadella, Assisi, 1992.

Bocconi A., *Viaggiare e non partire*, Guanda, Milano, 2002.

Bocconi A., *Il monaco di vetro*, Jaca Book, Milano, 2002.

Boggio Gilot L., *Disidentificazione e integrazione nella terapia psicosintetica: il ruolo della meditazione vedanta di autoosservazione*, in "Rivista di Psicosintesi Terapeutica", Anno II, n. 2.

Boggio Gilot L., *Lo sviluppo transpersonale verso la non dualità*, in Rosselli M. (edited by), *I nuovi paradigmi della psicologia*, Cittadella, Assisi, 1992.

Boggio Gilot L., *Crescere oltre l'io*, Cittadella, Assisi, 1997.

Bonacina P. M., *Appunti di un geografo su una rappresentazione dell'essere umano della psicosintesi*, unedited manuscript.

Bonacina P. M., *La coscienza e le funzioni psichiche*, in *Gulliver*, anno II, n. 2, 1993.

Bonacina P.M., *L'uomo stellare*, Giampiero Pagnini, Firenze, 1998.

Brunelli F., *Significato, scopo e valore della vita*, manuscript, 1971.

Caldironi B., *L'esistenzialismo positivo e Roberto Assagioli*, in "Rivista di Psicosintesi Terapeutica", Anno II, n. 2.

Caldironi B., *Atteggiamenti dinamici: regressione, adattamento, sviluppo, trascendenza*, manuscript, 1971.

Caldironi B., *Seminari di psicopatologia e psicoterapia*, Claudio Nanni, Ravenna, 1992.

Caldironi B., *Seminari di terapia immaginativa*, Claudio Nanni, Ravenna, 1992.

Caldironi B., *Semi di luce, audio* CD, Draghi Mizzau, Firenze, 1999.

Caldironi B., *Come, quando, perché agiscono le visualizzazioni*, Artestampa, Ravenna, 2006.

Cambi F., *Storia della pedagogia*, Laterza, Bari, 1995.

Capra F., *Il Tao della fisica*, Adelphi, Milano, 1982.

Capra F., *Il punto di svolta. Scienza, società e cultura emergente*, Mondadori - De Agostini, Novara, 1995.

Carotenuto A. (edited by), *Dizionario Bompiani degli psicologi contemporanei*, Bompiani, Milano, 1992.

Chevalier J., Gheerbrant A., *Dizionario dei simboli*, BUR, Milano, 1986.

Cirinei G., *La psicosintesi nell'educazione*, manuscript, 1964.

Cirinei G., *La volontà nell'educazione*, manuscript, 1965.

Cirinei G., *La visione della sintesi in Pierre Teilhard de Chardin*, manuscript, 1968.

Cirinei G., *L'energia e le energie. Introduzione alla psicoenergetica*, manuscript, 1968.

Cirinei M.L., *L'educazione integrale. Maria Montessori e la psicosintesi*, manuscript, 1971.

Cook R., *L'albero della vita*, RED, Como, 1987.

Cranston S., *Helena Blavatsky*, Armenia, Milano,1994.

Dattilo G. Y., *Psicosintesi e tradizione ebraica*, in "Rivista di Psicosintesi Terapeutica", Anno X, Nuova serie N. 19, Marzo 2009.

David M., *La psicoanalisi nella cultura italiana*, Bollati Boringhieri, Torino, 1966.

Demetrio D., *Manuale di educazione degli adulti*, Laterza, Bari, 1997.

De Paolis D., *La scoperta della volontà*, in Rosselli M. (edited by), "I nuovi paradigmi della psicologia", Cittadella, Assisi, 1992.

De Paolis D., *L'io e le sue maschere*, Istituto di Psicosintesi, Firenze, 1996.

Di Sazio C., *Roberto Assagioli: un contributo storico al padre della psicosintesi*, graduate thesis, Università degli Studi di Roma, academic year 1986- 87.

Ferrucci P., *Psicologia umanistica e transpersonale: Maslow e la psicosintesi*, manuscript, 1971.

Ferrucci P., *Il Sé: identità e molteplicità*, manuscript, 1975.

Ferrucci P., *Crescere – Teoria e pratica della psicosintesi*, Astrolabio Ubaldini, Roma, 1981.

Ferrucci P., *Esperienze delle vette*, Astrolabio Ubaldini, Roma, 1989.

Ferrucci P., *Introduzione alla psicosintesi – idee e strumenti per la crescita personale*, Mediterranee, Roma, 1994.

Ferrucci P., *La forza della gentilezza*, Mondadori, 2006.

Ferrucci P., *La bellezza e l'anima*, Mondadori, 2009.

Finotti A. M., *Sintesi: principio e tecnica*, in Rosselli M. (edited by), "I nuovi paradigmi della psicologia - il cammino della psicosintesi", Cittadella, Assisi, 1992.

Firman J., *A Suggested Change in the Egg Diagram*, in "Rivista dell'Istituto di Psicosintesi", anno XII, n. 2, ottobre 1995.

Firman J., Gila A., *La ferita primaria*, Pagnini e Martinelli, Firenze, 2004.

Franckl V., *Alla ricerca di un significato della vita*, Mursia, Milano.

Fresia G., *Esperienze transpersonali con l'immaginazione guidata*, manuscript, 1973.

Fresia G., *Dialogo interno quale fattore della sintesi interpersonale*, manuscript, 1978.

Fromm E., *L'arte di amare*, il Saggiatore, Milano, 1963.

Fromm E., *Essere o avere?*, Mondadori, Milano, 1977.

Fusini - Doddoli M., *L'attivazione della volontà nel reale, nell'immaginario e nel simbolico*, manuscript, 1970.

Galimberti U., *Dizionario di psicologia*, UTET, 1992.

Galimberti U. (edited by), *Psicologia*, Garzanti, Torino, 1999.

Galoppini A., *Il Sé transpersonale*, in Rosselli M. (edited by), "I nuovi paradigmi della psicologia", Cittadella, Assisi, 1992.

Gasparini- Riondino A., *Scritti giovanili di Roberto Assagioli*, manuscript, 1976.

Gerard R., *L'identificazione simbolica: una tecnica della psicosintesi*, Centro Studi di Psicosintesi "R. Assagioli", Firenze.

Giorni G., *L'azione nel processo formativo*, manuscript, 1977.

Giorni G., *Psicosintesi e cultura contemporanea*, manuscript, 1980.

Giovetti P., *Roberto Assagioli - la vita e l'opera del fondatore della psicosintesi*, Mediterranee, Roma, 1995.

Girelli M., *Psicosintesi e concezione dell'uomo*, in Rosselli M. (edited by), "I nuovi paradigmi della psicologia", Cittadella, Assisi, 1992.

Guidi F., *Iniziazione alla psicosintesi*, Mediterranee, Roma, 2005.

Haar B Carter., *L'integrazione della personalità*, Centro Studi di Psicosintesi "R. Assagioli", Firenze.

Harré R., Lamb R., Mecacci L., *Psicologia – Dizionario enciclopedico*, Laterza, Bari 1986.

Jung C. G., *Aion: ricerche sulla storia del simbolo*, in *Opere*, vol. IX, parte II, Bollati Boringhieri, Torino, 1951.

Jung C. G., *Psicologia e alchimia*, Bollati Boringhieri, Torino, 1981.

Keen S., *The Golden Mean of Roberto Assagioli*, in "Psychology Today", 1974.

Kull S., *Evoluzione e personalità*, Centro Studi di Psicosintesi "R: Assagioli", Firenze.

La Sala Batà A. M., *I sette temperamenti umani*, Nuova Era, Roma, 1990.

La Sala Batà A. M., *Lo sviluppo della coscienza*, Nuova Era, Roma, 1992.

La Sala Batà A. M., *La via del Tao (o l'armonia degli opposti)*, Nuova Era, Roma, 1993.

La Sala Batà A. M., *Cercando se stessi*, L'uomo edizioni, Firenze, 2007.

Lancia M., *La sessualità nel processo educativo - una visione psicosintetica*, Istituto di Psicosintesi, Firenze, 1998.

Legrenzi P. (edited by), *Storia della psicologia*, il Mulino, Bologna, 1980.

Legrenzi P. (edited by), *Manuale di psicologia generale*, il Mulino, Bologna, 1994.

Liguori V., *La sintesi in psicosintesi*, in Rosselli M. (edited by), "I nuovi paradigmi della psicologia", Cittadella editrice, Assisi, 1992.

Lunelli L., *Roberto Nella e Luisa*, Centro Studi di Psicosintesi "R. Assagioli", Firenze, 1991.

Luti G., *Firenza corpo otto - Scrittori, riviste, editori nella Firenze del Novecento*, Vallecchi, Firenze, 1983.

Luti G., *Roberto Assagioli e l'avanguardia fiorentina nel primo novecento*, in Rosselli M. (edited by) "I nuovi paradigmi della psicologia", Cittadella, 1992.

Macchia M., *Roberto Assagioli: La psicosintesi*, Nomina, Roma, 2000.

Malfiore L., *Psicosintesi - I tipi umani*, www.linamalfiore.it/index.php/psicosintesi.

Marhaba S., *Lineamenti della psicologia Italiana: 1870- 1945*, Giunti Barbera, Firenze, 1981.

Marhaba S., Armezzani M., *Quale psicoterapia?- Gli indirizzi psicoterapici in Italia: confronto e analisi*, Liviana, Padova, 1988.

Maslow A., *Verso una psicologia dell'essere*, Astrolabio Ubaldini, Roma, 1971.

May R., *Psicologia esistenziale*, Astrolabio Ubaldini, Roma, 1970.

Mecacci L., *Storia della psicologia del Novecento*, Laterza, Bari, 1992.

Miller S., *The Will of R. Assagioli*, in "Intellectual Digest", 1972.

Miller S., *La tecnica del dialogo col Sé*, Centro Studi di Psicosintesi "R. Assagioli", Firenze.

Musatti C., *Freud*, Bollati Boringhieri, Torino, 1970.

Nannelli R., *Il pensiero olografico*, Compagnia degli Araldi, Impruneta 1998.

Nocelli Petra G., *Conosci, possiedi, trasforma te stesso*, Xenia, Milano, 2016

Palombi I., *Analisi, sintesi e psicosintesi nella concezione assagioliana di educazione*, manuscript, 1976.

Parfitt W., *La psicosintesi – una guida all'autorealizzazione*, Xenia, Milano, 1993.

Parfitt W., *The Qabalist*, in "Rivista dell'Istituto di Psicosintesi", anno XIV, n. 1, aprile 1997.

Parietti P., *La funzione umanistica del medico*, manuscript, 1971.

Pasini F., *L'ombra e la sua luce*, Istituto di Psicosintesi (Centro di Milano), 1998.

Peresson L., *Il gruppo come momento formativo*, manuscript, 1977.

Peresson L., *La psicosintesi nel progresso delle scienze psicologiche*, in Rosselli M. (edited by), "I nuovi paradigmi della psicologia", Cittadella, Assisi, 1992.

Piccitto A., *La crescita psicologica attraverso il modello ideale*, in Rosselli M. (edited by), "I nuovi paradigmi della psicologia", Cittadella, Assisi, 1992.

Ramorino L., *Identificazione, disidentificazione, autoidentificazione*, in Rosselli M. (edited by), "I nuovi paradigmi della psicologia", Cittadella, Assisi, 1992.

Roche de Coppens Peter, *Lo sviluppo dell'uomo nuovo* (I, II, III parte), L'Età dell'Acquario, Torino, 1989.

Rosselli M., Alberti A., *Psicosintesi e nuovi paradigmi in psicoterapia*, in "Rivista di Psicosintesi Terapeutica", Anno I, n.1.

Rosselli M., *Psicoterapia e immagine dell'uomo: importanza della psicosintesi autoformativa nella terapia*, manuscript, 1975.

Rosselli M., *Metodo scientifico e prassi psicosintetica*, manuscript, 1979.

Rosselli M., *Introduzione alla psicosintesi*, Istituto di Psicosintesi, Firenze.

Rosselli M. (edited by), *I nuovi paradigmi della psicologia - il cammino della psicosintesi*, Cittadella, Assisi, 1992.

Rossi Monti M., Vitale S., *Dall'analisi esistenziale alla teoria dei sistemi*, Feltrinelli, Milano, 1980.

Russel B., *Storia della filosofia occidentale*, TEA, Milano, 2007.

Salvetti G., *La nascita del Novecento*, E. D. T., 1977.

Sannangelantonio L., *Paleologica, logica aristotelica e psicosintesi*, manuscript, 1966.

Sannangelantonio L., *La rivoluzione copernicana della psiche*, manuscript, 1968.

Santandrea M., *Frankl e la psicosintesi*, manuscript, 1973.

Santucci A., *Il pragmatismo in Italia*, Il Mulino, Bologna, 1963.

Sassi M., *Formazione e terapia o è terapia?*, in "Rivista dell'Istituto di Psicosintesi", anno XV, n. 2, ottobre 1998.

Scardovelli M., *Subpersonalità e crescita dell'io*, Borla, Roma, 2000.

Schaub R. e B., *Freedom in Jail: Assagioli's notes*, in "Rivista dell'Istituto di Psicosintesi", anno XIII, n. 1, aprile 1996.

Schnöller A., *Consapevolezza interna*, unedited manuscript.

Schnöller A., *La guarigione della memoria*, Travel notes, Roma, 2002.

Schnöller A., *La via del silenzio. Meditazione e consapevolezza*, Travel notes, Roma, 2007.

Staude J. R., *Dalla psicoanalisi alla psicosintesi: Freud, Jung e Assagioli*, in Rosselli M. (edited by), "I nuovi paradigmi della psicologia", Cittadella, 1992.

Talbot M., *Tutto è uno - L'ipotesi della scienza olografica*, URRA, Milano, 1997.

Tart C. T., *Psicologie transpersonali - La mente vista da sette grandi tradizioni spirituali*, Crisalide, Spigno Saturnia, 1994.

Tilli S., *Il momento esistenziale nella terapia psicosintetica- Alcune osservazioni*, manuscript, 1976.

Tilli S., *Autoformazione: parole stimolo e valori*, manuscript, 1977.

Tilli S., *Aspetti umanistici nella psicologia di Assagioli*, manuscript, 1978.

Tilli S., *Verso una visione umanistica della salute mentale*, manuscript, 1979.

Tilli S., *Concetti della psicologia umanistica di Roberto Assagioli*, Istituto di Psicosintesi, Firenze, 1980.

Tilli S., *Spunti per una lettura prospettica della "psicologia" di Roberto Assagioli*, in Rosselli M. (edited by) "I nuovi paradigmi della psicologia", Cittadella, 1992.

Toller G., *Prospettive umanistiche in sessuologia*, manuscript, 1979.

Tonini C., *Il carteggio Assagioli-Prezzolini dell'archivio contemporaneo del gabinetto Vieusseux di Firenze*, in Rosselli M. (edited by), "I nuovi paradigmi della psicologia", Cittadella, 1992.

Turus O., *La volontà nella psicosintesi autoformativa*, manuscript, 1975.

Viglienghi V., *Dalla morale all'etica: un percorso psicosintetico*, manuscript.

Viglienghi V., *Orizzonti psicosintetici - Antologia di scritti sulle applicazioni e le implicazioni della Psicosintesi*, Youcanprint, 2016

Walsh R., *I confini della psicologia*, in Rosselli M. (edited by), "I nuovi paradigmi della psicologia", Cittadella, Assisi, 1992.

Widmann C., *Le terapie immaginative*, Ma. Gi., Roma, 2004.

Wilber K., *Eye to eye: The Quest for the New Paradigm*, Anchor/Doubleday, New York, 1983.

Wilber K., *Oltre i confini- La dimensione transpersonale in psicologia*, Cittadella, Assisi, 1985.

Wilber K., *Lo spettro della coscienza*, Crisalide, Spigno Saturnia, 1993.

Wilber K., *Il progetto Atman. Una visione transpersonale dello sviluppo umano*, Crisalide, Spigno Saturnia, 2003.

3. Selected psychosynthesis works in the English language

Assagioli R., *Psychosynthesis: A Manual of Principles and Techniques (A Collection of Basic Writings)*, Viking Press, 1965

Assagioli R., *The Act of Will*, Penguin, 1974

Assagioli R., *Transpersonal Development: The Dimension Beyond Psychosynthesis*, Crucible/Harper Collins, London, 1991

Assagioli R., (edited by) Lombard C. A., *Freedom in Jail*, new series Quaderni dell'Archivio Assagioli, Istituto di Psicosintesi ed., 2016

Brode K., *Making Peace With My Body: Re-visualizing Cancer - The Psychosynthesis Guide to a new Life*, CreateSpace Independent Publishing Platform, 2015

Brown M. Y., *Unfolding Self: The Practice of Psychosynthesis*, Allworth Press, Revised edition, 2004

Brown M. Y., *Growing Whole: Self-Realization for the Great Turning*, Psychosynthesis Press, 2009

Doiron S., *Personal Transformation in the Counselling Process: The Integration of Psychosynthesis and Focusing Therapeutic Models*, VDM Verlag, 2008

Ferrucci P., *What We May Be: Techniques for Psychological and Spiritual Growth Through Psychosynthesis*, TarcherPerigee, 2009

Ferrucci P., *Inevitable Grace: Breakthroughs in the Lives of Great Men and Women: Guides to Your Self-Realization*, TarcherPerigee, 2009

Ferrucci P., *Beauty and the Soul: The Extraordinary Power of Everyday Beauty to Heal Your Life*, TarcherPerigee, Reprint edition 2010

Ferrucci P., *Your Inner Will: Finding Personal Strength in Critical Times*, TarcherPerigee, Reprint edition 2015

Ferrucci P., *The Power of Kindness: The Unexpected Benefits of Leading a Compassionate Life*, TarcherPerigee, Tenth Anniversary Edition 2016

Firman D., *Engaging Life: Living Well With Chronic Illness*, Healthy Learning, 2013

Firman J. and Gila A., *The Primal Wound: A Transpersonal View of Trauma, Addiction, and Growth*, State University of New York Press, 1997

Firman J. and Gila A., *Psychosynthesis: A Psychology of the Spirit*, SUNY series in Transpersonal and Humanistic Psychology, 2002

Firman J. and Gila A., *A Psychotherapy of Love: Psychosynthesis in Practice*, State University of New York Press, 2010

Hardy J., *A psychology with a soul: Psychosynthesis in evolutionary context*, Woodgrange Press, 1996

Horowitz M., *The Dance of We: The Mindful Use of Love and Power in Human Systems*, The Synthesis Center, 2014

Kramer S., *Transforming the Inner and Outer Family: Humanistic and spiritual approaches to mind-body systems therapy*, The Haworth Press, 1995

Macy J., Brown M. Y., *Coming Back to Life: The Updated Guide to the Work that Reconnects*, New Society Publishers, Revised edition, 2014

Parfitt W., *Psychosynthesis: The Elements and Beyond*, PS Avalon, 2006

Parfitt W., *Psychosynthesis: New Perspectives*, PS Avalon, 2009

Rueffler M., *Our Inner Actors: the Theory and Application of Subpersonality Work in Psychosynthesis*, PsychoPolitical Peace Institute Press, 1995

Schaub R., Schaub B. Gulino, *Transpersonal Development: Cultivating the Human Resources of Peace, Wisdom, Purpose and Oneness*, Florence Press, 2013

Schaub R., Schaub B. Gulino, *Dante's Path: Vulnerability and the Spiritual Journey*, Florence Press, 2014

Schaub R., Schaub B. Gulino, *The Florentine Promise: A Seeker's Guide*, Florence Press, 2014

Simpson S., Evans J., Evans R., *Essays on the Theory and Practice of a Psychospiritual Psychology: Volume 1*, Institute of Psychosynthesis, 2013

Simpson S., Evans J., Evans R., *Essays on the Theory and Practice of a Psychospiritual Psychology: Volume 2*, Institute of Psychosynthesis, 2014

Sørensen K., *The Soul of Psychosynthesis – The Seven Core Concepts*, Kentaur Publishing, 2016

Sorell S., *Psychosynthesis Made Easy: A Psychospiritual Psychology for Today*, Psyche Books, Reprint edition, 2011

Yeomans T., *Psychosynthesis Practice: Psychosynthesis Exercises for Personal and Spiritual Growth*, Psychosynthesis Distribution, 1990

Yeomans T., *Soul on Earth: Readings in Spiritual Psychology*, The Concord Institute, 1999

Whitmore D., *Psychosynthesis in Education: A Guide to the Joy of Learning*, Inner Traditions, 1986

Whitmore D., *Psychosynthesis Counselling in Action*, (Counselling in Action series) SAGE Publications Ltd, 4 edition 2013

Made in the USA
Coppell, TX
25 January 2023

11671861R00197